THE AUSTRALIAN POLITICAL SYSTEM
in action

NARELLE MIRAGLIOTTA
WAYNE ERRINGTON
NICHOLAS BARRY

THE AUSTRALIAN POLITICAL SYSTEM

in action

OXFORD
UNIVERSITY PRESS
AUSTRALIA & NEW ZEALAND

OXFORD
UNIVERSITY PRESS
AUSTRALIA & NEW ZEALAND

253 Normanby Road, South Melbourne, Victoria 3205, Australia

Oxford University Press is a department of the University of Oxford.
It furthers the University's objective of excellence in research,
scholarship, and education by publishing worldwide in

Oxford New York

Auckland Cape Town Dar es Salaam Hong Kong Karachi
Kuala Lumpur Madrid Melbourne Mexico City Nairobi
New Delhi Shanghai Taipei Toronto

With offices in

Argentina Austria Brazil Chile Czech Republic France Greece
Guatemala Hungary Italy Japan Poland Portugal Singapore
South Korea Switzerland Thailand Turkey Ukraine Vietnam

OXFORD is a trademark of Oxford University Press
in the UK and in certain other countries

National Library of Australia Cataloguing-in-Publication entry

Miragliotta, Narelle.

The Australian political system in action / Narelle
Miragliotta, Wayne Errington, Nicholas Barry.

9780195563177 (pbk.)

Includes index.
Bibliography.

Politics, Practical–Australia.
Australia–Politics and government.

Errington, Wayne.
Barry, Nicholas.

324.0994

Edited by Tim Fullerton
Cover design by Caitlin Ziegler
Text design by Patrick Cannon
Typeset by Cannon Typesetting
Proofread by Roz Edmond
Indexed by Russell Brooks
Printed in Hong Kong by Sheck Wah Tong Printing Press Ltd

Contents

Figures and tables   *vii*

Preface   *viii*

1   **Democracy and Liberalism in Australia**   **1**
Issue in focus: How healthy are Australia's political institutions?   16

2   **The Australian Constitution**   **25**
Issue in focus: Does Australia require a federal constitutional
bill of rights?   41

3   **Federalism**   **51**
Issue in focus: Is Australian federalism in need of reform?   64

4   **The Legislature**   **71**
Issue in focus: Is the Senate relevant and necessary to facilitate the
expression of the democratic will?   88

5   **Running the State: Executive Power**   **96**
Issue in focus: How can we keep the political executive accountable?   110

6   **The Public Service: Making and Implementing Policy**   **119**
Issue in focus: Has the Commonwealth bureaucracy been politicised?   131

7   **The High Court**   **141**
Issue in focus: How should High Court judges interpret the law?   151

8   **The Importance of Electoral Systems**   **160**
Issue in focus: Should preferential voting be replaced by a system
of proportional voting in the House of Representatives?   175

9   **The Australian Party System**   **187**
     Issue in focus: How relevant is the cartel party thesis to explaining
     new developments among Australia's major parties?   202

10   **The Australian Labor Party**   **213**
     Issue in focus: What does the Labor Party stand for today?   222

11   **The Liberal Party**   **234**
     Issue in focus: What does the Liberal Party stand for today?   247

12   **Minor Parties in Australia**   **256**
     Issue in focus: To what extent do minor parties enhance democracy
     in Australia?   276

     Glossary   *280*
     Bibliography   *290*
     Index   *307*

Figures and tables

Figure 1.1   The Australian political system   14
Figure 4.1   The structure of Australia's federal government   75
Figure 4.2   The passage of proposed laws through Parliament   85
Figure 6.1   Size of the Australian Public Service, Commonwealth public
              sector and Australian workforce, 1988–2007   130
Figure 6.2   New Commonwealth legislation since Federation   131

Table 1.1   Liberal and democratic features of selected political systems   4
Table 2.1   The Constitutions of Australia and its states and territories   33
Table 2.2   Overview of the eight chapters of the Australian Constitution   34
Table 4.1   The roles of the House of Representatives and the Senate
              compared   78
Table 4.2   Proportion of House time spent considering certain categories
              of business, 1995–2007   79
Table 6.1   Examples of Commonwealth public sector organisations   124
Table 8.1   Three major families of electoral system and their variants   164
Table 8.2   The electoral systems of the nine Australian jurisdictions   165
Table 8.3   Breakdown of the expenses for the 2007 federal election   178
Table 9.1   Different opinions on the functions of a political party   191
Table 9.2   Classifying Australian parties   196
Table 9.3   Political parties in Australia   198
Table 11.1   Liberal Party leaders   242

Preface

THIS book is designed to introduce the dynamics of the Australian political system in an interesting and readable way. It combines a thorough survey of the historical development of democratic institutions with lively critiques of the way democracy works in Australia today. Students will find definitions of all the key political concepts both in the text and a separate glossary. The book explains complex political ideas that can sometimes seem remote from students, beginning with the fundamental concepts and increasing the complexity of the discussion as the book unfolds. It caters both to those students who need to reinforce the basics of politics, as well as those seeking to engage with discussion and critique of the system.

Chapters are introduced with a colourful episode from Australian political life, which establishes the relevance of the material to follow. Boxes throughout the book highlight important ideas, people and events. Questions in the boxes challenge students to relate the material in each box to the wider themes of the chapter.

A significant part of each chapter comprises an 'Issue in Focus', which reinforces key concepts through analysis of contemporary debates about Australian political actors and institutions. Each Issue in Focus helps students to relate the discussion of political processes to 'real life' and underlines the relevance of the historical and theoretical material in the book.

The Australian Political System in Action begins by setting out some of the key concepts and institutions of democratic politics. Throughout the book, we show the way that the actors and institutions of Australian politics interact and develop, providing a sense of the operation of the system in addition to its key features.

Chapter 1 introduces some of the key concepts of the book, including democracy, liberalism and responsible government. It traces the historical development of these concepts and notes some of the tensions inherent in Australia's liberal-democratic system of government. In the Issue in Focus for this chapter, we examine the state of our democracy both on a system-wide basis and in its adherence to the principles of liberty, equality and participation.

Chapter 2 explains the importance of constitutions and traces their development in Australia and overseas. The various features of the Australian Constitution are then discussed. The Issue in Focus is the bill of rights debate: whether introducing a constitutional bill of rights would be a desirable move for Australia.

Chapter 3 discusses the way that federalism has evolved in Australia. It introduces the principles behind federalism, the way it is entrenched in the Constitution, and the decisions made by parliament and the High Court that have affected the course of federalism. The Issue in Focus analyses criticisms of the way federalism works in Australia and the attitudes of contemporary political leaders to reform of the system.

Chapter 4 outlines the role of parliament, describing the structure of the Commonwealth Parliament and the way it functions on a day-to-day basis. The Issue in Focus introduces historical and contemporary debates about whether parliaments are more effective with one or two chambers.

Chapter 5 sets out the role of the executive branch. It shows the importance of the historical development of cabinet to the flexibility with which it operates today. The challenge of keeping the executive branch accountable in a contemporary democratic system is the Issue in Focus for this chapter.

Chapter 6 builds on the discussion of executive government by analysing the public service. It introduces the concept of bureaucracy and traces the many changes in the structure of the Australian public sector in recent decades. The effect of these changes on the professionalism and non-partisanship of public servants is the Issue in Focus.

Chapter 7 discusses the role and development of the High Court. It sets out the types of cases settled by the Court, and the most important decisions in the Court's history. The Issue in Focus analyses the recent controversies over landmark decisions such as those securing native title, and the principles behind various approaches to legal interpretation.

Chapter 8 shows the importance of elections and electoral systems. It discusses the principles of representation implicit in a number of electoral systems, and outlines the various systems in use in Australia. The Issue in Focus analyses the consequences for democracy of the current and proposed electoral systems for the House of Representatives.

Chapter 9 describes the role of political parties in the Australian system. It shows the various phases of party development, introduces the idea of a party system, and traces the development of the party system in Australia. The Issue in Focus raises the concept of cartel parties, and provides a critique of the way modern political parties behave.

Chapter 10 provides an in-depth discussion of Australia's oldest political party— the Australian Labor Party. It describes the history and structure of the party, and analyses its founding principles. The contemporary relevance of those principles is the subject of the Issue in Focus.

Chapter 11 completes the discussion of the major parties by setting out the features of the Liberal Party. It shows the ways in which Australia's conservative parties have historically differentiated themselves from Labor, and the tensions inherent in the Liberals' coalition with the National Party. The Issue in Focus outlines the contemporary debates over the ideological direction of the Liberals.

Chapter 12 completes the survey of Australian political parties by looking at the role of minor parties. It traces the rise and fall of a number of minor parties and the conditions that allow them to flourish or perish. The question of whether minor parties are an advantage or a nuisance for Australian democracy is the Issue in Focus.

Democracy and Liberalism in Australia

1

THIS CHAPTER:

* critically examines the concepts of democracy and liberalism
* provides a brief introduction to the Australian political system
* shows the ways in which democracy and liberalism interact in our political system.

ISSUE IN FOCUS

How healthy are Australia's political institutions?

KEY TERMS

Bicameralism
Bipartisan
Bourgeois democracy
Checks and balances
Civil society
Consent
Constitutional monarchy
Constitutionalism
Democratic deficit
Electoral system
Elitist
Enlightenment
Federalism
Fourth Estate
Gough Whitlam
Great Depression
Humanism
James Madison
Jean-Jacques Rousseau
John Locke
Legitimacy
Liberalism
Lobbying
Malcolm Fraser
Mandate
Parliamentary system of government
Political ideologies
Political socialisation
Presidential system of government
Prime minister
Proportional representation
Representative democracy
Responsible government
Rule of law
Semi-presidential systems
Sir John Kerr
Social contract
Two-party system

In March 2003, as the American-led coalition forces prepared to invade Iraq, hundreds of thousands of Australians took to the streets of every major city across the country to protest the approaching war. The protesters were jubilant. How could any government ignore such a show of the popular will? Opinion polls showed that unease about the war was not confined to those who marched. Yet, the Howard Government was dismissive of these calls to stop Australia's involvement in the preparations for war. Having led his government to an election victory in 2001, and with another election not due until 2004, the prime minister was certain that any unpopularity associated with his decision to send Australian troops into battle would be temporary. Further, when the election came around, the prime minister could be confident that issues other than the war (such as interest rates and health) would dominate the campaign. This episode illustrates the limits on the ability of public opinion to affect decision-making in a democracy. A political community can make no more important decision than whether or not to become involved in a war. Yet, that decision is made by a handful of people. As citizens, we get to vote every few years, but just what does it mean to call a political system democratic?

Introduction

This chapter introduces the concepts of democracy and liberalism. It sets out the models of democracy that have been tested at various times over thousands of years, paying attention to the substance, as well as the form, of democracy. While the institutions that we associate with democracy, such as parliament, are easy to describe, many people have observed that the values originally associated with democracy have been left out of modern political institutions. Representative political systems, originally developed in North America and Europe, are usually designed to limit the power of governments rather than give effect to the popular will. The tension between liberalism (limiting and dividing the power of the state) and democracy is one of the major themes of this book. This chapter shows that both liberal and democratic traditions played a role in the design of Australia's political institutions. The resulting Australian Constitution provides for elections but also divides power between levels of government, upper and lower houses of Parliament and between three branches of government. The Issue in Focus in this chapter is an assessment of contemporary Australian democracy. The section considers whether one of the world's oldest continuous democracies has lived up to the promise of its foundation.

Democracy

The word 'democracy' is derived from Ancient Greek—literally *demos kratia*, or rule by the people. In ancient Athens, the citizens (although not everyone counted as a citizen) did just that. Citizens gathered in the city square to make the most important decisions in the running of the city-state. This method of political organisation is now known as direct democracy in order to distinguish it from the more common modern variant, **representative democracy**. Direct democracy is a means of citizens exercising power without the mediation of political institutions such as parliament. The citizens of ancient Athens regularly voted on a range of issues of state such as security and finance. In large, complex societies with big populations,

Representative democracy: a system whereby citizens delegate power to institutions elected by the people

direct democracy is not usually considered a practical form of government. The political community of Athens consisted of a small minority of the population that was usually made up of wealthy landholders. Women, slaves and foreign residents were excluded from the *demos*. Most people have neither the time nor the inclination to become involved in regular decisions of state. Large modern nation-states lend themselves more to representative political institutions (Held 1987, p. 64).

Today, direct democracy tends to be limited to occasional referenda on particular issues. Some jurisdictions, such as Switzerland, use direct democracy more than others. Australia requires a referendum to change the Constitution. Other democracies, such as the United Kingdom, rarely consult their citizens outside of parliamentary elections. For the most part, the citizens of modern democracies delegate power to elected representatives.

The term 'democracy' has come to describe any political system where the will of citizens with equal political rights is reflected in law-making and governing, whether the people exercise that power directly or indirectly. Within this broad definition, there are many models of democracy.

Democracies have historically been organised in a number of different ways. Political systems are rarely designed from the ground up. Their shape is influenced by tradition, the size and nature of the political community, and the ideas about politics dominant at crucial times in the development of each system. Even among contemporary democracies, **presidential** and **parliamentary systems**, as well as the many different types of **electoral system**, and varying levels of citizen participation provide quite different models of democracy. As democracy spread around the world in the twentieth century, local cultures and institutions ensured that the forms and values of democracy were interpreted slightly differently in each country.

All of the states featured in Table 1.1 have democratic political systems, yet each system is quite different from any of the others. Due to its unique history, Switzerland retains a good deal of direct citizen participation in government. The United States, on the other hand, was founded in response to heavy-handed colonial power, and its constitution seeks to limit the power of the majority to dominate the interests of the minority. Parliamentary systems, such as that of Great Britain, provide fewer checks on the ability of the majority to exercise its will. In spite of the different structure of their political institutions, all of the systems in Table 1.1 have enough in common for us to refer to them as democracies. Democracy has been defined differently, and has taken on positive and negative connotations, at different points in time (Sartori 1962, p. 250). We tend to think of democracy as an unambiguously good thing. As we will see, this was not always the dominant view in modern political history.

Presidential system of government: a system of government that separates executive and legislative power into different branches

Parliamentary system of government: a system where the members of the executive government are drawn from and are responsible to an elected legislature

Electoral system: the body of rules designed to turn the votes of citizens into representation in political institutions

Table 1.1   Liberal and democratic features of selected political systems

	More democratic features		More liberal features		
	Switzerland	New Zealand	UK	Australia	USA
Executive	Permanent formula for power-sharing between parties	Electoral system ensures coalition ministry	Ministers chosen from largest party or coalition	Ministers chosen from largest party or coalition	Directly elected president; separation of powers
Parliament	Strong bicameral (two houses with near equal power)	Uni-cameral (one house of Parliament)	Bicameral; lower house with greater power	Strong bicameral (two houses with near equal power)	Strong bicameral (two houses with equal legislative power)
Referenda	Citizen-initiated referenda to change the Constitution	May be called by the government to resolve contentious issues	May be called by the government to resolve contentious issues	May be called by Parliament to change the Constitution	Citizen-initiated referenda in some states

Source: Lijphart 1999

The various models of democracy represent not only different ways of achieving the same goal; they interpret the substance of democracy in different ways. Some democratic systems value direct public participation more than others. Some systems value human equality more than others. Some incorporate many **checks and balances** in their constitution in order to prevent a simple majority vote having too much influence. So, democracy may mean that the views of the majority are paramount, or it may mean that the views of all citizens (including vulnerable minority groups) should be taken into account—not just the views of those in the majority.

Different notions of equality, liberty and participation, as well as the various ways to structure political institutions, give us different types of democracy.

Checks and balances: a system that ensures that power is divided between different institutions

Liberalism: belief in the rights of the individual, the rule of law, and limited government

Liberalism

As representative democracy developed hundreds of years ago, it was often the rights of individuals in relation to the state, rather than participation in government, that were the primary concern of reformers and revolutionaries. Whereas democracy is an ancient concept, **liberalism** is a relatively recent human development.

Theorists of liberalism such as **John Locke** (1632–1704) sought to counteract the power of the state with the recognition of the rights of individual citizens. The **Enlightenment**, also known as the 'age of reason', which occurred during the eighteenth century, produced a range of ideas about the organisation of power within a state. Liberals debated among themselves the relative merits of liberty and equality, and the extent to which the intervention of the state is necessary to guarantee liberty.

John Locke: English philosopher most famous for his 1689 work, *Two Treatises of Government*

Enlightenment: an age of rapid developments in science and philosophy

Critics of liberalism argued that democracy is meaningless without a high degree of social equality. The ability to participate in and influence politics of citizens with vastly different financial means is inevitably different, so economic inequality leads to political inequality (DeLue & Dale 2009, p. 163). Whereas liberalism was arguably the product of an emerging middle class keen to limit the arbitrary rule of monarchs, Enlightenment philosophers drew on ideas about the equality of human beings from sources as diverse as Christianity and **humanism**. The notion that every person has some intrinsic moral worth was a radical one in a continent dominated by monarchical systems. The notion that the purpose of government is to provide freedom and justice to citizens undermined traditional systems of government. The very **legitimacy** of a system of government based on hereditary power and dating back hundreds of years was placed under question.

The idea that all people are equal goes to the heart of political power. What were the ends of government? By what right do some rule over others? More problematic still to both monarchists and some liberals was the argument of **Jean-Jacques Rousseau** (1712–78) in favour of self-determination. True democracy, Rousseau thought, could be achieved only with the participation of citizens in decisions that affect them (Heywood 1997, p. 73). These ideas continue to inspire those who believe that representative democracy fails to live up to the promise of human equality.

Humanism: an attempt to build a progressive and humane belief system that did not rely on religious principles

Legitimacy: the right to exercise power

Jean-Jacques Rousseau: a French philosopher whose ideas about politics were integral to the French Revolution of 1789

Locke and Rousseau provided quite different accounts of the purpose of government. Locke argued that citizens enter a **social contract** in order to live in a secure environment. Few obligations between citizens flow from such a contract, and government activity should therefore be limited. Rousseau, on the other hand, wrote in *On the Social Contract* that citizens form communities in order to realise a common set of goals and values (DeLue & Dale 2009, p. 170). Implicit in this conception of the social contract is that governments will do much more than provide security, and that citizens must expect to give up some of their rights for the good of the community as a whole.

Social contract: under a social contract, the relations between citizens are part of an explicit or implicit compact

Despite the association between democracy and liberalism in contemporary society, the relationship between the two principles has never been entirely reconciled. To the extent that the two principles were in conflict, in the eighteenth and nineteenth centuries liberalism was often preferred to democracy. Some liberals assert that liberalism is not only essential to democracy, but preferable to it (see Evans 2006). Other liberal thinkers have concluded that democracy is not so much undesirable as simply less important to the modern state than other political ideas, such as an independent judiciary, that have curtailed the arbitrary power of rulers (Weale 1999, p. 5). That is, popular participation in government is valuable only to the extent that it does not come into conflict with liberal principles of government.

Liberalism is a diverse body of thought. You will have heard the term 'liberal' being used to describe **political ideologies** of both the left and the right. Liberals tend to agree on the following tenets of government:

Political ideologies: bodies of thought, such as liberalism, socialism or conservatism, about the way society should be organised

Rule of law: where all power in a society is constrained by the legal system

- The rights' of individual citizens should be respected. Liberals disagree over the extent of these rights but they include basic freedoms of assembly, speech and religion.
- The **rule of law** should ensure that the state treats each citizen equally.
- Power should be divided. Executive and legislative functions should be separated. The government should be accountable to citizens. The judiciary should be independent of government influence.
- The above tenets are best secured through a written constitution.

These principles are rarely contested in modern societies. This represents a massive change in the way that human beings have been governed since Locke first wrote about liberalism (Heywood 1997, pp. 41–2).

Liberals were able to spread the message about their preferred form of government because by the eighteenth century freedom of speech was already to some degree protected in Britain. To liberals, the media is a unique political institution, essential to democratic debate and potentially powerful in its own right. So important is this role that the media is often compared in its influence to the three branches of government. The concept of the **Fourth Estate** was developed in the nineteenth century to justify the growing importance of newspapers in political debate. The Fourth Estate has come to represent a set of values about the role of the media and journalism in our democratic system. There are a number of ways in which the media plays its part in the political process. One is to provide a free exchange of ideas, exposing political institutions to criticism and helping to conceive of better ways to organise society. Another role of the media is to

Fourth Estate: a concept that sees the media in a democracy as so vital that it is often compared to that of the executive, legislative and judicial branches of government

provide a representative democracy with a means of holding governments account-able between elections.

The combination of liberalism and democracy in a single political system produces a paradox. Some degree of liberalism (such as freedom of speech) is essential to any democratic system yet liberalism expressly seeks to dilute the power of democratic institutions. The majority of citizens cannot take away the right to vote, the right to publicly debate issues and to form political parties without undermining the essence of democracy. Similarly, liberals have pointed out that self-determination, which is one of the underlying values of democracy, requires that the state recognise a sphere of private activity. Again, majority decision-making may undermine democracy if it results in laws that are too intrusive on citizens' lives. We can see the tension between democracy and liberalism in any number of areas: the balance between individual rights and the right of the community to act collectively; the ability of the state to prioritise the various claims of individuals and groups for recognition of their rights; the nature and degree of government and other collective activity in a market economy; and the extent to which the state can regulate private behaviour in the interests of morality or the protection of other citizens (Parkin 2006, pp. 16–17).

Types of representative democracy

We can see in these differing conceptions of liberty, equality and the social contract the roots of contemporary debates about the proper role of government and the market in our economy. Enlightenment thinking about the role of government helped to shape the representative institutions under development in Western Europe and North America during the eighteenth and nineteenth centuries. In parts of Europe, liberalism affected the development of parliamentary systems. In the United States, liberalism spawned a more radical form of government—the first presidential system.

Parliamentary systems

Liberalism had a gradual effect over European political institutions over centuries. This occurred partly though the influence of Enlightenment thinking, and partly because the liberal prescription of divided power reflected the reality of a society divided between the traditional aristocracy and a rising middle class. The role of parliament was essential to the develop-ment of European **constitutional monarchies**. Unlike in France, where the monarchy was overthrown in 1789, in Great Britain there was no clean break with the monarchical system. A crucial part of the changes to European politics was the growing acceptance of liberal and humanist views of the rights and worth of the individual.

> **Constitutional monarchy:** the combination of an hereditary but mostly powerless head of state with a parliamentary system of government

Responsible government: a system where the cabinet is responsible to the parliament and parliament is responsible to voters

Systems of **responsible government** contained many liberal features, such as freedom of speech and an independent judiciary.

Parliament gradually wrested power from monarchs over decades or centuries (Heywood 1997, p. 295). One of the most important developments in Britain was the inability of the Crown to raise taxes from subjects without the consent of Parliament. Parliamentary sovereignty, as opposed to the sovereignty of the monarch, placed few encumbrances on parliaments to legislate. For example, while the judiciary was independent, parliament could simply change the relevant law if it did not like the decision of a court.

These European parliaments were populated by the landed gentry and middle classes rather than by representatives of the population as a whole. However, they did establish the principles of responsible government that remain with us today. Centuries before the extension of voting rights to all adult citizens, the formal institutions of parliamentary government were established, with executive power in the hands of a cabinet drawn from the Members of Parliament. This chain of accountability from the ministers to parliament and from parliament to voters is at the heart of responsible government.

In parliamentary democracies, a deliberative, representative parliament was historically thought to be the best way to ensure that the rights of the people were protected. The growth of liberalism did not change the structure of parliamentary government. More recently European countries have taken on a different approach to democratic institutions, with the advent of the European Union and its courts, and through charters of rights and **proportional representation**, which ensure minority representation in parliament. While many of the changes in parliamentary systems have been evolutionary, the United States took a more radical route to its present political system.

Proportional representation: an electoral system that ensures that a party's share of the seats in parliament is in accordance with its share of all the votes cast

James Madison: contributor to *The Federalist Papers* and fourth president of the United States, 1809–17

Presidential systems

The American Revolution (1775–83) gave the residents of thirteen former British colonies the opportunity to build a new political system. Having fought a war against the world's foremost colonial power in the name of freedom from tyranny, liberty was the highest priority for the leaders of the new nation in designing a new political system. Many of the founders of the American constitution, such as **James Madison** (1751–1836), saw representative institutions as a deliberate check on the passions and interests of the majority. Men such as Madison had no intention of replacing a despotic king with a despotic electorate. The American system, therefore, is designed to limit the accumulation of power.

The American constitution separates executive, legislative and judicial power and provides a number of checks and balances (such as two houses of Congress with equal power) in order to limit the power of any single institution. Further, **federalism** limited the power of the central government. The United States adopted a Bill of Rights by amending its constitution soon after it was written. Perhaps most importantly, given the Americans' rebellion against the arbitrary use of power, was a sense among the citizenry that government must be subject to rules. This sense of **constitutionalism** is much more difficult for nations to develop than other elements of liberalism and democracy. The design of a constitution can easily be imported from elsewhere. The commitment of political leaders to constitutionalism—to obey the ruling of courts, for example—has historically proven much more elusive.

> **Federalism:** a division of government power between central and provincial levels
>
> **Constitutionalism:** the idea that government should and must be legally limited in its powers

The United States is the archetypal presidential democracy. Yet, while we tend to think of the President of the United States as a uniquely powerful figure, in fact the separation of powers places many restrictions on the president's freedom to act (Hague & Harrop 2001, p. 237). Further, the president is now limited to two terms in office. Outside the United States, presidential systems have been highly unstable. The basic form of a presidential system is simple to incorporate into a constitution. However, a true separation of powers has proved much more difficult to sustain because constitutionalism represents a set of values about government, not just a set of rules. Presidential systems in Latin America and Asia have proved susceptible to strong presidents, whose power overwhelms the legislative and judicial branches, leading to dictatorship. Many democracies limit the power of the presidency by formalising a system of power-sharing with parliament. The best known of these **semi-presidential systems** is France. Thus there are many ways to incorporate liberalism into a democratic system of government.

> **Semi-presidential systems:** semi-presidential systems divide executive power between a president and prime minister

Although liberalism was important to the development of political institutions designed to fragment and limit government power, it was not fundamentally concerned with advancing the rights of all people to vote and participate in politics. While some degree of human equality is implicit in liberalism, it took many liberal societies such as the United States and Britain hundreds of years to ensure that all members of the political community were treated equally. As these political systems became more democratic, the problem of balancing the will of the majority with the rights of the minority became more acute.

How much democracy is too much?

Most contemporary models of democracy have one thing in common. They have been designed to promote democratic processes but not necessarily democratic values such as equality. For most citizens, democratic participation begins and ends with an occasional vote at election time. In making representative, rather than direct, democracy the focus of political institutions in modern states, many observers argue that the essence of democracy was lost. In handing decision-making power to an elite, even an elected elite, the spirit of human equality and citizenship that was a distinctive part of ancient democracy struggled to find a place. While different in character, American and European approaches to democracy have much in common. Prior to the twentieth century, none of the countries we have discussed so far could have been classed as democracies, which according to modern definition includes a universal franchise. Until then, the right to vote was accorded to a minority of the population. The extension of the right to vote to all males, regardless of whether of not they owned property and regardless of race, was a widespread development in the nineteenth century (although not, as we shall see, in Australia). Similarly, votes for women became common from around the 1900s.

Equality between citizens was thus extended in a formal way throughout the twentieth century. Today, all adult citizens are entitled to vote in representative democracies. This extension of rights, though essential to realising the true meaning of democracy, has not taken away the focus in modern democracies on **consent** rather than participation (Held 1987, p. 182). Free and fair elections give governments the authority to act on behalf of citizens. We might interpret the movement towards universal franchise in the nineteenth and twentieth centuries as the process of democracy becoming wider but not necessarily deeper. Adult citizens could vote and form political parties, but there were few formal opportunities to influence government policies in between elections. Representation of all citizens, rather than popular participation, characterised most democratic systems.

Consent: the permission that citizens give to governments to act on their behalf

All sorts of political systems claimed to be democracies during the twentieth century. The value of liberalism to the democratic process was underlined by the experience of developing countries during this period. By this point in history, democracy was no longer something to be suspicious of; indeed many countries that were clearly not democracies, such as the Soviet Union, claimed that they were. Governments that could claim to act on behalf of all their citizens enjoyed a great deal of authority. However, notional equality through a universal franchise proved meaningless without liberal institutions such as an independent judiciary to give substance to the electoral process. Without the rule of law to guarantee free and fair elections, the electoral process in many states following the Second World War was simply a means of providing a veil of legitimacy for a dictatorial elite.

A number of advantages of mass participation in democracy have been advanced. The first is that participation in democratic politics allows the highest level of human development. Participation realises the full value of citizenship and encourages us to rise above our personal interests. Similarly, it is only right that citizens have some say over decisions that affect them directly. The second advantage is that widespread participation allows the widest possible range of views of people with a range of life experiences to influence the policy-making process.

Choosing political representatives is only one of a number of ways in which citizens might participate in politics. The notion of **civil society** denotes a level of political activity between periodic votes for elected representatives and full participation in the decision-making process. Thus, citizens and interest groups are free to raise and debate issues, organise themselves into trade unions or protest government decisions. It is important, though, that the concerns of a vibrant civil society are reflected in democratic parliaments. The idea of a **democratic deficit** has recently been coined to describe the difference between the ideals of democracy and the systems of government in industrialised societies that sometimes seem remote from the concerns of ordinary citizens. Formally bringing the kind of participation we see in civil society and social movements into a system of representative democracy, though, would be expensive. Parliaments already spend considerable time consulting community groups about proposed legislation. Critics of the notion of increased participation argue in favour of the right of private citizens to be left alone rather than being drawn into social conflict. Participation in politics is time consuming. Delegating that responsibility to elected representatives may be a rational response to the demands of a modern society rather than a democratic deficit.

Elite decision-making is inevitably influenced by well-resourced vested interests more so than the concerns of ordinary voters (Held 1987, p. 203). Representative democracy entails the risk, then, that the views of the wealthy minority will drown out the legitimate policy preferences of the majority. Decentralised decision-making would be less subject to **lobbying** by well-connected interests.

Advocates of democratic participation acknowledge the practical limitations of democracy in large industrialised societies. Rather than seeking to overturn representative democracy, some advocates look to social movements such as feminism and environmentalism for signs of stronger democratic participation. Social movements may include groups that attempt to influence party parliamentary politics and groups that prefer direct action such as protests and boycotts. The environmental movement, for example, is comprised of many organisations that deploy a variety of political methods to achieve their objectives. Sea Shepherd undertakes direct action to prevent whaling in the Antarctic while the Australian Conservation Foundation runs public awareness campaigns and lobbies governments.

Civil society: the free organisation of citizens outside the activities of the state

Democratic deficit: when notionally democratic institutions fail to reflect the views and interests of citizens

Lobbying: coined to describe people who populated the lobby of the US Congress: an attempt to influence the decisions of government officials

Where does power really lie in a democracy?

To some observers, representative democracy works best when rational, self-interested voters maximise their interests by choosing between groups of elites. We can thus analyse democratic institutions according to the efficiency with which they achieve this task by analysing whether elections are free and fair, or the extent to which the concerns and priorities of the majority of citizens are reflected in the agenda of elected governments. The spirit of democracy—citizenship and participation—is more difficult to identify and measure.

As a liberal pluralist, Robert Dahl recognised the limitations of representative democracy. In *Who Governs?* (1961), Dahl argued that while democratic societies often fell well short of democratic ideals of equality and participation, public offices in such societies are open to a greater range of candidates than in the past and the modern state is responsive to a range of interests. While some groups have demonstrably more resources than others, the state is also responsive to those with fewer resources because of their greater numbers, whether or not they participate in formal organisations (Held 1987, p. 189). C. Wright Mills, on the other hand, saw modern democracy as a means of legitimising the rule of a tiny elite. Under his formulation in *The Power Elite* (1956), Mills argued that it is the interests of business that are paramount to democratic governments. The **elitist** view of democracy sees voters as powerless because the power elite places limits on the types of issues and options that constitute political debate. The mass media, then, is a conservative force in the elitist conception of democracy. According to this view, the media filters the messages we receive in order to support the *status quo*.

Elitist: a conception of democracy that sees only very limited opportunities for public participation in representative political institutions

BOX 1.1   What is power? Three dimensions

Power as decision-making

Power is a fundamental concept in political science. It underlies everything we discuss in this book. Who has power? What do they do with it? How is power distributed or limited? Definitions of power affect our view of other political concepts such as democracy and liberalism. Considering how important this concept is to the study of politics, it is surprising that there is no consensus on just what power is. One of the most famous definitions of power comes from Robert Dahl (1970). Power, according to Dahl, is the ability of one political actor to change the behaviour or disposition of another political actor. This simple definition of power helps us understand the way in which political institutions decide who gets what and how.

Power as agenda setting

Naturally, such a simple definition fails to capture much of the complexity of power in our society. Steven Lukes (1974) argued that our understanding of power needs to be much more subtle if we are to truly understand how democratic systems work. Dahl's definition, Lukes maintains, applies only to political decisions that we can observe and measure. Lukes identified two further dimensions of power. The second dimension, originally identified by Bachrach and Baratz (1962), concerns the ability of office-holders (and others) to control the agenda of a public organisation. It is the nature of the issues that do not make it onto the public agenda that reveal this dimension of power. That is, we need to be aware of 'non-decisions' as well as the observable behaviour of political actors.

Power as political socialisation

Lukes's three-dimensional view of power goes further still in asking why some issues but not others are matters of public controversy. We need to think about the way that citizens are **politically socialised** in a liberal society—through the education system and the media, for example (1974, p. 24). We become used to debating politics within parameters acceptable to those in power. Radical alternatives to the current system are simply not debated, in part because those who might benefit from an alternative political system are not aware of just where their true interests lie.

> **Political socialisation:** the cumulative effect that the various institutions we come into contact with throughout our lives have on our view of the world

In these contrasting definitions of power, we can observe the differing attitudes of pluralists and elitists to democracy. Pluralists such as Dahl see in a representative democracy a system of government responsive to the needs of diverse groups of citizens. Elite theorists, on the other hand, share the view of Lukes that our political institutions hide more than they reveal, and that the promise of democracy is a long way from being realised in contemporary societies.

Q Which of these conceptions of power do you think is most useful in analysing politics? Is real power in a democracy easy to observe or do the most powerful political actors work outside the parliament?

The evolution of Australia's liberal-democratic system

The Australian Constitution was neither a product of a revolution (as in the United States) nor a long process of institutional struggle (as in Britain). It was designed by men who had respect for both systems of government. Just as the British had insisted on written constitutions for the Australian colonies, a written constitution was necessary for Federation in 1901. Indeed, Australia's constitution was in the first instance an Act of the British Parliament. The system of responsible government was not fully explained in the constitution. Attendees of the federation conventions during the 1890s were mostly drawn from colonial parliaments and simply assumed that the system of government with which they were familiar would persist at the Commonwealth level. The Australian Constitution thus says nothing about the office of **prime minister** or cabinet, and very little about political parties. A casual reading of the Australian Constitution gives the impression that the Governor-General is the most powerful actor in national politics. A lack of clearly codified rules for government is not as unusual as you might think. The United Kingdom has no written constitution at all, relying instead on conventions and certain pieces of legislation.

Prime minister: the head of government in parliamentary systems, usually the leader of the largest political party

Australia's Commonwealth Parliament plays a role in both responsible government and federalism. It holds the executive branch accountable, and in the upper house provides equal representation for each state. A powerful upper house at the

Figure 1.1　The Australian political system

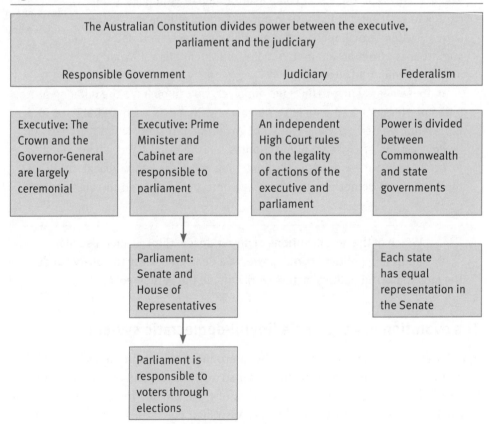

national level, similar to the American model, was a natural progression in Australia's political development since **bicameralism** was well entrenched in colonial political institutions prior to Federation. As the Australian colonies achieved self-government in the second half of the nineteenth century, all adopted powerful upper houses in their parliaments. Bicameralism was an expressly conservative institution. One of the fathers of self-government in New South Wales, William Charles Wentworth, had suggested that the upper house (the Legislative Council) consist of a hereditary aristocracy like the British House of Lords. The New South Wales constitution instead allowed for an upper house whose members were appointed by the Governor, which still had the effect of protecting the interests of wealthy landowners (such as Wentworth himself) from the popular passions of an elected lower house (Hirst 1988, pp. 34–7). Even in the more democratic Legislative Assemblies, property qualifications allowed wealthy citizens to vote in as many electorates as they held property, facilitated by elections held over multiple days.

> **Bicameralism:** parliaments that have an upper and a lower house

Importantly, the national constitution provided for elected representatives in both houses of Parliament. The appointed membership or property qualification for voting persisted in state upper houses well into the twentieth century. As late as 1973, South Australia abolished its property qualification. The democratic nature of the federal constitution served as an example for reform of state parliaments (although Queensland took the even more democratic step of abolishing its Legislative Council in 1922). However, the direct elections for upper houses gave them a legitimacy that supporters of responsible government did not welcome.

Even though bicameralism was an established part of Australian constitutional practice prior to Federation, the fusion of responsible government and federalism was in some quarters thought to create a potentially unstable hybrid (Emy & Hughes 1991, p. 265). The combination of an electoral system providing clear majorities to governments in the House of Representatives with an elected Senate carrying a different type of **mandate** led to an inevitable clash between the political principles of responsible government and federalism. The advent from about 1910 of disciplined political parties tilted the balance of the system away from its federalist principles towards that of responsible government. Leaders of those parties promoted the idea of responsible government (often referred to as the Westminster system) because it was that feature of the system that gave prime ministers the uniquely powerful position we see today. Even leaders of the Liberal Party, notionally a defender of federalist principles, have had an interest in promoting the idea of responsible government and the power-of-the-majority view when they win elections in the lower House. After winning the 1996 election, for example, Prime Minister John Howard insisted that he had a mandate to implement his policies by legislation without obstruction from the Senate.

> **Mandate:** a right to act

The decade before and after Federation was one of political experimentation in Australia. As was the case in Europe and the United States, liberal institutions were in place in Australia before they were given democratic substance with the introduction of the universal franchise. Australia was among the first countries to extend the electoral franchise to all adult men and women. Indigenous Australians did not fare so well in this democratic laboratory, with voting rights gradually extended to the first Australians by the 1960s. Introducing salaries for Members of Parliament was an important step in ensuring that those from backgrounds other than the wealthiest in society could afford to run for Parliament. The secret ballot was another Australian initiative, and is still referred to in some countries as the Australian ballot. Freedom of the press was an established principle in both the United States and Britain by 1901, although more firmly entrenched in the United States courtesy of the Bill of Rights. In Australia, the British model was preferred as a method of rights protection.

Although the United States Bill of Rights did not serve as a model of rights protection, federalism in Australia did necessitate a constitutional court to resolve disagreements about the division of power between the Commonwealth and the states. Elected governments from both sides of politics have had contentious legislation struck down by Australia's High Court. While supporters of responsible government might argue that the Court's role dilutes the democratic elements of the constitution, often the Court's decisions are designed to strengthen Australia's democratic processes. The Menzies Government's 1950 attempt to ban the Communist Party of Australia was rejected by the Court, although the reasons for that decision had as much to do with an over-reach of legislative power as with civil liberties.

The power of the High Court underlines the limits to democratic authority of the Parliament. If Parliament is not sovereign (as it was in the British model of responsible government), which of Australia's political institutions is the highest authority? Who has the final say? Galligan argues that the referendums endorsing the constitution were the true source of legitimacy for the Australian political system, and that the popular amendment process reinforces that feature of Australian democracy (1995, pp. 14–15). While a written constitution may constrain the actions of a popularly elected government, the constitution itself is in the hands of the Australian people. Thus, the people are sovereign in the Australian political system.

ISSUE IN FOCUS

HOW HEALTHY ARE AUSTRALIA'S POLITICAL INSTITUTIONS?

While the above discussion of the Australian political system shows that we have incorporated many key liberal institutions and embraced a representative model of democracy, not everyone is content with the system. A number of commentators, both historical and contemporary, have been at pains to denounce the Australian system as both undemocratic and illiberal. How, then, do we judge the health of a political system? One approach is to undertake a system-wide analysis, examining the cohesiveness (or the fit) between the various institutions that make up our political system. The importance of this approach is that while individual political institutions may be playing their role efficiently, it is the way in which the various institutions of democracy work (or fail to work) together that is most important.

One of the big debates to which system-wide analysis can be applied is in the relationship between the liberal and democratic elements of the Australian political system. The relationship between democracy and liberalism in Australia remains contested. One view is that liberalism provides a check on the undesirable elements of democracy. 'Democracy is not the essence of good government,' argued the Clerk of the Australian Senate, Harry Evans (2006). Many liberals, though, see checks and balances as an enhancement of democracy. Galligan, as we have discussed, sees no conflict between liberalism and democracy. The radical view, by contrast, argues that liberalism dilutes democracy in Australia by placing limits on the ability of elected governments to bring about the changes they have promised to the elector-ate. This applies not only to the liberal institutions designed to dilute the power of the majority but to a society where real power lies with a handful of citizens. That is, the notion of equality implicit in a democracy is inconsistent with a market-based economy, which promotes economic inequality.

We often take the nature of our market economy for granted. It provides most of us with a standard of living undreamt of by earlier generations. A market economy means, however, that managers and owners of capital exercise direct control over important aspects of the lives of Australian workers: their wages, hours of work and working conditions. In a liberal democracy, many of the decisions about how and where economic resources are deployed are made either by powerful private individuals in the market sector or by politicians with an eye to the needs of business. Workers are 'subject to the despotism of capital' (Kuhn 2005, p. 49). In addition, the inequality of wealth inherent in a market economy gives the wealthiest Australians a disproportionate ability to influence the political system. Businesses lobby for laws friendly to profit-making, make donations to political parties and build networks of contacts in politics and the media. For example, the Howard Government's response to global warming was heavily influenced by the coal industry. While many Australians professed concern about climate change, few of us were prepared to change our vote based on this single issue. The coal industry on the other hand, with much to lose if greenhouse emissions were to be reduced, lobbied aggressively in order to influence government policy. Even Labor governments need to take into account the profitability of business, so that Australian enterprises invest capital and employ workers (McGregor 1997, p. 233).

The limits of democratic control of Australian industry were firmly established in the 1940s when Ben Chifley's Government (1944–49) attempted to nationalise Australia's banks. Prime Minister Chifley was hardly a radical. Like many, he thought

Great Depression: a period of record unemployment during the 1930s

Bourgeois democracy: a political system with minimally democratic institutions and in which capitalism is able to thrive

that failures in the banking sector were an important cause of the **Great Depression** and sought to avoid a similar economic catastrophe. The private banks were joined in their protests against the proposed nationalisation by other industries fearing similar government intervention. The High Court ruled against the Government, causing many in the Labor movement to question their ability to implement socialist policies under the Australian Constitution (Crisp 1961, p. 337).

Critics of capitalism are pessimistic about modern democratic institutions. They argue that we live in a **bourgeois democracy** where the dominant class are the owners of capital. The election of a Labor government makes little difference to the direction of public policy. Others on the Left see some room for action by the state independent from the demands of big business. The interests of bureaucrats, workers and small businesses often come into conflict with those of big business, allowing a democratic state to make decisions about whom to favour, particularly when large companies are owned by remote foreign corporations with limited interest in Australian politics (Theophanous 1980, p. 84).

As well as this interaction between liberal and democratic principles throughout Australian society, the two principles continue to shape our political institutions.

Gough Whitlam: prime minister 1972–75

Sir John Kerr: Governor-General 1974–77

Malcolm Fraser: prime minister 1975–83

Seven decades after Federation, the constitution received its biggest test. **Gough Whitlam** led the Australian Labor Party to its second consecutive election victory on 18 May 1974. By 1975, the Whitlam Government faced a hostile Senate, and could not get its budget through the Parliament. On 11 November 1975 the Governor-General **Sir John Kerr** dismissed the Whitlam Government and appointed the Liberal Party's **Malcolm Fraser** as caretaker prime minister. This event, according to Graham Maddox, 'shook the foundations of Australian democracy' (2000b, p. 515).

How strong are those foundations if an unelected Governor-General can simply dismiss a government elected by millions of Australians? Political actors have been careful to avoid a repeat of the acrimony of 1975 and governments have had few problems passing their budget bills despite having a minority in the Senate for much of that period (Parkin & Summers 2006, p. 60). While the events of November 1975 may have been troubling, the end result was a free and fair election. The system has since continued to run smoothly. Others take a more critical view, seeing a calculated effort by the ruling class to deny the legitimacy of a democratically elected government. This was only possible because of the flaws in the Constitution that provide obstacles to the enactment of the will of the people as expressed at elections in 1972 and 1974. Maddox argues that the dismissal of the Whitlam Government 'placed democracy itself under question' (2000b, p. 515).

The 1975 crisis also raised the issue of the mix of democratic and monarchical features of the Constitution. The Governor-General's ability to dismiss an elected government is a vestige of the power of the British monarchy. The debate during the 1990s over whether Australia should become a republic revealed some interesting differences of opinion about Australian democracy. That move to cut Australia's ties with the British monarchy failed, at least in part, because of the widespread view that Australia was already a republic in all but name (see Maddox 2000a). That is, Australia's political institutions were already democratic and the powers of the monarch and the Governor-General were less important than the power of the people to elect their representatives and change the Constitution. Others saw the republic debate as an opportunity to raise longstanding concerns about the limitations of our political system. The Real Republic group argued that Australia, once a laboratory of democratic experimentation, had fallen behind democratic developments elsewhere in the world. The group was critical of the Australian Republican Movement proposal for a president appointed by the Commonwealth Parliament. In addition to direct election for any new head of state, Real Republic members supported a more proportional voting system, citizen-initiated referendums, and a bill of rights (Thompson 1999). It is interesting to note that many advocates for change in Australia's political system call for both liberal reforms such a bill of rights *and* more popular participation in decision-making. They don't necessarily see liberalism and democracy as conflicting values.

The combination in our constitution of federalism and responsible government causes concern not only when, as in 1975, the House of Representatives and the Senate are at loggerheads. The division of legislative responsibilities between two levels of government breaks up the clear chain of political accountability that is the primary strength of responsible government. It is difficult, for example, to hold state governments accountable for the state of public hospitals (owned and run by the states) when the funding of those hospitals is largely the responsibility of the Commonwealth.

Another approach to measuring the health of a democratic system is to analyse the system in accordance with the liberal-democratic concepts that we have discussed in this chapter: participation, freedom, and equality.

Equality

Australians like to think of themselves as living in an egalitarian society. This idea stemmed from the absence of inherited titles and the informal way in which the most powerful people in the country conducted themselves. This myth of equality, though, is belied by the level of economic equality between classes in Australia. Australia's ruling class is a network of business leaders, politicians, judges and journalists. Many company directors sit on numerous boards. Many went to exclusive private schools and network through clubs. The wealthiest 10 per cent of Australian families own nearly half of Australia's private assets while the poorest half own less than 10 per cent (Headey et al. 2004). Macquarie Bank CEO, Alan Moss, was reported in 2007 to have earned over $33 million, more than a hundred times the salary of the prime minister or 450 times the wage of a construction worker.

The level of social and economic inequality in Australia raises questions about our commitment to democracy. The lack of social equality in turn affects the ability of each citizen to participate in politics. Wealthy citizens and corporations can make donations to political parties. Middle-class citizens have the resources to organise themselves into interest groups. Australians enjoy a formal equality before the law. That is, the law applies equally to the prime minister as to the poorest citizen. With few exceptions, we have the right to vote and participate in politics. Yet, equality before the law does not guarantee equal access to the law. Hiring a lawyer is expensive and beyond the means of many. Australia's system of legal aid is modest.

Any substantial effort to reduce the level of social equality in Australia would involve a high degree of intervention on the part of the government. While our political system, with its divided power, is designed to prevent the rapid adoption of radical policies, Australia was a pioneer early in the twentieth century in many areas of policy designed to reduce social inequality, such as the aged pension and minimum wages and conditions for workers. Progressives argue that a renewed effort at achieving social equality is essential to the realisation of democratic values in the political realm.

Freedom

Many of the freedoms associated with liberalism are essential to a healthy democracy. Australians are free to join political parties, organise protest movements and petition against government decisions. The debate over the best way to protect these rights continues, with some advocates of rights protection acknowledging that a change to the Constitution in this area is unlikely and instead arguing in favour a bill of rights passed by state and Commonwealth Parliaments. While this would provide weaker rights protection than a constitutional measure, it would play an educative role by institutionalising the discussion of rights when measures to combat terrorism, for example, are debated (Williams 2007, p. 86).

When it comes to freedom of speech, Australia's ranking in the *Reporters Without Borders Worldwide Press Freedom Index* has fallen in the last few years to 35th, behind even some former Soviet states. Freedom of speech is one of the cornerstones of any liberal-democratic system. Unlike the United States, Australia has no express provision in its constitution protecting freedom of speech. The High Court has recognised an implicit but limited protection of political communication. However, this provision has not stopped Australian Parliaments from passing any number of restrictions on freedom of speech such as libel laws, contempt of court, and anti-vilification laws.

Concerned about anti-terrorism legislation that constrains the reporting of police investigations, the narrow interpretation by the public service and the courts of

Freedom of Information laws, and other restrictions on freedom of speech, a coalition of media organisations launched the *Australia's Right to Know* campaign in 2007. They argued that while any single restriction on the right of free speech might be justifiable on its own terms, the cumulative effect of hundreds of such restrictions casts a pall over political debate.

Participation

A lack of popular participation in politics is one measure of alienation from the political system. Voting is compulsory in Australia. For most of us, though, voting is the beginning and the end of our participation in politics. For instance, in the survey period for the *Australian Social Attitudes* report (2001–03), less than a third of people had contacted a political representative, while only 12 per cent had taken part in a protest or demonstration (Passey & Lyons, p. 70). Perhaps many Australians are sceptical about the value of political protest. Pluralists argue that instead of direct participation in the political system, the concerns of citizens are represented by the many interest groups active in politics and society. Australia certainly has a vibrant and growing set of interest groups. It is difficult to imagine a social group or political interest that is not represented in some way. A citizen does not need to be a formal member of an interest group for their views to be taken into account. When governments negotiate with, say, Seniors Australia, they are aware that this body is representative of the views of a great many people over and above the formal membership of the group. Of course, some interest groups have more resources than others. While some interest groups, such as environmentalists, like to protest directly, for example against a property development, other groups directly lobby governments behind closed doors. The lack of transparency in the lobbying industry is of great concern to those without the resources to influence politics in this way (see Warhurst 2007). The Australian Electoral Survey reported that in 2007, two-thirds of Australians thought that the government was run for the benefit of 'a few big groups' rather than 'all the people'.

The stability of Australia's **two-party system**, and the public perception that the two major parties are much the same in their policy platforms, discourages many people from direct involvement in politics. In spite of the fact that a declining proportion of voters identify with one of the main political parties, it has proved very difficult for minor party and independent candidates to win seats in the House of Representatives. A **bipartisan** consensus over issues such as globalisation and trade has left many Australians feeling alienated from the political system. This bipartisanship leaves room for populist parties such as One Nation to attract votes by offering simple solutions to complex problems.

Two-party system: a political system in which two parties are dominant and typically alternate between government and opposition

Bipartisan: when measures have the support of the two major parties

BOX 1.2   Types of interest (or pressure) groups

Sectional groups represent the interests of a clearly defined group of citizens. This might be a demographic group (the young or the elderly), a group with local or regional concerns, or citizens with something in common such as a motoring group or parents supporting children with a disability.

Producer groups are a subset of sectional groups that represent workers and businesses. They might be individual trade unions or local chambers of commerce, members of a profession, or large umbrella groups at the national level such as the Australian Council of Trade Unions or the Australian Industry Group.

Promotional groups advocate an ideological position on behalf of the community. Such groups might be environmentalists, refugee campaigners or road safety advocates.

Q Do you think that interest groups play a constructive role in democratic systems? Who looks after the national interest when so many organisations are geared towards looking after the interests of their members?

Membership of political parties is a useful measure of democratic participation. One of the reasons why party membership has fallen in recent decades is that the major political parties have become much more professional in their approach to winning elections. Members and volunteers were, in the 1950s and 1960s, essential to the success of a political campaign and membership was measured in the hundreds of thousands. Now, the major parties concentrate on expensive advertising campaigns and sophisticated policy-formulation strategies that target swinging voters. The membership of each of the major parties has slipped under 100 000. Party members find that they have little say in the running of their organisation. The only party willing to disclose its membership figures is The Greens, since their membership is growing, and is over 5000 (Jaensch et al. 2004, p. 53). Green parties around the world, by contrast, pride themselves on encouraging democratic participation. The Australian Greens promote grassroots democracy as one of the four principles of green politics. This is consistent with the direct action such as protests and blockades that environmental activists bring to politics.

For many years, the Democratic Audit of Australia has undertaken the task of measuring the effectiveness of democratic institutions. The Audit has published a series of reports on aspects of the Australian political system such as federalism, political fundraising, citizenship and public participation. Sawer finds that in many of these areas, incremental changes in the law and changing government practices are undermining political equality in Australia. The Howard Government's changes to electoral laws made enrolment more difficult, and removed the franchise for prisoners. In addition, corporate donations to political parties and the transparency of those donations; the poor representation of women and ethnic minorities in Parliament; the benefits to incumbent governments through the resources provided to Members of Parliament, government advertising campaigns and government funding skewed towards marginal seats, all bring the ability of all Australians to participate equally in the political system into question (Sawer 2007).

CHAPTER SUMMARY

After more than two and a half thousand years, democracy remains a vigorously contested concept. We tend to take our own system of representative democracy for granted, but it is in fact still taking shape. A hundred years is a relatively short time for a political system to evolve. While Australia has inherited political traditions from other countries, the unique nature of the resulting democratic system, and the flaws within it, are yet to be fully understood. There is no such thing as a perfect political system. Australian democracy is a blend of competing ideas, values and interests. The more controversial element of liberalism where democracy is concerned is the reach of the state. Liberals believe in a market economy. Infringement by a democratic state in the economic realm is always controversial, not just on the grounds of economic efficiency or social justice, but on the nature of the role that the state should play.

Whatever complaints we may have about aspects of our political system, Australians are generally happy with the way we are governed. In international surveys of trust in government, Australia ranks highly among the world's democracies (Donovan et al. 2007, p. 84). According to the 2007 Australian Electoral Survey, 86 per cent of Australians reported that they were happy with the democratic system. Central to living in a democracy, though, is the continual debate among citizens about the effectiveness of our political system and suggestions for improvement and refinement. Debates over a republic and the protection of rights show that the Australian political system continues to evolve.

WEBSITES

Centre for Democratic Governance Network:
http://www.ruc.dk/demnetgov_en/
A collaborative research centre that conducts research on the interaction within and among governance networks.

Democratic Audit of Australia:
http://arts.anu.edu.au/democraticaudit/
Publishes papers on the health of Australia's political institutions.

Documenting Democracy:
http://www.foundingdocs.gov.au/
A website that hosts 101 key foundational documents that have been central to the evolution of Australia's political and social history.

FURTHER READING

Galligan, B. 1995. *A Federal Republic: Australia's Constitutional System of Government*. Cambridge University Press, Cambridge.

Heywood, A. 1997. *Politics*. Macmillan, London.

The Australian Constitution

THIS CHAPTER:

★ defines a constitution and explains its purpose

★ explores the various categories that are used to classify constitutions

★ examines the essential attributes of the Australian Constitution and the circumstances that led to its creation

★ outlines the key features of the Australian Constitution.

ISSUE IN FOCUS

Does Australia require a federal constitutional bill of rights?

KEY TERMS

Act of Settlement
Affirmative rights
Bill of rights
Consensus democracy
Constitution
Conventions

Entrenched
Governor-General
High Court
Joint sitting of Parliament
Magna Carta
Majoritarian democracy
Republic

Separation of powers
Sovereignty
9/11 terrorist attacks
Westminster

In 1996, Albert Langer was imprisoned for ten weeks on contempt charges after breaching an injunction that prohibited him from advising voters to mark their ballot papers in a way that was discouraged by Australian electoral authorities. Langer's initial crime was to advertise a loophole in electoral law that permitted voters to cast what was essentially an optional preferential vote rather than a full preferential vote. Although Langer was ultimately jailed for contempt, his case raised concerns about the failure of the Constitution to adequately defend freedom of expression in Australia. The case led Amnesty International to declare Langer Australia's first prisoner of conscience in more than twenty years.

Introduction

An important measure of the health of a democracy is the extent to which there exists a clear set of rules that define the structure and operation of the political system. Most scholars and commentators agree that a good political system is one founded on rules that emphasise openness, order and the protection of basic political and civil rights. It is generally agreed that these rules, once established, must be applied in a uniform and consistent manner. The citizenry cannot be expected to understand their rights and obligations if the government can alter the rules on a whim. To this end, the laws should be written down to guarantee both their permanence and transparency. It is also vital that the rules be respected, adhered to and accepted by the citizenry and those who govern. The rules should not be a 'mere token' but correspond, in major respects at least, to actual political practice. The laws are only truly meaningful if there is a shared acceptance of their legitimacy and authoritativeness (Heywood 2007).

Constitution: a document that contains the rules by which the state is organised and governed and that describes the relationship between the government and the citizenry

The rules that are referred to in the preceding paragraph are typically set down in a **constitution**. A constitution is a device that provides a map of the institutions of the state and describes the powers they possess. Although no constitution is entirely comprehensive, nor are its rules always strictly adhered to, it does afford an important insight into the rules, processes, procedures and values that inform a nation's political practices.

This chapter provides an overview of constitutions and the Australian Constitution in particular. It begins with a discussion of the role of constitutions and the different forms they take. From here, we will explore the Australian Constitution and study some of its more important elements. In the Issue in Focus we investigate the status of rights protection within the Constitution.

Different types of constitutional models

One cannot possibly learn all there is to know about a country's political system by merely studying its constitution. All constitutions are incomplete in one way or another, some are misleading, either in whole or in part, deliberately or unintentionally, and they are rarely static, even if the rules remain unchanged in a formal sense. Whatever their faults, constitutions are important because they set down many of the key principles on which a country's political system is based. A constitution also reveals something about the political hopes of those who drafted it, the political values cherished by that society, the past mistakes it is hoping to correct, and the kind of polity it desires to create (Finer et al. 1995).

Constitutions are regarded as a recent development, even though scholars trace their lineage to the English **Magna Carta** of 1215, Bill of Rights of 1688 and the *Act of Settlement* of 1701. Heywood contends that the modern constitution is principally a creature of the late eighteenth century, precipitated by the enactment of the United States Constitution in 1787, the world's first written constitution, which was followed closely by the French Declaration of the Rights of Man and the Citizen in 1789. Both constitutions (and the United States Constitution more particularly) were to serve as templates for later constitution makers. Throughout the nineteenth century, the practice quickly spread throughout much of Europe and to a number of Asian states (Heywood 2007, p. 316). In the late twentieth century, a new wave of constitution making occurred. Many former authoritarian states and, to a lesser extent, a number of established democracies, such as Sweden and Belgium, adopted new constitutions (Hague & Harrop 2004, p. 209). In the ten-year period 1989–99 alone, 85 new constitutions were enacted (Derbyshire and Derbyshire quoted in Hague & Harrop 2004, p. 209).

Magna Carta: a charter signed in 1215, which was designed, among other things, to restrain the power of the British monarchs. Under the charter, the king was required to renounce certain rights, respect certain legal procedures and accept that the will of the king could be bound by the law.

Act of Settlement: the principal Act of 1701 governing the succession to the thrones of the United Kingdom and the other Commonwealth Realms

BOX 2.1   A typology of constitutions

In principle, all constitutions perform more or less the same functions, which are to 'mark out the existence of a state; identify and embody a nation's political goals and values; stabilise the state; and legitimise both the state and the ruling regime' (Heywood 1997, pp. 280–1). However, beyond this commonality of purpose, every constitution is different. As shown below, there can be significant differences in terms of its mode or status (the form of the constitution), its content, and the type of government it establishes.

Mode	Written v. Unwritten Entrenched v. Flexible Higher law v. Ordinary legislation (statute)
Content	Effective v. Facade Descriptive v. Limiting Bill of rights v. Limited or no rights protection
Form of government	Constitutional monarchy v. Republican Federal v. Unitary Presidential v. Parliamentary Dictatorship v. Democracy

As shown in Box 2.1, the range of constitutions is highly diverse and complex. Almost all countries have a constitution of some form, although no two are identical. This variation occurs because a constitution is drafted to suit the political, cultural and social realities of the people (and in some cases the rulers) it is intended to serve: 'different historical contexts have generated different preoccupations and priorities and this in turn has led to quite different constitutional structures' (Finer et al. 1995, p. 7). Consequently, any assessment of the merits of a constitution is inherently subjective, informed by different understandings about the kind of political structures needed to bring about an ideal system of government.

One of the ways scholars seek to bring order to the study of constitutions is by organising them according to their basic elements. A popular approach has been to distinguish between written and unwritten constitutions. Most countries have an identifiable written constitution that sets out the institutions and systems of government. According to Finer, written constitutions emerge out of one of two sets of circumstances: in order to 'replicate the old customary constitution' or 'when it is deemed desirable to innovate and replace it' (Finer 1988, p. 20). However, not every nation has enshrined their rules in a single instrument. It is not uncommon for a nation's constitution to be spread across any combination of multiple statutes (ordinary legislation) and/or **conventions**. An unwritten constitution is embodied in custom and tradition, commonly regarded as an 'organic entity', having evolved slowly in response to historical and political conditions. Unwritten constitutions are not the norm. There are only three nations—Israel, New Zealand and the United Kingdom—that continue to utilise an unwritten format. Some commentators regard the distinction between written and unwritten constitutions as specious, particularly because no written constitution can be sufficiently comprehensive that it describes all aspects of the political system. All constitutions incorporate written and unwritten features, 'although the balance between these varies significantly' (Heywood 2007, pp. 317–18).

Constitutions can be categorised according to whether they are **entrenched** (difficult to amend) or flexible (easy to amend). Unwritten constitutions are flexible because they can be easily altered. For example, there are few formal legal obstacles that stand between the British Parliament and the alteration of its constitution. While some would regard this arrangement as undesirable, the advantage is that it allows the lawmakers to update, revise and adapt the rules of government to the changing needs of society without having to wrestle with a complex legislative process. It is also worth noting that unwritten constitutions can be just as stable and durable as their written counterparts and do not necessarily provide any less substantive protections. As Finer et al. observed, 'constitutions are otiose: if the power holders exercise self restraint, the written constitution is unnecessary, and if they do not then it is useless' (1995, p. 2).

Conventions: informal practices that guide the operation of the constitution and which have moral rather than legal force

Entrenched: a constitution that is entrenched is more difficult to alter than normal law

Written constitutions, in contrast, are typically more difficult to amend because to do so requires formal alteration of an Act of legislation, involving a specific set of procedures and routines. Some written constitutions can be amended through the normal legislative process. However, some nations have incorporated special procedures for altering the constitution so as to ensure that the highest law in the land is not treated as any ordinary piece of legislation. Entrenchment can take the form of special majorities (i.e. more than 50 per cent of the parliament agreeing to the proposed alteration), the approval of state legislatures (in a federal system, amendment can only be approved if agreed to by a specified number of state legislatures), a referendum process (amendment put to the people to decide), or a combination of any of these mechanisms.

There are constitutions that concentrate **sovereignty** and those that devolve power to other political units within the state. Constitutions that divide power between one or more tiers of government are referred to as federal constitutions. Though there can be significant variation between federal constitutions, it is typical that where they operate the central government is allocated responsibility for matters of national concern while the regional governments attend to affairs within their particular jurisdiction. Federal constitutions are often the norm in divided societies because they allow for a structured devolution of 'sovereign' power while ensuring that a state's sovereignty remains intact overall (Heywood 2007).

> **Sovereignty:** the right of people living within a particular geographical community to claim ownership and authority over that particular territory

Some constitutions emphasise procedural rules and are 'largely restricted to justifiable rules of laws' whereas others contain 'manifesto-like' pronouncements, articulating a commitment to citizen rights (Finer et al. 1995, p. 6). The inclusion of citizen rights within constitutions became *de rigueur* in much of continental Europe and, most famously, the United States, but failed, up until quite recently, to be implemented in many former British colonies (Finer 1988, p. 30). Over the years, the concept of a bill of rights has undergone a transformation. Whereas early bills of rights were framed in very narrow terms (life, liberty and property), most modern declarations delineate a much more expansive suite of rights. Sartori notes that some contemporary charters include a commitment to **affirmative rights** and material entitlements, something that is absent in more traditional rights models (Sartori 1997, p. 197). While Sartori sees affirmative rights as important, he takes the view that they are ultimately 'quasi-suicidal', imposing duties and obligations on rulers that are near impossible to satisfy.

> **Affirmative rights:** also known as positive rights: the rights to be provided something, usually by the state, for example the right to employment or free education

A distinction is also drawn between constitutions that establish a frame of government and those that establish specific institutional structures to restrain government agency. Many constitutions are descriptive in that their only purpose is to map out the institutions of the state and the relationship of those institutions to one another. Such constitutions are not necessarily concerned with limiting the power of the governing body, but are simply intended to describe who has power. Some scholars argue that only those constitutions that limit the exercise of political power are worthy of the title of constitution (Sartori 1997, p. 196).

BOX 2.2   The problem of facade constitutions: the Democratic People's Republic of Korea (DPKR)

Despite the esteem in which modern societies purport to hold constitutions, they are sometimes worth no more than the paper they are written on. Consider the case of the Democratic People's Republic of Korea (DPRK).

The DPKR, or North Korea, was proclaimed on 9 September 1948, and was ruled by Kim Il-sung until his death in 1994. He was replaced by his son Kim Jong-il, who remains the current leader of the country. On the face of it, the DPKR's Constitution has much to recommend it. It sets down the fundamental principles on which the nation is founded, and describes the key political institutions of the country—a Cabinet, the Supreme People's Assembly (SPA), and a Court (Sung Chull Kim 2002)—indicating a similar separation of powers to that found in Western democracies. The Constitution also sets down a system of rights and obligations owed to the people, and these are unparalleled. For example, the Constitution guarantees the people the right to live tax-free, the collective ownership of the state's resources, access to housing, food and clothing, and free education, including crèches. Freedom of religion is guaranteed, as is the right to free speech, press, assembly, public demonstrations and the vote to all persons aged 17 years and over.

In practice, however, the Constitution delivers very little of what it claims to guarantee the North Koreans. The separation of powers between the key institutions, while overhauled in 1998, is ultimately subject to the whims of the nation's omnipotent leader (Sung Chull Kim 2002, p. 359). The political system that the Constitution describes far from reflects the realities of political life. Further, as Catherine Moller observed (2002), the fundamental rights of North Koreans are not protected:

> North Koreans are denied freedom of speech, the media, religion, movement, assembly, petition, emigration, and association. They do not have the right to peacefully change their government. Foreign travel is prohibited for nearly all. Workers' rights are not observed, and only government-controlled unions are allowed. The government regularly mobilises the population for compulsory labour projects in construction.

While the DPKR's Constitution is clearly a facade, some scholars claim that even the worst constitutions are not entirely without merit. Bogdanor suggests that 'to allocate functions, powers and duties is also *ipso facto*, to limit power'. There is, he argues, 'some gain to the citizen, however minimal, in living under a constitution which regularizes the way in which power is exercised; even where government is authoritarian it matters that it is not arbitrary' (Bogdanor 1988, p. 4).

Q Do you agree with Bogdanor that a constitution that regularises the exercise of governmental power is better for the citizenry than if there were no constitution?

Constitutions that limit government have their roots in liberalism. Liberalism is a political doctrine that is concerned with finding ways of restraining the exercise of government power. The important attribute of liberal constitutions is that they attempt to constrain government by assigning its key functions to separate institutions, a device which is known as the **separation of powers**. The concept of a separation of powers is associated with the ideas of the French philosopher Baron de Montesquieu. Montesquieu believed it was critical that the core functions of government be separated to weaken the power of those who govern. He proposed that responsibility for making laws should be conferred to the legislature; the business of implementing or executing law should fall to the executive or government of the day; while review of the laws and the manner in which they have been implemented should be carried out by the judiciary or the courts. The existence of three separate institutions ensures that each branch is able to check and balance the actions of the other, thereby acting as a brake on the abuse of state power.

> **Separation of powers:** an institutional separation of executive, legislative, and judicial functions of government

Of course, just because a constitution professes to limit government action, does not mean it occurs in practice. A commitment to constitutionalism must exist in order for a government to function in a manner consistent with the strictures of its constitutional system. Constitutionalism refers to the idea that government should and must be legally limited in its powers, and that its authority depends on it observing these limitations. However, the extent to which government adheres to and respects its constitutional arrangements is dependent on the prior existence of values and attitudes (political culture) that are compatible with the political values the polity deems important (Huggins 2002, p. 332). A constitution that lacks either authoritativeness or enforceability is likely to be ineffectual.

Constitutional formation and practice in Australia

If a country was to be judged on the number of constitutions it possesses then Australia would be rated as a top performer. Constitutions have been a vital part of Australia's political fabric for more than 150 years. There are a total of nine constitutions in Australia: one for each of the country's eight states and territories, and one for the nation. These constitutions have proven remarkably stable and durable.

The picture of constitutional abundance and continuity described above is the product of many forces. The initial proliferation of constitution Acts reflects the circumstances in which white Australia was established. Although initially founded as a single outpost, Australia was settled as a collection of separate colonies. When these colonies later sought greater control over their day-to-day political affairs, the British authorities insisted they adopt written constitutions as a precondition of self-government. Given the continent's distance from the motherland, codification offered the best hope of enforcing **Westminster** practice in the colonies. Despite later agreeing to federate, there was never any question that the colonies would surrender their constitutions, although, as we shall see a little later, they did relinquish some of their sovereignty by agreeing to the establishment of a national government. As a result, the formation of the Australian nation-state did not result in the abolition of any of the constitutions but a net gain of one. The durability of Australia's constitutions is a reflection, in part, of the success of the British in transplanting constitutionalism to Australia. However, it is also a reflection of the great peace and prosperity that has prevailed in this country. Australian nationhood did not arise out of the ashes of revolution (although it was at tremendous cost to the Indigenous inhabitants), it has not been invaded by foreign armies, and the country is not wracked by deep religious, sectarian or ethnic cleavages. There has been no serious or lasting crisis of confidence in our political system or the values on which it is based.

Westminster: the name given to the British Parliament and its system of government

While state constitutions remain important, the federal Act sits at the apex of Australia's system of constitutions. The federal Constitution was drafted by delegates of the Australian colonies, who came together to consider the terms and conditions under which they would unite. The final draft, once it was acceded to by the delegates, was put to a referendum of the Australian people, although a large section of the community, including most women and Indigenous Australians were excluded from voting. On receiving the people's imprimatur, the draft constitution was presented to the British Parliament for formal ratification and enactment, but not before Westminster had undertaken a fairly minor modification of at least one of its clauses (Williams 1999, pp. 29–30).

Although the Australian Constitution is now more than a hundred years old, it remains, in formal respects, very much unchanged from the original Act. The Constitution is a highly functional and serviceable instrument. The framers of

Table 2.1   The Constitutions of Australia and its states and territories

Jurisdiction	Name of constitutional Act	Link
Federal First enacted 1900	*Commonwealth of Australia Constitution Act 1900*	http://www.austlii.edu.au/au/legis/cth/consol_act/coaca430/
Australian Capital Territory First enacted 1988	*Australian Capital Territory (Self-Government) Act 1988 (Cth)*	http://www.austlii.edu.au/au/legis/cth/consol_act/acta1988482/
Queensland First enacted 1867	*Constitution Act 1867* *Constitution Act Amendment Act 1934*	http://www.austlii.edu.au/au/legis/qld/consol_act/ca1867188/ http://www.austlii.edu.au//au/legis/qld/consol_act/caaa1934289/
South Australia First enacted 1855	*Constitution Act 1934*	http://www.austlii.edu.au/au/legis/sa/consol_act/ca1934188/
Tasmania First enacted 1854	*Constitution Act 1934*	http://www.austlii.edu.au/au/legis/tas/consol_act/ca1934188/
New South Wales First enacted 1853	*Constitution Act 1902*	http://www.austlii.edu.au/au/legis/nsw/consol_act/ca1902188/
Northern Territory First enacted 1978	*Northern Territory (Self-Government) Act 1978 (Cth)*	http://www.austlii.edu.au/au/legis/cth/consol_act/nta1978425/
Victoria First enacted 1853	*Constitution Act 1975*	http://www.austlii.edu.au/au/legis/vic/consol_act/ca1975188/
Western Australia First enacted 1889	*Constitution Act 1889* *Constitution Acts Amendment Act 1899*	http://www.austlii.edu.au/au/legis/wa/consol_act/ca1889188/ http://www.austlii.edu.au/au/legis/wa/consol_act/caaa1899307/

Australia's Constitution were not idealists but pragmatic colonial politicians. As a result, the Constitution is largely absent of the prosaic language that is found in other constitutions, it stakes no great claim to the protection of citizen rights, nor does it describe a number of the institutions that are central to Australian political practice. Yet, the Constitution is the most important piece of legislation in this country, to which all other laws are inferior.

There are five attributes of the Constitution that are especially noteworthy. We shall now turn our attention to these features.

A written constitution

The Australian Constitution takes written form. It is a slight document, consisting of a mere 12 000 words. It is organised into two separate segments, one short and one long. The short segment is essentially the Act passed by the Imperial Parliament to establish the Commonwealth of Australia. While of historical importance, the nine clauses of which it is comprised are perfunctory and generally uninspiring. The long segment is the important part of the Act, setting out the Constitution proper. It is comprised of 128 sections divided into eight chapters (Howard 1986, p. 19). A brief overview of the structure of the Constitution is provided in Table 2.2.

Table 2.2 Overview of the eight chapters of the Australian Constitution

Chapter I—The Parliament	Describes the structure and organisation of legislative power, which is to consist of the Queen, a Senate (upper house) and a House of Representatives, and the scope of its policy-making competence.
Chapter II—The Executive Government	Establishes that formal executive power is vested in the Queen and her representative, the Governor-General. The Governor-General is to be advised by a Federal Executive Council, whose members must be drawn from Parliament.
Chapter III—Judiciary	Establishes the Judiciary. It describes the method by which Justices are to be appointed, the terms and condition under which they serve, and the scope and limits of their authority.
Chapter IV—Finance and Trade	Provides for the free movement of goods and people throughout the country as well as the rules for the appropriation and expenditure of monies.
Chapter V—The states	Preserves the constitutions and powers of the states. This section provides a solution to inconsistency between state and federal law where it involves an area that is not exclusive to the states.
Chapter VI—New states	Authorises the Commonwealth Parliament to admit or establish 'new states' as and when this might be required.
Chapter VII—Miscellaneous	Makes provision for the location of the Commonwealth Parliament and the appointment of deputies to assist the Governor-General.
Chapter VIII—Alterations of the Constitution	Describes the method for formal alteration of the Constitution.

As noted earlier in this chapter, written constitutions, by virtue of the inherent constraints that arise from the written form, only really make sense when read alongside a host of lesser laws and extra-legal instruments. This is especially so in the case of the Australian Constitution because important principles and features of our system of government are left out of the text. One important omission from the Australian Constitution is explicit reference to the conventions of responsible government. The conventions of responsible government refer to a set of practices that are designed to modulate the actions of the state's decision-makers through a continuous chain of accountability that directly links the people to the government of the day. In the simplest possible terms, the government (or the executive) is answerable to the parliament and retains office for as long as it enjoys the confidence (meaning majority support) of the lower house.

The conventions of responsible government play an important role in supplementing the Act. It is impossible to write down all the rules of government and, even if it were, it is not always desirable to do so. In explaining the absence of any explicit reference to the principles of responsible government in the Constitution, Samuel Griffith, one of its framers, claimed that the intention was 'to frame the Constitution that responsible government may—not that it must—find a place in it' (Griffith quoted in Quick & Garran 1901, p. 132). The framers believed that it was unnecessary to codify a principle that was an established part of colonial constitutional practice and that to do so would potentially stultify the natural evolution of this dynamic political concept.

It has long been argued that the conventions of responsible government do not sit easily alongside the federalist aspects of the Act. In recent times, and certainly in the wake of the constitutional crisis in 1975, some scholars declared the Australian model to be at best a 'hybrid' and at worst a 'mutation' (Parkin & Summers 2002, p. 5). At the root of Australia's so called constitutional troubles is the uneasy relationship between two of its most important political traditions: British **majoritarianism** and American **consensus**-style democracy. In its applied form, the tension is a product of the ability of a powerful Senate (which is commonly linked to the United States tradition of federalism) to force the removal of a government with a working majority in the House of Representatives (born from the British Westminster system of responsible government). Many commentators, including some of the delegates who drafted the Constitution, argue that the principles are irreconcilable.

However, not all scholars believe that Australia's primary constitutional arrangements are inherently dysfunctional.

Majoritarian democracy: described by Arend Lijphart as a model of democracy that aims to concentrate 'political power in the hands of a bare majority'. It is characterised as 'exclusive, competitive and adversial'. It creates political rules and institutions, which ensure 'government by the majority in accordance with the majority's interests' (Lijphart 1999, p. 3).

Consensus democracy: described by Arend Lijphart as a model of democracy that seeks to 'share, disperse and limit power'. It is characterised by inclusiveness, bargaining and compromise; endeavouring to maximise popular participation in decision-making through the establishment of rules and institutions that encourage 'broad participation in government' and 'broad agreement on policies' (Lijphart 1999, p. 3).

Sharman argues that there is no 'basic inconsistency' in the nature of the Australian system of government. Rather, Sharman proposes that the 'adoption of an entrenched constitution and powerful upper house … was quite consistent with existing colonial experience' and that the federalist aspect was not an 'alien import' imposed on British parliamentary practice, but very much 'derived from colonial experience' (Sharman 1990, p. 3). Sharman suggests that any tensions that exist within the system result from 'ambiguities of our British inheritance' and, more particularly, the rise of disciplined parties. It is this later phenomenon that has produced executive dominance in the lower house: the real culprit and primary cause of friction within the system. He claims that this development, along with the collectivist bias inherent in the writings of many Australian scholars, has resulted in the tendency to misdiagnose the cause of tension within the system (Sharman 1990, pp. 3–4).

The monarch's constitution

The Australian political system is a constitutional monarchy. Under this arrangement, the source of the nation's legal authority is the Monarch, although it is the people who enjoy the exclusive, legal authority to change the Constitution. It is the Monarch acting through her representative, the **Governor-General**, who is both the head of the Australian state and the repository of executive power.

While the Constitution makes it quite clear that the Monarch is the source of executive power, in practice it is the prime minister and the cabinet that exercise this power on a daily basis. According to the conventions of responsible government, the Crown takes her instructions from the Governor-General, who, in turn, takes her advice from the government of the day. In other words, 'government is administered in the name of the Queen, but it is *her advisers* who actually make the decisions' (Griffith 2006). In 1975, Queen Elizabeth II publicly avowed that she would not exercise her powers independently from the advice received by the Governor-General.

Despite there being benefits to Australia continuing as a constitutional monarchy, namely that a hereditary monarch, as opposed to an elected head of state, provide for 'an apolitical and impartial source of authority' (Lijphart 1984, p. 86), the model has many critics. In recent years, the voices calling for an Australian **republic** have grown in number and intensity and found strong support among the general public. However, as the outcome of the Republican referendum in 1999 revealed, changing these arrangements is not as simple as it seems. While polling shows that most Australians are keen to see an Australian citizen installed as the head of state, they are only willing to do so if the model is right.

Governor-General: the Monarch's representative, who is the formal head of state

Republic: a form of government in which sovereignty is based on consent of the governed and whose governance is based on popular representation. Sovereignty is vested in the 'people' and exercised on their behalf by government.

A liberal constitution

One of the most important influences on the Constitution is the liberal commitment to the principle of limited government. This is principally expressed in the tripartite separation of legislative, executive and judicial functions of government set down in the Act. The Constitution establishes that the power to make laws falls to the Parliament, the power to implement the laws is the responsibility of the Governor-General, who is advised by the Federal Executive Council, while the capacity to review those laws is a matter for the **High Court**.

Although the Constitution establishes what appears to be a fairly strict separation of powers, the demarcation between the executive and legislature is imperfect, and deliberately so. Executive power, in practice, is exercised by the government (the party or coalition that holds a majority of seats in the lower house of Parliament). Because the government commands a majority in the lower house, it effectively means it controls the legislative process in that chamber. One of the advantages of fusing legislative and executive power is that it minimises the incidence of gridlock between the two branches and, in doing so, improves the efficiency and stability of the law-making process.

> **High Court:** the highest court in the Australian judicial system. It was established in 1901 by s. 71 of the Constitution. It interprets and applies the law of Australia and is the custodian of the federal Constitution.

A rigid constitution

The federal Constitution is a rigid document insofar as special procedures apply to its formal amendment. These procedures are designed to ensure that proper consideration is given to the alteration of the highest law in the country. The process is set down in s. 128. It requires that any bill to alter the Constitution must be passed by an absolute majority in both houses of Parliament. If the chambers cannot agree on a proposed bill and if within three months one of the chambers again passes the bill with an absolute majority, there is a provision for the Governor-General to present the proposal to the people. Once either requirement has been met, the bill can then be put to the people to vote upon. Any proposed change must achieve a double majority in order to succeed: that is, a majority of the states and a majority of Australian electors overall must support the initiative.

Very few referendum proposals have been put to the people and, even then, the number of initiatives that have proven successful is even smaller. Of 44 proposals presented to electors, only eight have been approved. It is unclear why Australians have been so quick to reject so many of the referenda placed before them. Over the years, a number of hypotheses have been advanced (see Bennett 1999b; Saunders 2001). Some of these include:

- Australians are inherently conservative and unwilling to sanction any changes to the Constitution. Australians are essentially content with current arrangements and suspicious of any attempts to alter the status quo.

- The voters' reluctance to approve most of the referendum proposals is indicative of the poor quality of the questions on which they have been asked to cast a vote. Essentially, the high 'no' vote shows that Australian voters are highly discriminating in their political judgment, particularly when the referendum question will have the effect of increasing the power of the federal government.
- The Australian public does not fully understand the proposals they are being asked to consider. That is, Australian voters are ignorant and ill-informed and cast a vote without due consideration of the matters before them.
- Successive governments have failed to properly manage the referendum process. For example, the format of referendum proposals often rolls too many matters into a single question on the ballot paper. In doing so, voters are forced to vote against proposals they might otherwise support in order to prevent less desirable proposals from being enacted.
- The lack of bipartisan support for most referendum proposals divides the electorate.
- Complexities of the referendum process establish an unreasonably high threshold for success, i.e. the difficulty in achieving the double majority requirement needed for approval.

Although the public has been reluctant to amend the Constitution, this is not to say the Act is unchanged, even if the wording of the text remains mostly unaltered. One of the major influences on the Constitution is the High Court. The Constitution states that the High Court is responsible for interpreting the Act when there is disagreement about its provisions. Judicial interpretation has had a significant impact on the Constitution, greatly affecting its operation. While the Court's standing in constitutional matters is unquestioned, its judgments have been the source of much controversy because they are binding on both the executive and legislative branches.

A federal constitution

Those who drafted the *Commonwealth of Australia Constitution Act 1900* had the difficult task of reconciling a diverse and competing range of interests. By far the greatest challenge that faced the delegates was how to convince six independent colonies to cede a substantial measure of their power to a new political structure. In order for federation to proceed, a political solution had to be found for two key problems: how to protect the autonomy and independence of the colonies while ensuring that the new federal government had sufficient capacity to act in matters of agreed national interest; and how to quell the fears of the smaller states, who were anxious that their voice in national debate would be drowned out by the more populous states (Quick & Garran 1901, p. 931).

Attempts to resolve the first of these problems (the preservation of the colonies' autonomy) is found in the inclusion of ss. 106, 107 and 108 in the Constitution. These sections provide, among other things, for the continuation of the states' constitutions, parliaments and laws, unless these laws conflict with other sections of the federal Constitution. Further protection for the states is found in s. 51, which delineates, and thereby delimits, the scope of the federal government's powers. With few exceptions, most of the areas listed under s. 51, are areas of shared, rather than exclusive, policy-making responsibility. The Constitution confers very few exclusive powers to the federal Parliament (ss. 52 and 90). Additional safeguards for the states are found in the structure and powers afforded to the Senate. The Constitution states that the composition of the Senate 'shall be chosen directly by the people of the State'. It was the framers' intention to provide opportunities for the states to have a direct say in formulating national policy. To ensure the Senate is afforded proper consideration in legislative matters, the chamber is granted virtual parity in the law-making process with the House of Representatives (s. 53). The Constitution provides additional safeguards in the requirement that the number of members in the House of Representatives must be at least double that of the Senate (s. 24). Known colloquially as the 'nexus clause' this provision is designed to ensure that the Senate is not totally overshadowed by the House of Representatives in the minds of the people, or, more practically, in the event of a **joint sitting of Parliament**.

> **Joint sitting of Parliament:** when both houses of Parliament convene to debate and vote upon a bill or some other matter

The second problem that preoccupied the framers was how to equalise the voice of the states in the new law-making forum, particularly given their uneven population bases. Two important concessions were granted to the small states in the Constitution. First, the colonies were awarded equal representation in the Senate, and hence an equal voice in the formulation of laws, notwithstanding population size (s. 7). Second, any amendment to the Constitution must achieve the support of a majority of the states (see discussion above). This provision was included to ensure that the wishes of smaller states are not completely eclipsed by the more populous states at referenda.

While the framers evidently found enough common ground to eventually reach agreement, it is also clear that the resulting Act is very much the product of negotiation and compromise. The legal and political relationship between the federal and state governments, while fixed in writing, is dynamic and complex. While it was always assumed that the states would remain autonomous bodies, this has not quite eventuated (Carney 2006, p. 1). It is widely acknowledged that a major shift (some say a distortion) has occurred in the balance of power between the federal and state governments, with the federal government clearly in the ascendant.

BOX 2.2   Does the Constitution need a new preamble?

A preamble is a statement found at the beginning of a constitution that outlines the purpose of the Act. While all preambles do more or less the same thing, they vary in both style and content, but also with respect to the legal effect their words can have on the interpretation of the Act.

The preamble to the Australian Constitution is quite dry and uninspiring, particularly compared to the preambles of other nations' constitutions. The Irish constitution, for example, opens with a grand statement that pays homage to 'our obligations to our Divine Lord Jesus Christ, Who sustained our fathers through centuries of trial, Gratefully remembering their heroic and unremitting struggle to regain the rightful independence of our nation'. In contrast, the Australian preamble begins with:

> Whereas the people of New South Wales, Victoria, South Australia, Queensland, and Tasmania, humbly relying on the blessing of Almighty God, have agreed to unite in one indissoluble Federal Commonwealth under the Crown of the United Kingdom of Great Britain and Ireland, and under the Constitution hereby established …

As McKenna explains, the preamble 'embodies the three unifying features of federation in Australia: loyalty to the Crown, belief in God and the shared need to provide national unity for white Australians through the introduction of a federal government' (1996).

Up until the late 1980s, the preamble was considered to be of little public interest or constitutional significance. However, in 1999 Australians were asked to vote on a new preamble, which had been written by Australian poet Les Murray (in consultation with then-prime minister John Howard), with revisions by the Parliament. The proposed preamble read as follows:

> With hope in God, the Commonwealth of Australia is constituted as a democracy with a federal system of government to serve the common good. We the Australian people commit ourselves to this Constitution: proud that our national unity has been forged by Australians from many ancestries; never forgetting the sacrifices of all who defended our country and our liberty in time of war; upholding freedom, tolerance, individual dignity and the rule of law; honouring Aborigines and Torres Strait Islanders, the nation's first people, for their deep kinship with their lands and for their ancient and continuing cultures which enrich the life of our country; recognising the nation-building contribution of generations of immigrants; mindful of our responsibility to protect our unique natural environment; supportive of achievement as well as equality of opportunity for all; and valuing independence as dearly as the national spirit which binds us together in both adversity and success.

The preamble question was resoundingly defeated at the referendum. Only 39.34 per cent of the population supported the initiative (for more information on this topic see McKenna 2000).

Q Do you think Australia should adopt a new preamble to the Constitution and, if so, what should it contain? What, in your opinion, are some of the difficulties in rekindling debate on this issue?

ISSUE IN FOCUS

DOES AUSTRALIA REQUIRE A FEDERAL CONSTITUTIONAL BILL OF RIGHTS?

Almost all countries have codified a set of basic rights belonging to the citizenry. These rights, known as human rights, are designed to ensure that the freedom and liberties of the people are protected, particularly against intrusions from the state. A codified statement of this type, known as a **bill of rights**, takes one of two basic forms: a statutory bill of rights, which is an Act of parliament; or a constitutional bill of rights, which is considered a body of higher law and, as a result, theoretically beyond the reach of parliament. As shown in Box 2.3, there are cogent arguments both for and against having a rights bill.

> **Bill of rights:** a list of rights and liberties belonging to the people and which the government cannot trespass upon

BOX 2.3   Arguments for and against a bill of rights for Australia

Arguments for a bill of rights

- Guarantees fundamental liberties and rights that are not currently fully protected under Australian law.
- Gives recognition to international universal rights to which the Australian government is a signatory.
- Allows those who are otherwise powerless a basis from which they can assert their rights and seek redress for wrongdoing.
- Brings Australia into line with other comparable democracies.
- Ensures that rights are elevated beyond the world of petty politics.
- Improves policy-making, enhances legislative oversight and enriches administrative decision-making because it creates standards against which government action can be judged.

- Promotes tolerance and understanding in society.
- Provides inspiration for Australians to take a greater interest in politics, thereby enhancing the quality of Australian democracy.

Arguments against a bill of rights

- The rights of Australian citizens are not at peril and never have been.
- The courts have demonstrated an inclination, willingness and capacity to protect and extend fundamental rights through their interpretation of the Constitution and common law.
- Further entrenches the rights and privileges of wealthier members of society.
- The structure, configuration and values that inform the political system afford the best possible protections to the public. The best protections come from devices contained within the Constitution that limit the scope of government power and hence the chance for official abuse of citizen rights.
- In defining rights we risk limiting them.
- Can politicise the judiciary because government officials may feel compelled to appoint judges who are sympathetic with the government's political views.
- Produces endless litigation, ultimately costing governments (and ultimately taxpayers) millions of dollars in defending specious and vexatious claims.
- May protect rights that prove objectionable to later generations.
- Does not guarantee that the rights of Australians will not be trespassed. For example, the United States Bill of Rights provides little protection against capital punishment for anyone but the insane and children under the age of 16.
- A bill of rights is contrary to Australian political traditions and practices, which have served this country well.

Q The range of arguments within the 'for' and 'against' camps is diverse. Proponents within the same camp often reach similar conclusions about the necessity or otherwise of a bill of rights; however, the reasoning that led them to their conclusion is often quite different. Looking closely at the arguments advanced in the 'for' and 'against' camps, are you able to discern the different motivations that underpin the arguments?

Source: Williams 2000, pp. 35–6; Griffith 2006

One thing that sets Australia apart from many of its democratic (and undemocratic) counterparts is that it does not have a national bill of rights (Galligan & Morton 2006, p. 18; O'Neill et al. 2004, p. 1). It is curious that Australia, one of the oldest democracies in the world, has failed to implement a national rights charter.

In fact, the Constitution, confers remarkably few explicit rights to the Australian people. The more important of these include:

- the acquisition of property on 'just terms' (s. 51(xxxi))
- jury trial for certain offences against the Commonwealth (s. 80)
- freedom of interstate trade (s. 92)
- freedom of religion (s. 116)
- non-discrimination based on state residence (s. 117).

Moreover, these fairly modest protections apply only to the actions of the federal government. The state legislatures are not constitutionally bound by these sections of the Act and are free to ignore them to the extent that their own constitutions permit. Although Australians are not entirely defenceless against the government, it is also true that most of the rights the public possess exist almost entirely at the discretion of Australia's legislators.

The omission of a bill of rights within the Constitution is no accident. The framers knew that it was within their powers to enshrine basic civil and political rights in the new Constitution. One delegate, Tasmanian Andrew Inglis Clark, was particularly keen to see this eventuate and drafted a clause which, if adopted, would prohibit the Parliament from passing laws that sought to 'deprive any person of life, liberty or property' or to 'deny to any person within its jurisdiction the equal protection of its laws'. Clark's clause was debated but was defeated by a vote of 23 to 19 (Williams 1999, p. 40).

There are at least three reasons that Clark's recommendations were rejected. First, the framers of the Constitution had, in their view at least, a much more important issue to tackle than the development of a rights charter. The purpose of the new Constitution was to codify the federal agreement. The sheer import of this task—the political sensitivities that needed to be accommodated and assuaged—consumed the delegates' time and energies. As Patapan notes, 'federalism was about all the innovation the framers of the Constitution could handle' (1997, p. 3). As a result, the issue of rights protection assumed a very low priority. Second, there was a view among the delegates that a bill of rights was unnecessary and even offensive. Some of the delegates believed that the codification of rights represented a personal attack on the good character of colonial legislators and also the institutions and practices of parliamentary democracy. They argued that between English common law and Parliament, Australians would be afforded adequate protections and had been well served by both (La Nauze 1972, p. 231). This sentiment is best encapsulated in the words of John Cockburn, one of the delegates at the convention, who remarked, 'Have any of the colonies ... ever attempted to deprive any person of life liberty without due process of law? ... People would say, "pretty things these states of Australia; they have to be prevented by a provision in the constitution from doing the grossest injustices"' (Cockburn quoted in La Nauze 1972, p. 231).

Lastly, the view was robustly put that the codification of human rights would undermine both existing and future colonial legislation designed to discriminate against Indigenous and Asian persons (Malcolm 1998). The delegates feared that Inglis's clause might get in the way of discriminatory legislation already enacted by some of the colonial parliaments. As one delegate remarked,

> It is of no use for us to shut our eyes to the fact that there is a great feeling all over Australia against the introduction of coloured persons ... I do not want this clause to pass in a shape which would undo what is to be done in all colonies ... in regard to that class of person (Forrest quoted in Williams 1999, p. 42).

While it was argued that such problems might very well be circumvented by defining citizenship in such a way so as to ensure that the protections were not applied to all persons living in Australia, a majority of the delegates were not prepared to chance it.

Over the years, rights proposals have been discussed, debated and, on occasion, even put to the Australian people to vote at referendum (see Box 2.4). Both Victoria and the ACT have introduced a bill of rights, with many other states currently investigating the option. Various scholars, commentators and activists, with surprising regularity, have pressed for a federal charter. There is even evidence to suggest that the public is receptive to a national bill of rights, even if they have not always embraced opportunities to insert rights in the Constitution. The Rights Project opinion survey conducted in the early 1990s revealed that 72 per cent of those polled expressed strong support for a bill of rights, with only 7 per cent registering opposition (Galligan & McAllister 1997, p. 147). This raises an interesting question: why hasn't public support for a bill of rights translated into the development and implementation of a national rights charter?

BOX 2.4   The bill of rights debate in Australia

This chronology provides an overview of some of the important developments in the debate on whether Australia should have a bill of rights. The chronology draws heavily on information sourced from the Australian Parliamentary Library's Civil and Human Rights Internet Guide and the Gilbert and Tobin Centre for Public Law.

1890s	Andrew Inglis Clark proposes that four basic rights be enshrined in the new Constitution: trial by jury for all crimes (clause survives but weakened); prohibition on the establishment of religion by the federal government (clause survived); freedom of religion (clause negatived); and equal protection of the laws (clause negatived).

1944	*Constitution Alteration (Post-War Reconstruction and Democratic Rights) Bill* is presented at referendum. Among other things, the Bill includes constitutional guarantees of freedom of speech and religion and safeguards against the abuse of delegated legislative power. The proposal is rejected by the people.
1959	Queensland Premier Frank Nicklin introduces the *Constitution (Declaration of Rights) Bill* into the Queensland Parliament but is forced to abandon the Bill owing to lack of support in Parliament.
1973	*Human Rights Bill.* Not passed; lapsed with the double dissolution of April 1974.
1976	The federal government ratifies *The International Covenant on Economic Social and Cultural Rights*.
1980	The federal government ratifies *The International Covenant on Civil and Political Rights*.
1984	Draft *Australian Bill of Rights Bill* is given limited distribution by Attorney-General Gareth Evans and later released under the Freedom of Information Act. An amended version is introduced by Attorney-General Lionel Bowen in 1985.
1985	*Australian Bill of Rights Bill* is not passed. Passed by the House of Representatives but is later withdrawn by the government in the Senate.
1988	*Final Report of the Constitutional Commission*, established by the federal government, recommends inserting a bill of rights into the Constitution. The federal government rejects the recommendation. *Constitution Alteration (Rights and Freedoms) Bill* proposes four-year maximum terms for federal parliaments; to recognise local government; to guarantee 'one vote one value'; to extend the right to trial by jury; to extend freedom of religion; and to ensure fair terms for persons whose property is acquired by any government. The proposal is defeated at referendum.
1998	The Queensland Legislative Assembly Legal, Constitutional Administrative Review Committee, following an investigation of the utility of a bill of rights, finds against the proposition.
2000	*Australian Bill of Rights Bill 2000* drafted by Senator Andrew Murray, which would later be introduced as the *Parliamentary Charter of Rights and Freedoms Bill 2001*.

2001	*Australian Bill of Rights Bill 2001*, a Private Member's Bill introduced by Dr Andrew Theophanous MP, does not proceed to a second reading.
	Parliamentary Charter of Rights and Freedoms Bill 2001, originally the *Australian Bill of Rights Bill 2000*, introduced into the Senate by Australian Democrats leader, Meg Lees. The Bill does not progress beyond its second reading.
	An inquiry by the NSW State Parliament into the efficacy of a statutory bill of rights finds that it would not be in the public's interest to introduce a bill of rights.
2004	*Human Rights Act* is passed by the ACT Legislative Assembly: the first bill of rights enacted in Australia.
	Sandra Kanack introduces the *Human Rights Bill* in the South Australian Legislative Council.
2005	Senator Stott-Despoja unsuccessfully reintroduces the *Parliamentary Charter of Rights and Freedoms Bill 2001*.
2006	The Victorian State Parliament enacts the *Charter of Human Rights and Responsibilities Act 2007*.
	The Tasmanian Attorney-General engages the Law Reform Institute to investigate suitable options for human rights protections.
2007	The Western Australian Attorney-General releases a draft *Human Rights Bill*.
	NSW Attorney-General, John Hatzistergos, rejects calls for a rights charter.
2008	Federal Attorney-General, Robert McClelland, reveals the government's intention to undertake community consultation on a charter/bill of rights.

Source: Australian Parliamentary Library's Civil and Human Rights Internet Guide;
Gilbert & Tobin Centre for Public Law

Some commentators argue that Australians have not actively pushed for a national bill of rights because there is simply no necessity for such an instrument. Although Australia continues to 'largely rely upon parliamentary and political means for rights protection …', it has been suggested that it is 'probably just as successful in achieving a rights revolution as comparable bill of rights countries' (Galligan & Morton 2006, p. 37). Simply put, the Australian political system has been designed to both protect and advance the rights of Australian citizens. In the absence of any serious or sustained attack on individual rights, particularly those of citizens, the imperative for a rights charter is, in the public mind, significantly diminished.

Others claim that Australia's failure to adopt a bill of rights has more to do with the influence of political culture than it does the public's faith in their political institutions to keep the government in check. It is argued that Australian political culture has created an atmosphere of rights apathy. Australian political life is thought to be defined by a commitment to group rights over those of the individual, which is believed to result from the influence of utilitarianism on Australian political culture. Utilitarianism is a political philosophy dating from the eighteenth century that defines the role of the state in terms of the protection and improvement of society's 'average welfare' (Kildea 2003, p. 2). The state should act to develop and enhance the nation's capacities and to provide 'the greatest happiness of the greatest number' (Jeremy Bentham 1789). In order to achieve this outcome, individual rights must be subordinated to the collective will. Individual rights are viewed, therefore, with suspicion, particularly where they are believed to undermine or conflict with the rights of the majority (McAllister 1997, p. 244).

The influence of utilitarianism on Australian culture, while difficult to prove, is reflected in the public's acceptance of occasional intrusions into their personal freedoms. Australians tend to support initiatives that might be regarded as invasive by citizens of other comparable countries. A good example of this is the public's reaction to terrorism legislation introduced by the federal government in 2004. The Anti-terrorism Acts were enacted following the **9/11 terrorist attacks** and were justified by the government as a national security imperative. The legislation significantly encroached on individual rights, strengthening the state's capacity to detain individuals without charge and to prosecute those connected with proscribed terrorist organisations. While many commentators and civil libertarians regarded the legislation as Draconian, the public's reaction to the initiatives was mostly acquiescent. When asked about the federal government's response to the threat of a terrorist strike, almost one in two voters (49 per cent) believed the government had shown about the right amount of respect for civil liberties, and 15 per cent thought the government had shown too much respect. Only 29 per cent believed the government had not shown enough respect for individual rights and liberties (Mann 2006).

However, others claim that the most significant obstacle to the introduction of a national rights charter is Australia's federal law-makers. With few exceptions, Australian prime ministers have been openly derisive of a bill of rights. Former prime minister John Howard made clear his position on the issue when he declared: 'I belong to that group of Australians who is resolutely opposed to such a course of action. It is my view that this nation has three great

> **9/11 terrorist attacks:** a series of coordinated Islamist terrorist attacks carried out in the USA on Tuesday, September 11, 2001. Nineteen men affiliated with al-Qaeda, a network of militant Islamist organisations, hijacked four commercial airliners. They crashed one into each of the two towers of the World Trade Center in New York City, and a third into the Pentagon in Washington DC.

pillars of its democratic life. A vigorous parliamentary system … a strong independent and incorruptible judiciary; and a free and skeptical media' (Howard 2003). As Box 2.4 shows, the few attempts to introduce a national bill of rights have been rejected by Parliament. It seems that the views of Australia's political elites are, on balance, out of step with the public on this issue. Survey data shows that only 54 per cent of legislators believe a national bill of rights is desirable compared to just over 70 per cent of the public (Galligan & Sampford 1997, p. 149). Moreover, it is Coalition parliamentarians who tend to be the strongest opponents of a bill of rights: the group that held office federally between 1996 and 2007. From the perspective of government, a bill of rights increases bureaucracy and limits the government's scope for action. Parliamentary sovereignty will be eroded, enabling judges to strike down legislation (if a constitutional bill of rights) or bring political pressure to bear by exposing any inconsistency (if a statutory bill of rights). In introducing a bill of rights, the political cost to government is likely to outweigh the benefits. Even the ALP, which has historically been sympathetic to the introduction of a rights charter, has made it abundantly clear that 'any proposal for legislative change in this area must maintain sovereignty of the Parliament and shall not be based on the United States Bill of Rights' (ALP National Platform 2007). In 2008, the Attorney-General revealed that while the government was committed to 'consulting the Australian people on the further protection of human rights and responsibilities', he was at pains to 'emphasise that the consultation will not pre-suppose any outcome' (McClelland 2008).

BOX 2.5   The bill of rights experience in other liberal democracies

Making the decision to commit to a bill of rights is, in some respects, the easy part for many countries. What can prove challenging is reaching agreement on the types of rights that require protection (affirmative rights versus limited rights); the form in which the rights will be enshrined (statutory versus constitutional); and the scope of judicial interpretation.

In most liberal-democratic countries, there is broad agreement about the type of rights that should be protected. For the most part, liberal-democratic states tend to emphasise the protection of basic civil and political liberties, such as the rights to free speech and the vote, rather than aspirational or affirmative rights. However, it is quite a different picture in relation to the other two matters. As shown below, there is dissensus on the best approach to enshrining rights and how much latitude the judiciary should be afforded in interpreting such rights.

■ United States—*Bill of Rights* (1789)—rights are framed in 'absolutist terms'; constitutionally entrenched; judiciary is the final arbiter in conflicts over rights. Congress can only nullify the judiciary's judgment by formal alteration of the Constitution.

- Canada—*Charter of Rights and Freedoms* (1982)—rights are subject to 'justi-fied limits'; constitutionally entrenched; judiciary can strike down legislation, however any finding of unconstitutionality can be set aside by express enact-ment of ordinary legislation by either Provinces or Federal Parliament.
- United Kingdom—*Human Rights Act* (1998)—enshrined in statutory form; judiciary cannot strike down legislation inconsistent with Act but can issue a 'declaration of incompatibility'. A declaration of incompatibility can trigger a request from the Government that Parliament amend the relevant legislation to ensure its conformity.
- New Zealand—*Bill of Rights* (1990)—enshrined in statutory form; judiciary cannot strike down legislation that is inconsistent with the Act.

Q Explain which is better in your view: a constitutional bill of rights or a statutory charter of rights?

CHAPTER SUMMARY

The first part of this chapter explored the diverse and complex world of con-stitutions, explaining their function and their different forms. One of the most important differences between constitutions is the extent to which they seek to limit the power of the government. The chapter then investigated the key attributes of the Australian Constitution. It was suggested that while the Constitution is imperfect, it has proven to be a stable and durable political insti-tution. The success of the Australian Constitution owes much to its ability to live up to the ideals of liberal constitutionalism. The Issue in Focus examined the bill of rights debate in Australia. It considered possible explanations for Australia's failure to adopt a national bill of rights, despite the growing trend worldwide for rights statements to be incorporated into national law. It argued that many fac-tors account for this omission, the most significant of which are political culture and the conservative, self-interested attitude of many federal legislators.

WEBSITES

Australian Federal Constitution: Net Resources Guide:
http://www-personal.edfac.usyd.edu.au/staff/souters/constitution/
This site provides references to various articles and papers written about the Australian Constitution.

Centre for Comparative Constitutional Studies:
http://cccs.law.unimelb.edu.au/.
This centre, based at the University of Melbourne, undertakes and promotes research on the constitutional law and government of Australia and of other countries.

Constitution Finder (University of Richmond):
http://confinder.richmond.edu/
A database that provides links to constitutions from around the world.

Constitutions Compared (Australian Broadcasting Corporation):
http://www.abc.net.au/concon/compare/default.htm
This site provides researchers with an opportunity to compare aspects of the Australian Constitution with other countries' constitutions.

Gilbert & Tobin Centre of Public Law:
http://www.gtcentre.unsw.edu.au/resources/charterofhumanrights.asp
This site contains excellent information and resources related to the issue of bills of rights.

FURTHER READING

Bennett, S. 1999. *Australia's Constitutional Milestones*. Politics and Public Administration Group. Australian Parliamentary Library, Canberra.

Irving, H. 2004. *Five Things to Know About the Constitution*. Cambridge University Press, Cambridge.

La Nauze, J. 1972. *The Making of the Australian Constitution*. Melbourne University Press, Melbourne.

Williams, G. 1999. *Human Rights Under the Australian Constitution*. Oxford University Press, Melbourne.

Federalism

THIS CHAPTER:

★ explains the nature of federalism and the key institutions associated with a federal system of government

★ outlines the variety of federal systems around the world

★ highlights the key elements of federalism in Australia

★ examines the major challenges confronting federalism in Australia, including the growth in Commonwealth power and the vertical fiscal imbalance.

ISSUE IN FOCUS

Is Australian federalism in need of reform?

KEY TERMS

Concurrent federalism
Confederation
Coordinate federalism
Corporations power

Cosmopolitanism
Executive branch
Executive federalism
Literalist
National sovereignty

Parliamentary sovereignty
Residual powers
Vertical fiscal imbalance
Welfare state laggard
Welfare state retrenchment

In November 2006, the High Court of Australia handed down its decision in the *WorkChoices case*, ruling that the Howard Government's controversial WorkChoices industrial relations reforms were a valid use of the Commonwealth's power to legislate in respect of corporations. The Court's expansive interpretation of the corporations power paved the way for greater Commonwealth interference in the activities of the states, a move that one commentator described as 'a shipwreck of Titanic proportions' (Craven 2006b). *WorkChoices* was the latest in a long list of Court decisions in Australia that shifted power from the states towards the Commonwealth, leading to serious questions about the relevance of federalism to Australia in the twenty-first century.

Introduction

In the lead-up to the 2007 federal election, federalism was firmly on the political agenda. Alongside the High Court's *WorkChoices* decision, the Howard Government had announced plans to take over the Mersey Hospital from the Tasmanian State Government and it had intervened in Northern Territory Aboriginal communities. The Labor Opposition, on the other hand, had announced plans to reform Australian federalism, establishing greater cooperation between the Commonwealth and the states. It was not surprising to see federalism playing such a crucial role in Australian political debate, as the federal nature of Australian government has major implications for public policy, the design and operation of our major political institutions, and even the character of our democracy. This chapter will outline the key elements of Australian federalism before focusing on the growth of Commonwealth power. The Issue in Focus will examine whether Australian federalism is in need of reform.

What is federalism?

In essence, '[f]ederalism is the principle of sharing sovereignty between central and state (or provincial) governments; a federation is any political system that puts this idea into practice' (Hague & Harrop 2001, p. 202). In other words, there are two levels or 'spheres' of government, and neither level has absolute authority over the other (Galligan 2006, pp. 263–4). This means that the central government cannot simply abolish the state governments, or vice versa. For example, in Australia, the Commonwealth Parliament does not have the power to abolish the New South Wales Parliament. This contrasts with a unitary state in which 'sovereignty lies exclusively with the national government' (Hague & Harrop 2001, p. 208). Although there may be local governments and other subnational authorities in a unitary system, they are not sovereign entities, and are able to be both established and abolished by the central government.

In its modern form, a federation can be distinguished from a **confederation**. In a confederation, the national government is simply made up of representatives of the various states, and in this sense it is not a sovereign entity. Agreement between the different states is needed to get things done, and this tends to result in a weak central government. It also means that there is no national citizen-ship—individuals are citizens of a state political community, but not a national political community. In contrast, citizens in modern federations enjoy dual citizenship because they are members of a state political community as well as a national political community (Galligan 2006, p. 264).

Confederation: a political system in which there is a weak central government and strong state or sub-national governments that exercise exclusive sovereignty

Underlying federalism is the idea that within a liberal-democratic political system power should be dispersed rather than concentrated.

This conception of democracy was most famously defended in the *Federalist Papers* (1788), which were written by the framers of the United States Constitution to convince the American people to support the model of government they had created. The framers, particularly James Madison, proposed a Constitution that would establish the United States of America as a compound republic where power was dispersed through federalism and a variety of other institutional mechanisms. Federalism has since spread to other parts of the world, and there are currently 26 federations in existence (Hueglin & Fenna 2006, p. 56). In recent years, federalism has grown in popularity with a number of new federations forming since the early 1990s. This has led to claims that federalism is particularly well suited to the nature of politics in the twenty-first century (see Box 3.1).

The 26 federations tend to share four key institutional characteristics (Lijphart 1999; Watts 1999; Galligan 2006). The first of these is an entrenched constitution, which is needed to protect the continuing existence of each level of government, and to determine how responsibility for different policy areas should be divided between them. The second common institutional feature of federal systems is strong bicameralism. One of the major concerns that smaller states have is that their interests will be ignored or even threatened by the national government because they have smaller populations, and thus fewer voters. A way of addressing this concern is to have a powerful second chamber in the national legislature that gives special representation to the smaller states. A third common institutional characteristic is intergovernmental machinery, which helps to facilitate cooperation between the two levels of government, and to resolve conflicts that arise between them. A fourth characteristic is a supreme court—in Australia, the High Court—which is needed to adjudicate in cases where intergovernmental machinery is unable to resolve conflict between the central government and the states.

BOX 3.1   Federalism in a global age

Federalism seems well suited to politics in the early twentieth-first century. This is because '[t]he world environment has changed from the twentieth century's primary focus on **national sovereignty** and centralized government to the twenty-first century's concern with **cosmopolitanism** and multiple sphere government' (Galligan 2006, p. 262; see also Watts 1999, pp. 4–6; Hueglin & Fenna 2006, pp. 11–29). Many political scientists believe that due to globalisation, nation-states are more interdependent and this has undermined their autonomy. As events in one nation-state affect other nation-states, negotiation and cooperation between governments over a wide range of issues is an increasingly important feature of global

National sovereignty: the idea that each nation-state is the supreme source of legal authority over its territory

Cosmopolitanism: the belief that human beings are members of a global community with obligations to those living beyond the borders of the state in which they live

politics. In this way, the power of the nation-state is spread around rather than concentrated. This parallels the sort of interdependence and power dispersal that characterises federal systems of government.

Since the end of the Cold War (1945–90), the power of the nation-state has also been challenged from within as ethnic groups or particular regions push for greater autonomy from the national government, or even the right to establish a new, separate nation-state. Sometimes the struggle for independence has turned violent, and there has been a resurgence in bloody ethnic conflict since the end of the Cold War. Federalism has often been viewed as an effective response to these conflicts because it provides a way of giving greater autonomy to particular regions without a break-up of the nation-state. Even in the United Kingdom, which has historically had a highly centralist system, the devolution process has seen the establishment of parliaments in Scotland and Wales. Devolution is not the same as federalism because the Westminster Parliament retains ultimate authority over Scotland and Wales, but it is an example of the sort of decentralisation of power that is associated with federalism.

Q   Is the adoption of a federal system of government likely to provide a long-term solution to ethnic conflict?

Despite these similarities, there are also important institutional variations among the world's federations. One of the major differences relates to whether federalism is combined with a presidential or parliamentary system of government (Hueglin & Fenna 2006, pp. 58–9). In a presidential system of government the **executive branch** of government is independent of the legislative branch. Thus, in presidential federal systems, such as the United States, power is dispersed between both the different branches of government (legislative, executive and judicial), and different tiers of government (the national government and the states). In parliamentary federalism, on the other hand, the executive branch of government is fused with the legislative branch. The members of the executive branch are drawn from the legislature, and they are dependent on the ongoing support of the legislature to govern. Thus, although parliamentary federalism divides government power between different tiers of government, executive and legislative power is more concentrated than in presidential federalism. Australia, Canada, India and Germany are all examples of parliamentary federalism.

Another important distinction relates to the way in which the responsibilities of government are divided between the two tiers of government. Administrative federalism means that the emphasis is on dividing the functions rather than the powers

Executive branch: the branch of government responsible for carrying out the law, headed by the prime minister and cabinet

of government (Hueglin & Fenna 2006, pp. 61–3). This approach is particularly associated with the German model. Although the *Lander* (the German equivalent of states in Australia) have the exclusive right to make and administer laws in certain policy areas, the national government possesses most legislative power. However, it is the *Lander* rather than the national government that have the chief responsibility for *administering* these national laws, and delivering the bulk of government services. Thus, in general, the German model splits the law-making and administrative functions of government between the two tiers.

An alternative approach is legislative federalism, which characterises federalism in countries such as Australia, the USA and Canada. Rather than assigning the principal responsibility for law-making to one level of government and the principal responsibility for administration to the other, in legislative federalism 'each level of government is responsible for policy-making in its entirety—from policy initiation and formulation to legislation and on to implementation and administration' (Hueglin & Fenna 2006, p. 62). It is the legislative powers of government that are divided between the two tiers, with the central government generally taking responsibility for areas that are best handled at the national level, such as foreign affairs and defence.

A further distinction is drawn between federations based on the way they divide legislative power. **Coordinate federalism** is when the different levels of government each have 'separate and distinct … policy responsibilities' (Galligan 1995, p. 192). This means that it is clear which level of government has jurisdiction over a particular policy area and, in theory, it reduces the need for the different levels to cooperate with each other to get things done. Generally, states have responsibility for areas such as education and health, while the central government concerns itself with issues such as defence and foreign relations. In contrast, **concurrent federalism** is when the policy responsibilities of the different levels overlap, leading to a high degree of intergovernmental interaction. However, it is important not to exaggerate the differences between the two models. In reality, almost all federal systems have some degree of overlap between the different levels of government partly because policy areas are interrelated rather than discrete. Nonetheless, if the power of central and regional governments becomes too uneven, cooperation between the two tiers of government can turn into coercion by the more powerful central government. Organic federalism is when the central government becomes so dominant over the states that we 'may hesitate to describe the result as federal at all' (Sawer 1969, p. 125). As we will see below, there is debate over how to characterise Australian federalism according to these models.

Coordinate federalism: a federal system in which the tiers of government have distinct responsibility for separate policy areas

Concurrent federalism: a federal system in which the tiers of government have shared or overlapping policy responsibilities

Finally, although a bicameral legislature is one of the institutional characteristics of a federal system of government, there are important variations in the nature of bicameralism in different federal systems (Hueglin & Fenna 2006, pp. 59–61). In particular, upper houses can be based on the council principle of second chamber representation, or the senate principle. The council principle is particularly associated with the German model of federalism in which the members of the *Bundesrat* (the Federal Council or German upper house) are appointed by the *Lander* governments to serve as their representatives. This gives the *Lander* a direct role in the national legislative process. This contrasts with the senate principle of second chamber representation, which is associated with bicameralism in countries such as Australia and the USA. In this approach, members of the upper house (which is referred to as the Senate in Australia, the USA and elsewhere) are representatives of the people of the states rather than state governments, and in both Australia and the USA (at least since 1913), they are elected at regular elections. The Senate represents the interests of the states because each state is represented by the same number of senators, regardless of the size of its population. The aim of doing this is to ensure that the interests of less populous states are not overlooked.

Although federalism takes different forms in different countries, it is clear that there is a general link between federal institutions and the dispersal of government power. Entrenched constitutions, strong bicameralism, judicial review, legislative federalism, administrative federalism, coordinate federalism, and concurrent federalism all tend to limit and divide the power of government. Many federalists view this as a great strength of federalism because it helps to achieve the liberal objective of protecting individual rights and liberties from overbearing government. However, federalism is also criticised and defended on other grounds. In particular, some argue that it undermines responsible government, resulting in an inefficient decision-making process. Others believe it tends to promote more responsive government and better policy outcomes. As we will see in the second half of the chapter, these debates have particular relevance for contemporary Australian politics.

Federalism in Australia

Prior to 1901, Australia did not exist as a sovereign nation. Instead, there were simply six self-governing colonies—New South Wales, Victoria, Queensland, Tasmania, South Australia, and Western Australia. The decision for these colonies to come together to become one country was motivated by a variety of considerations, including the desire to create a larger internal market by removing tariff barriers on trade between the colonies, and concerns about immigration and defence (Castles & Uhr 2005, p. 54). However, the six self-governing colonies were reluctant to give up all their power to a central government, and this made federalism a logical step.

In designing a federal system of government, the founders could draw upon the experience of other liberal-democratic federations, such as the USA, Canada and, to an extent, Switzerland. The decision to develop a federal system of government had important implications for the institutional design of the Australian system. Australia has an entrenched Constitution that prevents the abolition of the states by the Commonwealth, outlines the division of powers (rather unsatisfactorily as we shall see below) and which can only be changed at a referendum. The Constitution also provides the basis for the High Court, which is the final court of appeal in Australia and is responsible for interpreting the Constitution and adjudicating on disputes between the states; and it establishes a strongly bicameral Parliament.

Historically, many Australian politicians and political scientists have been hostile towards these power-dispersing institutions, and to federalism more generally. A key reason for this is that federalism conflicts with the principle of responsible government, which is also central to the Australian system (see Chapter 1). Responsible government is the idea that the executive branch is responsible to the Parliament. If the prime minister and cabinet lose the support of Parliament, then they lose office. In Britain the idea of responsible government is closely associated with the idea of **parliamentary sovereignty**, which means that the Parliament exercises supreme legal authority. No other institution—including a court or entrenched constitution— can lawfully prevent the Parliament from passing whatever laws it wants. Although Australia has a system of responsible government, it does not have parliamentary sovereignty because the authority of

> **Parliamentary sovereignty:** the idea that the Parliament is the ultimate source of legal authority

the Commonwealth Parliament has been limited by an entrenched Constitution, and the existence of independent state governments. Many Australian politicians and political scientists have regarded this as a deeply regrettable state of affairs because the British approach was seen as the most efficient and democratic form of government. The federal, power-dispersing aspects of the Australian system upset what is otherwise an essentially British model of government.

This view has been strongly challenged by other political scientists, who point out that the federal design of the system is not an accident (Sharman 1990; Galligan 1995). Rather, federalism is a crucial principle at the heart of the design of Australian government, with its roots in the colonial era. The decision to embrace federalism was not alien to the Australian political tradition, but reflected the fact that there were six self-governing colonies in place when Australia federated. These colonial political systems also had the very power-restraining features that were adopted as part of Federation—entrenched constitutions, strong bicameralism, and judicial review. As Sharman puts it, the framers designed Australia to be a compound republic, drawing on the experience of colonial self-government (Sharman 1990). In a related argument, Galligan emphasises that Australia is a federal republic (Galligan 1995). Although we have a system of responsible government, sovereignty is invested in a Constitution that was democratically approved by the people, and which establishes a federal system. For both Sharman and Galligan, the federal nature of the Australian system and the accompanying emphasis on the dispersal of power is a deliberate and desirable feature of government in Australia.

The division of powers: intention and reality

For many Australian politicians and political commentators, the ideal form of federalism is the coordinate model, and the fact that there is so much overlap between federal and state government policy responsibilities in Australia is regrettable. Mathews holds that the framers designed Australian federalism with the coordinate approach in mind, and that the division of powers matched up to this ideal in the early years of the Federation (1901–1920s). However, this has changed significantly over time. He argues that the 1920s and 1930s was a 'cooperative' period in which there was greater interaction between the Commonwealth and the states, with both tiers of government agreeing 'on machinery for joint decision-making in a number of important areas of public policy' (Mathews 1977, pp. 12–13). The period from the Second World War to the 1970s was an example of 'coercive federalism' because it was marked by an aggressive expansion of Commonwealth power. Mathews also makes the tentative suggestion that a new era of 'coordinative federalism' had begun in the mid 1970s, with the establishment of 'machinery for coordinating planning, programs and policies among the different levels of government' and across a wider range of policy areas than in the earlier period of cooperative federalism (Mathews 1977, p. 13).

More recent accounts have challenged the idea that Australian federalism was designed with the coordinate approach in mind, claiming instead that the Constitution establishes an essentially concurrent division of powers (Galligan 1995, pp. 199–203; see also Painter 1998, pp. 12–13). The powers of the Commonwealth are clearly outlined in the Constitution, predominantly in ss. 51 and 52, but the states' powers are residual. These **residual powers** are granted by s. 107, which assigns the states jurisdiction over policy areas that

> are not exclusively vested in the Parliament of the Commonwealth or withdrawn from the Parliament of the State.

This means that the states have residual powers in areas that are not assigned to the Commonwealth in the Constitution, and in areas that are assigned to the Commonwealth but not *exclusively*. As the majority of the Commonwealth's powers are non-exclusive, 'the essential design principle of the Australian Constitution in dividing federal powers is one of concurrency, not coordinacy' (Galligan 1995, p. 199).

Despite their differing views on the constitutional design of Australian federalism, both sides in this debate agree that there has

Residual powers: state powers that were not granted exclusively to the Commonwealth in the Constitution

been a significant increase in the Commonwealth's power since Federation. A key cause of this centralisation of power has been the High Court's changing interpretation of the Constitution (Galligan 1995, pp. 170–4). The residual powers of the states have been undercut over time by the High Court's decision to adopt a more expansive interpretation of the heads of power assigned to the Commonwealth in the Constitution, and by the decision not to take into account the broader implications of particular decisions for the overall balance of Commonwealth and state power.

Initially, the High Court's approach to Constitutional interpretation took into account the broader principles of federalism. In particular, it applied the doctrine of implied immunities, which 'saw the Commonwealth and States as having more or less separate spheres of jurisdiction so that each ought to be free from the interference and control of the other', thus reflecting a coordinate view of federalism (Galligan 1995, pp. 172–3; Zines 1989, pp. 19–20). The states were also protected by the doctrine of reserved state powers and implied prohibitions. This doctrine held that the states possessed certain exclusive powers, and that the Commonwealth was prohibited from exercising its enumerated powers in cases where this would interfere with a state power (Galligan 1995, p. 173; Zines 1989, p. 20).

However, the High Court's approach changed in the *Engineer's case*, in 1920. Rather than explicitly taking into account broader political values such as federalism, the High Court adopted a **literalist** interpretation of the Constitution that looked simply at the literal meaning of the words of the Constitution. In the *Engineer's case*, the Court held that Commonwealth arbitration legislation applied to an industrial dispute between a national union and an engineering and saw-milling works owned by the WA State Government. The Court held that Commonwealth law applied because s. 51(xxxv) of the Constitution gave the Commonwealth the power to deal with 'industrial disputes extending beyond the limits of any one state', thus overturning the immunities doctrines, which had previously protected the states (Galligan 1995, p. 174). The Court also overturned the doctrine of reserved state powers, rejecting the idea that the scope of the Commonwealth's enumerated powers was limited by a set of exclusive state powers that were implied, but not explicitly stated, in the Constitution (Zines 1989, pp. 21–2). Overturning implied immunities and interpreting the Commonwealth's enumerated powers literally was important because it meant that the Commonwealth would be deemed to have legal superiority to the states in any dispute that conceivably fell within the ambit of one of these heads of powers. Thus, the attempt to protect the states by listing a limited range of the Commonwealth's powers in the Constitution and assuming that the states had extensive residual powers, unravelled as the High Court adopted a literalist approach to Constitutional interpretation. Australia is not alone in experiencing this phenomenon and, ironically, it is countries such as Canada, which list explicitly a more limited range of state

> **Literalist:** an approach to judicial interpretation that focuses on the words in the Constitution, rather than taking into account broader principles and values

powers in the Constitution, that have actually enjoyed greater success in protecting the autonomy of the states (Zines 1989, pp. 22–3).

In the 1980s, the *Koowarta case* and the *Tasmanian Dam case* led to a further increase in the legal power of the Commonwealth. The Court held that the Commonwealth could legislate in a policy area that was previously the exclusive preserve of the states, if it was made the subject of an international agreement (Galligan 1995, pp. 177–9; Zines 1989, pp. 30–3). This was justified by s. 51(xxix) of the Constitution, which gives the Commonwealth power over external affairs. Although this could have led to a massive increase in Commonwealth power, in practice political constraints have placed limits on the Commonwealth government's preparedness to exercise this legal power. A good example of this is the Hawke Labor Government's decision to abandon plans to pass a statutory bill of rights that would have applied to state governments as well as the Commonwealth (Galligan 1995, pp. 178–9).

Most recently, the Court's expansive interpretation of the **corporations power** has created scope for even greater Commonwealth interference in a variety of areas that were traditionally the preserve of the states. In 2006, the states and unions challenged the Howard Government's WorkChoices industrial relations reforms in the High Court, arguing that the reforms relied upon an invalid use of the corporations power (Kildea & Gelber 2007, pp. 653–5). However, the Court found in favour of the Commonwealth, ruling that its use of the corporations power was valid. Moreover, the Court adopted a wide interpretation of the corporations power that would allow the Commonwealth to regulate corporations in a variety of respects beyond workplace relations. Given the key role played by corporations in Australia, this gives the Commonwealth enormous regulatory power (Kildea & Gelber 2007, p. 657).

Corporations power: s. 51(xx) of the Constitution, which gives the Commonwealth the power to legislate in respect of '[f]oreign corporations, and trading or financial corporations formed within the limits of the Commonwealth'

The Howard Government's decision to use the corporations power to force industrial relations reform on the states was also a clear indication of a centralist shift in Liberal Party ideology. Historically, the Liberal Party has tended to support federalism, largely because a belief in limited government is one of the Party's key principles. Federalism and the political institutions associated with it, such as the Constitution, the High Court, and a strong Senate, also limit the power of Labor Governments, checking their ability to implement radical socialist reforms. Nonetheless, despite the Party's traditional support for federalism, and its introduction of the GST (discussed in more detail in the following section), the Howard Government adopted a more centralist approach to government (see Parkin & Anderson 2007). Along with the WorkChoices industrial relations reforms, the Howard Government's policies in areas such as school report cards, and vocational education and training, interfered with areas that had traditionally been considered the responsibility of the states (see Chapter 11 for a more detailed discussion).

Prime Minister Howard defended centralisation by appealing to what was, in essence, a kind of conservative nationalism. The Commonwealth would use its powers 'to expand individual choice, freedom and opportunity, not to expand the reach of the central government … The goal is to free the individual, not to trample on the States.' While the Howard Government would not take over state powers for its own sake, it would exercise its might where necessary to advance conservative policies that it felt were in the national interest:

> I am, first and last, an Australian nationalist … I have little time for State parochialism … [O]ur first impulse is to seek cooperation with States and Territories on national challenges where there is overlapping responsibility. But I have never been one to genuflect uncritically at the alter of States' rights (Howard, cited in Parkin & Anderson 2007, p. 309, quotation abridged).

As we shall see in the Issue in Focus, the view that the Commonwealth is a superior policy-maker to the states is one of the key issues at stake in the debate over the merits of federalism in Australia.

Vertical fiscal imbalance

The second key source of Commonwealth dominance is the **vertical fiscal imbalance**, which refers to the fact that whereas the states have the responsibility for delivering expensive services such as health and education, it is the Commonwealth that has vastly greater revenue-raising capacity. The states' tax powers are so limited that they depend on the Commonwealth to provide them with the funds needed to deliver the essential services for which they are responsible.

> **Vertical fiscal imbalance:** the disproportionate revenue-raising capacities and spending responsibilities of the Commonwealth and states

At the time of Federation, the major source of government revenue was excise taxes (taxes on goods for the domestic market), but the power to tax customs and excise was given to the Commonwealth as the framers believed that it was necessary to create a national economic union (Galligan 1995, pp. 217–18). Initially, the Commonwealth was obliged to pass on a fixed amount of the revenue generated to the states, but this only applied for the first ten years following Federation, with the expectation that the Commonwealth and the states would be able to reach a more permanent agreement after that. However, no agreement was ever reached and the Commonwealth continued to negotiate regularly with the states over the sharing of tax revenue (Galligan 1995, pp. 221–3).

Over time, income tax became a more important source of revenue than excise, and both Commonwealth and state governments had the power to raise funds this way. However, this changed after the Second World War when the Commonwealth threatened to cut its funding to any state that levied income tax. The states challenged this arrangement in the High Court, but the Court ruled in favour of the Commonwealth and the arrangement has continued ever since (Galligan 1995, pp. 175–6). Subsequent Court decisions have also ruled out other revenue sources for the states, including taxes on alcohol and cigarettes.

Further undermining the fiscal autonomy of the states was the increasing use of tied grants, which are technically known as specific purpose payments. The basis for these payments is s. 96 of the Constitution, which states

> the (Commonwealth) Parliament may grant financial assistance to any state on such terms and conditions as the Commonwealth sees fit.

This allows the Commonwealth to provide states with grants on the proviso that they spend the money in a particular way, leading to further Commonwealth encroachment in policy areas that are predominantly a state responsibility. In 2002–03, 40 per cent of all Commonwealth grants to the states were tied grants (McLean 2004, p. 25).

The biggest recent change in Commonwealth–state financial relations occurred in 2001 when the Howard Government introduced a Goods and Services Tax (GST). Although this tax is collected by the Commonwealth, the revenues raised are passed on to the states to spend as they see fit. In effect this gives the states access to a major growth tax, which consequently increases their financial autonomy (Parkin & Anderson 2007, pp. 297–300). However, although the GST has increased the states' revenue base, it is not a sure-fire way of securing their financial independence. In particular, the states still receive specific purpose payments from the Commonwealth, which they use to fund their activities. The Commonwealth could use this as leverage to force the states to behave in a certain way, threatening to reduce these payments if the states do not accede to the Commonwealth's wishes. In the future, there is also a risk that the Commonwealth will try to depart from the current unconditional allocation of GST revenue to the states. Comments from Howard Government Treasurer Peter Costello in 2006 have been interpreted as implicitly threatening to go down this path (Parkin & Anderson 2007, p. 299). Thus, although the situation has improved since the introduction of the GST, the states' financial autonomy is still significantly constrained.

BOX 3.2   Horizontal fiscal equalisation

Horizontal fiscal equalisation is another crucial element of fiscal federalism in Australia. It refers to the redistribution of financial resources across the federation in order to equalise the relative position of each state. It is based on the idea that '[w]ithin reasonable limits citizens in all parts of a federation … [should] have comparable access to public services, universities, hospitals, or cultural institutions' (Hueglin & Fenna 2006, pp. 52–3).

In Australia, the Commonwealth Grants Commission plays a central role in the process of horizontal fiscal equalisation. It advises the Commonwealth on how the revenue raised through the GST should be allocated, working on the principle that 'each State should be given the capacity to provide the average standard of State-type public services, assuming it does so at an average level of operational efficiency and makes an average effort to raise revenue from its own sources' (CGC, italics removed). In effect, this means that part of the GST revenue raised by people in one state may be transferred to fund services that are provided to people in another state. The motivations for horizontal fiscal equalisation are equity and social solidarity (Hueglin & Fenna 2006, pp. 52–3). If citizens in one state feel that they are much worse off than citizens in the rest of Australia, then this may undermine the unity of the federation, ultimately leading to secession. Interestingly, 'Australia has the most egalitarian equalisation regime of any democratic federation' (MacLean 2004, p. 25), leading one United States economist to describe Australian federalism as 'Fair Go Federalism' (Gramlich, cited in Galligan 1995, p. 234).

Q Is horizontal fiscal equalisation fair on the financially strong states, which subsidise the weaker states?

Intergovernmental machinery

The expansion of the Commonwealth's legal power since Federation, combined with the vertical fiscal imbalance, means that government in Australia is characterised by a high degree of interaction between the Commonwealth and the states. Yet, for the most part, the Australian Constitution does not establish the intergovernmental institutions that are needed to facilitate effective interaction between the different levels of government (Painter 2001, p. 139). Nonetheless, a variety of such institutions have developed over time as governments came to recognise their necessity.

One of the chief characteristics of these institutions is that they involve interaction between members of the executive branch of Commonwealth and state governments. That is, intergovernmental interaction generally occurs between the prime minister and premiers, ministers, and public servants, rather than between backbench MPs in different jurisdictions. This **executive federalism** reflects the dominance of the executive branch over the legislative branch in Australia (Sharman 1991; Painter 2001, p. 138).

Executive federalism: interaction between the different tiers of government that primarily involves members of the executive branch

There are myriad intergovernmental institutions in Australia. Some arise from the Commonwealth's use of special purpose payments (Painter 1998, pp. 97–100). Although the Commonwealth provides this funding with specific purposes in mind, it is the states that must spend the funds to achieve the Commonwealth's objectives. If the Commonwealth wishes to assess whether these objectives have been achieved, communication between Commonwealth and state bureaucrats is needed. This can occur through formal meetings as well as informal communication.

However, throughout the history of Australian Federation, the most high-profile intergovernmental institution was the Premiers' Conference. These meetings were held at least once a year between the prime minister and premiers, who discussed a variety of issues, although Commonwealth–state financial relations generally received the most attention (Sharman 1991, pp. 26–7). The Premiers' Conference largely played a 'symbolic and political rather than administrative' role because the broad outline of the Commonwealth budget was determined prior to the meeting (Sharman 1991, p. 27). Similarly, while there was greater scope for bargaining over non-financial issues at the Premiers' Conference, it was mostly an occasion for signing agreements that had been decided upon prior to the meeting, or referring issues to committees for further examination. The importance of the Conferences lay in the way it gave the prime minister and premiers the opportunity to communicate their views to a national audience, and to the national media based in Canberra. The Conferences also gave each head of government the opportunity to assess their counterparts, and to share information about key political issues (Sharman 1991, pp. 27–8).

In 1992, a new intergovernmental institution, the Council of Australian Governments (COAG), was formed. The members of COAG include the prime minister, state premiers, territory chief ministers, and the head of the Australian Local Government Association. The COAG meeting was introduced in the wake of the Hawke Labor Government's New Federalism reforms, and it originally met twice a year to discuss issues that were not covered in the Premiers' Conference (Galligan 1995, p. 211). However, after the introduction of the GST in 1999 by the Coalition Government, John Howard announced that the Premiers' Conference would be abolished, leaving COAG as the pre-eminent institution for intergovernmental cooperation. In December 2007, at the Rudd Labor Government's first COAG meeting, it was announced that COAG would meet four times a year. In addition to COAG, there are also 40 Commonwealth–State Ministerial Councils, featuring ministers from different levels of government who share the same portfolio area and who meet to discuss important policy issues.

ISSUE IN FOCUS

IS AUSTRALIAN FEDERALISM IN NEED OF REFORM?

Australian federalism has been subjected to strong criticism throughout its history. While some politicians and political scientists have attacked the whole idea of a federal system of government, more recent criticisms have tended to focus on the problems associated with the centralisation of power, and the high degree of overlap between the Commonwealth and the states (Fenna 2007).

Federalism and liberal democracy

One of the long-standing arguments against federalism in Australia is that it undermines accountability and responsible government. Because so many government powers in Australia are concurrent, it can be difficult to determine which level of government is ultimately responsible for problems in a particular policy area. For example, hospitals in Australia are largely a state responsibility, which suggests that problems with the hospital system are matters for which the states should be held accountable. However, when faced with criticism over the state of the public hospital system, the states often respond by blaming the Commonwealth for underfunding.

In recent times, the states have also argued that the chronic shortage of aged care places in Australia has put pressure on the hospital system, as elderly patients who would be more suitably cared for in aged care facilities take up hospital beds. As aged care is largely a Commonwealth responsibility, this means that the Commonwealth must again share a large portion of the blame for the problems in the hospital system. In reply, the Commonwealth claims that the states have sufficient funding to properly run hospitals, but that they have directed the money to other areas, or mismanaged the hospital system. With these sorts of arguments dominating the debate, it makes it very difficult for voters to determine which level of government is responsible for policy failure, and to hold them accountable through the electoral process. Thus, there is a sense in which federalism undermines the notion of accountability that is crucial to democratic government.

A further criticism of Australian federalism is that it results in over-government. After all, Australia has a relatively small population, and it seems wasteful to have multiple tiers of government. A related criticism is that Australia lacks the geographical concentration of ethnic and linguistic minorities that makes federalism appropriate (Riker 1964, p. 151). Instead, many of these critics would prefer to abolish the states, give their power to the national government and strengthen local government, which would deliver some of the services that were formerly provided by the states.

In response, other political scientists emphasise that liberal-democratic principles are at the heart of federalism. In particular, the existence of multiple levels of government is a way of dispersing government power, as are the institutions that are associated with federalism such as entrenched constitutions, judicial review, and strong bicameralism. Rather than constituting over-government, federalism is an important mechanism for achieving the crucial liberal-democratic objective of dispersing government power in order to protect the rights and liberties of the individual (Sharman 1990; Galligan 1995). Federalism also enhances democracy by providing citizens with a greater opportunity to access and influence government. If different levels of government are dealing with issues within the same policy area, then there are two sets of policy-makers whom citizens can lobby, rather than being forced to deal with a single central government that is geographically remote from the vast majority of citizens (Galligan 1995, pp. 52–3, 202–3).

If these claims are correct then federalism is even relevant in countries such as Australia, which lack large, geographically concentrated ethnic communities. In fact, as Galligan has argued, there is reason to think that federalism is actually more likely to be successful in countries with relatively homogeneous populations and political stability (1995, p. 55). Moreover, although Australia has a relatively small population, it is a large country in geographical terms, and this makes the idea of centralised government less appealing, particularly to residents of states such as Western Australia which are a long way from Canberra. It is also questionable whether local governments would do a better job of running services than state governments which, for all their faults, are currently run by full-time, professional politicians, who have a large bureaucracy to advise them, and who are subjected to close media scrutiny.

Reform, rights and redistribution

Another criticism of federalism is that it results in bad public policy. This follows from the problems with government accountability mentioned earlier: in difficult policy areas such as health, both levels of government can deny that they are responsible for dealing with problems in the system. Moreover, even if a government has the political will to address a problem, implementing the policies they support means cooperating with the other tier of government, which may obstruct the reform process. In recent times, this line of argument has often been used by supporters of neo-liberal economic reform in Australia who believe that the states are impeding the reform process. They have also argued that it is expensive for businesses to have to adapt to different regulations in each state.

However, others have defended federalism against these criticisms, arguing that it has beneficial consequences for the policy-making process. First, they argue that a faster process is not necessarily a better one, and slowing the process down and consulting more widely is actually likely to produce better policy in the long term, and more durable reforms that reflect the wishes of the public (Galligan 1995, pp. 202–3; Lijphart 1999). Federalism also allows for policy experimentation (Fenna 2004, p. 183). In the Australian context, a commonly cited example is South Australian Labor Premier Don Dunstan, whose pioneering social reforms were later adopted by governments in the other states. More generally, federalism encourages policy competition between the states, who compete with each other in order to attract citizens and investment to their state. This gives the states a strong incentive to come up with good policies and provide better quality goods and services. This sort of thinking should appeal to neo-liberals who are committed to the idea of free markets and greater competition (Pincus 2008). It is also important to note that federalism did not prevent Australia from undergoing a far-reaching process of economic reform in the 1980s and 1990s, which required extensive interaction between the two levels of government (see Painter 1998).

Recent comparative research also casts doubt on the claim that federalism hinders economic performance. Lijphart does not find any evidence that countries with a federal system and its associated institutions (an entrenched constitution, a supreme court, and strong bicameralism) perform any worse economically than non-federal countries (1999, pp. 272–4). This is not to deny that federalism places obstacles in the way of policy reform, but it does suggest that the economic impact of federalism is more complex than some of its critics suggest.

Those on the Left of the political spectrum have also criticised federalism, mainly for obstructing the policy reform that is needed to achieve social, political and economic change. Federalism can create barriers to the redistribution of social resources, and the protection of citizens' rights. Critics often cite the example of the USA where southern states resisted federal attempts to end racial segregation (Riker 1964). However, things are more complicated than this picture suggests. As mentioned earlier, federalism can encourage policy innovation as successful reforms are adopted by other states. For example, the Dunstan Government's social reforms (see above) were clearly designed to enhance rather than weaken individual rights and liberty.

Another criticism from the Left is that federalism inhibits the growth of the welfare state. While Australia was an early leader in the development of social support, it became a **welfare state laggard** over the course of the twentieth century, spending far less on social security than other liberal democracies. For some, federalism was partly to blame for this state of affairs, because it made policy reform difficult and prevented the Commonwealth from delivering the resources to which all Australians were entitled. However, while federalism played some role in explaining Australia's relatively low levels of social expenditure during the postwar years, other factors are likely to have been more significant, particularly the electoral dominance of the Coalition government, which was in power for 23 years during this era, and less sympathetic towards welfare state expansion than Labor (Castles & Uhr 2005, pp. 276–81). Moreover, Castles has disputed the claim that Australia is a welfare state laggard, arguing instead that social protection in Australia occurred predominantly through other mechanisms, most notably regulated labour markets, which ensured that all workers earned wages sufficient to support a family (Castles 1985). Moreover, the last few decades have seen a process of **welfare state retrenchment**,

Welfare state laggard: a country with an underdeveloped welfare state that provides less social protection for its citizens than other countries

Welfare state retrenchment: a reduction in the size of the welfare state rather than expansion, and in this context federalism's capacity to slow down the rate of change may actually help to protect the welfare state. However, while a recent study found that some associated aspects of Australian federalism such as strong bicameralism had placed a check on welfare state retrenchment in Australia, it has not prevented the erosion of key aspects of social protection, such as labour market regulation (Castles & Uhr 2005).

Reforming federalism

Although some criticisms of federalism in Australia are overstated, many policy-makers and political scientists continue to express their dissatisfaction with the current state of federalism. There is particular concern at the way the vertical fiscal imbalance affects the states' ability to provide a high quality of public services such as health and education. There is a perception that these services are performing below community expectations in Australia, and some believe that the vertical fiscal imbalance is to blame, along with the problems this creates for government account-ability. In recent times, there have been suggestions that the Commonwealth should take over these areas as a national government is more likely to properly fund and manage them.

Conversely, some believe that there are advantages associated with the increasing interaction between the Commonwealth and the states, but express concern at the degree to which the Commonwealth is able to dominate this interaction. Recent decisions such as the *WorkChoices* case heighten this problem by expanding the Commonwealth's powers even further, leading to a situation where a federal govern-ment can threaten to act unilaterally if the states do not cooperate with it. The vertical fiscal imbalance is another crucial mechanism by which the Commonwealth can set the policy agenda and dominate the states. Moreover, the vertical fiscal imbalance is inherently concerning because it means that the level of government that is responsible for running essential services such as health and education lacks the capacity to set the tax rate at the level needed to fund those services. This undercuts one of the key advantages of federalism—that it is responsive to the diverse preferences of citizens who live in different political communities.

A variety of reforms have been proposed to help address these problems. For a start, there are some who support adopting a clearer demarcation between Commonwealth and state responsibilities (Beattie 2007). They seem to have in mind something like the coordinate model of federalism where there is a clear division between the Commonwealth and the states. Yet strengthening the states need not involve adopting the coordinate approach. For example, the states' autonomy could be increased by reinstating their power to collect income tax. Addressing the legal sources of the Commonwealth's dominance is likely to prove more difficult because it is largely a result of the way the High Court interprets the Constitution, but it would be possible to improve the situation by strengthening the extra-constitutional intergovernmental institutions such as COAG, which are so crucial to the operation of the system (Galligan 1995, p. 189).

The Rudd Labor Government has also emphasised that properly addressing some of the key problems confronting Australian policy-makers will require improvements to the functioning of Australian federalism. In a speech to Australian Business Economists prior to the 2007 election, Kevin Rudd argued that Australia's future prosperity depended on its ability to develop and utilise its human capital, and that achieving this required greater cooperation between the Commonwealth and states, rather than 'the buckpassing, cost shift and blame shift which has become such a tired component of our nation's political theatre—contributing in turn to policy inertia and policy failure' (Rudd 2007a). Labor's National Health Reform Plan reflected this thinking, emphasising the role of COAG in the reform process, but also raising the prospect of a referendum on a Commonwealth takeover of hospitals if the states did not implement the reforms by mid-2009 (Rudd & Roxon 2007). Within a month of Labor winning office, COAG met and set up a National Health and Hospitals Reform Commission to assist with the process of health reform. COAG also established seven working groups in areas that were identified as priorities (COAG 2007). It seems that the Rudd Government is intent on using COAG and other intergovernmental processes to cooperate with the states, at least in the first instance, in order to achieve policy reforms in problem areas. However, if the states' commitment to these reforms waivers, the Commonwealth has also signalled that it is prepared to act unilaterally to implement the reforms that it believes are necessary. This dual approach makes it difficult to determine, at this early stage, whether the centralisation of power will continue under the Rudd Government.

CHAPTER SUMMARY

Australia has a federal system of government, which means that power is divided between governments at the national and state level. This is of fundamental importance to the Australian political system, and leads to other power-dispersing political institutions that are discussed throughout the book, including the Constitution, the High Court, and the Senate. Although the Constitution was designed to ensure that the states remained powerful, over time there has been a centralisation of power, facilitated by the High Court's literalist interpretation of the Constitution, and the vertical fiscal imbalance.

Over the years, a variety of criticisms have been made of federalism from the Left and Right of the political spectrum. Although many of these criticisms are exaggerated, there is significant unease at the current division of powers in Australia, with federalists concerned at the erosion of state power, and others concerned at instances of apparent policy failure. After the relatively centralist

Howard years, the Rudd Government has foreshadowed a more cooperative approach to intergovernmental relations in Australia. However, in the area of health policy, the Government has also stated that it is prepared to move towards greater Commonwealth control if the states do not embrace the reform process. Either way, federalism is likely to continue to occupy a prominent place in Australian political debate.

WEBSITES

Council of Australian Governments (COAG):
www.coag.gov.au
COAG is an intergovernmental forum that brings together the heads of different levels of government in Australia to discuss national policy reforms. It is chaired by the prime minister and its membership also includes the state premiers, the territory chief ministers, and the president of the Australian Local Government Association.

Commonwealth Grants Commission:
www.cgc.gov.au
A statutory body that is responsible for advising the Australian Government on, among other things, the share of GST revenue and health care grants that each state should receive.

The Federalism Project, Socio-Legal Research Centre, Griffith University:
http://www.griffith.edu.au/centre/slrc/federalism/
Provides information and materials on the social, economic and political roots of Australian federalism, and likely or desirable directions for federalism to evolve towards in response to the challenges of the twenty-first century.

FURTHER READING

Galligan, B. 1995. *A Federal Republic*. Cambridge University Press, Melbourne.

Parkin, A. & Anderson, G. 2007. 'The Howard Government, Regulatory Federalism, and the Transformation of Commonwealth–State Relations.' *Australian Journal of Political Science*. Vol. 42, No. 2, pp. 295–314.

Hueglin, T.O. & Fenna, A. 2006. *Comparative Federalism: A Systematic Inquiry*. Broadview Press, Toronto.

The Legislature

4

THIS CHAPTER:

* ★ examines the design and function of legislatures
* ★ analyses the nature and composition of the Australian Parliament
* ★ explains the operation of the Australian Parliament.

ISSUE IN FOCUS

Is the Senate relevant and necessary to facilitate the expression of the democratic will?

KEY TERMS

Alternative vote	Constitutional Crisis of 1975	Malapportionment
Chairperson of the	Divisions	Money bills
Committee	Federal system of	'No confidence' motion
Clerk	government	*Odgers' Senate Practice*
Commonwealth Gazette	*House of Representatives*	Speaker
	Practice	

In 1992, Prime Minister Paul Keating denounced the Senate as 'unrepresentative swill' when the powerful upper house demanded that the Treasurer appear before a Senate inquiry. Two years later, Keating repeated the insult when again confronted with an assertive Senate. Keating was not the first Australian prime minister to vent his frustration at the Senate nor is he likely to be the last. Over the years, a succession of prime ministers and ministers from both sides of the major party divide have been quick to express publicly their dissatisfaction when the Senate has exercised its full constitutional power and rejected proposed laws passed by the House of Representatives. The Senate's formidable power makes it one of Australia's most important political institutions.

Introduction

This chapter will investigate the nature of contemporary legislatures and survey some of the areas in which they can differ. It will then examine four key roles served by the Australian federal Parliament and explore some of the tensions that scholars have identified in its ability to perform these functions. In the Issue in Focus we will examine the role of second chambers in the Australian federal context and pose the question: What function is served by the Senate and is it an impediment to the fulfilment of the democratic will?

Legislative assemblies are entities that 'join society to the legal structure of the authority of the state' (Olsen quoted in Hague & Harrop 2004, p. 247). The modern legislature serves as a forum in which the collective will can be represented in the most efficient terms possible. The origins of most modern European assemblies can be traced to the thirteenth century when noblemen were forcibly required by the Monarch to provide counsel on affairs of the state. The early medieval parliaments lacked deliberative powers and were established either to 'acclaim the action of the Monarch or to give solemnity to certain events', particularly in matters relating to taxation (Birch 1971, p. 25). Over time, and owing to the force of 'revolutionary ideas and movements', the powers and authority formerly possessed by absolutist Monarchs were transferred to the parliament (Birch 1971, p. 31).

While almost every modern state possesses a legislative assembly of some description, there are significant differences in the structures, powers and responsibilities that are assigned to such bodies. One area in which assemblies differ is in the number of seats or the number of members who sit in the chamber. There is often a strong relationship between the size of an assembly and the size of a country's population. India, which has a population of over 1 billion people, has a 788-member legislature, whereas Papua New Guinea, which has 6 million inhabitants, has a 109-member Parliament. However, not all large assemblies are created to satisfy democratic principles but are designed in some cases to achieve anti-democratic outcomes. There is a strong correlation between the numerical size of a legislature and its capacity to act in a coherent and constructive manner. Hague and Harrop contend that big legislative bodies are often chaotic and unwieldy due to the large number of actors that compete within them, making it difficult for interests to aggregate successfully to achieve their legislative objectives (2004, p. 248).

There is also variation in the number of chambers a legislature may possess. While many of the feudal European assemblies were multiple chamber entities, in the modern era it is common to find either single-chamber bodies, referred to as unicameral assemblies, or dual-chamber bodies, known as bicameral assemblies (Hague & Harrop 2004, p. 249). Unicameral legislatures are the most popular, accounting for approximately 60 per cent of all deliberative assemblies. They are particularly common in countries that are geographically small. In contrast, nations that occupy a significant land mass or that have a **federal system of government** are more likely to favour a bicameral structure. However, deciding whether to adopt a unicameral or bicameral legislature is not always informed by the need to satisfy practical/functional considerations. It can sometimes also reflect a broader disagreement about the nature of democracy and how best to operationalise it (Hague & Harrop 2004, p. 249). We will return to this theme in the Issue in Focus.

> **Federal system of government:** where political power is divided between one central, national government and several regional governments

Legislatures also differ in the methods used to select representatives. The typical method of appointment in liberal-democratic states is on the basis of free and direct elections, although the choice of electoral system varies significantly from nation to nation. In addition to direct elections, there are two other methods that are used to constitute a legislature. *Indirect election* is where a second democratically elected body, such as a regional or local government, selects the members. The German *Bundesrat*, for example, is composed of the prime minister and cabinet ministers drawn from the 16 *Lander* or state parliaments that make up the German federation. The *appointment model* involves the selection of members on the basis of a hereditary entitlement or some other principle. For example, members of the British House of Lords have either inherited their seat or 'owe their appointment to the exercise of prime ministerial patronage' (Shell 1999, p. 199). According to Russell's 2001 study of selection procedures for 66 upper chambers, the most used method is direct election (41 per cent), followed by indirect election (32 per cent) and appointment (25 per cent) (Russell 2000, p. 23).

One of the significant areas in which legislatures differ is in terms of the relationship between the executive and legislative branches (Heywood 1997, p. 295). There are two core institutional arrangements: parliamentary systems and presidential systems. Lijphart observes three crucial differences between parliamentary and presidential systems. First, whereas the functional head of government can be dismissed from office by the legislature in a parliamentary system, the same is not true in a presidential system. Second, the functional head of government is selected by the legislature under the parliamentary system and by direct election in the presidential model. Third, the parliamentary system has 'collective or collegial executives' whereas the presidential model has a one-person or 'non-collegial' executive (1999, pp. 117–18).

The parliamentary system was pioneered in the United Kingdom, evolving over eight centuries. The defining characteristic of the parliamentary system is the interlocking of the executive and legislature functions of the state. According to its supporters, parliamentary systems deliver effective and responsive government. The executive's effectiveness is said to be enhanced because it resides in the legislature. Co-habitation affords the executive a greater opportunity to persuade the assembly of the merits of its proposals, thereby expediting the passage of its legislative program in parliament. At the same time, the government is kept responsive or accountable to the legislature because parliament not only can reject legislation that it does not support but it also has the capacity to dismiss government. Essentially, an executive that fails to deliver can be removed through a vote on a 'no confidence' motion.

'No confidence'
motion: a motion put in
parliament that censures
the government

Not all political communities are confident that a parliamentary system will effectively constrain the executive. This has given rise to the presidential model, which seeks to create friction in the relationship between the executive and legislative branches by formally dividing them into discrete entities. A presidential system strictly applies the doctrine of separation of powers so that law-making and law-implementing functions are embodied in independent agencies, thereby limiting the capacity of the executive to exert undue influence on the legislature. A famous example of a presidential system is found in the USA. The dual-chamber legislative assembly, known as the Congress, enjoys the exclusive right to make laws, while the executive branch, embodied in the office of the President, can veto legislation passed by Congress. In the event that Congress disagrees with the President's veto, an override is triggered on a two-thirds majority vote in both houses of Congress. Just as the parliamentary system has its critics, so too does the presidential model. One of the chief criticisms of the presidential system is that disagreement between the two branches can produce institutional deadlock, resulting in policy inertia and 'government gridlock' (Heywood 2007, p. 340).

Anatomy of the Parliament of Australia

Australia's federal Parliament formally came into existence in 1901, following the enactment of the Australian Constitutional Act. Since that time, 42 parliaments have come and gone, and 60 new ministries have been formed and disbanded. For the first 26 years of the new Parliament's existence it was located in Melbourne. In 1927, in accordance with s. 125 of the Constitution, it was moved to Canberra—a distance 'not less than 100 miles from Sydney'. In 1988, a new Parliament was constructed at a cost of $1 billion dollars.

The Constitution states that the legislative power of the Commonwealth Parliament is vested in three entities—the Queen and two elected houses of Parliament: the House of Representatives and the Senate.

While the Queen is rarely seen in Australia, she is an intrinsic element of the legislative process. According to the Constitution, the Monarch's assent is required to enact laws passed by Parliament. The Governor-General performs this task for the Queen when she is not *in situ*, acting as her representative. The Monarch's powers were originally far-reaching and included the formal, legal right to stop legislation

Figure 4.1   The structure of Australia's federal government

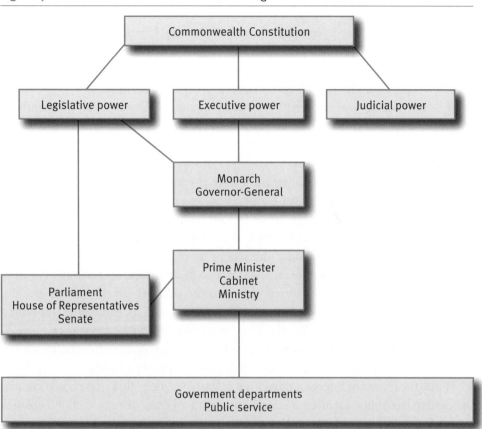

Adapted from Australian Parliamentary website: http://www.aph.gov.au/parl.htm

from being enacted. Many of the Queen's powers under the Constitution, such as the authority to disallow legislation, are now obsolete because of changes in Australia's constitutional relations with Britain. The Queen now plays an unobtrusive role in the day-to-day making of law in this country and the Governor-General acts only on the advice of the prime minister. It is almost inconceivable that the Governor-General would refuse to ratify legislation lawfully passed by the Parliament.

The second critical institution of law-making in Australia is the Parliament. The Australian Parliament is bicameral; that is, it is comprised of two chambers that meet separately, and which have their own members, procedures, meeting chamber, administration and personnel. Two considerations influenced the decision to adopt a bicameral structure. First, bicameralism was intended to provide protection to the states by ensuring that they had effective representation in the national Parliament. Second, and in keeping with the commitment to liberal-democratic principles, the bicameral arrangement was intended to ensure that all proposed legislation was given due consideration before being enacted. We will return to the issue of bicameral parliaments in the Issue in Focus.

The House of Representatives is established by Chapter I, Part III of the Constitution. The Constitution expressly requires that members of the House of Representatives serve a term that shall not exceed three years. Over the years, membership of the House of Representatives has grown from 75 to 150 members: New South Wales, 49 members; Victoria, 37 members; Queensland, 29 members; Western Australia, 15 members; South Australia, 11 members; Tasmania, 5 members; Australian Capital Territory, 2 members; and Northern Territory, 2 members.

There are only three formal restrictions on the composition of the House of Representatives. First, the chamber must have twice the number of senators, which is a provision known as the nexus clause. The nexus clause was incorporated so as to prevent the House of Representatives from completely eclipsing the Senate in the event of a joint sitting. Second, each of the original states must have at least five elected members, notwithstanding the size of its population. Third, to be eligible to sit in Parliament, a person must be at least 18 years of age; an Australian citizen; and an elector (or a person qualified to become an elector). To this list we can also include the possibility of disqualification if the member is an existing member of a state or territory Parliament; is serving a prison sentence of 12 months or more; is an undischarged bankrupt or is insolvent; is holding an office of profit under the Crown; or is a permanent member of the Australian Defence Force.

While the House of Representatives is recognised principally as the people's house, the Senate has a dual identity: a states' house and a house of review. The Senate is established by Chapter I, Part II of the Constitution and is composed of senators from each state. Each state is represented equally with senators enjoying six-year terms. The longer electoral term afforded to senators is designed to insulate them against the pressures of regular elections and to allow them to develop the expertise and knowledge that befits a chamber charged with the responsibility of defending the interests of the states and reviewing legislation. As with the House of Representatives, the Senate has been enlarged since 1901, when there were originally only 36 senators. Today there are 76 senators. While each of the states is entitled to 12 senators, the territories are only permitted two senators apiece and for three-year terms.

The Senate is equal to the House of Representatives in all but three respects. Section 53 forbids the Senate from initiating **money bills**; amending money bills; or amending any bill so as to increase any proposed charge or burden on the people. At first glance it might appear that s. 53 is designed to prevent the Senate from having involvement in money matters, however the reality is very different. Section 53 does not prevent the Senate from sending a money bill back to the House of Representatives with suggested changes, nor does it prohibit the Senate from withholding its assent. While the Constitution ensures that the Senate's legislative power is almost equal to that of the

Money bills: any bill that seeks to raise money

House of Representatives, this situation has also led to strong criticism of the Senate, and to allegations that it abuses its power. We will return to this debate in the Issue in Focus section.

The four faces of the Australian Parliament

Conceptually, the House of Representatives and the Senate play quite different roles in the legislative process (see Table 4.1). The different roles reflect the different purpose for which the chambers were constituted, particularly the Senate. For example, *Odgers' Senate Practice* specifies that the Senate provides 'adequate representation of the people of all the states' while no similar function is listed in the *House of Representatives Practice*.

Odgers' Senate Practice: the rule book of the Senate, which sets out the rules, procedures and practices to which the chamber must conform

While Table 4.1 identifies a number of functions performed by Parliament, there are *four key roles* that are especially significant. First, a critical function of the Parliament is drafting new laws, amending existing laws and abolishing redundant legislation. This is one of the only tasks that the Constitution explicitly ascribes to Parliament. According to figures collated by the *House of Representatives Practice*, the House devotes 54 per cent of its time considering proposed laws (Table 4.2). While law-making absorbs slightly more than

House of Representatives Practice: the rule book of the House of Representatives, which sets out the rules, procedures and practices to which the chamber must conform

half of its total business, Parliament's law-making authority is constrained by the Constitution. Any laws passed by Parliament that exceed the powers granted to it by the Constitution can be overturned by the High Court.

Two concerns are frequently expressed about the quality of the legislative function performed by Parliament. First, commentators have noted that there has been a significant increase in the volume of the Parliament's legislative program without a corresponding increase in the amount of time that it convenes. In the 1930s, Parliament considered an average of 80 bills and met for 64 days of the year (541 hours). In 2004, Parliament was presented with 223 bills but met for only 59 days in the year (or 594 hours) (Odgers 2004, p. 791). At the same time, the 'environment of Australian governance' is not only changing, but is becoming increasingly complex, which is putting Parliament under increased strain (Uhr & Wanna 2000, pp. 26–9). This raises the concern that proposed legislation is not always afforded the close scrutiny that it warrants or deserves.

Quite apart from the additional workload that burdens the modern parliament, others point to another, interminable problem, which is the dominance of the executive in the law-making process. While the parliamentary model is based on a dominant role for the executive in the formulation of policy and the initiation of new laws, it also presupposes that the legislature is able to exercise sufficient power to block or to amend proposals that are not in the national interest.

Table 4.1   The roles of the House of Representatives and the Senate compared

House of Representatives	Senate
▪ Making and unmaking government. ▪ The initiation and consideration of legislation. ▪ Seeking information on and clarification of government policy. ▪ Surveillance, appraisal and criticism of government administration. ▪ Consideration of financial proposals and examination of public accounts. ▪ Inquiry by committee. ▪ Ventilation of grievances and matters of interest or concern. ▪ Receiving petitions. ▪ Examination of delegated legislation. ▪ Prerequisites for fulfilling functions.	▪ To ensure adequate representation of the people of all the states. ▪ To balance domination of the House of Representatives by members from the more populous states. ▪ To provide representation of significant groups of electors not able to secure the election of members to the House of Representatives. ▪ To review legislative and other proposals initiated in the House of Representatives, and to ensure proper consideration of all legislation. ▪ To ensure that legislative measures are exposed to the considered views of the community and to provide opportunity for contentious legislation to be subject to electoral scrutiny. ▪ To provide protection against a government, with a disciplined majority in the House of Representatives, introducing extreme measures for which it does not have broad community support. ▪ To provide adequate scrutiny of financial measures, especially by committees considering estimates. ▪ To initiate non-financial legislation. ▪ To probe and check the administration of the laws, to keep itself and the public informed, and to insist on ministerial accountability for the government's administration. ▪ To exercise surveillance over the executive's regulation-making power. ▪ To protect personal rights and liberties which might be endangered if there were a concentration of unrestrained power in the House of Representatives. ▪ To provide effective scrutiny of governments, and enable adequate expression of debate about policy and government programs.

Source: *The House of Representatives Practice* (5th edn); *Odgers' Senate Practice* (11th edn)

Table 4.2 Proportion of House time spent considering certain categories of business, 1995–2007

	38th Parliament				39th Parliament						40th Parliament		41st Parliament	
	1995	1996	1997	1998	1999	2000	2001	2002	2003	2004	2005	2006	2007	Average
Legislation														
Government sponsored	48.7	48.0	53.8	49.8	54.2	54.9	51.9	51.5	50.7	56.7	58.0	50.4	58.6	52.9
Sponsored by Private Members	0.4	0.9	0.2	0.5	0.4	0.5	0.9	0.2	0.3	0.1	1.3	7.1	0.2	1.0
Total	49.2	48.9	54.1	50.4	54.5	55.3	52.8	51.7	51.0	56.9	59.3	57.5	58.7	53.9
Motions														
Government initiated	9.1	2.4	2.2	1.3	3.7	1.7	5.0	4.4	7.9	2.0	1.2	1.5	0.8	3.3
Initiated by Private Members	6.5	5.0	4.7	6.5	6.4	5.1	3.5	4.7	5.1	3.0	4.0	5.6	3.7	4.9
Total	15.7	7.5	6.9	7.8	10.1	6.9	8.4	9.1	13.0	4.9	5.1	7.1	4.5	8.2
Statements														
Ministerial statements	0.6	1.7	1.6	0.7	0.8	0.5	0.3	0.5	0.7	0.2	0.2	0.3	0.1	0.6
Statements by Private Members	0.9	0.8	1.0	0.7	1.0	0.7	0.6	0.5	0.7	0.5	1.0	0.6	0.5	0.7
Total	1.5	2.4	2.6	1.4	1.8	1.2	0.9	1.0	1.4	0.7	1.2	0.8	0.6	1.4
Matters of public importance	**5.5**	**5.5**	**6.5**	**5.5**	**5.8**	**6.5**	**6.2**	**6.1**	**5.7**	**7.6**	**7.6**	**7.5**	**8.8**	**6.5**
Adjournment debates	**5.1**	**4.6**	**5.2**	**5.6**	**5.1**	**5.1**	**5.4**	**4.9**	**4.8**	**4.8**	**5.0**	**5.0**	**5.2**	**5.1**
Grievance debates	**2.7**	**3.0**	**3.5**	**3.0**	**3.6**	**3.0**	**3.0**	**2.8**	**3.0**	**2.6**	**2.8**	**2.8**	**2.4**	**2.9**
Address-in-reply	—	**3.3**	—	**3.4**	—	—	—	**2.5**	—	**3.0**	—	—	—	**3.1**
Motions to suspend standing orders														
Government initiated	0.8	1.8	0.3	0.7	0.4	0.2	0.0	0.4	0.3	0.2	0.3	0.3	0.5	0.5
Initiated by Private Members	1.3	1.7	1.7	0.6	0.7	1.0	1.3	1.5	1.8	0.7	2.2	1.8	0.6	1.3
Total	2.0	3.5	2.0	1.3	1.1	1.2	1.3	1.9	2.1	0.9	2.4	2.2	1.1	1.8
Business of the House	**18.3**	**21.3**	**19.2**	**21.6**	**18.1**	**20.9**	**21.9**	**20.0**	**18.9**	**18.5**	**16.4**	**17.1**	**18.6**	**19.3**

Source: *House of Representatives Practice*, p. 835

However, the parliamentary model was conceived in an era when loose coalitions occupied the benches of parliament and not the highly disciplined partisan foot soldiers that are now the norm. Since the emergence of disciplined political parties, MPs rarely cross the floor to vote against their party and with the opposing side, particularly MPs from the two big political groupings. A recent study confirmed how rare such an occurrence is in the Australian context. Of over 14 000 **divisions** between 1950 and 2004, only 3 per cent of members crossed the floor to vote with the opposing party (McKeown & Lundie 2005).

Divisions: a device used in parliament to gauge the support of the chamber for a motion

A second function performed by the Australia Parliament is to provide the nation with a government. Governments are formed in the House of Representatives owing to convention. Voters help to realise this convention at election time when they are called to the ballot box. The leader of the party or coalition that holds a majority of seats in the lower house is sworn in as the government. While the Senate plays no role in making governments, it does have the ability to unmake a government—a power that many scholars believe is contentious and inconsistent with Westminster parliamentary practice. We will return to this debate in the Issue in Focus.

The third important function of the parliament is to scrutinise the government. In a parliamentary system, government is accountable to the legislature between election periods. This is achieved through a range of tools, procedures and practices that permit parliament to critically evaluate the government's performance (see Box 4.1).

BOX 4.1   Devices to scrutinise Parliament

- *Censure motion*: A motion in which the government, a minister, a member or the opposition is formally censured for wrongdoing or misconduct of some description. The most crucial censure motions are those in which a majority of MPs in the House of Representatives moves a vote of no confidence in the government. A successful censure motion, or vote of no confidence, requires the government of the day to resign their commission. For more information see: http://www.aph.gov.au/house/pubs/PRACTICE/chapter9.htm#cen

- *Committees*: These are made up of a small group of members or senators appointed by one or both chambers to investigate specific matters of policy or government administration. Committees are able to call persons to appear before them, such as public servants, or inspect official documents relevant to the inquiry. While there are as many as eight different types of committees, there are four that are especially well known: standing (continuous); select (convened on a needs basis); joint (consists of members from both houses); and the main committee (established as an alternative to the chamber, for detailed discussion of a bill). For more information see: http://www.aph.gov.au/house/info/infosheets/is04.pdf

- *Parliamentary privilege*: Members of Parliament are entitled to special legal rights and privileges, which are designed to ensure that they have maximum freedom while in Parliament to freely debate, question, and conduct investigations without fear of prosecution. For more information see: http://www.aph.gov.au/house/info/infosheets/is05.pdf
- *Procedure*: There are separate standing rules for each chamber, which are designed to bring order and certainty to the conduct of business. The business of the Parliament is typically dealt with as a series of motions, which are formal proposals that some kind of action be taken by the chamber. The purpose of maintaining formal rules is to ensure that all matters that are presented to Parliament for its consideration are dealt with fairly. For more information see: http://www.aph.gov.au/house/info/infosheets/is14.pdf
- *Questions*: The standing orders of Parliament, or the rules set by Parliament that inform its conduct, permit two types of questions to be put to ministers. These are oral questions, which are questions without notice, and written questions, which are typically questions of which the minister is given advanced warning. Question Time is intended to allow the Parliament to scrutinise the actions of the government. For more information see: http://www.aph.gov.au/house/info/infosheets/is01.pdf
- *Urgency debates*: Known colloquially as the 'guillotine', urgency debates are designed to ensure that discussion on certain matters is subject to a strict time limit. A guillotine occurs when a minister moves that a bill be considered 'urgent' and the motion is carried, resulting in a specified time limit being applied to the various stages of the bill.

In much the same way that party discipline has served to undermine the legislative function of the Parliament, so too has it had an adverse effect on Parliament's ability to hold the government to account. The extent to which these mechanisms can be successfully deployed against the executive depends upon the government's willingness to allow them to be used for such a purpose. Governments typically have very little interest in subjecting either their policies or personnel to scrutiny, particularly if the government's credibility is undermined as a result.

Parliamentary scrutiny is less effective where the government has a clear majority of seats in the lower house. The electoral system helps to cultivate stable majorities in the House of Representatives, leading to cohesive voting blocks in Parliament. The **alternative vote** (or preferential voting) is notorious for inflating the winning party's majority in the House of Representatives, delivering them far

Alternative vote: an electoral system that requires voters to rank all candidates in order of preference. The candidate who receives 50 per cent + 1 of the vote is deemed elected. Also known as preferential voting.

more seats in the chamber than they need in order to govern. At the 2007 federal election, for example, the Rudd ALP government won only 43.38 per cent of the primary vote but claimed 83 of the 150 lower house seats (55 per cent). This affords the government an unassailable majority in the lower house and the capacity to manipulate parliamentary procedure to its advantage.

A fourth task performed by Parliament is to represent the popular will. Neither the House of Representatives nor the Senate's description of their responsibilities explicitly emphasises this function although one could argue that this task is implicit in the constitutional requirement (s. 24) that Parliament is

directly chosen by the people of the Commonwealth ...

However, there is significant disagreement over what it means for Parliament to represent the people (see Box 4.2). Many academics believe that Parliament can only fulfil its representative function if the social composition of the legislature closely approximates the broader social, ethnic, economic and political cleavages within society. That is, a representative body, such as parliament, should constitute a micro-cosm of the larger society and contain members drawn from a cross-section within society that is 'proportional to the size of the groups in society at large'. A parliament that fails to mirror society risks marginalising or even completely ignoring certain interests (Heywood 2007, p. 252).

The Australian Parliament, not unlike most liberal-democratic parliaments, is far from a microcosm of the broader community. While the composition of the modern federal Parliament is more diverse than its antecedents, it remains the 'domain of white middle aged men' (Miskin & Lumb 2006). Miskin and Lumb's 2006 survey of 226 MPs in the 41st Parliament showed that even women, a cohort that comprises one-half of the population, make up only 28.5 per cent of the total number of federal MPs. A more recent study by Miragliotta & Errington (2008) revealed that in the last twenty years there has been a continued narrowing in the pre-parliamentary occupa-tions of MPs from the three major parties. The paper found a significant increase in the number of major party MPs previously employed as political staffers, leading some commentators to lament about the emergence of 'cookie-cutter' politicians.

Some countries have sought to tackle the problem of under-representation of certain groups by imposing quotas on the normal process of election. In New Zealand, seven of its 69 electoral seats have been set aside as Maori electorates. Both NSW and Queensland have, in recent years, considered proposals for the creation of dedicated Indigenous seats within their parliaments. These proposals have been considered within the context of the under-representation of Indigenous people at all levels of political life in Australia (see Iorns 2003; Legal, Constitutional and Administrative Review Committee 2002). On the other hand, many argue that quotas are an artifice that interferes with the 'normal processes of election' (Hague & Harrop 2004, p. 253). They assert that the use of quotas 'portrays representation in narrow and exclusive terms' and, moreover, if realised, risks 'social division and conflict, with no one being able to advance the common good or advance a broader public interest' (Heywood 2007, p. 252).

Based on the above discussion, it is tempting to conclude that Parliament is a dysfunctional institution. One Australian scholar declared that Parliament is 'in eclipse, a pale, even sickly pale, moon reflecting but a little of the shining light of Executive power' (Crisp quoted in Smith 1994, p. 107). Such claims are not new and nor are they made solely in relation to Australia's federal Parliament. Rodney Smith points out that the since the 1960s the 'view of parliaments as largely moribund' has become 'political science orthodoxy' (1994, p. 306). While it is true that the operation of the Australian Parliament is far from ideal, it remains a bedrock institution. Perhaps more important is evidence that shows that the public views Parliament as an indispensable element of the Australian political system (Uhr & Wanna 2000, p. 23).

Making laws in Parliament

Parliament is critical in helping to fulfil the democratic ideal. But how does the Commonwealth Parliament make laws? What are the processes that lead to the creation of new legislation? Before we discuss the mechanics of passing legislation, it is important to outline the principle of responsible government, which sits at the heart of the Australian parliamentary system.

The Australian parliamentary tradition is based on a modified version of the English Westminster model. Central to Australian parliamentary practice is the system of responsible government, which involves a chain of accountability designed to keep government 'responsible'. According to the theory of responsible government, parliament is charged with the task of holding to account those who the public have elected to run the state, which is the government. While the principle of responsible government is considered fundamental to Australian parliamentary practice, like so many other features of the Australian political system, it is not expressly mentioned within the Constitution. The only real clue to this is found in s. 64 of the Constitution, which states that ministers must be Members of Parliament.

BOX 4.2   Theories of representation

One of the classical debates within political science is the vexed question of representation: what considerations should guide members of parliament when representing those who voted them into office. There are three principal models of representation and no agreement on which best conforms to liberal-democratic practice.

The *Trustee* model requires members to act in what he or she believes is in the best interests of the constituent. The ideal is best summed up by Edmund Burke, who in 1774 declared that your 'representative owes you, not his industry only, but his judgment; and he betrays, instead of serving you, if he sacrifices it to your opinion'. The Trustee model advocates that representatives have a moral duty to act in what they believe is best for the electorate on the grounds that elected members possess both superior judgment and enlightened conscience whereas the masses, devoid of such capabilities, are not always the best judge of their own true interests.

The *Delegate* model demands that the member faithfully convey the interests and wishes of the electorate. Unlike the Trustee model, the Delegate model requires the member to act only as his electorate dictates and not according to the member's own opinions and beliefs.

The *Mandate* model is a response to the emergence of modern political parties. It is different to both the Trustee and Delegate model in that it proposes that members represent and give expression to the programs and policies of the party that pre-selected them to office. According to this conception of representation, parties, via their members, are given a mandate to deliver those policies on which the party campaigned at the election.

Q   What are the pros and cons of each of these models of representation and which of them is most appropriate for the modern political age?

The passage of proposed laws through Parliament is a highly routine affair. All new legislation initially takes the form of a bill, which is the name given to proposed new legislation that has yet to be enacted (see Box 4.3 for other procedures for making legislation). Most of the new bills that are presented to Parliament begin their journey in the House of Representatives rather than the Senate (see Figure 4.2). This is in keeping with the convention that governments are formed in the lower chamber. In 2007, 154 of the 168 new bills introduced, commenced in the House of Representatives (*House of Representatives Practice*).

The first stage consists of what is known as the *first reading*. At this point the bill is introduced into the House of Representatives (House) by reading out its title. There is no real discussion on the bill. Almost immediately following the first reading of the bill, the minister who is responsible for bringing it before the House will propose a motion for a *second reading*. At the second reading the minister will give a short speech outlining the merits of the bill and offer reasons why it should be passed. When the minister has finished describing the bill, the opposition and the government begin the task of debating the merits of the proposal. At the completion of the debates, the House will decide whether it will support the bill in principle.

Figure 4.2   The passage of proposed laws through Parliament

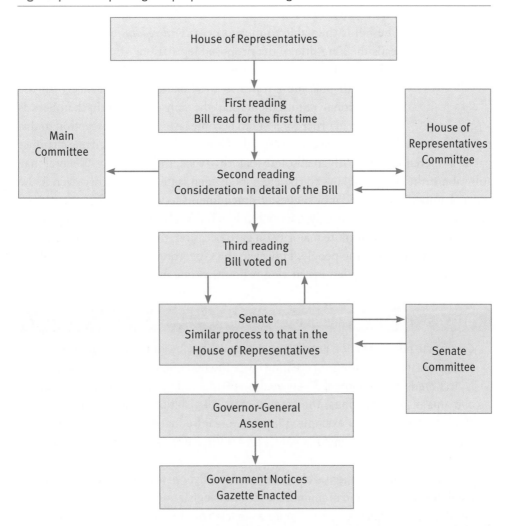

Source: Adapted from *House of Representatives Practice* (5th edn)

Once the bill has cleared the second stage it moves into the committee stage where each clause of the bill is sometimes considered separately. The House transforms itself into a committee of the whole, or the Main Committee. This is achieved by the **Speaker** of the House vacating the seat for the **Chairperson of the Committee**. In some cases the bill is referred to a specialist Select Committee of the House, which considers the whole bill in detail. Once the bill has been sufficiently debated and a majority view has been reached, the Chairman of the Committee then

Speaker: the person elected by the members of the House of Representatives to chair meetings of the chamber and to preside over proceedings. In the Senate, this office is referred to as the President.

Chairperson of the Committee: the person selected to chair and to manage proceedings of the Committee

Clerk: the person responsible for ensuring that the business of the Parliament runs smoothly and in accordance with the procedural rules

reports to the Speaker, who resumes the chair and the Committee of the Whole is disbanded and reverts to its usual status as the House. The bill is then able to move into a *third reading* where the **Clerk** reads the long title of the proposed legislation.

Bills that have been dealt with by the House then proceed to the Senate. All bills must travel to the Senate in accordance with the constitutional requirement that the consent of both chambers is necessary in order for a bill to become law. The only exception to this rule is referendum proposals. Section 128 of the Constitution states that if one chamber passes a referendum bill with an absolute majority twice, the Governor-General may still submit the proposed laws to the electors in each state and territory even if the other chamber has rejected it or suggested amendments to which the first-mentioned house does not agree. Essentially, if a referendum bill has been passed twice by one of the chambers with an absolute majority on each occasion, the Governor-General can present the proposal to the people. However, the Governor-General is only likely to do this if they receive explicit instruction from the prime minister.

BOX 4.3   Laws made outside of Parliament

Contrary to popular belief, not all laws are made in or by Parliament. There are at least three major methods for creating laws. The first and most obvious of these is *Acts made by Parliament*. Every year, the Parliament passes many new laws and amends existing ones. The amount of new legislation created each year is significant. In 2006, for example, 188 bills were introduced to Parliament and of this number 172 were transformed into an Act (*House of Representative Practice*, 5th edn).

In addition to Acts, there is also *delegated legislation*, which typically includes regulations, by-laws and ordinances. Delegated legislation is the term applied to legislation that is made by government agencies or the Governor-General under Acts of Parliament and is sometimes known as subordinate legislation. In recent years, there has been a sharp increase in the volume of delegated legislation, largely due to the increase in the legislative burden that modern parliaments shoulder. In order to help expedite matters, non-controversial legislation that deals with matters of administrative detail are granted to an appropriate government agency. The problem with delegated legislation is that it is not subjected to the same level of scrutiny as ordinary Acts of Parliament. However, as Jordan (2003) notes, whatever the deficiencies of the system of delegated legislation, it is subject to 'fairly standard and well-established procedures', which makes it subject to review.

A third type of legislation is known as *Letters Patent*, which is an ancient form of law-making that initially existed so as to enable the monarch to make laws independent of the parliament. While the instrument is considered out-moded, Letters Patent survive in the modern era. Today, Letters Patent are used to grant awards and honours. The Monarch uses Letters Patent when advised by the government of the day. One of the interesting features of Letters Patent is that, unlike Acts of Parliament and delegated legislation, they are made entirely outside of Parliament and are not subject to stringent routines, procedures or reporting requirements that govern the other methods of making laws.

Q Should Letters Patent be permitted to persist? Does the continuation of this form of law-making, along with delegated legislation, usurp the Parliament's authority?

Source: Jordan 2003

Apart from this one exception, all bills must be ratified and approved by both houses of Parliament. Once the House has dealt with the proposal it is then presented to the Senate for its consideration. The process by which the Senate does this is much the same as in the House: there is a first and second reading interspersed with a committee stage and finally a third reading of the bill.

If the Senate passes the bill without any qualifications or changes it is then ready for the final stage. This involves the bill being presented to the Governor-General for royal assent. Once the Governor-General has signed off on the legislation, consent must be notified in the **Commonwealth Gazette** in order for the legislation to be activated.

It is not uncommon for the House and the Senate to disagree on legislation. The Senate does, on occasion, reject government bills or suggest amendments to a government-sponsored bill. This situation is most likely to occur when the executive lacks a majority in the Senate. When the two houses are in conflict over a bill, there are specified deadlock procedures used to resolve the conflict. The deadlock procedures are found in s. 57 of the Constitution. The rules are quite simple. If on three separate occasions, separated by intervals of three months, the House passes a bill that the Senate rejects or passes it with amendments with which the lower house does not agree, the Governor-General can dissolve both houses simultaneously and call a new election. If after the new election the House presents the same bill to the Senate and it again rejects it or makes recommendations that the House believes are unsuitable, the Governor-General may convene a joint sitting of members of both houses so that they can vote on the bill. In order for the bill to be passed, an absolute majority is required, which gives a decided (numerical) advantage to the government of the day.

Commonwealth Gazette: the *Government Notices Gazette* is published by the Attorney-General's Department each Wednesday, except for the Christmas–New Year period. The *Gazette* contains a range of legislation, including proclamations, information about legislation, notices of Commonwealth government departments and courts, and other notices required under Commonwealth law.

ISSUE IN FOCUS

IS THE SENATE RELEVANT AND NECESSARY TO FACILITATE THE EXPRESSION OF THE DEMOCRATIC WILL?

> The Senate, of course, is the B Grade, as our colleagues like to refer to us, or unrepresentative swill, or whatever you want to call us. Swill and proud, that's my view. The Senate is the Chamber of Parliament where all the real politics are played out. I mean the House of Representatives is the House for the big bang. The Senate is the place for the slow grind … (Senator Bob Collins 1996).

Australia is unique among parliamentary federations in having strongly bicameral parliaments at the regional level as well as at the national level (Stone 2002, p. 267). The Australian partiality for bicameralism was imposed on the colonies by the British authorities, who insisted on this arrangement as a precondition of being granted self-government (Sharman 1990, p. 84). As a result, parliaments in Australia tend to be bicameral rather than unicameral. Currently, there are only three Australian parliaments that are unicameral: those of the ACT, Northern Territory and Queensland.

Despite its association with radical liberal-democratic principles, bicameralism in Australia has fairly conservative beginnings. The British variant of bicameralism was initially designed to protect the landed classes from the radical policies that might occur as a result of a directly elected lower house giving legislative expression to the collective will. In order to prevent the tyranny of the masses, second chambers, constituted on the basis of a limited franchise, were viewed as an important checking mechanism to preserve the power and status of the landed nobility (Russell 2000, p. 21). In the modern era, however, bicameral parliaments are viewed as an instrument to protect the citizenry from the excesses of elected governments.

Second chambers (or upper houses) tend to look quite different from first chambers (or lower houses). Second chambers are often smaller than first chambers, and their members typically enjoy longer, staggered terms in office. While such differences have an important bearing on the operations of second chambers, they have, on their own, limited influence on the power the second chamber is able to exert over the legislative process. According to Lijphart, the extent to which a second chamber is capable of constraining and checking the activities of the first chamber is contingent on the second chamber possessing at least three additional attributes. First, it must possess identical (or near identical) powers to the first chamber. A second chamber that does not enjoy parity with the first chamber will simply be rendered redundant because the latter will be able to ignore the wishes of the second chamber. Second, Lijphart notes that the method by which the second chamber is elected also has a significant bearing on its status. Second chambers that are not directly elected will lack the legitimacy enjoyed by the first chamber and may therefore have less power. Third, Lijphart points out that the method of election to the second chamber must be different from the first chamber so as to increase the possibility that the partisan composition of the members within each chamber is different. Lijphart argues that the greater the incongruence between the chambers in terms of the political composition of its members, the greater the likelihood that the second chamber will enjoy independence from the first house (1999, pp. 205–8).

The Australian Senate meets Lijphart's three criteria for a strong second chamber. The Senate enjoys virtual parity with the House of Representatives, is directly elected, and is selected using a different electoral method to that used to elect MPs to the first chamber. In combination, these features make the Australian Senate one the most powerful second chambers currently in existence.

While possessing great power makes the Senate a force to be reckoned with, it also brings with it a great many enemies. A second chamber, by its very nature, is a political target, regardless of whether it possesses great power. Abbe Sieyes describes the plight of second chambers aptly: 'if a second chamber dissents from the first, it is mischievous; and if it agrees it is superfluous' (quoted in Hague & Harrop 2004, p. 249). A strong second chamber is especially vulnerable in parliamentary systems, which naturally accord much greater emphasis on first chambers that alone are thought to posses the democratic legitimacy to make and break governments.

The Senate is frequently subject to criticism whether it is flexing its significant powers or not. When the Senate was controlled by the government, as it was largely during the period between 1910 and 1977, it was accused of being a rubber stamp, blithely pushing through the government's legislation. Yet, on the rare occasions where the Senate has had the temerity to challenge or question proposed legislation it has been attacked for being obstructionist and undemocratic. While open and frank debate about our political institutions is vital to the health and well-being of democracy, one might be tempted to argue that the Senate has been the target of particularly strong abuse, which its lower house counterpart, for all its innumerable flaws, has not been forced to endure.

While many believe that the Australian Senate only emerged as a powerful and independent presence in the 1980s, this is not strictly true. From its inception, the Senate differentiated itself from the House of Representatives on procedural matters, reflecting the first Senate President's belief that the chamber 'should develop its own practice and procedure, rather than just follow Westminster practice' (Bennett 2004). In doing so, the Senate established for itself 'a procedural independence which was to become a major factor in its subsequent history'. This has had implications for how the Senate operates. As Bennett explains: 'This determination to be seen as a place separate from the House has permeated Senate thinking, even in times when it was controlled by the government of the day, and it forms an important backdrop to its latter-day relations with the lower house' (Bennett 2004).

Despite the resentment that many modern governments feel towards the Senate, they have rarely called for its abolition in recent decades. This may reflect the fact that the Senate has come to enjoy strong public support, in contrast to the early decades of Federation when it was viewed with suspicion, and any attempt to abolish it is likely to be rejected by the people at a referendum (see Bennett 2004 for figures). The major parties also have a vested interest in the continuation of the chamber. The major parties often reward those who have served their party faithfully with a safe seat in the Senate. It is further claimed that the major parties use senators as 'shock troops' in marginal seats and those held by their opponents. Senators' generous member entitlements, fewer constituency obligations and longer electoral terms make the chamber an increasingly indispensable resource that can be directed for partisan advantage (van Onselen & Errington 2005, p. 359).

Most of the proposals for Senate reform have focused on curtailing its powers rather than calling for its abolition. Over the years a number of proposals have been put forward, the most recent of which was by the Howard Coalition Government in 2003. Prime Minister Howard released a paper entitled *Resolving Deadlocks: A Discussion Paper* in which he argued that reform of the Senate was vital in order to 'rebalance the relationship between the two houses' (Howard quoted in Summers 2006, p. 88). Howard proposed reform to the double dissolution provisions within the Constitution so as to significantly truncate the conditions under which a joint sitting of the Parliament could be triggered (Summer 2006, p. 88). While at pains to defend the institution of the Senate, Howard argued that 'without such reform, governments will be unable to implement policies which have both a popular mandate and are essential to promoting good government' (Howard 2003).

Three key arguments are advanced to justify changes to the Senate. These are that the Senate no longer functions as intended by the framers of the Constitution, that reforms are needed to correct a fundamental weakness in the institutional design of the Parliament, and that the Senate is dominated by vexatious minority senators. The three arguments are explained below.

A states' house no more?

The first of the three arguments is that the Senate's claim to parity with the House of Representatives can no longer be supported on the grounds that it does not perform the role that had been envisaged at the time of Federation. The emergence of disciplined political parties has resulted in a situation whereby senators no longer actively represent the interests of their home state but serve the interests of the party that pre-selected them. Often this criticism is linked to questions about the legitimacy of the Senate on the grounds of perceived democratic/representational inequality between the states. In a 2003 speech, Helen Coonan, a senator in the Howard Government, argued:

the constitutional entitlement to equal representation of Senators irrespective of population has led to entrenched inequality between voters. New South Wales, with 34 per cent of the population, is confined to the same representation in the Senate as the smallest state, Tasmania, with only 2.6 per cent of the population. Although undoubtedly part of the federal design and entrenched in the Constitution, can it be defended as a democratic outcome for a Tasmanian's vote to be worth thirteen times that of New South Wales voters, or a South Australian's vote to be worth four times that of New South Wales voters in the Senate?

The claim that the Senate no longer acts as a states' house is difficult to argue against. Scholars and commentators are under no illusions that the Senate is no longer an advocate for states' rights. However, it is also incorrect to define the role of the Senate in such narrow terms. To do so ignores the fact that the Senate was conceived to perform a dual function—as both a states' house and a house of review.

The second problem identified in the above quote, the issue of constitutional **malapportionment**, also affects the House of Representatives, although not to the same extent as the Senate. Tasmania, for example, is entitled under the terms of the Constitution to five members in the House of Representatives, even though its population is only big enough to support three members. Moreover, some of the ill effects of malapportionment in the upper house are partially offset by the more proportionate electoral system used to elect senators. As Goot (1999, pp. 332–3) explains:

> **Malapportionment:** refers to the problem of some electoral districts containing significantly more people than others. In Australia, malapportionment has historically taken the form of deliberate rural over-representation.

> if one calculates election results on a national rather than state basis (so that all votes count equally regardless of where they were cast) and then compares the votes cast with the seats won in the Senate and the House of Representatives, it has almost always been the Senate since 1949—not the House of Representatives—that has better mirrored the nation's mind.

So while the principle of one vote one value has not be instituted in the Senate, its use of proportional representation means that it can be considered a more representative chamber than the House of Representatives because seats are awarded in closer approximation to the wishes of each of the state electorates.

Correcting poor institutional design

The second of the three arguments is that the institutional basis of the Australian Parliament is flawed and in need of correction. In describing the Parliament, academics are fond of claiming that it is a 'hybrid' or a 'mutation' because of the dual commitment to federalist principles, which strongly support the institution of a powerful upper house, and responsible government, which is based on the idea that governments are both made and broken in the lower house. The coexistence of both sets of design principles is thought to destabilise the very foundations of the Parliament, particularly when it results, as it did in 1975, with the Senate triggering the forced removal of the Whitlam Labor Government from the House of Representatives.

The problem with this claim is that Australia's powerful Senate is not quite the institutional oddity that many writers suppose. Sharman reminds us that strong bicameralism was inherited from the British and is not an aberrant political structure inconsistent with the liberal ideal that underpins the British parliamentary tradition (Sharman 1990, pp. 84–5). Nor has the Senate been the source of significant political and institutional instability. Despite the tumult of the **Constitutional Crisis of 1975**, no permanent damage was incurred to the Australian political system, which recovered relatively quickly and effortlessly from the resultant strife. If anything, the events of 1975 served to clarify the so called ambiguity implicit in the Australian model by confirming what politicians and scholars had long known, which is that the Senate has the power to bring down a government under certain conditions.

Constitutional Crisis of 1975: In 1975, the Governor-General took the unprecedented step of exercising his reserve powers to dismiss the Whitlam Labor Government. The Governor-General justified the dismissal on the grounds that the Government had lost the support of the Parliament due to its failure to secure the passage of its supply bills in the Senate.

Rule of minority parties and independents

The third of the criticisms levelled against the Senate is that the introduction of proportional representation has allowed minor parties too great a role in determining the fate of proposed legislation. This has resulted in the claim that the national, popular interest is often derailed by minority voices operating in the Senate and that a small coterie of minor-party and independent senators are holding the will of the majority to ransom.

One of the weaknesses of this argument is that one does not need to reform the powers of the Senate in order to fix this problem, if indeed the presence of minor parties in the chamber is a blot on the system. This problem is easily solved by replacing proportional representation with an electoral system that makes it more difficult for minor parties to get elected. Even then, the public might not take too kindly to the Parliament tinkering with the Senate's electoral system. In a Roy Morgan poll conducted in 1999, nearly three-quarters (72 per cent) of the sample thought the electoral system 'should stay the way it is' rather than be changed 'to make it easier for the Coalition or the Labor Party to have a majority in the Senate' (Goot 1999, p. 338).

More importantly, perhaps, is that the argument that minor parties are capable of holding the majority will to ransom ignores s. 23 of the Constitution, which states that: 'questions arising in the Senate shall be determined by a majority of votes, and each senator shall have one vote'. Minor parties and independents cannot, by simply voting against the government legislation, prevent its enactment. They can only do so if the major opposition party is also opposed to the proposed legislation.

The arguments put by the major parties (particularly when in government) for reforming the Senate often conceal other motives for wanting to meddle with the upper house. Despite couching their arguments using appeals to 'democracy', 'equality' and even the 'national interest', there is no escaping the fact that governments object to the powers possessed by the Senate because it produces the very constraints that a powerful upper chamber is intended to engender. This certainly became the case following the entry of minor parties to the Senate from the 1980s onwards, which saw the Senate transformed from a 'rubber stamp' to what some scholars now describe as a genuine 'house of review' (Smith 1994, p. 131). Some commentators even claim that the inability of the government to command a majority in the Senate has helped to create an atmosphere of greater collegiality within the Senate, with senators adopting a slightly less partisan mindset when considering proposed legislation.

Despite government claims about the injustice of an oppositional Senate, very little of its legislative timetable is held up by the Senate and there is even some evidence that Senate amendments have improved the quality of legislation, particularly where the upper house has been able to glean drafting or other errors in the proposed legislation. Bach's study showed that while the government has been 'compelled [to] compromise' when it does not command an outright majority in the Senate, the fact is 'more often than not, government bills have survived Senate legislative consideration unscathed; and also more often than not, the Senate has not insisted on its amendments when the House has disagreed to them' (2007, p. 66). The reality is that the major opposition party tends to support the government's bills through the Senate and it is only on rare occasions that a government is forced to negotiate with minor parties and independents.

While many of the criticisms levelled against the Senate are easy to dispel, this is not to say that the Australian political system is necessarily more democratic because it has a bicameral parliament and a strong bicameral structure more particularly. Scholars are divided on philosophical grounds over whether two chambers are necessarily better than one. Not everyone believes that bicameralism delivers better government, better legislative outcomes or better representation of the people's will, which are all claims that proponents of bicameralism assert in its favour. Proponents of unicameral chambers argue that quick, efficient and expeditious outcomes are best achieved by a single-chamber parliament. Moreover, they contend that unicameralism increases government accountability, making it difficult for the executive to dodge responsibility for ill-conceived legislation by blaming it on the second chamber.

One cannot claim with great certainty that bicameralism is better than unicameralism or vice versa. As with many of the debates about Australia's political institutions, it taps into the essential tension that is at the heart of the liberal-democratic system.

Bicameralism stresses the 'liberal' element of the liberal-democratic model, which is the view that a healthy political system depends on constant surveillance of those in power. A second chamber increases the possibility of constraining government action by offering checks and balances as a bulwark against an oppressive majority in the lower house. In contrast, unicameral structures are much more consistent with the 'democratic' half of the liberal-democratic equation. Democracy assumes popular, majority rule. An assembly that has been appointed on the basis of direct popular election reflects the popular will and should be entitled to exercise its mandate without obstruction or obfuscation.

CHAPTER SUMMARY

The chapter has examined the role of the Australian Parliament and the functions it performs. It has also highlighted one of the key debates about Australian parliamentary practice, which is the role of the nation's powerful second chamber, the Senate. While the public appears to be broadly supportive of the Senate, the same cannot be said for Australian governments. A long line of Australian governments have argued that a powerful Senate capable of blocking the government's proposed legislation is inherently undemocratic because it subverts the collective will. However, the Issue in Focus demonstrated that Australia's bicameral Parliament is hardly the impediment to democracy that governments are fond to declare. This is not to suggest that there are not legitimate grounds for the argument that unicameral legislatures are better than bicameral chambers and vice versa. In the end, the preference for either arrangement depends on one's conception of what structures best realise their particular vision for a robust democracy.

WEBSITES

Australian Parliament:
http://www.aph.gov.au/
The website of the Australian Parliament contains much information on the operation of the Parliament.

International Parliamentary Union:
http://www.ipu.org/english/home.htm
The IPU is the international organisation of Parliaments of sovereign states and was established in 1889. The IPU claims to be a focal point for worldwide parliamentary dialogue and works for peace and cooperation among peoples and for the firm establishment of representative democracy.

Commonwealth Parliamentary Association (CPA):
http://www.cpahq.org/default.aspx?id=2116
The CPA consists of the national, provincial, state and territorial parliaments and
legislatures of the countries of the Commonwealth. Its mission is to promote the
advancement of parliamentary democracy by enhancing knowledge and understanding
of democratic governance.

FURTHER READING

Bach, S. 2003. *Platypus and Parliament: The Australian Senate in Theory and Practice.*
Department of the Senate, Parliament House, Canberra.

Reid, G.S. & Forrest, M. 1989. *Australia's Commonwealth Parliament 1901–1988*. Melbourne
University Press, Melbourne.

Tsebelis, G. & Money, J. 1997. *Bicameralism*. Cambridge University Press, New York.

5 Running the State: Executive Power

THIS CHAPTER:

★ traces the origins of executive power in parliamentary systems of government

★ outlines the difficulties for the political executive in running a government while competing for political power

★ discusses the day-to-day responsibilities and processes of senior executive office-holders—ministers, prime ministers and premiers

★ shows the growing pressures on the executive through increasing work-loads, lobbying and increasing public expectations on governments.

ISSUE IN FOCUS

How can we keep the political executive accountable?

KEY TERMS

Cabinet	Conflict of interest	Parliamentary secretaries
Collective cabinet responsibility	Federal Executive Council	Political executive
	Ministerial responsibility	Presidentialisation
	Ministers	Senate Estimates Committee

In April 2006, Prime Minister John Howard was called before the Cole Inquiry into the hundreds of millions of dollars in bribes paid to Iraqi officials by an Australian company, Australian Wheat Board Ltd (AWB). The events in question occurred on the eve of an armed conflict against Iraq in which Australia was to be involved. It had been more than twenty years since a prime minister had been called to give evidence before such an inquiry. It had taken a United Nations inquiry to uncover the role of an Australian company in what became known as the 'wheat for weapons' scandal (so called because of allegations that the money from the bribes was used to purchase weapons possibly used against Australian soldiers). Iraq had been under strict United Nations trade sanctions and only a small number of wheat contracts were available under the Oil-for-Food program.

Howard was aware of allegations that the Oil-for-Food program was corrupt but he denied having seen documents that raised allegations of bribery against AWB. Trade Minister Mark Vaile and Foreign Affairs Minister Alexander Downer were also forced to appear and made similar denials. The inquiry heard that the Howard Government was repeatedly warned about the bribery but conducted minimal investigations into AWB. Yet, no minister was forced to take responsibility for the affair. Executive government is so large and complex that ministers, including the prime minister, can maintain the position that they simply didn't know what was happening. Yet, accountability for the actions of the executive supposedly lies at the heart of our system of responsible government.

Introduction

When we talk about government, or 'the Australian government', we are usually talking about the executive. It is the executive functions of government that most of us come into contact with on a day-to-day basis. The other branches of government—parliament and the judiciary—are important but if parliament didn't sit for months on end, most of us wouldn't notice. If judges went on strike, few of us would be inconvenienced. We would, however, notice if the executive branch of government did not function—if police weren't patrolling the streets, if our garbage wasn't being collected, or if the Youth Allowance was not paid.

This chapter is concerned with the senior decision-making elements of the executive—prime ministers, premiers and ministers. These positions are known as the **political executive**. They are known as the executive because they execute, or give effect to, the laws passed by the parliament. Parliament may pass a law regulating the level of pensions or other government payments. It is up to the executive to find a fair and efficient way of distributing those payments. The executive is also central to a nation's leadership. The executive sets the priorities for government policy and legislation, makes the key decisions in government and defends those decisions in public, and manages crises as they arise (Hague & Harrop 2004 p. 268). The nature of that leadership—how it is constrained and which other political and social actors can offer leadership—continually evolves. Executive leadership varies according to the institutional arrangements of the day but also depending on the personality of the leader or leaders who comprise the executive. The next chapter

> **Political executive:** the group of decision-makers at the highest level of government

will examine the bureaucratic elements of the executive, which provide advice to and carry out the policy decisions of the political executive—the public service, the police and security apparatus, as well as service delivery agencies such as Centrelink.

Executive power: origins and conventions

To some extent, the history of politics is the history of the struggle to gather or constrain executive power (Heywood 1997, p. 315). Even in democratic societies, the need for an individual or a small group to take timely decisions has always been recognised. In ancient Athens, an executive council carried out the day-to-day administration of laws passed by the citizens. In times of conflict, the political executive argues in favour of the need for emergency powers—to have fewer checks and balances on their ability to make decisions and take action. A crucial part of the process of democratisation has been to subject the actions of the executive to constitutional limits (Hague & Harrop 2004, p. 268).

The role of **cabinet** at the heart of executive government in parliamentary democracies evolved over centuries. Cabinet was originally a group of advisors to the British Crown. Struggles over the power of the Crown versus the power of parliament were central to British politics even before the English Civil War of 1642–51, when Royalists and Parliamentarians took to the battlefield. Cabinet was an important part of the solution to the power struggle between Crown and Parliament because it was able to link the two institutions. By choosing ministers who had some influence in parliament, monarchs found it easier to pass legislation. Constitutional developments don't always come about through careful design. Cabinet became more influential under King George I (1714–27) because the king spoke little English. By the middle of the eighteenth century, executive power had mostly passed from the monarch to the cabinet (Anderson 2006, p. 95). It was this model of executive power, where the monarch acts on the advice of **ministers**, that Australia inherited in colonial parliaments and at Federation in 1901.

> **Cabinet:** the central decision-making body of the executive that coordinates government activity, adjudicates disputes between ministers, and allocates resources to government departments
>
> **Ministers:** those politicians responsible for the development of and conduct of government policy in a particular area

In many parliamentary systems this fluid development of the structure of the political executive is possible because there are few constitutional rules setting out the day-to-day requirements of government. The political executive has historically evolved as the demands of government have changed. The size and power of cabinet, as well as the power of the prime minister and individual ministers varies over time, depending on the personalities of the people filling those positions, on the complexion of the parliament, and on the nature of the challenges facing the political community. Prime ministers have become relatively more powerful in most parliamentary systems throughout the twentieth century. However, in some systems, such as those of Italy and Japan, there is a frequent turnover of prime ministers, which limits their power (Heywood 1997, p. 325). The composition of cabinet depends on which parties have the largest representation in the parliament. In Britain, where a single party usually has a majority in the lower house, cabinet is composed of members of that single party. Strong representation of minor parties in a parliament may require the representation of minor parties in the ministry, if not in the cabinet (Hague & Harrop 2001, p. 239). In Germany, where the electoral system makes a single-party majority very difficult, multi-party coalitions are the norm.

In our system, ministers are appointed by the Governor-General on the advice of the prime minister. The Australian Constitution requires ministers to be Members of Parliament within three months of their appointment (s. 64). In presidential systems and some parliamentary systems, people with expertise in business or science can be called upon to serve as ministers. In presidential systems, where there is a clear separation of the executive and legislative branches, cabinet secretaries serve at the pleasure of the president. Systems of responsible government expect ministers to be accountable to the parliament. The power of individual ministers varies in line with developments in cabinet and the prime ministership. When the centralised leadership of cabinet or the prime minister is weak, individual ministers can wield a good deal of power (Hague & Harrop 2001, p. 243).

BOX 5.1   Who's on top? Head of state or head of government?

When Australia debated the possibility of becoming a republic during the 1990s, the republic movement underlined the symbolic importance of having an Australian as head of state. Republicans wished to replace the Queen with an Australian citizen. Supporters of the constitutional monarchy retorted that Australia's head of state was already an Australian—the Governor-General. In a constitutional monarchy, the role of the head of state is usually ceremonial. As we discovered in 1975, however, Australia's Governor-General enjoys important reserve powers, including the right to dismiss an elected government.

On reading the Australian Constitution, you could be forgiven for thinking that the Governor-General is the most powerful figure in Australia. While there are some powers that the Governor-General can exercise independently, most decisions are taken on the advice of the prime minister. That makes the prime minister the most important figure in Australian government—or the head of government. The head of government exercises day-to-day decision-making power, often in controversial circumstances.

In recognition of the partisan role of the prime minister, the Governor-General embodies a wider sense of nation and duty. The Governor-General greets foreign dignitaries, speaks at memorial services, opens museums and festivals, and makes other appearances as a representative of the Australian people. Increasingly, though, prime ministers have been taking on these roles. Prime ministers crave opportunities to be portrayed as national leaders above the fray of party politics.

Q Why do we need a head of state? How important are the ceremonial roles of the Queen and the Governor-General? Could Parliament instead exercise their non-ceremonial roles, such as appointing and dismissing the prime minister?

The Australian Constitution vests executive power in the Queen, which 'is exercisable by the Governor-General' (s. 61). Formally, the Governor-General acts on the advice of a body called the **Federal Executive Council** (s. 62). As we saw in Chapter 1, the text of Australia's Constitution omits the conventions that make up our system of responsible government. The most important decisions in government are made by a group of senior ministers known as the cabinet. You won't find anything about cabinet in the Constitution. While cabinet is the supreme decision-making body in the executive, its rules are unwritten so as to provide maximum flexibility to the government of the day to decide how cabinet will operate. Cabinet can delegate important decisions to the prime minister (or, at state level, the premier) or other ministers, or insist on making most of the important decisions itself. The decisions of the political executive are then communicated to the Governor-General by the Executive Council, which is made up of ministers. This seemingly archaic division of executive authority between the Crown and the elected government reflects the way that executive government evolved in the United Kingdom.

Federal Executive Council: a group of ministers who convey the wishes of cabinet to the Governor-General

Cabinet consists of senior ministers who are each responsible for the management of a policy area (portfolio) and the relevant government department (say, the Department of Defence or the Department of Health). Ministers are responsible for the way their department manages legislation related to their portfolio, as well as the day-to-day running of the department. Not all ministers serve in cabinet. The extent to which individual ministers can reasonably be expected to be accountable for departments that are staffed by thousands of public servants is one of the most controversial aspects of executive government, and will be discussed later in this chapter. Ministers must be Members of Parliament and can be drawn from either the House of Representatives or the Senate. Ministers are appointed by the prime minister in consultation with the party or parties in government. You will often hear ministers referred to as 'front-benchers' because they sit in the front row in Parliament.

Collective cabinet responsibility: one of the conventions of responsible government; all cabinet ministers take responsibility in parliament for the decisions of cabinet. If a minister cannot publicly defend a cabinet decision, he or she must resign from the government.

Cabinet deliberations are secret in order to allow robust debate without media headlines about how divided the government might be over a given issue. Cabinet documents are withheld from the public for thirty years. The secrecy of cabinet deliberations enables another convention, that of **collective cabinet responsibility**. All members of cabinet are expected to support government decisions regardless of any contrary position they may have taken in cabinet. Any minister who cannot publicly support a decision of the cabinet must resign from the government—something exceedingly rare in Australia. This gives the government unity of purpose and prevents endless debate of divisive issues. Like many constitutional conventions, it is the political imperative behind the convention, rather than the convention itself, that guarantees adherence (Ward & Stewart 2006, p. 234). In this case, all politicians know that disunity ensures a lack of public confidence in the government.

Individual **ministerial responsibility** is one of the cornerstones of responsible government. Ministers must answer questions in Parliament and from the media and face parliamentary committees. Precisely what ministers should be held accountable for is more controversial. Holding ministers accountable for their own actions seems straightforward. Where personal misbehaviour, such as misappropriating public money or misleading Parliament, is concerned, ministerial responsibility is clear enough. Where ministers have acted in good faith based on the advice of their officials, or where government departments have taken decisions of which the minister was not made aware, the situation is more complex. Often, questions of ministerial responsibility come down to electoral concerns. A prime minister may take office determined to hold his ministers to higher standards than their predecessor but soon find that toughing out political controversy is a better strategy than forcing ministers to resign.

> **Ministerial responsibility:** the accountability that individual ministers have to parliament for their decisions and the actions of their department

Ministerial responsibility now works something like this: ministers are responsible to the prime minister; the prime minister is responsible to the electorate. The prime minister will sack a minister if he or she believes that it is politically necessary to do so. Ministers almost never resign over a matter of principle. Parliament plays a role in investigating the activities of the executive but rarely does the composition of parliament allow for it to insist that a minister resign (Anderson 2006, p. 106). Elections prove to be the ultimate forum for political accountability. While no Howard Government minister resigned over the AWB affair, for example, the government was defeated at the 2007 polls.

BOX 5.2   Difficulties in holding ministers to account: cases from the Howard Government

During its first term, seven ministers and parliamentary secretaries were forced to resign from the Howard Government over financial scandals. These scandals were mostly about the ministers' failure to disclose personal interests related to their portfolios or making inflated claims for travel allowances. By contrast, some of the most controversial episodes of the Howard Government resulted in no ministerial resignations. In the 'Children Overboard' affair during the 2001 election campaign, a number of ministers repeated claims (later shown to be false) about asylum-seekers throwing their children into the ocean to Australia's north. The Australian Wheat Board scandal (described above) also proved controversial but no minister was forced to take responsibility.

There is an important difference between the two types of scandals. While the two later scandals were considerably more important than the earlier financial scandals, the lines of responsibility in each case were quite different. The travel rorts and **conflict of interest** cases involved a clear (if unintentional) breach of a set of rules by individual ministers. The events of Children Overboard and AWB scandals were not so clear, and the roles and responsibilities of the ministers concerned were complex enough for the government to avoid a public backlash. Ministers could plausibly claim that they were not informed of key events or reports of misconduct. The question then becomes: *Should the relevant ministers have known more about the Children Overboard and AWB scandals?* Did members of their staff or departments make the decision that it was better to keep some information from their ministers to save them from later political embarrassment? (Tiernan 2007, p. 208)

Conflict of interest: a situation in which a minister has the power to make decisions on an issue where they stand to gain or lose personal benefits

Q Why is it important for the political executive to be held accountable? Can we expect ministers to be responsible for everything their departments do?

Executive roles and party politics

A visitor to Australia who spent a week or so reading the daily newspapers and watching the news on television would quickly learn that the prime minister is the most powerful figure in our political system. The prime minister becomes the head of government because he or she is leader of the largest political party or coalition in the Parliament. Thus, the prime minister exercises the power of the state but has access to this power by virtue of their position in a political party. Members of the political executive are the key figures in both the noble art of government and the competitive practice of politics. They get to the top by mastering party politics. To stay there, they must find a balance between governing for the nation as a whole and retaining their edge in the partisan contest. They will face challenges from rival parties and from within their own party.

Political leaders must also manage relationships with public opinion and interest groups. Policy development and implementation is very difficult without public support. Popular leadership is thus one of the key requirements of executive government (Heywood 1997, p. 318). Prime ministers, in particular, are conscious of their role as national leaders. The vision of an individual leader can set the tone and direction of political debate (Uhr 2001, p. 7). Prime ministers are both the chief combatants in electoral contests and one of the few members of the community whose rhetoric of nation-building is guaranteed significant media coverage. Each role makes the conduct of the other problematic. Most Australians do not enjoy seeing their national leaders yelling abuse at each other across the Parliament. Paul Keating (1991–96) found that the prime ministership was a unique position from which to launch a debate on the possibility of Australia becoming a republic (Uhr 2001, p. 19). Yet, the combative Keating also gathered enemies who were reluctant to allow their adversary to take credit for such an important move, regardless of their own position on the matter. John Howard, too, found that attempts to deal with questions of national values and identity were inseparable from the conflict of party politics.

The balance between good policy and good politics is one that governments are always trying to manage. Decisions that may benefit the country in the long term, such as cutting tariffs on international trade, will be politically sensitive in the short term as the lives of citizens are adversely affected. Ministers require sensitivity to the concerns of the electorate on the one hand, and sufficient policy expertise to make decisions crucial to the future of the nation on the other (Weller 2004, p. 64). The role of the opposition in policy debates is crucial. Most opposition spokespeople are aware of the importance of cabinet conventions such as the need for secrecy. Yet, the demands of political competition give incentives for the opposition to play a destructive rather than a constructive role in policy debate. A leaked cabinet document may cause endless embarrassment to a government conscientiously exploring a range of policy options. As Keating and Weller note, 'adversarial politics is often the enemy of a policy debate' (2000, p. 52). At the beginning of each meeting of the Howard cabinet, time was set aside for discussion of partisan political matters. How was the government's standing in the community? Does the government's performance in the media need attention? Are there any issues on the horizon that might cause embarrassment to the governing parties? (Errington & van Onselen 2007, p. 324)

'Cabinet in Australia,' Richard Lucy wrote in 1985, 'is not a formal governmental institution but the executive of the governing party.' He argued that the role of political parties in our system of government is so important that the system should be characterised as 'Responsible Party Government'. Lucy characterised the system thus: 'The prime minister is responsible to the party room for his own political performance. Ministers are responsible to the prime minister for their own political performance' (Lucy 1985, p. 6). According to this view, the conventions of our system remain important not because power to enforce government responsibility lies formally in the Parliament but because the public expects the government to adhere to that tradition. The real decisions are made elsewhere.

Part of the difficulty in characterising the Australian political system, Lucy argued, was that the Labor and Liberal parties had such different methods of electing leaders and ministers. More recently, and particularly in light of Kevin Rudd's appointment of his ministry without a caucus vote following the 2007 election, the practices of the major parties have converged in these areas. More problematic for a thesis that places parties at the centre of government has been the enmeshing of cabinet in the bureaucracy (or, perhaps, vice versa) in recent decades. Cabinet ministers are heavily dependent on the public service in the conduct of their offices.

The political executive in action

The strategies for the day-to-day running of cabinet and ministerial portfolios vary over time, between parties and across ministerial portfolios. Some portfolios, such as treasury, are highly complex and the minister relies heavily on expert advice. In other areas, such as industrial relations, each political party has a quite different idea of directions and priorities. Recent Australian governments have also allocated portfolios to junior ministers and **parliamentary secretaries**, who do not attend cabinet meetings unless they have business from their portfolio to discuss. The effectiveness of a minister might depend on such factors as their level of authority among their government colleagues.

> **Parliamentary secretaries:** the most junior members of the political executive, who are delegated portfolio responsibilities from ministers

---

BOX 5.3   Executive responsibilities

- Coordinating the activities of government.
- Declaring and waging war.
- Proposing a budget to Parliament and administering the budget of each department.
- Making all sorts of day-to-day decisions.
- Appointments to statutory authorities (such as the ABC), diplomatic posts and other government bodies.
- Establishing inquiries, Royal Commissions (including, importantly, the commissioners and their terms of reference, or scope of the inquiry).
- Announcements of policy initiatives; communicating decisions to citizens affected.
- Answering questions from journalists, MPs and the public.
- Gathering support for government policy in the media and Parliament.
- Crisis management—responding to natural disasters, stock market crashes.
- Ceremonial duties such as memorial services.
- Managing the bureaucracy.

Each government department is responsible for administering a number of Acts of Parliament. Many of the requirements of each Act will be administered by junior officials. Some Acts require policy decisions taken at ministerial level, and may be divided between a senior and junior minister, or a parliamentary secretary. For example, Centrelink employees make decisions every day about who is or is not entitled to a benefit. The policy framework within which each application is decided, though, by the relevant minister if it is not expressly set out in the legislation. Decisions by more junior officials might be appealed to or overturned by ministers.

In arriving at each decision in their portfolio and as well as in cabinet, ministers have access to many sources of information. Each issue will carry with it position papers from the relevant department, inter-departmental committees and interest groups, petitions, correspondence from citizens, minutes of meetings and direct advice from departmental experts as well as partisan political advisors.

BOX 5.4   Buying time with a minister?

Time is precious to ministers, who have an endless list of documents to read and people to meet. How do ministers decide who they have time to meet and who has to make do with more junior officials? In a democracy, where citizens are equal under the law, we expect ministers to meet ordinary people as well as powerful individuals and lobby groups. We know, however, that the views of some citizens carry more weight than the views of others. It would be a brave minister for communications for example, who made a decision on the future of television broadcasting without meeting representatives from the major media corporations.

The idea that money may affect decisions about who gets access to ministers is more troubling. Ministers tend to be senior figures within each political party. They know which businesses and groups make donations to their party. Spending time with ministers has become big business. Donors might pay money to attend a dinner where they know a minister (even the prime minister) will be present. In some cases, ministers' time has been auctioned at party fundraisers (van Onselen & Errington 2004). Ministers are quick to point out that all that party donors receive for their time is a hearing, and that party fundraising does not affect decision-making. At the very least, though, wealthy citizens are in a better position than most of us to get their message across to the nation's most powerful politicians. The Rudd Government's code of conduct bans party fundraising at the two prime-ministerial residences—The Lodge and Kirribilli House—but this represents a cosmetic change.

A large part of the problem is that political parties are constantly in need of money to pay for election advertising. Since 1984, parties have had part of their election expenses reimbursed by taxpayers. Such public funding of elections is designed to limit the need for funding from private sources, something that has proved unsuccessful. More radical measures, such as bans or limits on donations, may need to be considered in future. Opponents of such measures point to our fundamental political freedoms, and argue that political parties should be able to organise themselves however they see fit.

On a related note, a number of ministers have taken lucrative jobs in their areas of ministerial responsibility upon leaving office. Bob Carr, former premier of New South Wales, took a position with Macquarie Bank, a company that makes infrastructure deals with governments worth many millions of dollars. Former health minister Michael Wooldridge was one of a number of Howard Government ministers to face criticism for similar moves. Wooldridge took a consultancy with the Australian College of General Practitioners shortly after awarding them a $5 million government grant (van Onselen 2007). The Rudd Government's code of conduct bans ministers from acting as lobbyists for twelve months after leaving office. Overseas jurisdictions apply such restrictions for longer periods of time.

Q Should ministers use the status of their office to help raise funds for their party? How do such activities affect their ability to discharge their ministerial duties in the national interest?

While cabinet takes collective responsibility for its decisions, it is also a centre of conflict within the government. Government departments compete for resources and attention through their ministers. Cabinet is where the most senior members of the executive meet on a regular basis to coordinate the activities of government. Cabinet is chaired by the prime minister and usually meets weekly. Some past prime ministers preferred lengthy cabinet meetings where all sides of an issue were extensively discussed. John Howard's cabinet was an example of a more business-like approach, with meetings rarely lasting more than a couple of hours (Weller 2007, p. 186). In addition to the conventions of responsible government discussed above, cabinet employs a set of rules that may vary from government to government. These concern the timing and content of policy submissions; the power and number of committees to which cabinet will delegate decisions; whether decisions are made by consensus or by a majority vote; the priority that cabinet will give to each policy area; the extent to which cabinet will discuss party political problems; as well as matters of state (Keating & Weller 2000, p. 49).

There are no simple rules for deciding which matters need to be decided by cabinet and which can be handled by individual ministers. Any measure requiring legislative action must make its way through cabinet. Ministers will send anything likely to raise controversy to cabinet in order to ensure that the government is not embarrassed in public. Substantial spending increases or changes would also come into this category.

In early 2007, Prime Minister John Howard announced $10 billion of spending on the Murray–Darling river system. It soon emerged that the plan had not been approved by cabinet. Then-finance minister Nick Minchin explained that 'If the cabinet's not meeting but there is an appropriate level of consultation ... then a decision is made' (cited in Peatling 2007). This type of ad hoc decision-making is likely to cause problems for governments, though, since ministers and departments with an interest in such decisions may not be properly consulted.

Government overload and executive responsibility

At Federation in 1901, the Commonwealth of Australia had few government departments and therefore few cabinet ministers. The responsibilities of the state governments were more relevant to the day-to-day lives of Australians. The Commonwealth was chiefly responsible for trade, immigration and defence. Over the course of the twentieth century, the Commonwealth took on more and more responsibilities from the states in areas such as health, education and industrial relations. Governments across the world have also taken on additional responsibilities in areas such as welfare and the environment.

It is the responsibility of the political executive to make choices about the adding of new responsibilities to government. The executive of today, however, is left to deal with the totality of choices of previous governments that have gradually added to the size and complexity of public administration. The contemporary executive can change priorities but cannot ignore the changing public expectations of what governments are supposed to do. Further, these growing expectations of government coincide with doubts among some groups about the representative nature of Australian governments. As Keating and Weller (2000, p. 51) ask, can our cabinet ministers, who are predominantly white and male, be expected to make decisions in the interests of a diverse and increasingly sophisticated society?

Interest groups have become more professional in the way they deal with government, employing lobbyists to put their case to ministers, producing large volumes of information supporting their cause and entering public debate in a fashion that demands a response from the relevant minister.

One role of cabinet that is of growing importance is that of coordination. Cabinet stands at the heart of the growing public sector. One problem caused by the increasing number of decisions made by the political executive is that cabinet ministers, already overloaded with material in their own portfolio, don't have time to properly assess submissions to cabinet from other portfolios. Cabinet may therefore not be in a position to make the most appropriate decision on each issue (Weller & Grattan 1981, p. 198). The sheer volume of decisions to be made by the political executive has led to continual restructuring of the cabinet process in recent decades. As Keating and Weller (2000, pp. 50–1) point out, these changes include:

- more administrative and advisory support for cabinet in the form of senior public servants, ministerial advisors and policy units. The role of these advisors may be administrative—to ensure, for example, that cabinet has all the information it needs to make decisions. However, these positions are often charged with assessing the partisan political consequences of cabinet decisions.

- increased coordination across portfolios to ensure that separate departments are not working at cross-purposes or duplicating work.
- development of public relations strategies aimed at influencing public expectations of government capacity in difficult policy areas such as drug abuse and the ability of governments to respond to social problems in a realistic time-frame. Extensive opinion polling is used to assess the public reaction to major decisions and initiatives.
- increased use of information technology to manage the volume of documents and other information generated in the policy-making process.
- enabling the executive to make use of expertise outside government including consultancies, think tanks, interest groups and universities.

The size of cabinet and the outer ministry has become a trade-off between the large number of decisions required of each minister and the coordination problems inherent in a political executive that grows too large. One of cabinet's most important decisions is to establish guidelines that govern the level at which decisions need to be made and to which information needs to flow.

BOX 5.5   Cabinet portfolios 1901 and 2007

Barton Government 1901	Rudd Government 2007
Prime Minister and External Affairs	Prime Minister
Treasurer	Deputy Prime Minister, Education, Employment and Workplace Relations, Social Inclusion
Trade and Customs	Treasurer
Home Affairs	Immigration and Citizenship
Attorney-General	Special Minister of State and Cabinet Secretary
Defence	Trade
Post-master General	Foreign Affairs
2 Ministers without portfolio	Defence
	Health and Ageing
	Community Services and Indigenous Affairs
	Finance and Deregulation
	Infrastructure, Transport and Regional Development, Local Government, Leader of the House
	Broadband, Communications and the Digital Economy
	Innovation, Industry, Science and Research
	Climate Change and Water
	Environment, Heritage and the Arts
	Attorney-General
	Human Services
	Agriculture, Fisheries and Forestry
	Resources and Energy, Tourism

Q What does the ever-increasing number of ministerial portfolios tell us about the way we are governed? Could a cabinet of nine run the national political executive today, as they did in 1901?

The business of government is becoming increasingly complex. Parliament has created a number of important government agencies, such as Centrelink, that are part of the executive (rather than independent authorities; see Chapter 6), and these have added to the responsibilities of ministers. Society more generally is becoming too technologically complex for any one person to be expert in a single policy area (let alone multiple areas). For example, can the minister for communications be expected to be fully aware of the consequences of introducing a new mobile phone technology? Some portfolios are managed by numerous ministers. The defence portfolio in the first Rudd ministry, for example, contained a junior minister and a parliamentary secretary in addition to the defence minister. The lines of responsibility between these members of the executive are not always clear. Further, the importance of portfolios such as Defence ensures that the Department of Prime Minister and Cabinet keeps the prime minister briefed on security and economic issues. The prime minister might be called upon to answer questions in Parliament or by journalists on any number of policy areas. On important issues, the prime minister will intervene directly in the decision-making process. All of this makes accountability in government an increasingly complex matter.

Cabinet delegates many of its decisions to cabinet committees. One of the most famous of these is the Expenditure Review Committee—known as the 'razor gang'—which looks for wasteful government spending in order to save resources or redeploy them to higher priority areas. The National Security Committee, consisting of the prime minister, defence minister and other senior ministers, makes the most important decisions on security matters, which may arise when cabinet is not scheduled to meet. Decisions taken by cabinet committees tend to be adopted by the full cabinet without debate, making them an important streamlining mechanism for executive government.

BOX 5.6   Too much power?

When incoming Immigration Minister Chris Evans took over his portfolio in 2007, one of his first actions was to order a review of his own powers. 'I have formed the view that I have too much power,' Evans told the Senate. He said he was uncomfortable with 'playing God'. The Immigration Minister makes final decisions on who should or should not be granted a visa to stay in Australia. Labor had long criticised the Howard Government for its decisions in this area. Evans was concerned about the transparency, accountability and lack of rights to appeal ministerial decisions (cited in Lane 2008). Immigration can be an emotional issue. Decisions made by politicians by their very nature become the subject of partisan political competition.

Q   While a reduction in the number of decisions made by the Immigration Minister would reduce his workload, would any other process for making decisions on immigration cases be any more accountable?

Much of the growth in decision-making in recent decades has fallen on individual ministers rather than cabinet. Further, ministers are usually the source of legislation and other policy initiatives. Given the breadth of their portfolios, ministers rely heavily on their advisors to choose between competing priorities and policy ideas (Weller 2004, pp. 63–4). Ministers are lobbied by Members of Parliament and interest groups. They can also be constrained by the promises that the government made to get itself elected. Advice on handling these competing priorities and ideas can come from the public service or from ministerial offices usually staffed by partisan political actors.

In taking on new roles, governments have burdened themselves with rising expectations. There may be little that governments can do, for example, to avoid a downturn in the economy or rising prices. Nevertheless, voters will hold governments to account for poor economic conditions—and why not, when political leaders are quick to take credit when the economy is strong?

ISSUE IN FOCUS

HOW CAN WE KEEP THE POLITICAL EXECUTIVE ACCOUNTABLE?

Parliament

In this chapter we have outlined a number of ways in which the operation of executive government has evolved since Federation. The workload of ministers has increased while their responsibility to Parliament has decreased. Since so many of the rules governing the Australian political system are unwritten, these substantial changes in the way we are governed have been accommodated without formal changes to the Constitution. To many observers, however, our democratic system of government is struggling to keep up with the way that the political executive now functions.

Our system of government has both British and American influences. Democratic accountability operates through elections to Parliament and, indirectly, for competition for executive power. The American system of checks and balances, however, also influences the Australian system. The liberal elements of our political system are designed explicitly to limit executive power. Is it possible to both limit the power of the executive and hold ministers accountable for their actions and for the way they have governed? If the legislation through which a government claims it needs to solve a particular problem is blocked by the Parliament, who does the electorate hold responsible for failing to solve the problem? As Sawer (cited in Summers 2006, p. 85) wrote about the 1975 constitutional crisis, our governments are: 'committed to economic management and a multitude of welfare services. This is not possible if the initiatives of a government based on a House of Representatives majority are to be constantly "checked" by a hostile majority in the Senate.' Governments, according to this view, have a responsibility to carry out their activities in the manner expected by those who elected them.

The liberal dimensions of our Constitution might play a role in ensuring that the executive is held to its promises but they might equally prevent a government from carrying out its electoral mandate. The concept of a mandate tends to be closely tied to political convenience. With each house of Parliament elected separately, each can claim a mandate. Governments elected in the House of Representatives have rarely achieved a majority of the primary vote, which questions the extent of any democratic mandate. Responsible government assumes that ministers are ultimately accountable to the electorate for their actions. Other checks on government power can make elections a problematic method of accountability. In any event, elections are 'a crude device for recording a reaction to the diverse policy and administrative actions' of government (Lovell et al. 1998, p. 57). Elections are often about the future whereas government accountability is inherently about past actions.

Parliamentary systems, particularly where bicameralism makes control of parliament by the executive difficult, are designed to hold the executive accountable to one or both chambers. This can occur in a variety of ways (see Box 5.7). As we discussed earlier, the notion of ministerial responsibility tends to be neater in theory than in practice. Even if parliament cannot force the resignation of a minister, though, it plays a crucial role in ensuring that the public is informed of the activities of the political executive. These accountability functions start with legislation proposed by the executive, which parliament can amend as it sees fit. Parliamentary committees hold inquiries into most legislation, inviting members of the public and interest groups to comment on how the legislation might affect them, or how legislation might have effects that cabinet had not counted on when it approved the proposed bills.

BOX 5.7   Investigating the executive

There are a number of bodies whose responsibility it is to hold the executive accountable for its actions. In some cases, these bodies make binding judgments on executive office-holders as well as investigating them.

Ombudsmen

Parliament has long provided for an ombudsman to investigate complaints from citizens at state and Commonwealth levels. We now have specialist ombudsmen for telecommunications and privacy. Similar bodies, such as the Police Integrity Commission in New South Wales, also investigate particular arms of the executive.

Human Rights Commissions

These commissions ensure that state and Commonwealth legislation pertaining to human rights and anti-discrimination are observed. They hear complaints about other groups, as well as executive government. There are specialist commissioners for Indigenous people and women at Commonwealth level.

The media

Investigative reporting is crucial to our ability to know what our politicians are up to.

It is often stories in the media that lead to government inquiries into government corruption or maladministration.

Question Time

Ministers are expected to answer any question raised by a Member of Parliament.

When Paul Keating restricted his appearances in Parliament to two a week, the opposition was able to portray his government as hostile to accountability.

Parliamentary committees

Committees investigate legislation, the activities of government departments, or any issue of public concern. The effectiveness of these committees usually depends upon opposition parties having a majority on the committee.

Royal Commissions and other inquiries

As their name suggests, Royal Commissions are creatures of executive power. Their effectiveness depends on the terms of reference under which they are established. While these and other inquiries, such as the Wood Royal Commission into police corruption in New South Wales, can be very effective in uncovering wrong-doing or mismanagement, inquirers can only investigate problems as directed by the political executive.

Since the early 1970s, parliamentary committees have improved the way in which they investigate the activities of the executive. One important development has been that the **Senate Estimates Committee** has provided opportunities for senators to ask questions of ministers and their departmental advisors. While notionally about budget matters, estimates hearings provide a unique opportunity for opposition senators to bring up all manner of topics (Evans 2007, p. 210).

Government control of the Senate makes all of these parliamentary functions more difficult for the opposition. While individual senators

Senate Estimates Committee: a committee in which ministers and departmental office-holders are questioned about the activities of their departments

can still ask difficult questions in estimates committees, they have little recourse if ministers instruct their officers not to answer them. While Parliament still investigates legislation when the government enjoys a majority, those hearings may be very brief and the resulting reports may reflect the wishes of the government MPs. The Howard Government controlled the Senate between 2005 and 2007, taking advantage of its majority to make the Senate committee system less onerous (from the Government's point of view). The result was less information available to the public about the activities of the political executive and less scrutiny of legislation (Evans 2007, p. 221). Of course, the Howard Government argued that it had won control of the Senate in a democratic election. Yet, the scrutiny of the Parliament is not only for the benefit of the opposition. Greater scrutiny of legislation can alert governments to problems that cabinet had not considered. Indeed, had the Senate amended the Howard Government's 2005 WorkChoices legislation to give effect to the Coalition's 2004 industrial relations election policy, that legislation would not have been so unpopular. Gaining control of the Senate may have thus cost John Howard the prime ministership (Brett 2007, pp. 75–6).

It was the rise of disciplined political parties during the twentieth century that made the contemporary political executive in parliamentary systems possible (Heywood 1997, p. 325). Party discipline allows the executive to rely on a stable majority in at least one house of parliament. Party discipline essentially means that the executive is able to influence the behaviour of MPs from the same party or coalition. Few members of the major parties now cross the floor to vote against legislation proposed by their own party. This party discipline in turn strengthens the power of the executive, providing for stable government and some predictability where the passage of legislation is concerned. Executive dominance of the parliament is generally seen as a problem in our system of government rather than a boon for executive accountability to the electorate. Paul Keating (1991–96) famously refused to allow his ministers, much less himself, to be questioned by Senate committees. The Senate, he thundered, was 'unrepresentative swill' and his ministers would not 'slum it' by appearing there (Uhr 2001, p. 23). Keating may have paid a price for these types of sentiments at the 1996 election, where his government lost in a landslide, but accountability at the ballot box every three years needs to be complemented by a rigorous set of 'continuous accountability' measures controlled by Parliament (Lovell et al. 1995, p. 57). The problems that Parliament has experienced in keeping the political executive accountable underline the central role of parties in our political system, and the relevance of Lucy's characterisation of the system, discussed above, as *responsible party government*.

Prime ministerial government?

In addition to the problems with the various ways in which parliament is supposed to hold the executive accountable, it is not always clear precisely where executive power lies. Ultimate executive authority may lie with cabinet, the prime minister or with individual ministers. The various responsibilities can change not just between different governments but may be fluid over the course of a single government in reaction to changing government priorities, the personalities of political leaders, and the standing of the government in the electorate. The advantage of a presidential system lies in holding a single actor accountable for the activities of the executive.

Centralising power in the office of prime minister or premier has been a long-term trend in Australia. Parliamentary systems tend towards collective decision-making within the executive, since the prime minister needs to ensure that the government has the confidence of the parliament. That is, cabinet allows a more diverse representation of the governing party or coalition in the executive and can alert the party leadership to discontent among backbenchers. Yet, a single political leader might provide strength and direction to a government that collective leadership does not. There are few constitutional restraints on executive power being concentrated in the office of the prime minister if that is the way the system evolves (Heywood 1997, pp. 324–5).

BOX 5.8   Should Parliament or the executive have the power to declare war?

The Australian Constitution provides the Commonwealth Parliament with power over defence (s. 51(vi)). This applies to laws pertaining to defence and the military, yet, under the conventions of responsible government, the power to declare war is held by the executive branch. The Constitution vests the Governor-General with 'command of the naval and military forces' (s. 68), although that is in practice a ceremonial role.

Prime ministers recognising the importance of public debate surrounding such a crucial decision may allow Parliament to debate a motion on involvement in a conflict. The final decision, though, rests with cabinet. The argument in favour of retaining this system is the same as the reason for vesting any power in the executive—that decisions sometimes need to be made quickly. Parliament only sits for part of the year and may not be easily recalled to debate a motion on declaring war.

In the wake of the Howard Government's decision to commit Australian troops to the United States' invasion of Iraq in 2003, the Australian Democrats introduced legislation that would require the consent of Parliament for such an action. This bill addressed the need for quick decision-making by allowing troops to be deployed overseas provided parliamentary approval is received within two days. Labor joined the government in voting down the legislation. Executive prerogatives are not surrendered lightly. Such a change, though, would not be unprecedented. In 2007, incoming British prime minister Gordon Brown, conscious of popular discontent with Britain's involvement in the Iraq War, announced his intention to cede the prime minister's power to declare war to the British Parliament.

Q **What are the advantages and disadvantages of allowing the political executive to make the decision to declare war?**

In explaining his decision to appoint Labor Members of Parliament to cabinet rather than following Labor tradition and accepting a vote of caucus after his election victory in 2007, Kevin Rudd explained, 'I was elected as this country's next prime minister. I think it is incumbent upon me to put forward the best possible team for the nation' (cited in Anon. 2006). In fact, at the election a day earlier, Rudd had only been elected as the Member for his local seat of Griffith. Nevertheless, he was encapsulating the view that Australians vote to choose between party leaders rather than party platforms or local candidates. Australians have been responding rationally to the centralisation of power in the prime ministership. They know they may be formally electing a local MP, but they are in fact choosing between competing candidates for the prime ministership.

Rudd's leadership was certainly central to his party's defeat of the Howard Government. You may remember the 'Kevin 07' slogan from that campaign. Rudd used the mandate that he received by winning that election to increase his power *vis-à-vis* the Labor caucus. Future Labor prime ministers will jealously guard this power.

This was just one step in a lengthy process by which prime ministers in Australia and other parliamentary systems have centralised power in their own offices.

An important dimension of the power of a chief executive is their ability to hire and fire. If a prime minister can choose his or her own cabinet members, their position as leader of the government is more assured. There are, of course, constraints on just who might be left out of cabinet, but Australian prime ministers have become adept at managing cabinet to ensure that their position on policy matters is rarely overruled. Prime ministers were once *primus inter pares* (first among equals). This was especially the case in the first Australian cabinet, where Prime Minister Edmund Barton (1901–03) left ministers who were all prominent colonial politicians largely to run their own portfolios. Provided they are secure in their leadership, prime ministers have many advantages over their cabinet colleagues (whom, in any event, they appoint and dismiss). They control the cabinet agenda, chair cabinet committees, and make appointments to government departments, the judiciary and diplomatic posts.

> **BOX 5.9   The department of everything**
>
> While Australia has had a government department dedicated to supporting the prime minister for almost a hundred years, it was not until the Fraser Government (1975–83) that the Department of Prime Minister and Cabinet began to take on its present shape. The Department supports the prime minister in the management of cabinet—circulating policy proposals and keeping records. More troubling is the growth of the advisory capacity of the Department of Prime Minister and Cabinet, which now contains expertise that duplicates that found in most of the departments for each policy portfolio. This change both reflects and reinforces the growing power of the prime minister compared to other cabinet ministers.
>
> *Q*   Why would the prime minister wish to have a source of policy advice independent of ministers and their departments?

The prime minister's power of patronage is crucial to the office. Most Members of Parliament are, have been or would like to be part of the executive (as ministers or as appointees to other government positions). Their loyalty to the prime minister is important to their career paths. This process of strengthening the prime ministership has not gone unnoticed by the media and the public. An increasingly sophisticated electorate expects governments to explain their decisions. The prime minister is the government spokesperson with the most authority and greatest knowledge of policy areas across the whole of governments (Keating & Weller 2000, p. 58). Journalists take notice of the prime minister more so than other ministers, whose wishes can be overruled. Television, with its demands for pithy comments on the news of the day from a familiar face, has played an important part in these developments. The party leader has become an essential part of the 'brand image' of the party (Heywood 1997, p. 325). The prime minister becomes central to the electoral fortunes of the government, and in turn demands loyalty and unity from ministers and MPs. These trends have been mirrored at state level, where premiers are by far the most recognisable members of their cabinets.

Such a crucial office as prime minister or premier must be properly resourced. The Department of the Prime Minister and Cabinet and the private office of the prime minister have both gradually increased in size in recent decades. While the precise structures vary from government to government, bodies such as the Cabinet Policy Unit or a dedicated Cabinet Secretary fall under the authority of the prime minister and assist the occupant in mastering the cabinet and policy agenda (Weller 2007, pp. 186–7). These developments, combined with the increase in ministerial workloads described above, give the prime minister a unique advantage over other cabinet ministers. The prime minister is the only minister who knows (or should know) about policy developments and problems across all ministerial portfolios.

It is important to characterise these changes as prime ministerial government rather than **presidentialisation**. While some of the campaign and media management methods used by Australian party leaders have been imported from the United States, the degree of power that prime ministers can accumulate is indigenous to parliamentary systems. Provided they can maintain party discipline, prime minsters are assured that legislation can pass at least one house of Parliament. Where American presidents must bargain with Congress, Australian prime ministers can threaten a recalcitrant Parliament with a double dissolution election. The crucial difference is that prime ministers can be deposed by their party room whereas presidents are elected for fixed terms. While this has only happened once (when Paul Keating deposed Bob Hawke in 1991) in the last thirty years, the possibility of a leadership change makes prime ministers attentive to the concerns of the party. While the power of a prime minister can be formidable, that power is 'built on shifting sands' (Ward & Stewart 2006, p. 245). Thus, the extent to which prime ministerial government is a serious departure from our system of responsible government depends on whether or not the prime minister respects the role of cabinet. Former British prime minister Tony Blair was accused of sidelining cabinet in his decision-making. Australian prime ministers, on the other hand, while they have increased their ability to control it, still regard cabinet as the central body for executive decision-making (Keating & Weller 2000, p. 59).

> **Presidentialisation:** the notion that power centralised in the office of prime minister makes parliamentary systems more like presidential systems

A considerable amount of power, of course, remains outside the purview of the prime minister. Interest rates, for example, are set by the Reserve Bank. In 2007, the Bank raised interest rates in the middle of a federal election campaign. Naturally, when, until the 1990s, such decisions were in the hands of politicians (in this case, the treasurer), rising interest rates close to an election were unheard of. In putting the decision-making process outside the hands of the political executive (precisely to avoid a conflict of interest over when rates should rise and by how much), our politicians have given up some of their power. Yet, voters cannot hold the Reserve Bank accountable for interest rate rises (the Bank is accountable to the Parliament). Federalism also divides the political executive in Australia, and therefore makes accountability more complex. State and federal elections are held at different times. Health is one example of a policy area divided between levels of government. The Commonwealth plays a considerable role in funding services but it is the states that have the day-to-day responsibilities of managing hospitals. Who is responsible when things go wrong—the financiers or the managers? Thus, while we as voters can hold governments accountable for their management of the country, there are limits on just what the political executive can do. Accountability in a liberal democracy, then, is never as simple as the model of responsible government suggests.

CHAPTER SUMMARY

The political executive is the core of government at both state and Commonwealth levels. The rules of cabinet government—most notably collective and individual ministerial responsibility—are not spelt out in the Constitution. Government in Australia is becoming more complex as society becomes more complex. The political executive has both increased this complexity by promising citizens more and more at election time and attempted to solve it by constantly re-organising the structure of government.

Responsible government assumes a chain of accountability from cabinet to parliament and from parliament to the electorate. Parliament plays an important role in holding the executive accountable. However, many voters identify with politicians not as Members of Parliament but as members of the political executive (and their shadow ministers). The prime minister has become by far the most powerful and most visible member of the executive. With the principle of ministerial responsibility evolving towards something like responsibility to the prime minister, public opinion is becoming more important than Parliament in holding ministers accountable.

WEBSITES

Prime Minister:
www.pm.gov.au
The prime minister's website contains details of the activities and speeches of the current Australian prime minister.

National Archives of Australia:
http://primeministers.naa.gov.au/
The National Archives site on Australian prime ministers provides a history of each occupant of that office.

FURTHER READING

Hague, R. & Harrop, M. 2004. *Comparative Government and Politics: An Introduction*. Palgrave Macmillan, London, chapter 15.

Grattan, M. (ed.). 2000. *Australian Prime Ministers*. New Holland, Sydney.

Weller, P. 2007. *Cabinet Government in Australia: 1901–2006*. University of New South Wales Press, Sydney.

The Public Service: Making and Implementing Policy

6

THIS CHAPTER:

★ discusses the role and composition of the public sector
★ outlines the changing structure of government agencies and the reasons for these changes
★ traces the influences of economic rationalism and managerialism on the Australian public sector.

ISSUE IN FOCUS

Has the Commonwealth bureaucracy been politicised?

KEY TERMS

Executive agencies
Government
    departments
Government trading
    enterprises
Managerialism
Natural monopolies
Policy networks
Privatisation
Public–private partnerships
Stakeholders
Statutory authorities
Whistle-blowing

In April 2008, a thousand Australians, all brimming with bright ideas, gathered at Parliament House in Canberra for the Rudd Government's *2020 Summit*. Among the ideas passed on to the Prime Minister for consideration were proposals for a host of new government agencies. These included a community corps, life learning centres, a global centre of excellence for education, a federation commission, a bipartisan agency to review regulation, an Indigenous knowledge centre, a climate information authority, a landscape and carbon commission, a national preventive health agency, a ministry of creative industries, and a new public television network (Commonwealth of Australia 2008). A month later, the Treasurer, Wayne Swan, delivered the government's first budget, which included spending cuts of hundreds of millions of dollars aimed at increasing the budget surplus in order to help keep inflation under control.

These two episodes illustrate a tension at the heart of public administration in Australia. We all expect a well-resourced and responsive government but a decades-long squeeze on public funds has led to a continual restructuring of the public sector.

These changes have been aimed at providing better value for money while ensuring that public servants are accountable to the elected government for their actions. The result has been a public service that has often been demoralised and lacking the capacity to fulfil its fundamental role. It seems unlikely, though, that the restructuring of the public sector is coming to an end.

Introduction

In the previous chapter, we introduced executive government, concentrating on the party political dimension of that branch such as the prime minister and cabinet. The executive branch, however, consists of much more than the political executive; it consists of the public service and other government agencies, including the police and military. We are much more likely to interact with this face of executive government in our daily lives than we are with politicians. Public servants administer laws and provide a range of government services—everything from welfare to the defence of the nation. Governments need to raise hundreds of billions of dollars to pay for those services, so public servants are also involved in raising revenue.

We often use the terms 'public service' and 'bureaucracy' interchangeably. Bureaucracy, though, has a particular meaning—rule by officials (Hague & Harrop 2001, p. 254). One of the pioneers of the study of bureaucracy in democratic societies, Max Weber (1864–1920), argued that policy-making in such systems was characterised by rationality, impartiality and efficiency (1967 [1915], p. 367). Yet, while this may be said of bureaucracy in democracies *in comparison to other political systems*, where corruption may flourish, there are a number of institutional and political pressures that make policy processes in our system less than ideal. Even in cases where there is consensus over which policies are in the public interest, a number of factors can conspire to produce sub-standard policies. We will examine some of those pressures in this chapter. Kevin Rudd (2008) underlined the tension between policy rationality and the pressures of day-to-day politics when he promised that in his government 'policy design and policy evaluation should be driven by analysis of the available options, and not by ideology'.

Around the world, the public sector varies enormously in size, structure and role. Many of the big debates in politics revolve around the role that governments play in society and the economy. The more active the government, the larger the public sector. While there is a good deal of variation between countries in the size of the public sector it generally increased across the developed world throughout the twentieth century (Hague & Harrop 2001, p. 256). More recently, some states have reduced the size of their public sector through **privatisation**. European states tend to have a larger public sector than other states. Among developed countries, governments in Scandinavia such as those of Sweden and

Privatisation: the removal of activities from the public sector through asset sales or service contracting to the private sector

Denmark undertake over half of all spending across the economy. The South Korean government, on the other hand, spends about a quarter, with Australian governments accounting for 35 per cent of all spending here (OECD statistics). The organisation of public sector entities differs in other ways. They can come under the direction of democratically elected politicians, or they can be independent of political control. They can be staffed by independent experts or by appointees loyal to the government of the day. Public servants may have security of tenure or serve at the pleasure of politicians. In some countries, such as Japan, senior public servants can be as powerful as senior politicians, in part because the public servants have permanent positions while the politicians come and go (Heywood 1997, p. 350). The ideas that fuel debates in Australia about the size and role of the public sector, then, are often imported from overseas.

The structure and values of the Australian public sector

By the time the Australian Commonwealth public service was formed in 1901, the principles of professionalism and neutrality were well entrenched in what was known as the Westminster tradition. Prior to the development of that tradition in the nineteenth century, in Britain and its colonies (including Australia) many public positions had been the subject of political patronage, where government jobs were distributed to trusted allies of the political executive. Some revenue-raising jobs were even sold to the highest bidder, who would take a percentage of the revenue. Reducing patronage and establishing principles such as recruitment and promotion on merit were essential elements of the development of responsible government (Singleton et al. 2003, p. 196).

Traditionally, in the model Australia inherited from Britain, the role of the public service was to provide advice to ministers and carry out the duties required of them under the relevant body of law applying to each ministerial portfolio. Governments could come and go with the expectation that they would inherit a professional and non-partisan public service from their predecessors. Over the course of the twentieth century, Australian governments expanded the range of activities in which they became involved. Governments built and managed infrastructure such as transport and telecommunications. The size of the public service grew in concert with the development of the country. From around the 1970s, however, concerns about the size and efficiency of the public sector saw a series of reforms undertaken by governments from both sides of politics. This chapter examines the reasons behind those changes and sets out some of the arguments still under way about public sector restructuring—over privatisation, organisational restructuring, the alleged politicisation of the public service and the role of ministerial advisors.

It is important to differentiate between the public sector and the public service. The public sector refers to all government activity (see Box 6.1). It includes public service departments as well as businesses owned by governments, such as power stations, railways and Australia Post. The Australian Public Service consists of those employed under the *Public Service Act 1999*. The public service is a sub-set of the public sector, made up of government departments and related agencies. For example, the Department of Human Services provides policy advice to the political executive on welfare matters while Centrelink provides welfare services to the public. Both agencies are staffed under the *Public Service Act* (Ward & Stewart 2006, p. 247). Government departments are historically very hierarchical organisations. They follow a chain of responsibility up to a single department head, and then to the relevant minister.

As we saw in the previous chapter, each government department is accountable to at least one government minister. Whereas the political executive is drawn from Parliament, the bureaucratic executive is expected to be apolitical. Its role is to provide advice and support to ministers in the administration of their portfolio. The public service is funded by the taxes of all Australians, and citizens expect that public servants will be politically neutral. They should act and provide advice in the public interest, not in the interests of the party in power or in the narrow interests of a government minister. By contrast, when the United States elects a new president, thousands of senior office-holders in the executive branch lose their jobs and the president appoints new officials who can be trusted to follow the orders of the new chief executive. In a Westminster system, public servants should be secure enough in their jobs to provide frank and fearless advice to their political masters. In return, public servants carry on their duties largely anonymously, leaving ministers with the public responsibility for the actions of government departments (Wanna & Weller 2003, p. 86). Consequently, public servants who wish to enter the political arena are forced to stand down from their positions while campaigning.

Statutory authorities, as the term implies, are created by statutes (laws). Government departments, while they are subject to the law, are often created by the executive (although subject to various laws) to assist with the day-to-day running of government. Under our system of responsible government, all public sector agencies are accountable to Parliament. Statutory authorities, such as the Australian Broadcasting Corporation (ABC), were created separately from government departments so that they could be free from partisan bias in their management. Other statutory authorities are housed within government departments and report to the relevant minister as well as to Parliament. Where the ABC is concerned, non-partisanship is essential to the fulfilment of its charter. The Auditor-General's Department, with its role in investigating the financial operations of other government authorities, requires a similar level of independence. Other statutory authorities such as utility companies and the Commonwealth Scientific and Industrial Research Organisation (CSIRO) were created separately from government departments because they require expert management more so than ministerial direction.

BOX 6.1   Types of public sector organisations

One of the consequences of public sector restructuring in recent decades has been continual changes to the way in which public organisations are classified. A single area of public responsibility, such as health, may contain numerous types of government authorities. **Government departments** such as state and Commonwealth departments of health are under the direction of a responsible minister. Public hospitals (or regional health services), on the other hand, are **statutory authorities**, managed by expert administrators and accountable directly to the Parliament rather than to a government minister.

Not all public servants are at the beck and call of the minister of the day. Some senior public servants, such as the Commissioner of Taxation, need statutory independence from partisan direction even if their agencies—in this case the Australian Taxation Office—report to a government minister. Similarly, *police* and *military* chains of command are independent from ministerial direction in order to ensure their operational freedom, although this independence is usually a matter of tradition and public expectation rather than legislation. Government departments can also be broken down into the main departments where policy development takes place and those **executive agencies**, such as Centrelink, that deliver government services (Wettenhall 2003a, pp. 9–10).

Government trading enterprises, such as Australia Post, are owned by the government but operated according to private-sector management principles. They report to Parliament. **Public–private partnerships** combine the long-term considerations of government in areas such as roads and other infrastructure with the construction and management expertise of private enterprise.

Government departments: a division of the public service responsible for the administration of a given portfolio

Statutory authorities: statutory authorities are independent public organisations created by law and accountable to parliament

Executive agencies: agencies that are responsible to government ministers for the delivery of services to the public

Government trading enterprises: businesses owned and operated by the state

Public–private partnerships: where private sector funding and expertise are used to build and operate public infrastructure

There are hundreds of statutory authorities across all levels of government: some are staffed under the *Public Service Act* while others have their own Act of Parliament. The CSIRO continues to operate under the *Science and Industry Research Act 1949*. It is accountable both to the Parliament and to the relevant minister. Statutory authorities have their own parliamentary reporting requirements such as annual reports and appearances by managers before relevant parliamentary committees. Those statutory authorities outside the main government departments are not immune from the influence of the political executive, which can affect the character of such agencies through appointments to their management and boards, through proposals for cuts or increases to their budgets, and through other government-initiated legislation. It is worth noting that the Howard Government employed a retired businessman, John Uhrig, and not a retired public servant, to provide a vital report on the restructuring of statutory authorities in 2002. The Uhrig Report recommended greater ministerial direction and oversight in the management of statutory authorities, recommendations that the Howard Government was more than happy to implement (Halligan 2008, pp. 34–5).

Table 6.1   Examples of Commonwealth public sector organisations

Policy area	Government departments	Executive agencies	Agencies outside the public service
Health	Department of Health and Ageing	Cancer Australia	Australian Institute of Health and Welfare
Law	Attorney-General's Department	Emergency Management Australia	Australian Security Intelligence Organisation
Communications	Department of Broadband, Communications and the Digital Economy		Australian Communications and Media Authority
Education	Department of Education, Employment and Workplace Relations	Office of Early Childhood Education and Childcare	Australian University Quality Agency

Throughout this chapter we will be referring to a number of trends and reviews that have provided challenges to both the traditional Westminster model of the public service and to the nature and size of the public sector as a whole. Privatisation and **managerialism** have reduced the size of the public sector and transformed the management of the remaining agencies. Critics of the restructuring of the public service (sometimes referred to as New Public Management) argue that it has compromised the political neutrality of public servants. Politicisation can manifest itself in a number of ways. The promotion of senior public servants may depend on them being seen to be sympathetic to the aims of the government of the day. Public servants may be circumspect in the advice they give to ministers if they do not have security of tenure. The extent to which the principles of merit and neutrality have been compromised during the various public sector reforms in recent decades is the Issue in Focus for this chapter.

Managerialism: the application of private sector principles of efficiency and goal-orientation to the public sector

> **BOX 6.2   The greatest public servant: H.C. 'Nugget' Coombs**
>
> Trained as an economist, Dr H.C. 'Nugget' Coombs became Australia's most influential public servant. He advised six prime ministers from Curtin (1941–45) to Whitlam (1972–75) from both sides of politics. He was a driving force behind reconstruction and banking policies following the Second World War (1939–45), the creation of the Australian National University and a number of arts funding bodies, and was an advocate for the rights of Indigenous Australians. Coombs led the 1974–76 Royal Commission that recommended greater accountability for the Commonwealth public service. In 2008, Coombs was singled out by Prime Minister Kevin Rudd in a speech to public servants as proof that 'independence, excellence and absolute integrity can all go together'.

Policy-making and the public service

Making public policy is a complex process. Due attention needs to be paid to the testing of proposals and consideration of consequences, preparation of any necessary legislation, implementation, public information campaigns and policy reviews.

The Westminster model assumes that policy advice and policy decision-making are separate functions. In practice, ministers delegate many of their decision-making powers to individual public servants. Parliament, too, passes laws that leave detailed regulations to be decided upon at departmental level. Further, the advice provided by the public service constrains the decision-making process by limiting the choices available to ministers (Ward & Stewart 2006, p. 251). This is a matter of necessity, since the number of possible options in a single policy area can be limitless. Public servants make important decisions about which of a range of policy options are to be developed and presented to a minister. The public service also makes policy when it administers the law. The laws governing social security benefits, for example, cannot possibly anticipate every possible circumstance under which citizens might be entitled to welfare. Centrelink managers require some discretion in administering such laws. Ministers cannot be expected to be accountable for every such decision within their department. Appearances by public servants before parliamentary committees are important venues for understanding the way in which legislation is implemented.

The sheer size of some government departments makes responsibility to a minister and the Parliament problematic. With Parliament creating an ever-increasing body of law for the bureaucratic executive to administer, the problems of oversight and accountability multiply. The notion of a permanent public service naturally lends itself to institutional beliefs and practices unique to each agency that will be difficult to change in the short term. Politicians, by contrast, respond to short-term changes in public sentiment. Government and opposition make claim and counter-claim in the same news cycle (Weller 2008, p. 73).

Politicians and public servants must also find a balance between the representations of interest groups seeking to initiate or change government policy and the often-contentious notion of the public interest. As part of the process of providing advice to ministers, public servants are required to consult with any **stakeholders**, such as business, welfare, other interest groups and state and local governments likely to have a view on policy proposals. Some stakeholders are more proactive (and better resourced) than others in making their views on those policy proposals clear both to the public service and the political executive. Senior public servants, in particular, are part of **policy networks**, which might include academic experts, business representatives and politicians (Rhodes 2007, p. 1244). Such networks can provide the public service with the latest thinking on new theories and practices in their area of expertise. Policy networks are also used by stakeholders to influence government policy. Media ownership is one area that has historically been notorious for the extent to which incumbent interests (owners of newspapers or television stations) have been able to influence politicians and regulators to favour them in decision-making processes. The result has been demonstrably sub-standard public policies over a number of decades, such as delays in licensing new media technologies to protect the profits of incumbent corporations (Errington & Miragliotta 2007, p. 156).

Stakeholders: groups likely to be affected by policy changes

Policy networks: formal and informal groups of government and non-government actors with a common interest in a policy area

---

BOX 6.3   Influencing public policy

Around the world, democracies have struggled to come to terms with a well-funded and well-organised lobbying industry. While lobbying is often associated with powerful corporate interests, parliaments are the subject of lobbying from all sorts of interest groups including charities and religious organisations.

In Western Australia, disgraced former premier Brian Burke made use of his network within the Australian Labor Party to run a lucrative lobbying business. That state's Crime and Corruption Commission uncovered extensive contacts between Burke and his partners, cabinet ministers, opposition MPs and senior public servants. While cabinet ministers and public servants were forced to resign, Burke himself faced no charges.

It is difficult to clearly separate the right of all citizens to petition their elected representatives, organised lobbying of public officials, and clear-cut cases of undue influence and corruption. The latter crime most often occurs over town planning, where a single public official is in a position to make a decision that will benefit or cost a company a good deal of money. That company naturally has a strong incentive to influence the decision-maker. In New South Wales in 2008, a number of local government officials were found to have accepted bribes for decisions favourable to particular businesses.

Warhurst (2007) argues that transparency is the most important principle in regulating lobbyists. One of the first actions of the Rudd Government was the establishment of a register of lobbyists as part of a Lobbying Code of Conduct. While that register was criticised for some of its limitations (in applying the code to those lobbying ministers rather than all Commonwealth MPs, for example), it represents an important step towards disclosure of this important practice.

Q   What constraints should we put on contact between lobbyists and public servants? Is transparency enough to ensure fair dealing?

The expertise of the public service can put ministers in the position of having little choice but to accept the advice of trained professionals in the bureaucracy. Senior public servants with their wealth of experience can give ministers valuable advice about the unforseen consequences of their policy ideas. Yet, a department comfortable with the way things have always been done may swamp ministers with technical and administrative objections to government reforms. This can set up a conflict between ministers keen to achieve their policy goals and make a public impression and a staid public service that prefers to proceed with caution. Further, the incentives for public service departments to increase their own influence, in absolute terms and with respect to one another, sometimes leaves the ethos of the public service a long way from the Westminster ideal. The interests of the political and bureaucratic wings of the executive, then, are not always in concert. Ministers sometimes mistakenly see the characteristic caution of the bureaucracy as hostility to the government's policies.

BOX 6.4   Women in the public service

The position of women in the public service has changed a lot since the 1960s, when the ban on married women holding positions there was lifted. According to the Public Service Commission, the number of women in the public service has been growing faster than the number of men for some time. Women comprise 57 per cent of Commonwealth public service employees, although they are dispro-portionately represented among those on short-term contracts. There is a large variation in employment by gender among different government agencies. The Bureau of Meteorology employs the highest proportion of men (79 per cent) and Medicare Australia the highest proportion of women (81 per cent), suggesting that men still hold the majority of highly-trained public service positions. Similarly, there is a stark gender division at the most senior ranks of the public service. Whereas women comprise less than one-third of the most senior employment classification, they comprise almost two-thirds of the lowest classification.

Q Why are women still under-represented at senior levels of the public service? Should governments make greater efforts to redress this imbalance?

Source: Australian Public Service Commission 2007

In addition to ministers coming and going from each portfolio, governments regularly restructure the public service to take account of new portfolio areas and to streamline service delivery. The largest of these reorganisations occurred under the Hawke Government in 1987 when the number of departments was reduced from 27 to 18. Departments with similar responsibilities and expertise were merged. The creation of 'super-departments' such as Foreign Affairs and Trade was designed to increase political control of the bureaucracy by putting a cabinet minister in charge of each department (Singleton et al. 2003, p. 205). Often, though, such reforms leave constituent units of the public service in place, with only the lines of political responsibility changing.

There is no ideal organising principle for a large and complex public service. Governments reduce some of the complexity through the use of inter-departmental committees to scrutinise policy portfolios using the expertise of a range of departments (Halligan 2008, p. 20). For instance, a large road project will be of interest not only to the Department of Transport and Regional Development but to the Department of Environment, Heritage and the Arts (to assess environmental impact), relevant state authorities, and the Treasury. Complex proposals also need to be assessed for their legal consequences, with the Attorney-General's Department or lawyers within each agency giving advice on proposals. As we saw in Chapter 5, the Department of the Prime Minister and Cabinet duplicates all the areas of expertise throughout the public service, since successive prime ministers have 'wanted advice on everything' (Walter & Strangio 2007, pp. 49–50). That department plays the main coordinating role in policy development. The exhaustive process of policy-making is designed to ensure that the short- and long-term consequences of all decisions are carefully considered. All of this takes time and resources, the latter of which, as we shall see in the next section, have been under continual pressure since the 1970s as the Australian economy has been restructured.

A shrinking public sector?

The Australian government has always played a strong role in our national development. A big country with a relatively small population and a limited pool of private capital has required government intervention in transport, communications and other infrastructure. W.K. Hancock long ago noted that the Australian characteristic of individualism rested comfortably with a powerful state so long as the primary role of the state lay in assisting individuals to tame the wide open spaces of the continent (1945, p. 62). Australia was a pioneer in the provision of aged pensions and other welfare services. All of this required a strong public sector. Australian governments have traditionally invested in such areas as electricity, water, roads, banks, airlines and telephone companies. Some of these areas are **natural monopolies**. In other areas, such as banking, the government sought to intervene to correct problems in the marketplace.

> **Natural monopolies:** services, such as water supply, that are most efficiently provided by a single entity

As Hancock anticipated, the last few decades have seen a rethink over how these services should be delivered. In some industries, such as water and electricity (usually the responsibility of state governments), government intervention remains extensive in terms of price-setting and environmental protection but many of the service providers have been privatised. In other industries, such as airlines and banking, privatisation has been accompanied by deregulation, resulting in minimal government intervention. Enterprises such as Telstra, the Commonwealth Bank and Qantas have been privatised since the late 1980s. Some areas long thought to be the preserve of governments, such as prisons and immigration detention centres, have had their operations privatised in the midst of great public controversy.

Government departments have also been influenced by privatisation. Services within a large government department such as cleaning, human resources, or the provision of information technology may be undertaken by private providers in a process known as outsourcing. Some frontline government services have also been privatised. The Howard Government introduced the Job Network to allow private (often not-for-profit) agencies to tender for employment and training services previously undertaken by a government agency—the Commonwealth Employment Service (Aulich 2005, pp. 71–2). Some of these policies, such as the practice of selling government buildings and leasing them back from their private owners, have come under criticism for providing poor value to taxpayers.

In addition to changing the nature of the relationship between the government and citizens, the result of these various forms of privatisation has been a large reduction in the number of Australians employed by the government and government-owned firms (the public sector). Figure 6.1 shows the effects of three decades of public sector restructuring on the number of Australians employed by the Commonwealth government. A large number of employees have been shifted from the public sector to the private sector. This is important since public sector employees have historically enjoyed a more stable employment environment and more generous working conditions (if not higher wages) than those in similar positions in the private sector. However, while privatisation of public enterprises has reduced the total number of public sector employees, regular cuts in the number of public servants inevitably seem to give way to restoration of a long-run average as governments discover the need for new government programs, sources of advice and expertise.

Figure 6.1   Size of the Australian Public Service, Commonwealth public sector and Australian workforce, 1988–2007

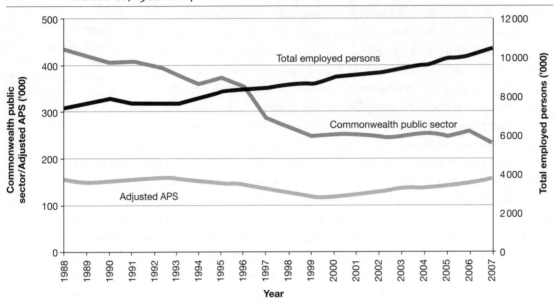

Source: Australian Public Service Commission

Such statistics, though, do not necessarily reflect the reach (as opposed to the size) of government. Employing fewer workers does not mean that Australian governments are doing less. Many private firms, from construction companies to advertising agencies, rely heavily on winning government contracts. Many public servants who lost their jobs during the regular rounds of government cost-cutting have subsequently won lucrative contracts as consultants. Governments spend increasing amounts of money on private consultants to provide policy advice in competition with the public service. One of the most controversial of these episodes was the Howard Government's use of a Melbourne consulting firm to advise it on changes to industrial relations laws. In the past two decades, while governments have been reducing the overall size of the public sector, they have been legislating at a record pace. For example, the telecommunications industry may have been privatised, but that sector faces an enormous amount of government regulation since Australians have become used to a certain level of service. A 2005 study by Access Economics found that the last two decades had produced by far the largest volume of Commonwealth legislation since Federation. This trend gives government agencies responsibility for more and more areas of our lives in spite of the trend towards privatisation of service delivery. Moon and Sayers describe this trend as one of government increasing its scope while decreasing its intensity (1999, p. 149).

Figure 6.2   New Commonwealth legislation since Federation

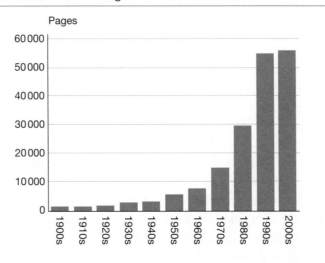

Source: Access Economics 2005

ISSUE IN FOCUS

HAS THE COMMONWEALTH BUREAUCRACY BEEN POLITICISED?

Three decades of public service reform

While the basic structure of the Commonwealth public service has remained constant since Federation, the way in which it operates has changed considerably in recent decades. A series of reviews and Acts of Parliament have reflected the wishes of the political executive to make the bureaucratic executive more responsive to their wishes. The extent to which these changes have led to a politicised public service has been much debated. Politicisation is a broader concept than partisanship. Partisanship is to prefer the government over the parliamentary opposition. Politicisation refers to the pressures on public servants to serve the interests of the government of the day over and above the interests of the nation—not just their political rivals. It may, for example, involve the appointment of a public servant known for their sympathy with a certain policy direction (Mulgan 1998). A series of such appointments would undermine the ability of the public service to give independent advice to ministers.

The quality and political neutrality of bureaucratic advice increasingly came to be doubted by governments by the 1970s. Some of the problems associated with ministers' workloads were discussed in the previous chapter. As government took on more and more responsibilities during the course of the twentieth century, they became increasingly reliant on the public service for advice and expert administration. Today, ministers make policy decisions only in part on the advice provided by the bureaucracy. They also rely on the platform and beliefs of their party, advice from their political advisors, policy networks and lobbying from interest groups. Senior public servants tend to know more about politics than ministers know about their portfolio. While it is important that an experienced public servant can tell a minister things they may not wish to hear, it is equally important that the public service assists rather than obstructs the government of the day.

Ministers found that the public service 'mandarins', as permanent department heads were known, 'came to be associated with belligerence and complacency' (Tiernan 2007, p. 4). In the early 1970s, the introduction of ministerial advisors provided an alternative to the permanent public service. The Whitlam Government, elected in 1972, was suspicious of senior public servants who had advised Coalition Governments during the long period of Liberal–Country Party rule from 1949. While paid for through government revenue, ministerial advisors are not public servants and are employed under a separate Act of Parliament. The number of ministerial advisors has steadily increased since the 1970s, although new governments make a show of paring back their numbers before settling into the pattern of justifying more and more staff. Cuts in this area in the early weeks of the new Rudd Government were quickly followed by concerns that ministers did not have sufficient staff. The growth of ministerial advisors feeds into a much longer-running debate about just how the public service should be structured in order to ensure that ministers are receiving the best possible advice.

Public servants are often frustrated that due to their physical location inside the minister's office, political advisors have the last word on policy proposals before the minister makes a decision. One view of ministerial advisors is that 'they intervene in departmental processes; they mediate between the political and administrative domains; they drive, sieve and skew advice; and they insist on what the minister wants as opposed to the public interest or the integrity of the policy process' (Walter & Strangio 2007, p. 54). By contrast, then-prime minister John Howard argued that the increase in ministerial staff actually underlines the apolitical nature of the public service. Their presence allows ministers to receive impartial advice from public servants and test it against politically attuned advisors in their private office (Ward & Stewart 2006, p. 263). Many public servants don't see things that way. Tales of ministerial advisors yelling down the telephone line to bully public servants into providing advice more amenable to the minister's wishes are sadly common. The role of political advisors in shielding ministers from information that could damage them down the track has never been fully exposed. Howard Government scandals over refugees (the children overboard affair) in 2001 and bribes paid by the Australian Wheat Board exposed in 2006 both involved damaging information circulating in the public service apparently failing to reach the desk of relevant ministers. The lack of accountability of ministerial advisors means that they 'operate in the shadows of Australian politics' (Tiernan 2007, p. ix).

BOX 6.5   Freedom of information

The public's ability to navigate the increasingly complex public sector was enhanced by the Commonwealth's *Freedom of Information Act 1982*. The Freedom of Information (FOI) legislation was a response to growing concerns that the bureaucracy was unaccountable. Governments nevertheless maintain that the importance of public servants giving free and frank advice often outweighs the principle of disclosure. They argue that the release of documents giving ministers advice on a range of policy proposals would cause public servants to become more circumspect in their advice. For example, the Treasury refused to release documents on taxation data sought by *The Australian* newspaper (ABC 2006). Critics argue that the political executive is only saving itself from public embarrassment by withholding such documents. The principle of the public interest in keeping the documents secret put forward by the relevant minister was upheld by a High Court decision over *The Australian*'s FOI application in 2006, leaving (in the eyes of news organisations at least) a large loophole in the FOI legislation.

In 2008, the Queensland Government released a review of its *Freedom of Information Act*. The review authors argued that governments should, as a routine matter, release much more information to the public than they are inclined to at present. This would reduce the costs of FOI requests since more information would already be in the public domain (Solomon 2008).

Q   What is the public interest in limiting the free flow of government information? Is secrecy an essential part of good government?

Also beginning in the 1970s the principle of public service neutrality was challenged by the twin intellectual currents of economic liberalism and the demand for a politically responsive bureaucracy. The former led to privatisation of some public sector agencies and pressure on spending across the whole of government. The latter saw successive governments reform the public service to ensure that democratically elected governments could more easily put their policies into practice.

A series of reports into the public service saw the introduction of a number of important reforms. The Administrative Appeals Tribunal was created to provide a review of the decisions of public servants that affect citizens. Cabinet processes were streamlined, giving the Department of Prime Minister and Cabinet a higher profile. The Department of Finance was created to separate the public sector management role from the Treasury.

The allegedly creaking Commonwealth Public Service proved quite adept at remaking itself. A further round of reforms accompanied the election of the Hawke Government in 1983. Hawke's ministers were determined to avoid the experience of the Whitlam Government, which believed that the public service resisted many of the policy reforms in Labor's platform. Hawke made his position clear: 'It will be the government who will be making the policies for this country, not the public servants' (cited in Ward & Stewart 2006, p. 252). The Senior Executive Service (SES) was created to bring modern corporate management techniques to the public service. Managers were given greater freedom to go about their jobs but they would be held accountable for their success or failure. Short-term contracts undermined the notion of a career bureaucracy dedicated to the service of the nation—not just the government of the day. This managerialism saw the introduction of such principles as performance bonuses, risk management, success indicators, computer modelling, budgets linked to specific programs, detailed reporting requirements, and efficiency dividends that required regular cuts in the budget of most departments (Thompson 1997, pp. 149–50).

Management structures are now less hierarchical, with public servants working in teams to achieve goals. Departmental secretaries have become expert managers capable of shifting between departments. Competition for these positions has increased with the capacity for the government to make senior appointments from outside the public service (Halligan 2008, p. 22). There has been much debate around the world as to whether or not management techniques imported from the private sector have much relevance to the public sector (Hague & Harrop 2001, p. 265). In the private sector, measures of corporate health such as revenue and profits, can serve as markers of management effectiveness. Finding similar performance benchmarks in the public sector is more difficult. Citizens expect governments to be concerned with issues such as fairness and social justice that are not easily captured through statistics.

A number of departmental heads were chosen by the Howard Government from outside the public service. Some of these incoming secretaries had managed bodies representing business. Another had a close association with the Liberal Party. The ability of governments to hire and fire departmental heads was confirmed by a Federal Court judgment in 1999, denying the right of appeal to the sacked secretary of the Department of Defence on the basis of 'loss of trust and confidence' in the incumbent on the part of the minister (cited in Barker 2007, p. 142). One concern with an open selection process is that the ability of the political executive to choose senior public servants results in an overly narrow range of policy advice making its way to the desks of ministers. This criticism often comes from the Left of politics, wishing to see within the bureaucracy alternative ideas to the dominant neo-liberal paradigm of economic efficiency and market-based provision of services.

Another of the principles of public service that has been compromised is that of anonymity. Senior public servants now play a role in promoting government policy through speeches. At the state level, in particular, senior public servants can be more effective policy advocates than their ministers. At Commonwealth level, senior public servants maintain a lower profile but nevertheless play an important role in ongoing policy debates (although their remarks are usually cleared by ministerial offices—see Box 6.6). This can lead to confusion about their role, as one departmental secretary explained:

> When I speak on public issues I tend to be quite strong, forceful and passionate and therefore it is assumed that I'm *supporting* 100 per cent the policies of the government of the day whereas I think I am *communicating* 100 per cent the policies of the government of the day (Anon. cited in Weller 2008, p. 74).

Having the experience and expertise of senior public servants on the public record raises the quality of policy debates. From the perspective of opposition parties struggling for the resources to effectively participate in those debates, however, the distinction between senior officials *supporting* and *communicating* policy could easily be lost.

BOX 6.6 Speaking out

The executive branch of government must speak with one voice. The principle behind collective cabinet responsibility, where ministers must resign if they cannot support government policy, is that mixed messages reduce public confidence in the government. Governments have long sought to extend this principle beyond cabinet to the entire executive branch. Ministers are politically responsible for the activities of their departments, so controlling the flow of information is consistent with that responsibility. The extent to which governments should be able to control information, though, is hotly debated.

Cabinet documents leaked to the media have long been a source of embarrassment to governments. Such leaks often produce police investigations into the source of the leak, although they rarely find the culprit. Historically, journalists could be forced to reveal in court the source of any classified documents they receive. More recently, however, legislation at state and Commonwealth level has provided limited immunity to journalists to protect their sources so that they can conduct investigations into government corruption. Contracts for public servants include clauses about the secrecy of government documents and the circumstances under which employees can speak to the media. With governments increasingly using private firms to provide services, the contracts involve a high level of secrecy (Funnell 2001, p. 138). Similarly, Freedom of Information legislation has limitations on what can be released in the public interest (see Box 6.5). When Australian Federal Police Commissioner Mick Keelty contradicted the prime minister's preferred explanation of an overseas terrorist incident in 2003, he came under intense pressure from the PM's office to 'clarify' (change) his remarks (Errington & van Onselen 2007, p. 334).

Civil libertarians argue that government media management is more often a matter of political convenience than the public interest. An example of the tension between secrecy and the public interest arose when a customs officer, Allan Kessing, leaked a classified report critical of security at Sydney Airport to a journalist. Kessing was found guilty but not jailed for his actions (Marr 2007). Legislation to protect this kind of **whistle-blowing** from prosecution was promised by the incoming Rudd Government in 2007. There are a number of such Acts at state level.

Whistle-blowing: actions by public servants to publicly expose corruption or mismanagement

Q Under what circumstances should public servants be free to publicise sensitive public documents? How can we assess whether too much government information is withheld from the public?

A further round of public sector reforms under the Howard Government reduced the job security of all public servants and gave more flexibility to managers to decide the wages and conditions of employees under their control. These reforms also made it clear that it is the prime minister who appoints departmental heads. One former incumbent has pointed out the tension between departmental heads being account-able to a minister but also the prime minister and the head of the Department of the Prime Minister and Cabinet (Podger 2007, p. 144). Such tensions reflect the power struggle within cabinet for control of the policy agenda.

The *Public Service Act 1999* provides for a statement of public service values, including its apolitical and professional status, merit-based appointment and promo-tion, anti-discrimination principles, ethical standards, as well as its accountability to the government, Parliament and public. Conscious of criticism that recent reform of the public service may have undermined Westminster traditions, the values state that the service is 'responsive to the government in providing frank, honest, com-prehensive, accurate and timely advice' (APSC 2002). As far as the government is concerned, then, there is no conflict between the principles of a responsive and a frank public service.

Allegations of a politicised public service

Many of the reforms to the public service since the 1970s have been aimed at making government departments more responsive to the wishes of the elected government. While this is not inconsistent with the need for public servants to be accountable to a minister and to Parliament, the reforms have brought into question the notion of a politically neutral public service—that serving the government of the day and serving the Australian public are not always the same thing. In 1996, incoming prime minister, John Howard, replaced six departmental heads believed to be sympathetic to the agenda of the Keating Government (1991–96). Labor criticised Howard's move as an unnecessary politicisation of the SES. To some extent, a more responsive public service can create a vicious cycle where perceptions about partisanship matter more than reality. Howard was suspicious of senior public servants who had enthusiastically served Keating when, in fact, those officials were simply doing what modern public sector management expects of them (Weller 2008, p. 74).

Some departmental secretaries were more sceptical of the notion of politicisation than others. Max Moore-Wilton was used by a number of Australian governments to shake up the bureaucracy (his nickname, 'Max the Axe', conveys some idea of his approach). As head of the Department of Prime Minister and Cabinet under John Howard, Moore-Wilson commented that 'a number of people have confused frank and fearless with just being a bloody nuisance' (cited in Errington & van Onselen 2007, p. 241). The ethos of managerialism is not, of itself, hostile to political neutrality, but its goal-centred approach to public sector management at the very least came into conflict at times with the historical principles of the public service.

Writing in the wake of the Howard Government's shake-up of the top levels of the SES, Mulgan (1998) argued that while:

> the great majority of public servants, including secretaries, still see themselves as politically neutral professionals, capable of serving alternative governments with equal competence and loyalty, incoming governments may be increasingly tempted to appoint new management teams as a means of imposing new policy directions on the bureaucracy. Such a convention, if it becomes entrenched, will erode the principles of a professional service with damaging long-term consequences for the morale and competence of the APS as a whole.

By contrast, secretary of the Department of Prime Minister and Cabinet in the latter years of the Howard Government, Peter Shergold, was confident that the public service retained the utmost standards of professionalism. He argued that 'public servants do what is required of them' not because they are politicised but for the very opposite reason—'they would do it for any government' (cited in Barker 2007, p. 127). While arguing against the idea of politicisation, Shergold was in fact confirming Mulgan's point. Again, the distinction between partisanship and politicisation is crucial. Enthusiastically serving the government of the day may not be partisanship but it can mean politicisation.

Critics of public service reform point to a number of episodes during the Howard Government of public servants serving the interests of the elected government rather than the interests of the nation. One of these was the provision of intelligence about

Iraq's alleged weapons of mass destruction in the period prior to the United States and its allies declaring war on Iraq in 2003. Former intelligence insiders claimed that the Office of National Assessments selectively presented intelligence to the prime minister that supported the government's case that Iraq was attempting to build nuclear weapons. Doubts at lower levels of the intelligence services about such claims were filtered out of the reports that reached the office of the prime minister (Wilkie 2007, p. 191). The fact that the intelligence services may well, as Shergold argued, 'do it for any government' is not very comforting.

On other occasions, Howard chose to reject advice from the public service that may have been politically beneficial to him in due course. For example, solutions to global warming proposed by the Department of the Environment were rejected in favour of the preferred course of action of the fossil fuels industry (Walter & Strangio 2007, p. 14). The government missed an opportunity to address an issue that eventually contributed to its demise in 2007 (McAllister & Clark 2008). Industry lobbying more so than a politicised public service proved to be the problem in that policy area.

Kevin Rudd is the first Australian prime minister with a long history as a public servant. He joined the diplomatic service and then served as head of the Queensland Cabinet Office (Weller 2007, p. 72). He brought a unique perspective, then, to the debate over politicisation of the public service. On coming to power in 2007, Rudd left all the public service heads in place in pointed contrast to the Howard Government. Aware of the problems caused by insecurity of tenure, Rudd sought to express confidence in the professionalism of the public service. Importantly, however, Shergold was due to retire as head of the Department of Prime Minister and Cabinet just months into the Labor Government's tenure, allowing Rudd to place a new face in that most important of public sector positions. In an address to senior public servants shortly after becoming prime minister, Rudd (2008) spoke of 'reinvigorating the Westminster tradition'. Siding with those who believed that the bureaucracy had become politicised under Howard, he said: 'We cannot afford a public service culture where all you do is tell the government what you think the government wants to hear.'

Barker argues that the host of reforms since the 1970s have left Australia with a politicised public service in the American style without the checks and balances that characterise the United States system of government (2007, p. 128). Short-term contracts for senior managers put obvious pressures on the notion of frank and fearless bureaucratic advice. Weller cites a former minister in setting out the stakes of recent reforms to the public service: 'It was an institutional struggle between the democratically elected governments and the public service for control of the public service. And in that struggle the elected governments have won.' (2007, p. 72) The prize for winning that institutional struggle, though, may be a public service that is unable or unwilling to provide ministers with all the advice and support they need to avoid the unexpected political disasters that often accompany policy changes (Wanna

& Weller 2003, p. 88). Ministers may have won control but lost the most important thing that the public service can provide—unbiased expertise.

In terms of responsible government, the public service is now more accountable than ever for its actions. Former departmental head and public service commissioner, Andrew Podger, while conceding that while the shift from the 1970s to a more politically responsive public service was 'overdue', wonders whether 'the balance has shifted too far towards responsiveness and away from apolitical professionalism and its focus on the long-term public interest' (2007, pp. 143–4). Some observers have recommended new reforms in the interests of rebalancing public service norms in favour of impartiality. These include a partial restoration of the security of tenure of departmental heads through longer contracts; a code of conduct and parliamentary accountability for ministerial advisors; and increased protection for whistle-blowers (Podger 2007, p. 145; Walter & Strangio 2007, pp. 74–5). Whether or not the political executive will be responsive to such calls must be doubtful.

CHAPTER SUMMARY

The Australian public sector has recently undergone its most significant period of reform since Federation. The Westminster traditions of political neutrality, independence and permanent employment have come under pressure from a political executive concerned chiefly with the responsiveness to ministerial direction. Privatisation and managerialism have swept through the public sector since the 1970s. While the number of employees in the public service has been relatively stable, the size of the wider public sector has been reduced. Concurrent changes to the public service culture have made it more responsive to the wishes of elected governments.

There is little doubt, though, that this increased political responsiveness has come at some cost to the ethos of political neutrality that was once the cornerstone of the public service. Neutrality is now one principle among many to which the bureaucratic executive must aspire.

WEBSITES

Australian Public Service Commission:
http://www.apsc.gov.au/
This site publishes regular reports on the structure, composition and values of the Commonwealth public service.

Government Sites by Portfolio:
http://www.australia.gov.au/Government_Sites_by_Portfolio
Exploring the websites of public organisations is a good way of understanding the structure of the government. Start at the 'Government Sites by Portfolio' site.

FURTHER READING

Aulich, C. & Wettenhall, R. (eds). 2008. *Howard's Fourth Government: Australian Commonwealth Administration 2004–2007*. University of New South Wales Press, Sydney.

Australian Public Service Commission (APSC). 2003. 'The Australian Experience of Public Sector Reform', Occasional Paper No. 2. Commonwealth of Australia, Canberra.

Hamilton, C. & Maddison, S. (eds). 2007. *Silencing Dissent*. Allen & Unwin, Sydney.

The High Court

THIS CHAPTER:

★ outlines the origins of the High Court and its role in Australian democracy
★ discusses the most important decisions of the Court, and their role in the direction of Australian federalism
★ provides an understanding of the importance of the appointment of High Court justices
★ distinguishes between the originalist, legalist and activist approaches to judicial decision-making, and outlines the arguments for and against each approach.

ISSUE IN FOCUS

How should High Court judges interpret the law?

KEY TERMS	*Coup d'état*	Legalism
Activism	Defamation law	Originalism
Common law	Judicial review	Precedents

The High Court of Australia found itself at the centre of political controversy on numerous occasions during the 1990s. After one particularly contentious decision, the then-Queensland Premier referred to the Court as 'an embarrassment'. The leader of the federal National Party called for the appointment of 'capital C conservatives' to the Court. A series of decisions on matters as diverse as Indigenous land rights and freedom of speech sparked debate across the political spectrum about the role of the Court.

An independent judiciary is one of the liberal principles that allows democracy to operate smoothly. The judiciary, though, is not immune from political influence.

The justices who came under fire for their controversial decisions had been appointed by the Fraser and Hawke Governments. The government of John Howard was determined to make appointments to the Court who would make more conservative, predictable decisions. By and large, Howard was successful in that endeavour. The Court is widely believed to have become less adventurous in the area of rights protection, for example, as a result of Howard's appointments.

While we can (and do) debate the extent to which decisions of the High Court should be the result of strict legal reasoning or attuned to changing social mores, the more conservative posture of the High Court in the last decade or so is a reminder that the Court is a political as well as a legal institution. The appointment of High Court judges is one of the most important things that the Commonwealth government undertakes.

Introduction

The independence of the judiciary is one of the liberal concepts that underpins democracy. Without an independent judiciary, the executive and the legislature would be free to trample our fundamental rights and freedoms, including those that guarantee free and fair elections. However, beyond this generally agreed upon function of the judiciary, the role of Australia's High Court in interpreting both the Constitution and the **common law** has been a matter of considerable controversy in recent decades. The Parliament expects the judiciary to be sympathetic to its attempts to keep Australians secure in times of turmoil. At other times, the judiciary leads the way in finding new ways of protecting the rights of citizens under threat from government decisions. Liberal institutions are designed to ensure that no single political institution can dominate the efforts of a democratic society to settle such complex arguments.

Common law: the body of decisions by courts on legal matters not covered by statutes and that provide precedents for contemporary decisions

One important point of contention is whether the High Court is a legal or political body. Certainly insofar as the Court makes decisions of great political significance, such as interpreting the division of power between the Commonwealth and the states, it is a body of great political weight. Yet, High Court Justices have traditionally been at pains to underline the fact that their decisions are always based on legal reasoning, not on partisan or ideological bias. Even those Justices who are innovative in their interpretation of the law are at pains to be seen to be above the hurly-burly of party politics. All judges need to be independent in their decision-making. However, one consequence of judicial independence is that judges are not accountable to Parliament or to the people for their decisions. Their power, then, is of quite a different type to that of Parliament or the executive. This chapter briefly outlines the history of the High Court in Australia, highlighting the most important decisions and changes of judicial philosophy that have affected the course of Australian politics and society. The Issue in Focus for this chapter is the ongoing debate between those who favour a strict interpretation of the law and those who prefer what is often referred to as 'judicial activism'.

The origins and function of the Court

While each country has a court recognised as its highest legal authority, the powers of those courts can differ markedly. In countries with written constitutions, the supreme court plays a crucial role in arbitrating in disputes over the division of power in that constitution. However, in countries where parliament is sovereign, such as the United Kingdom, the courts can be overruled on constitutional matters by the parliament. Supreme courts can also differ in their composition (the number of justices and their backgrounds), the types of cases they typically handle, and the method of appointment (and removal) of justices. For example, while Australia's High Court hears both constitutional matters and appeals from lower courts, some countries, such as South Africa, have dedicated courts for each of these functions (Hague & Harrop 2001, p. 189). One of the weaknesses of emerging democratic systems is the inability of courts to rule against powerful government figures because judges lack security of tenure. Judicial independence is crucial to the realisation of liberal ideals of freedom and equality before the law.

The independence of Australia's High Court is signified by its distinctive build-ing on the shores of Lake Burley Griffin near Parliament House in Canberra. The public's trust in this important political institution is the result of hundreds of years of development of the notion of judicial independence. Both British and American influences contributed to the Australian conception of an independent judiciary. The principle of judicial independence was firmly entrenched in Britain before Australia was colonised. Historically, the courts were made independent by allowing parlia-ment rather than the monarch (or, later, his or her ministers) to remove judges. Courts could thus behave truly impartially in matters concerning the Crown. Indeed, today the executive branch is inevitably the chief litigant in courts at all levels of government, underlining the importance of public confidence in the judiciary to the smooth operation of our democracy. Security of tenure assists judges in carrying out their roles from the High Court to the local Magistrates' Court. The rule of law only exists when those in power are held accountable to the law on the same basis as ordinary citizens. That is, all government actions must have their ultimate basis in the law (Spigelman 2007, p. 3). Australian colonies instituted these principles prior to Federation.

The Australian Constitution, of course, was in part designed to protect an American concept—federalism—and American ideas influenced Australia's federation debates. Judicial independence was guaranteed in the United States by an institutional separ-ation of executive, legislative and judicial functions. It was inevitable, then, that some form of judicial independence would be an integral part of the Australian political system at Federation (Patapan 2000b, p. 155). However, the distinction between a separation of powers and an independent judiciary is important. The notion of judicial independence is not a controversial one, although methods of appointment and removal of judges at all levels naturally impinges on just how independence is secured. The Constitution provides High Court Justices with security of tenure unless both Houses of Parliament agree on removal on the grounds of 'proven mis-behaviour or incapacity' (s. 72(i)). This has never happened, although Justice Lionel Murphy died while being investigated by Parliament in 1986. A 1977 referendum changed s. 72 of the Constitution to require High Court Justices to retire at age 70. Of course, many judges would be perfectly capable of serving on the Court well past age 70. The retirement age is arbitrary, although probably necessary.

There is more to the separation of powers than judicial independence. Both the United States and Australian constitutions separate the executive, legislative and judicial functions, yet Australia's largely unwritten system of responsible government in part fuses executive and legislative powers. In addition to this overlap in the com-position of parliament and the executive, the line between the parliament's function of writing law and the judicial function of interpreting the law is not always clear. It is the High Court, through its power of **judicial review**, which makes the final decision on the nature of Australia's separation of powers, meaning that the Court makes rulings about its own power. This ability of the High Court to interpret the powers of the judiciary includes finding the power of judicial review itself, which is not spelt out in the Constitution. With respect to the tradition of responsible government, the Court has held that the Parliament can delegate some legislative powers to the executive for the purposes of efficient government regulation, but that judicial power must be retained by the courts (Patapan 2000b, p. 159).

Judicial review: the ability of the judicial branch to overrule the actions of the other branches of government within the limits of the constitution

The principle of judicial review was well established in the United States by the time of Australia's federation debates. Judicial review allows the Court to disallow actions by the Parliament or the executive on the basis that they are unconstitutional. Thus, the American tradition of the role of the courts was quite different from the British model of parliamentary sovereignty, where decisions of any court could be quashed by legislative action. The High Court, then, has the final say over whether crucial pieces of legislation can take effect. Even if judges are careful to limit their decisions involving judicial review to established legal reasoning, the act of striking down government legislation or ministerial decisions brings the Court squarely into the political arena.

While provided for in Chapter III of the Constitution, the High Court was formally created by an Act of Parliament in 1903, with places for three justices. The number of justices was increased to five in 1906 and seven in 1913. The full bench of the Court hears constitutional cases, but appeals can be heard from lower courts by smaller numbers of justices. The Court can sometimes arrive at a majority decision with individual justices using different reasoning to arrive at the same conclusion.

Until the *Australia Acts* of 1986, the Privy Council in the United Kingdom was the final court of appeal for state matters, the Commonwealth having legislated in 1975 to prevent High Court decisions being appealed. Most of the High Court's work comes from appeals from state courts and lower federal courts. In 1976, the Federal Court of Appeals was established in order to leave the High Court to consider only the most important cases. The Court itself decides which cases these will be. Parties to a case must seek leave to appeal to the High Court, which agrees to take on such cases only when important points of law are at stake. Decisions of the High Court are binding on all lower courts.

Interpreting the Constitution

We can divide the types of cases that come before the High Court into those dealing with constitutional matters, and those that arise either from interpretation of statutes (laws) or from the common law. Statute and common law cases tend to be heard as appeals from lower courts, although the Court can choose to hear cases that bear on the interpretation of the Constitution as a matter of urgency. A number of common law cases, such as those dealing with native title, are discussed in the Issue in Focus. Constitutional cases usually fall into two broad categories—the division of state and Commonwealth powers, and the separation of powers between executive, legislature and judiciary. This section deals with constitutional cases.

Many of the constitutional cases argued before the United States Supreme Court require an interpretation of that country's Bill of Rights. Without such a bill to interpret, the most important role for Australia's High Court has been the division of powers in the Constitution between the Commonwealth and the states. Section 51 of the Constitution gives the Commonwealth Parliament

> the power to make laws for the peace, order, and good government of the Commonwealth with respect to

39 policy areas including immigration, marriage and divorce, currency and the census. Deciding whether or not a law passed by the Commonwealth Parliament, and challenged by one or more state governments, is allowed under s. 51 is one of the High Court's staple roles. The constitution explicitly reserves few policy areas for the states. While the constitution does not prevent states from legislating in areas concurrent with Commonwealth power, any contradiction between state and federal law is resolved in favour of the Commonwealth (s. 109). Because the Court has interpreted Commonwealth power very broadly, the trend towards the centralisation of power within the Federation was continuous throughout the twentieth century, as we saw in Chapter 4.

Australia has changed considerably since the Constitution first came into use in 1901. The text of the Constitution, however, has changed little. This necessitates a good deal of interpretation on the part of the Court as to how modern developments in technology, social organisation and values fit into a constitution designed over a hundred years ago. For example, s. 51(v) gives the Commonwealth power over

postal, telegraphic, telephonic and other like services[.]

Radio and television broadcasts, barely envisioned when the Constitution was written, logically come under the power of the Commonwealth. Similarly, aviation was not anticipated in the Constitution, but its role in interstate commerce (s. 51(i)) naturally lent aviation to Commonwealth regulation.

Each High Court decision has importance beyond the case at hand, since the principles on which the decision is based can become **precedents**, which future justices will often follow in subsequent cases. There have been a number of milestone cases in the judicial interpretation of Australian federalism (see Box 7.1). After an initial period in which the Court largely contained Commonwealth power, the *Engineers' case* (*Amalgamated Society of Engineers v. Adelaide Steamship Co. Ltd* (1920) 28 CLR 129) marked a turning point. In that case, the justices found that the Constitution was to be interpreted through its text rather than through an effort to determine the intentions of those who wrote it. Any implied prohibitions on Commonwealth power due to the fact that the Constitution is federal in nature and purpose could not outweigh that the text of the document reserves many powers for the Commonwealth but few for the states. For those supporting the principle of federalism, this is a major design flaw in our Constitution. Most of the early High Court justices had taken part in the federation debates. They could not help but interpret the intent of a document they had themselves taken part in writing. Since that initial period, very few justices have taken the original intent of the founding fathers into account.

> **Precedents:** legal decisions that courts will in future use as the starting point in their deliberation in similar cases

While the trend towards greater centralisation of power within the Commonwealth has been consistent since the *Engineers' case*, not every attempt by federal governments to increase their power has been tolerated. An attempt to nationalise the private banking sector by the Chifley Government was disallowed in 1947. Later decisions on the power of the Commonwealth to regulate corporations suggest that such legislation may not be struck down today. The Menzies Government's attempt to ban the Communist Party of Australia was struck down (and a subsequent referendum to achieve the same goal was lost). In *Communist Party of Australia v. The Commonwealth* (1951) 83 CLR 1, the Court ruled that banning a political party was beyond the scope of the defence power under s. 51(xi) of the Constitution. While this decision was, in practice, a defence of the individual freedom of assembly, the Court relied on the maintenance of the federal division of powers in the Constitution rather than any notion of rights implied in the Constitution.

Decades later, in *Thomas v. Mowbray* (2007) 237 ALR 194, the Court *did* allow the Commonwealth to impinge on civil liberties by legislating for control orders that limit the freedom of movement of individuals suspected (but not proven) to have supported terrorist groups. Even though Australia was not formally at war with terrorist groups, the Court found that terrorism was a threat to Australia, which allowed for the use of the defence power by the Commonwealth (Saul 2007). This decision, supported by five of the seven justices, was the starkest indication yet that a series of conservative appointments by the Howard Government had altered the balance of power of the Court away from the protection of civil liberties, which in part had characterised the Court's most prominent decisions of the 1990s. The role of the High Court, then, since its character depends much on the judicial philosophy of the seven justices, will vary over time.

BOX 7.1   Key decisions: power in the federation

The *Engineers' case: Amalgamated Society of Engineers v. Adelaide Steamship Co. Ltd* (1920) 28 CLR 129

The High Court ruled that a Western Australian Government instrumentality came under the jurisdiction of laws made under the Commonwealth's arbitration power in s. 51(xxxv) of the Constitution. The powers of the Commonwealth under s. 51 could not be restricted by an implied prohibition on intervening in areas of state responsibility. This marked the end of the implied prohibition doctrine and the beginning of a long period of literal interpretation of the Constitution. Since there are few explicit powers granted to states under the Constitution, this case proved a turning point in the balance of power within the federation.

The *Uniform Tax case: South Australia v. The Commonwealth* (1942) 65 CLR 373

During the Second World War (1939–45), the Commonwealth took control of large parts of the Australian economy for the purposes of war planning. The states challenged Commonwealth laws giving the federal government a monopoly over income taxing powers. The Court not only ruled that the relevant Acts were constitutional, but that the Commonwealth's income taxing powers could continue during peacetime. The states have since relied on the Commonwealth to pass on revenue to pay for state-run services such as hospitals and schools.

The *Tasmanian Dam case: The Commonwealth v. Tasmania* (1983) 158 CLR 1

While not the first decision of its kind, the *Tasmanian Dam case* gained a high public profile when the Court ruled that the Commonwealth had the power to legislate to stop the construction of a dam in south-west Tasmania. By signing an international treaty on environmental protection, the Commonwealth could use the external affairs power under s. 51(xxix) to overrule a state government in the area covered by the treaty.

The *WorkChoices case: New South Wales v. The Commonwealth* (2006) 229 CLR 1

The Howard Government's industrial relations legislation was upheld by reference to the corporations power under s. 51(xx). Combined with the powers confirmed in the *Tasmanian Dam case*, the Commonwealth now has few constitutional or financial restrictions on the areas in which it may legislate. While the result of this case was not unexpected, it confirmed a trend in the Court's interpretation of the corporations power that is hostile to the powers of the states.

While the High Court's posture towards civil liberties and the separation of powers has been liable to change, its attitude to federalism has not. A single clause in the Constitution has given the Commonwealth power over many areas, though, to be the preserve of the states. Treaties with other countries are signed by the Commonwealth executive without reference to Parliament. The High Court has given such treaties added significance by interpreting the external affairs power of s. 51(xxix) in such a way as to greatly expand the scope of Commonwealth power. Australia is subject to thousands of treaties concerning any number of issues, including racial discrimination, the rights of women and children, and prohibited drugs. The *Tasmanian Dam case* (see Box 7.1), which was important to the course of Australian federalism, was a 4–3 decision, indicating how fine the margin can be in such important political developments. In a later case, *Minister of State for Immigration and Ethnic Affairs v. An Hin Teoh* (1995) 183 CLR 273, the Court ruled that an international treaty gives the Commonwealth duties as well as power. The majority found that the executive must take into account Australia's treaty obligations in such areas as human rights when making decisions. The Court is still in the process of marking out the place of international law in the Australian political system. More recent decisions suggest that the principles found in *Teoh's case* are no longer supported by a majority of the Court.

We noted earlier an industrial relations case concerning s. 51(xxiii), which deals explicitly with industrial disputes that cross state boundaries. The Howard Government's 2005 WorkChoices legislation was an attempt to create a single national system of industrial relations. The Commonwealth thus relied on s. 51(xx), the corporations power, in defending its legislation from a challenge in the High Court (see Box 7.1). While the decision in this case was expected, it nevertheless confirmed the fears of federalists that there are now few limits on the ability of the Commonwealth to intervene in matters traditionally within the sphere of state responsibilities. One federalist referred to the decision as 'a shipwreck of Titanic proportions' (Craven 2006b).

The High Court has largely determined its own role in the Australian political system. While the Court has undergone a number of phases where its direction has changed or been less pronounced (such as the shift in 1920 in the way that the Constitution is interpreted), a number of trends are now clear. The Court's role of judicial review of parliamentary powers is clear, with the role as an arbiter of federal versus state powers unambiguously favouring the former. The Court's role in protecting the independence of the judiciary is also clear. More ambiguous has been judicial review of the decisions of the executive, in which the Constitution gives the Court little basis to act (Gelber 2006, p. 439). Since the composition of the seven-member High Court can affect the direction of the country so much, it is important to discuss the method of appointment of the justices.

The selection of High Court justices

As we can see from the way that High Court decisions affect the distribution of power in Australia, the Court is a political as well as a judicial institution. High Court justices can sit on the court for decades. They face no formal periodic review of their performance, and no process of reappointment until their retirement. Since there are only seven justices, the decision-making approach of just one new appointee can change the complexion of the Court. The appointment of a High Court judge is thus one of immense importance. The current process for selecting those judges hardly reflects that importance. High Court justices are appointed by politicians who by their nature are in a constant struggle for partisan advantage. In the United States, the Senate processes of investigating and voting on appointments to the Supreme Court lays bare the political role of the judiciary. Indeed, the type of judges candidates propose to appoint to the Supreme Court is frequently a matter of debate in presidential elections.

In Australia, a facade of legalism surrounds the appointment of High Court judges. The Governor-General appoints justices on the recommendation of the Attorney-General (who acts on behalf of cabinet). Like almost all of the operation of the executive in our system of responsible government, much is left to convention and is therefore liable to change. Since 1979, the Attorney-General has been required by law to consult state Attorney's-General. In practice, the prime minister—as on all matters—has the greatest say. Naturally, governments prefer to appoint judges of similar ideological complexion to their own. In all likelihood, a judge appointed by a politician will be on the bench long after the politician has left the scene. Yet, rarely has the appointment of High Court judges been raised as an election issue in Australia. Nobody doubts that the appointment of justices should be made on the basis of merit. It is the precise meaning of merit that inevitably sparks debate (Spigelman 2007, p. 15). Experience in practising law is essential—whether as barrister, judge or government solicitor. The *High Court of Australia Act 1979* requires only that appointees have practised law for five years.

The most controversial appointments to the Court are inevitably those of serving or former politicians. A number of government ministers have gone on to become High Court justices. In the case of H.V. Evatt, a ministerial career in the Curtin and Chifley Governments followed his time on the Court. Appointed to the Court in 1930 aged only 36, Evatt remains the youngest appointee. One of the most controversial episodes of alleged politicisation of the High Court came during the constitutional crisis in 1975. The Governor-General consulted Chief Justice Garfield Barwick (1964–81), a former cabinet minister in the Menzies Government, about the crisis. Barwick arguably became a participant in a matter on which he may have subsequently been required to rule as a High Court justice. While there is no reason why politicians experienced in law-making are not suitable for appointment, such candidates inevitably raise the prospect of partisan decision-making. An appointment process with more public input would, for good or ill, probably prevent a politician being appointed to the High Court. Fear of public opprobrium at the appointment of a politician to the bench has in any case prevented such an appointment since the Whitlam Government appointed one of its ministers, Lionel Murphy, to the Court in 1975. The controversy over Murphy seems to have chastened subsequent governments, since no politician has been appointed to the High Court since (Ward & Stewart 2006, p. 43). While some of the appointments of the Howard Government to federal courts caused controversy owing to the appointees' lack of legal (as opposed to political) qualifications, these appointments gain much less attention than appointments to the High Court. Perhaps more troubling, given the secrecy of the appointment process, is not the prospect of a politician serving on the bench but the selection of a lesser known figure with some sort of partisan allegiance. A more transparent appointment process would reduce the prospect of such partisan appointments.

BOX 7.2   A diverse institution?

The overwhelming majority of High Court justices have been men. The notion of diversity where High Court justices are concerned is inevitably constrained. The expectation of the highest order of legal qualifications and experience (or, where applicable, the right political connections) rules out Australians from most walks of life from ever qualifying for the job. While the Constitution does not require an appointee to be a lawyer, non-lawyers have not been and are unlikely to find themselves on the bench. The values of High Court judges are the values of an elite group of highly educated and wealthy Australians.

Geographic diversity has been one important consideration of governments, although South Australia is yet to be represented on the bench. The appointment by the Howard Government of Susan Kiefel in August 2007 had much to do with the fact that she was from Queensland. With the northern state expected to play a key strategic role in the 2007 election, the replacement of one Queenslander, the retiring Ian Callinan, with another, Kiefel, was a logical step. The Government also won plaudits for appointing Justice Kiefel as only the third woman to the Court. Attorney-General Philip Ruddock was careful to claim that gender played no role in Kiefel's appointment. Others, however, welcomed the appointment on precisely that basis.

Q How important is the gender or ethnicity of High Court justices? If judges are expected to incorporate the values of society into their legal reasoning, which values have historically been dominant among Australia's judicial appointees?

ISSUE IN FOCUS

HOW SHOULD HIGH COURT JUDGES INTERPRET THE LAW?

Originalism, legalism or activism?

The 1990s saw heated public debate surrounding the role of the High Court in Australia. At stake were some of the most important political ideas outlined in this book, such as the separation of powers between the executive, legislature and judiciary. Decisions of the Court upset governments, lobby groups and business interests. One commentator likened the High Court's decisions to a *coup d'état* (McGuinness 1992). When the Court makes a new interpretation of common law that is not to the Parliament's liking, that interpretation can be overturned through legislation. Not so for constitutional decisions, which would require a change to the text of the Constitution in order to be overturned, and such changes have been historically difficult for Australian governments to achieve. While the High Court has attracted less public controversy of late, the legal and political debates surrounding its role continue.

Since 1920, when the Court ruled that the intent of the founding fathers to preserve the principle of federalism carried no weight in the interpretation of the written Constitution, legalism (sometimes called literalism) has been the dominant approach of the Court.

Coup d'état: the overthrow of a government by a small group

Legalism: the principle that legal statutes and the constitution must be interpreted as they are read rather than according to the intentions of the authors

Former Chief Justice Sir Own Dixon argued for a 'strict and complete legalism' (cited in Patapan 2006, p. 62). This style of judicial interpretation leads to a view of the judge's role as a technical one, applying the facts of a case, however complex, to the relevant statute. Supporters of legalism argue that it removes the courts from political controversy, since the values of judges are not influencing decisions. Whatever the merits of this argument, the legalistic decisions of Australian courts have not been without public controversy.

Legalism was at its height in the 1970s, when the Court under Chief Justice Garfield Barwick handed down a series of decisions on income tax law that provided headaches for successive Australian governments. Barwick argued that 'the citizen is bound to pay no more tax than the statute requires him to pay according to the relevant state of his affairs' (1996, p. 229). This legalistic approach prevented the Australian Taxation Office and the lower courts from enforcing taxation law according to the intent of the Parliament. The Barwick Court's legalism forced the Parliament to continually rewrite taxation laws to prevent income tax avoidance, which in turn had the effect of making taxation legislation horribly complex. Barwick's former role as a cabinet minister in a Coalition Government hardly reduced the political tensions surrounding his leadership of the High Court.

While legalism replaced **originalism** as the dominant approach of the High Court in 1920, the concept itself has not died. Supporters of originalism argue that the constitution itself, and the High Court in particular, were designed to protect federalism. In his dissenting judgment in the *WorkChoices case*, Justice Ian Callinan cited the arguments of the founding fathers, such as Alfred Deakin and Edmund Barton, in their debates prior to Federation about the Commonwealth Constitution, in support of his finding against the Howard Government's industrial relations laws. 'The founders never intended the Constitution to confer any intrastate industrial power upon the Commonwealth,' he wrote. The majority of justices disputed Callinan's originalist view: 'To pursue the identification of what is said to be the framers' intention, much more often than not, is to pursue a mirage.'

Originalism: a form of legal interpretation that attempts to take into account the intention of those who wrote the law or constitution in question

The main argument against originalism is that the interpretation of the constitution must change as community values change. Australia is a vastly different place now than it was when the Constitution was first ratified by the people. The original intentions of the authors of the Constitution should not get in the way of the smooth operation of our modern political institutions. While this approach seems democratic, allowing for the changing views of the community to be incorporated into the law, the Australian people have rejected at referendum most attempts to change the text of the Constitution. Is it the business of judges to give contemporary relevance to the Constitution when the people have not seen fit to change it? Further, the ability of judges, well-paid and well-educated members of the governing class, to give voice to community attitudes must be questioned. Nevertheless, originalism has long since ceased to be the dominant method of interpreting the Australian Constitution.

The eclipse of originalism as an approach to legal interpretation does not end the debate over the role of judges. The words of a written document can be interpreted in any number of ways. While legal language is designed to be precise, legislation is often the result of compromise and bargaining, leading to ambiguous or hastily drafted clauses. The meaning of words can change over the years. A strict application of legalism could thus lead perfectly logically to different decisions in different social eras. **Activism** (sometimes called realism) is a term (often applied pejoratively) to the argument that legalism is an inadequate guide to jurisprudence, since judges inevitable apply some set of values to their interpretation of the meaning of legislation or the constitution. This sometimes requires an understanding of the original intent of legislation, even though those promoting activism and those promoting originalism often have very different political values. In one of the landmark decisions of the 1990s, Justice Anthony Mason pointed out that the explicit rejection of a bill of rights by the framers of the Australian Constitution limited the extent to which he would be prepared to find implied rights in the Constitution (Solomon 1999, p. 45).

> **Activism:** the legal reasoning by which contemporary social values are applied to the law

There are any number of differences, then, over the task of judicial interpretation, and more nuanced positions than it is possible to do justice to in this book. One of the most clear-cut differences between legalists and activists is whether courts interpret the law or, on occasion, make the law. Activist judges readily concede that making the law is at times an important function of the judiciary. According to this view, the nature of a law is only finally revealed when it is interpreted by judges. The Court was at its most adventurous in this regard under the leadership of Chief Justice Anthony Mason (1987–95). This 'new politics' of the Court (Patapan 2000b) was not simply a matter of different theories of legal interpretation. It raised much wider questions about our system of government. Where does the prospect of judges making law fit in the concept of a separation of powers? If the courts are to play a more important role in the country's direction, should judges be more accountable to the people? These matters were debated extensively during the 1990s. As is often the case in Australia, the result was not a change to the formal political institutions but an accommodation by the Court itself, modifying the extent of some its most controversial rulings (see Box 7.4).

BOX 7.3   Key decisions: common law

As well as dealing with constitutional cases, the High Court is the final court of appeal in Australia for decisions based on the common law. Such cases were among the most controversial during the 1990s.

Native title: *Mabo v. Queensland* (*No. 2*) (1992) 175 CLR 1 and *Wik Peoples v. Queensland* (1996) 187 CLR 1

The *Mabo case* overturned the long-held principle of *terra nullius*—literally 'empty land'. *Terra nullius* was a legal fiction, holding that Australia had no legal system of land management prior to European settlement. In the *Wik case* the High Court found that pastoral leases did not extinguish native title, widening considerably the amount of land otherwise subject to claim. Both decisions sparked public controversy and in 1993 and 1998 the Commonwealth Parliament passed laws on native title. On the latter occasion, the law overturned the findings of the Court that had been most supportive of Indigenous land rights.

Right to a fair trial: *Dietrich v. The Queen* (1992) 177 CLR 292

A man charged in Victoria with drug trafficking was unable to pay for his defence, but his trial went ahead, as had often been the case in Australian courts, and Dietrich was convicted and sentenced. A majority of the High Court ordered a new trial, finding that Dietrich had been denied a fair trial. Two of the justices also referred to the separation of powers, denying the right of the legislature to define the functions of the judiciary.

After his appointment as Chief Justice in 1998, Murray Gleeson advocated legalism as the basis of deliberation, while conceding that statutes were always open to interpretation (Patapan 2001). By that point, the Court had consolidated, rather than expanded, its earlier decisions. Meanwhile, advocates of 'deep-lying rights', such as Justice Michael Kirby (2004), also looked to international human rights instruments to find a legal foundation for rights protection. According to such an interpretation, the Constitution is not simply a legal document but a contract between the Australian people and their government. Kirby, appointed by the Keating Labor Government, was during his tenure invariably in the minority of a Court appointed predominantly by the conservative Howard Government.

Until the 1990s, the practice of legalism kept public debate over the political role of the High Court to a minimum. Yet, at the same time legalism arguably played an overtly political role, albeit a conservative one. The legalism of the High Court was traditionally a greater hindrance to Labor governments than those of a conservative stripe (see Galligan 1987). While not all the decisions of the High Court during the 1990s suited the Labor Party (it was Hawke Government legislation that was struck down in the name of free speech in 1992), the direction of the Court in its activist phase has undoubtedly been progressive, favouring human rights and placing limits on executive and legislative action.

What these different approaches to judicial interpretation have in common is that they all see the role of the Court through a legal framework, even though they differ over the method and scope of interpretation open to judges. Craven, on the other hand, argues that understanding judicial activism requires a political approach to the role of the Court—an understanding that High Court judges exercise power and the Court has garnered a powerful role for itself within the political system. The swings in judicial interpretation between legalism and activism underline the political nature of the Court. Craven points out that the nature of High Court cases brings the Court into the centre stage of partisan political debate, a different atmosphere than judges and lawyers are used to (Craven 1999, p. 220).

BOX 7.4   Key decisions: implied rights

Implied right of free speech: *Australian Capital Television Pty Ltd & New South Wales v. The Commonwealth* (1992) 177 CLR 106

The Hawke Government's attempt to ban advertising by political parties was struck down on the basis that the freedom of political communication was fundamental to Australia's system of representative government. The extent of this freedom was later clarified by the Court in later cases. In *Theophanous v. Herald and Weekly Times* (1994) the Court held that the implied right to freedom of communication extended to **defamation law**, normally a state matter. However, in *Lange v. Australian Broadcasting Corporation* (1997), the Court sought to strike a balance between freedom of communication and the ability of the legislature to pass laws aimed at protecting reputation.

> **Defamation law:** defamation is the false or unjustified injury to one's reputation

Limits on democratic rights: *McGinty v. Western Australia* (1996) 186 CLR 140

The Court ruled against a challenge by the state Labor opposition to the malapportionment of Western Australian electorates. The plaintiffs argued that malapportionment infringed the principle of democratic equality implicit in the Constitution. The Court has held, then, that the implied rights stemming from the democratic nature of the Constitution are quite limited.

While the legal fraternity has been debating these principles for centuries, the debate sometimes captures the attention of the public, usually after decisions that affect large numbers of Australians. The High Court decisions on *Mabo* and *Wik* during the 1990s (see Box 7.3) sparked controversy among farmers and miners concerned about the security of their land leases. Native title is an old concept in the common law but the High Court had long accepted the principle of *terra nullius*—that for legal purposes Australia was unoccupied before European settlement. The Court's change of direction on this issue followed some years where the Parliament dithered over the issue of Indigenous land rights. The justices in the 6–1 majority in the *Mabo case* were frank in their application of changing attitudes to the status of Aboriginal people in Australian society as one of the reasons for their decision. Of course, the anger with which the decision was met in some quarters indicates that this change of heart was not universal. Yet, even the finding in the *Wik case* that the rights of pastoralists prevail in the event of a clash with the rights of native title-holders did not prevent a noisy public backlash against the decision. The premier of Queensland, Rob Borbidge, declared the Court 'an embarrassment' (Patapan 2000b, p. 167). Prime Minister Howard argued that the Court was making the law instead of interpreting it (Brennan 1998). Both cases were followed by Commonwealth legislation responding to the Court's finding. The Howard Government's legislation in response to the *Wik* decision limited the opportunities for Aboriginal groups to be granted native title—a reminder that the Parliament has the final say on non-constitutional matters.

The debate over the supposed politicisation of the judiciary often ignores the fact that conservative decisions are not apolitical. They stem from a view of society and the place of the judiciary within it as surely as do many of the more radical decisions of recent decades. Deputy Prime Minister Tim Fischer responded to the *Wik* decision (see Box 7.3) by calling for the appointment of judges who would be 'conservative with a capital C' (cited in Patapan 2000b, p. 38). Just what it means to be a conservative judge, however, is not as obvious as it must have seemed to Mr Fischer. Conservatives disagree over whether legalism or originalism is the correct way to interpret the Constitution. Where federalism is concerned, these two approaches can take High Court justices in opposite directions. Most of the Howard Government's appointees to the Court took a more legalistic approach to their jobs than either Callinan or the appointees of the Fraser and Hawke Governments, who delivered the more activist decisions of the 1990s. While the Court has attracted less public attention as a result, decisions such as those over WorkChoices will have far-reaching consequences. Just because a decision of the Court is predictable does not make it unimportant.

The debate between legalists and activists should not be portrayed as a simple Left–Right divide. Critics of the Court's decisions on federalism, such as Craven, usually come from a liberal or conservative position. Yet, Justice Kirby argued that the majority view in the *WorkChoices case* would leave a 'profound weakness in the legal checks and balances which the founders sought to provide to the Australian Commonwealth'. Kirby was not relying on legalistic reasoning, but was making a conservative argument about the nature of the Australian political system. Equally, the terms of the debate should not be set by those on either extreme. As Chief Justice Mason has pointed out, the requirement that judges look beyond the text of a statute in order to interpret its meaning is centuries old. Constitutions, by their nature, are designed to be flexible enough to deal with political and social circumstances undreamed of by the founders (Mason 1995, p. 239). That is, the democratic nature of our Constitution has implications for the way that the Court interprets it, but those implications are not necessarily those that were in the minds of the men who wrote it.

Should we place limits on political criticism of the courts?

One reason for the changing public perceptions of the role of the Court is the changing nature of the cases brought before it. With the number of criminal cases appealed before the court having been reduced in recent decades, justices find themselves dealing with a higher proportion of constitutional and other cases of a ground-breaking nature. The Courts are more likely today to be a forum for social and political activism than was the case for much of the twentieth century (Gleeson 1997). High Court cases are expensive to mount, and have historically been the preserve of governments, big business and well-funded lobby groups. More recently, public advocacy groups have taken, for example, cases of refugee determination before the Court on behalf of appellants who could not ordinarily afford to fund their own appeals. This is a reminder of the political nature of the court system.

The intemperate reaction to some High Court decisions has led to calls for the Court to be protected from the worst excesses of the criticism directed at it. One of the most troubling episodes of criticism of a High Court judge involved not a decision of the Court but allegations of impropriety directed under parliamentary privilege at Justice Michael Kirby in 2002. The claims by Liberal Senator Bill Heffernan were quickly discredited and Heffernan apologised to Kirby and to the Parliament and was forced to resign his position as a parliamentary secretary, but not before many observers expressed their concerns about the motives for the attack and the public standing of the Court (Patapan 2006, p. 171). While not defending the more outlandish criticism of individual justices, Craven argues that it is the 'solemn duty' of legal observers to criticise the Court when that criticism is warranted (Craven 1999, p. 217). The role of public defender of the independence of the judiciary has historically belonged to the Attorney-General. Judges have been reluctant to comment publicly on cases so that they are seen to be impartial. Then-Attorney-General Daryl Williams announced during the first term of the Howard Government that he would no longer speak for the Court due to the possible conflict of interest with his role as a member of the executive government (Patapan 2000b, p. 168).

Those who argue that the Attorney-General should play a role in defending the Court from public criticism often express a concern for the independence of our judicial institutions. Yet, there is little evidence that criticism of decisions represents a threat to judicial independence. Indeed, the volume of criticism of the Court from Commonwealth ministers and state premiers underlines their frustration at their inability to influence the decisions of the Court. Robust public debate is to be expected given the political nature of the High Court. Indeed, the justices themselves are often in furious (if inevitably polite) disagreement. In his dissent in *Thomas v. Mowbray* (2007) (see above), Justice Michael Kirby argued that Australians will 'look back with regret and embarrassment' at the ruling of the majority (cited in Saul 2007, p. 10). Much is at stake in decisions of the Court. Robust debate over their deliberations is to be expected in a democratic society.

Public confidence in the courts is another matter. Criticism of High Court decisions, in concert with fierce debate over the alleged leniency of lower courts on criminal matters, has dented public confidence in the legal system (Bean 2003, p. 130). Naturally, criticism of the High Court runs the risk of undermining public confidence in that institution but, by the same token, so does any effort to limit public debate on inherently controversial issues. As the Court itself has found, freedom of political communication is essential to the working of a liberal democracy. The solution to the problem of vitriolic debate over High Court decisions, if it is indeed a problem, may lie in more effective communication of Court decisions. To this end, the High Court employs a public relations officer and its decisions are easily available on the internet (Patapan 2006, p. 171). In a similar vein, Justice Kirby, a regular dissenter from the majority, consistently made speeches throughout his tenure outlining his judicial philosophy. Suffering criticism may simply be the price that the judiciary must pay for its independence. Blunting that criticism with counter-arguments may be the most effective response.

CHAPTER SUMMARY

The High Court is the arbiter of disputes over the nature of the Australian Constitution. While structured as a judicial body, the role of the Court inevitably leads it to the centre of political debate. The High Court has two major functions: it is the final court of appeal for matters of federal and state law, and the common law; and it adjudicates on matters of dispute pertaining to Australia's Constitution, in particular the division of powers between state and federal governments. It is the latter role that has for most of its history underlined the political nature of the Court. The legalistic reading of the Constitution since 1920 has tipped the balance of power in the federation firmly in the direction of the Commonwealth.

More recently, controversial common law decisions and a move away from a strictly legalistic reading of the Constitution have embroiled the Court in new controversies. There is no objective way of arbitrating between the legalistic and activist approaches to the law. They represent differing political as well as judicial philosophies. A democratic society settles such matters through the interplay of its political institutions. If Parliament doesn't like the common law decisions of the Court, it can change the law. If the people don't like the Court's rulings on the Constitution, they have the ultimate power to change that document. The sharply political role of the Court raises the question of judicial appointments, and whether the appointment and role of High Court justices should be more extensively publicly debated. The Howard years showed that a government with some longevity and a determination to alter the tenor of the Court can ultimately influence High Court decisions.

WEBSITES

High Court of Australia:
www.hcourt.gov.au
The High Court's website provides information about the role of the Court and its justices, including speeches on matters such as judicial interpretation.

AustLII:
http://www.austlii.edu.au/au/cases/cth/HCA/
The AustLII database of High Court decisions provides access to the reasoning behind the decisions of the Court as well as dissenting opinions.

Samuel Griffith Society:
http://www.samuelgriffith.org.au/
The Samuel Griffith Society is a conservative organisation dedicated to federalist principles.

FURTHER READING

Galligan, B. 1987. *The Politics of the High Court*. University of Queensland Press, Brisbane.

Patapan, H. 2000. *Judging Democracy: The New Politics of the High Court of Australia*. Cambridge University Press, Melbourne.

The Importance of Electoral Systems

THIS CHAPTER:

★ describes the various elements of the different electoral systems used in Australia
★ outlines the circumstances that gave rise to the Australian electoral system
★ explains the Australian electoral system and its strengths and weaknesses.

ISSUE IN FOCUS

Should preferential voting be replaced by a system of proportional voting in the House of Representatives?

KEY TERMS

Australian Electoral
   Commission (AEC)
Cleavage
Competitive elections

Electoral roll
First Past the Post (FPP)
Half Senate election
How-to-vote card
Issue of the writ

Party system
Private members bill
Prorogue
Threshold
Universal suffrage/franchise

Every three years, Australian citizens aged 18 years or older are required to make their way to one of the thousands of electoral stations set up around the nation to choose their federal parliamentary representatives. Strangely, Australians have no constitutionally guaranteed right to vote but are forced to do so under law. Compulsory voting has been a feature of federal elections since 1924 and Australia is one of a handful of Western nations that persist with enforcement.

Private members bill: a proposed new law that is introduced to the Parliament by a person other than a government minister

It seems counterintuitive that in a democracy it is acceptable to force people to participate in the democratic process. Although compulsory voting was introduced at the federal level as a **private members bill**, the initiative had bipartisan support. It was implemented in response to concerns about declining levels of voter turnout on election day. The major political groupings recognised that mandatory voting would greatly reduce the costs associated with campaigning. Parties would no longer have to expend their energies on convincing people to turn out to vote but only on encouraging electors to vote for their party. To this day, compulsory voting remains an unchallenged canon of the Australian electoral system.

This brief history of the introduction of compulsory voting for federal elections tells us something about the importance of elections, if only that political interest plays a key role in shaping the rules of the electoral game. Even in advanced liberal democracies, the political elite are tempted to interfere with the electoral process, although they typically do so using available legal avenues. Australia's electoral history is replete with examples of where the short-term interests of a particular party have been prioritised above democratic values. While many of the electoral reforms introduced to Australia have been justified on democratic principles, the reality is that more often than not they have directly assisted the government that has initiated the change and the major opposition party that supported the passage of the proposal in the Parliament. Nonetheless, there are often unintended consequences of tampering with the electoral system. As Graham states, 'parties rarely obtain voting methods entirely appropriate to their needs, for they generally lack the combination of experience and foresight necessary to assess correctly their own situation, and further, to make predictions on the basis of such an assessment' (1968, p. 219). There is always the distinct possibility that the electoral system may eventually bite the hand of those who contrive to bend laws for narrow partisan gain.

In this chapter we will examine the importance of electoral systems and explore some of the key elements that make up any system, including the distortions that these elements can sometimes generate. In the Issue in Focus we will consider the suitability of the preferential voting system used to elect the House of Representatives and pose the question: is a system of proportional representation more appropriate in the modern age?

What are electoral systems and why are they important?

Elections are 'fundamentally important components of a democratic political system' (Jaensch 1995, p. 2), although this was not always the case. Nationwide elections based on **universal suffrage** or **franchise** are a relatively recent invention and are intimately linked to the appearance of representative institutions in the nineteenth century (Harrop & Miller 1987, p. 7). Elections emerged as something of a necessity following the birth of the modern liberal-democratic state. Since it was impractical to implement a system of direct democracy whereby all citizens would participate directly in public decision-making, the modern solution was to set up a process that would allow citizens to select representatives to act for them in the nation's most important deliberative institutions. In liberal representative democracies this

Universal suffrage/ franchise: a guarantee of the right of all adult citizens to vote

Competitive elections:
where the election
outcome is not pre-
determined and the
final result influences
the composition of the
legislative body

is achieved through a system of episodic and **competitive elections** in which citizens are called upon to choose those who will represent their interests in parliament. However, it would be a mistake to think that elections are only about choice and freedom. Elections are also about constraint and control (Harrop & Miller 1987, p. 1). Elections are not simply a mechanism for facilitating representation but they are also an instrument to hold elected representatives accountable. Elections enable the public to reward those who they believe have served them well and to cast from office those who have failed to live up to the electorate's expectations.

While voters in liberal democracies are ultimately free to choose their elected members, they have very little input into the rules that shape and regulate the activities associated with elections. These rules, known collectively as an electoral system, are important because they translate the will of the people into members of a legislative body, thereby determining which party or parties will govern. More importantly, perhaps, the electoral system influences and shapes how the political system will function on a number of different levels:

- the quality, levels and frequency of citizen participation and involvement in the electoral process
- the conditions under which parties and individuals compete
- how parties organise, campaign and even interact with one another (including the composition of the party system)
- who wins and who loses, including government formation
- the public's perception about the legitimacy of the political system.

It should come as no surprise that electoral system design is the subject of discussion and disagreement among the nation's political elite.

An electoral system is a bundle of processes, laws and formulae that serve to translate votes into seats and to determine which party or coalition will form government. How any particular system operates is influenced by the different variables that make up the system, as well as the interactions between the variables of which it is composed. There are four variables that are especially important in influencing the dynamic that an electoral system produces: the electoral formulae; the ballot structure; the district magnitude; and the laws and regulations that shape the context in which elections are held.

Electoral formulae

The electoral formulae refer to the mathematics used to convert votes into actual representation in Parliament. As Rae states, the electoral formula 'interprets' voting returns 'as the basis for the legitimate distribution of parliamentary seats among the competing parties' (1967, p. 22). There are three broad families of electoral system or formulae, each of which generates quite a deliberate tendency in terms of the electoral **threshold** it generates: plurality, majoritarian and proportional systems (see Table 8.1).

Plurality formulae (or systems) award the seat to the person who wins the most number of votes in absolute terms. The threshold in this case is the attainment of more votes than any other candidate. Basically, the candidate who wins the most votes claims the seat. One of the key strengths of plurality formulae is that the basic mechanics of these systems are easy for the voter to comprehend. Some scholars argue that it is important that voters understand the actual counting arrangements so that they are able to cast their vote to best effect (Newman & Bennett 2006, p. 3). Plurality systems are used in some of the largest democracies in the world, with a high uptake rate among former British colonies. While they are not necessarily the most utilised electoral formulae on a nation by nation basis, they are 'used by a plurality of the world's voters' (Farrell 2001, p. 7). Examples of plurality formulae include **First Past the Post (FPP)**, which is used for elections of the British House of Commons, and the Cumulative Vote, which is used in the Norfolk Islands.

> **Threshold:** the minimum percentage of the vote that is required to win a seat
>
> **First Past the Post (FPP):** an electoral formula in which the candidate with the highest number of first preference votes is elected

Majoritarian systems are a cluster of formulae that require the winning candidate to obtain an absolute majority of the vote. That is, in order to claim victory the candidate must have achieved more than 50 per cent of all votes cast. While majoritarian systems have much in common with plurality systems, they are designed to ameliorate some of the less desirable effects found in the latter. Like plurality systems, majoritarian systems operate on a fairly straightforward premise, aiming to ensure that the candidate who wins the most votes wins the seat. However, these systems seek to improve the legitimacy of the outcome by ensuring that the winning candidate can claim to have secured the support of more than half of the electorate, or 50.1 per cent of the vote. Examples of majoritarian electoral formulae are preferential voting (known outside of Australia as the Alternative Vote), which has wide usage at Australian lower house elections, and the Two-Ballot, used for presidential elections in France.

Proportional systems are designed to encourage quite a different set of outcomes from those of the other two formula. Proportional systems were developed in direct response to some of the shortcomings that had been identified in the plurality and majoritarian voting systems. Proportional systems have been constructed to ensure that seats are awarded roughly in proportion to the popular vote received. In theory, if a party receives 20 per cent of the vote, then they are allocated 20 per cent of the seats in the legislature. According to Hague and Harrop, proportional systems are the most pervasive and they have emerged as the preferred method in most new democracies since the 1920s (2004, p. 150). While there are a 'bewildering number of proportional systems', they can be grouped into two basic categories: List Systems and the Single Transferable Vote (STV) (Newman & Bennett 2006, p. 15).

Table 8.1   Three major families of electoral system and their variants

Electoral system	Variants of system formulae
Plurality: The seat is awarded to the candidate who wins more votes than any other candidate.	*First Past the Post:* Single-member electoral districts in which the leading candidate is elected. Used in Canada, the UK and the USA.
	Single Transferable Vote: Multi-member electoral districts in which the candidates with the highest number of votes are elected. Each elector has one only vote to award to candidates listed on the ballot paper. Used in Japan.
	Cumulative Vote: Multi-member electoral districts in which the candidates with the highest number of votes are elected. Each elector has as many votes as there are candidates to be elected. For example, if there are ten vacancies to be filled, each voter has ten votes. However, should they so choose, voters can allocate all of their vote entitlement to one of the candidates. Used in the Norfolk Islands.
Majoritarian: The seat is awarded to the candidate who obtains an absolute majority of the vote.	*Preferential Vote* (*Alternative Vote*): If no candidate obtains an absolute majority of the vote, low-scoring candidates are eliminated and their votes are redistributed to remaining candidates. Used in Australia.
	Two-Ballot Systems: If no candidate wins an absolute majority on the first ballot, a second election takes place between the top two scoring candidates. Used in presidential elections in France.
Proportional: Seats are awarded in proportion to votes received. There are four common methods used to calculate quotas: *Hare:* valid votes/number of vacancies *Hagenbach–Bischoff:* valid votes/number of vacancies + 1 *Droop:* valid votes/number of vacancies + 1 (+1) *Imperali:* valid votes/number of vacancies + 2	*List System* (*Largest Remainder*): Voters are presented with lists, which are compiled by parties. Quotas are mostly calculated using the Hare method. Following the allocation of full preferences, remaining seats are allocated on the basis of the largest number of remaining votes.
	List System (*Highest Average*): Voters are presented with lists, which are compiled by parties. A quota may or may not be used although typically where it is, the quota is calculated using the Hagenbach–Bischoff method. Each party's votes are divided by a series of divisors to produce an average vote. Different divisors are used (e.g. the d'Hondt system uses 1, 2, 3, 4 etc. as divisors). The party with the highest average vote after each stage wins a seat and its vote is then divided by the next divisor.
	Single Transferable vote: Voters vote for candidates by rank, ordering the candidates on the ballot according to their preference. To be elected, a candidate must achieve a quota of first preference votes. Any of the methods for calculating the quota can be used, such as the Droop or the Hare methods. A candidate who does not meet the threshold is excluded. When a candidate is excluded, or if an elected candidate has a surplus of first preference votes, voter preferences are then re-allocated among other candidates.

Sources: Hague & Harrop 2004, p. 148; Newman & Bennett 2006

The electoral formula is important because it determines the threshold that candidates must attain in order to claim a seat. Among other things, this has implications for the structure and composition of the **party system**. While it is thought that all electoral formulae assist bigger parties, plurality and majoritarian systems are believed to foster a two-party–dominant system by favouring stronger parties at the expense of weaker ones (Rae 1967, p. 137). The high thresholds associated with majoritarian and plurality formulae can have the effect of over-representing the major parties and freezing out minor parties, particularly those whose voter support is geographically diffuse. This, in turn, is thought to set up a 'psychological' reticence both on the part of voters and political elites to support smaller parties. Voters are potentially averse to casting a vote for a party that they do not believe will win, while elites are unlikely to invest time or energy into the creation of a new party vehicle that they believe is unlikely to succeed. In contrast, proportional systems are much more conducive to multi-partism and small party electoral success due to the lower thresholds they impose (Lijphart 1999, p. 165). Thus the choice of electoral system can have a bearing on the number of political parties that a party system will yield.

> **Party system:** refers to the interrelationship between parties within a polity and the manner in which they co-exist

Table 8.2 gives an overview of the variety of electoral systems found in the Australian Commonwealth, and its states and territories.

Table 8.2   The electoral systems of the nine Australian jurisdictions

Jurisdiction	Voting system		
		Lower House	Upper House
Commonwealth *Commonwealth Electoral Act 1918, Commonwealth Referendum (Machinery Provisions) Act 1984, Representation Act 1983 & Commonwealth of Australia Constitution Act*	Term	3 years	6 years
	Members	150, single-member electoral districts	76, elected from 6 states and 2 territories
	Electoral	Alternative vote (full preferential)	PR-STV (full preferential)
New South Wales *Constitution Act 1902, Parliamentary Electorates & Elections Act 1912 & Election Funding & Disclosures Act 1981*	Term	4 years fixed	8 years
	Members	93, single-member electoral districts	42, single state-wide electoral district
	Formula	Alternative vote (optional preferential)	PR (optional preferential)
Victoria *Electoral Act 2002, Electoral Boundaries Commission Act 1982 & Constitution Act 1975*	Term	4 years fixed	4 years fixed
	Members	88, single-member electoral districts	40, elected from 8 regions
	Formula	Alternative vote (full preferential)	PR-STV (partial preferential)

Table 8.2 *(cont.)*

Jurisdiction	Voting system		
		Lower House	**Upper House**
Queensland *Electoral Act 1992*	Term	3 years	*not applicable*
	Members	89, single-member electoral districts	
	Formula	Alternative vote (optional preferential)	
Western Australia *Election of Senators Act 1903, Electoral Act 1907 & Electoral Distribution Act 1947*	Term	4 years	4 years fixed
	Members	59, single-member electoral districts	36, from 6 regions
	Formula	Alternative vote (full preferential)	PR-STV (full preferential)
South Australia *Electoral Act 1985*	Term	4 years fixed	8 years
	Members	47, single-member electoral districts	22, single state-wide electoral district
	Formula	Alternative vote (full preferential)	PR-STU (full preferential)
Tasmania *Constitutional Act 1934, Electoral Act 2004, Electoral (Registered Parties) Act 1995, Legislative Council (Electoral Boundaries) Act 1995 & Referendum Procedures Act 2004*	Term	4 years	6 years
	Members	25, elected from 5 regions	15, single-member electoral districts
	Formula	PR Hare–Clarke (partial preferential)	Alternative vote (partial preferential)
Northern Territory *Electoral Act 2004*	Term	4 years	*not applicable*
	Members	25, single-member electoral districts	
	Formula	Alternative vote (full preferential)	
Australian Capital Territory *Australian Capital Territory Electoral Act 1992 & Referendum (Machinery Provisions) Act 1994*	Term	4 years fixed	*not applicable*
	Members	17, elected from 3 regions	
	Formula	PR Hare–Clarke (optional preferential)	

Source: Electoral Council of Australia (http://www.eca.gov.au/index.htm)
& Australian Electoral Commission (http://www.aec.gov.au/index.htm)

Ballot structure

A second key element of an electoral system is ballot structure. This refers to the design and structure of the ballot paper that is presented to the voter on polling day. There is remarkable variation in ballot design. While all ballots require voters to 'choose among the contestants in some way … they vary in the kind of choice they demand' (Rae 1967, p. 16). Ballot structures can differ in terms of how many votes each elector is entitled to cast. Is the voter required to express a single preference or is the voter permitted to express preferences for multiple candidates? This is known as the difference between an *ordinal* and a *categorical* ballot structure. Categorical ballots require the elector to choose which party or candidate he or she most prefers without qualification or equivocation. In contrast, ordinal ballot structures allow the voter to 'express a more complex, equivocal preference by rank ordering the parties' (Rae 1967, p. 17).

While the requirements of a categorical ballot are fairly straightforward, ordinal ballot structures place additional demands on the voter on polling day. Where a voter is permitted more than one preference, they may be required to rank candidates in sequential, numerical preference. That is, voters may be compelled to compulsorily rank all the candidates listed on the ballot paper in their order of preference. In some cases, the voter may have full discretion to determine how many candidates listed on the ballot paper they will rank. Under these conditions, the allocation of preferences is optional, with the voter possessing the right to rank only those candidates they support. Some ordinal ballots allow the voter to allocate as many preferences as there are candidates or to allocate more than one preference to a single candidate up to a specified maximum. Further again, some ordinal ballots may deny the voter the ability to control the order in which candidates are elected and only permit them to choose between lists composed by the parties. Known as *closed list* systems, these ballots only enable the voter to select the party group but have no discretion to prioritise the candidate from the party list that they most prefer. In *open list* systems, there is the flexibility for the voter to rank a party's candidates in whatever order they choose, regardless of how the parties have ranked their candidates.

The ballot structure has an effect on many different aspects of the electoral environment, from influencing the level of control the party is able to exert over its candidates, to even shaping the relationship between the parties competing at elections. Consider, for example, the requirement that voters must compulsorily allocate all of their preferences to every candidate listed on the ballot paper. In Australia, this has had the effect of transforming voters' subsequent preferences into a form of electoral property that can be traded, swapped and exchanged between parties. At elections, parties enter into agreements with their opponents to swap preferences, which they do via offering to competitor parties a favourable position on a **how-to-vote card** distributed to voters on polling day. Sharman et al. (2002) explain that parties exchange preferences with other political groupings to achieve any number of ends, such as to bolster the party's own electoral hopes, in exchange for policy concessions, or merely to punish their opponents. This has encouraged parties to

> **How-to-vote card:** a pamphlet printed and distributed by parties to voters on polling day that outlines the order in which a party desires their supporters to rank the candidates listed on the ballot paper

enter into strategic partnership with parties with whom they are competing, thereby influencing the competitive dynamic at elections.

District magnitude

The third variable that plays an important role in shaping an electoral system is district magnitude, which refers to how many members or candidates will be returned in each electoral district. It is important not to confuse district magnitude with either the geographical size of the electorate or how many voters it contains (Lijphart 1999, p. 150). District magnitude takes one of two basic forms: either single-member, in which one member is returned, or multi-member electoral districts, in which two or more seats are assigned to the district.

District magnitude is a very important element of any electoral system and can have a startling impact on the outcome. The greater the district magnitude (that is, the greater the number of candidates to be returned from the one electoral region), the lower the quota that a candidate will require in order to gain election. Consider, for example, the effect of district magnitude on Preferential Voting (PV). If only one candidate is to be returned in an electoral district, the winning candidate must attain upwards of 50.1 per cent of the vote in order to win the seat. However, if three candidates are to be returned, they will each have to achieve a maximum of 33.3 per cent of the vote to secure election. Generally speaking, district magnitude and electoral thresholds 'can be seen as the two sides of the same coin' and have implications particularly for smaller and micro parties and their likelihood of electoral success (Lijphart 1999, pp. 150–1).

Electoral laws

The fourth factor that is critical to the operation of an electoral system is the set of laws and regulations that shapes the context and processes in which elections are conducted. In the context of this chapter, the term *electoral laws* is being used as a coverall, applying to those variables that have yet to be mentioned but which are important nonetheless. The *electoral laws* refers to the rules or to the machinery provisions of elections, such as: who is permitted to vote; which individuals or political organisations are entitled to compete (that is, who have ballot access); and who is charged with responsibility for the carriage of elections and how much freedom and independence they are accorded in this respect.

One of the ways in which the law can affect electoral outcomes is in relation to the accessibility of the franchise (see Orr 2004, pp. 5–16). In most advanced liberal-democratic states, the right to vote is a largely settled matter. The introduction of universal franchise to Australia, beginning in 1894, granted the right to vote to adult citizens (except for Aboriginal people, see comment below). Today, all citizens are eligible to vote provided they are 18 years of age; of sound mind; have not committed an act of treason against the state; or have served a prison term of three or more years.

However, small and seemingly innocuous changes to the laws can potentially have an impact on voter entitlements and, in subtle ways, the electoral outcome. For example, the Howard Coalition Government's decision to introduce early closure of the **electoral roll** in 2005 had an important indirect impact on voter eligibility. Prior to the new amendment, voters had a week after the **issue of the writ** to enrol to vote or update their enrolment details. However, the new reform effectively closed the election roll on the day the election was announced. The seven-day reprieve, under the old system, essentially gave voters a small window of opportunity to get their enrolment details in order, particularly first-time voters. Orr estimates that over 350000 enrolments are processed during this reprieve period (2004, p. 16). While the Howard Government claimed that the reform was necessary in order to preserve the integrity of the electoral roll, others strongly criticised the reform on the grounds that it would disenfranchise young voters. It has been suggested that the Howard Government's motive for introducing the initiative was because the cohort most likely to be affected by the reform (first-time voters) are less inclined to vote for conservative parties (Costar 2006, pp. 189–90).

> **Electoral roll:** a register compiled by the electoral authorities that lists the names of eligible persons who are registered to vote
>
> **Issue of the writ:** a document that commands an electoral officer to hold an election

The administration and oversight of elections is another important factor that can influence the outcome of an election. Are the bodies that are put in charge of elections independent and non-partisan and are they relatively well shielded from political interference? Hague and Harrop make the point that 'how the rules are applied is as important as the rules themselves' (2004, p. 41). It is important that elections are administered by a body that is nominally independent from those that have a vested interest in the outcome, particularly the government. Key tasks, such as the maintenance of the electoral roll, the drawing up of electoral boundaries and the counting of votes, should not be susceptible to corruption and should be free from any such taint. Over the years, the independence of many of Australia's electoral authorities has been strengthened by a significant measure. In 1983, the **Australian Electoral Commission (AEC)**, the federal electoral authority, was accorded the status of a statutory commission in order to insulate it from undue political interference from the government of the day. While there is 'the potential for the nibbling of the AEC's independence', Hughes asserts that the potential for overt partisan interference in its activities on a 'serious scale' is 'unlikely' due, in part, to the manner in which the organisation has been constituted (2003).

> **Australian Electoral Commission (AEC):** the federal statutory agency responsible for conducting federal elections and referendums and maintaining the Commonwealth electoral roll

Other regulations that shape an electoral outcome are the rules relating to ballot access. Almost all countries have imposed rules about who can and cannot stand for elections and the conditions under which electoral competition between opposing interests occurs. The rules pertaining to ballot access are important because they determine which persons are permitted to nominate and which parties are authorised to field candidates. It is very easy to exclude persons or parties based on the imposition of narrow residency requirements or onerous nomination thresholds (such as payment of a candidate deposit in order to stand) that may be beyond the reach of resource-poor individuals or parties to satisfy. (For a discussion on such matters in the Australian context, see Orr 2004.)

The Australian federal electoral system

The previous section has shown that an electoral system consists of many different elements, which in combination have an important impact on voter behaviour, electoral outcomes, and the number of parties competing at elections. Although some effects produced by an electoral system are intended, others are not. This section examines the Australian federal electoral system using the four electoral variables identified in the previous section.

The electoral formulae for federal elections

The electoral formulae used at federal elections for the House of Representatives and the Senate are different, principally because it is recognised that the two chambers perform different roles and, as a result, should be elected on a different basis. The electoral formula that has been adopted to elect each of the chambers is designed to ensure representation that is consistent with their different legislative responsibilities.

For elections of the House of Representatives, the electoral formula is known as preferential voting (PV), a system that Farrell and McAllister (2006, p. 52) describe as 'quintessentially' Australian. Under this system, a candidate must obtain 50 per cent + 1 of the formal vote in order to claim a seat. This means that if there are 85 000 formal votes cast, the winning candidate needs to win 42 501 votes, or 50.1 per cent. If none of the candidates achieves an absolute majority following the initial count, then a new round of counting is activated whereby the candidate with the smallest share of the first preference vote is eliminated and their votes redistributed to the remaining candidates, according to the second preferences indicated on the ballot papers of the excluded candidate. This procedure continues until one candidate has more than half of the total votes cast and is declared 'elected'. Box 8.1 provides a practical overview of how the votes are counted.

Senate elections are conducted using an electoral formula known as Proportional Representation using the Single Transferable Vote (PR-STV). The quota for election is obtained using the Droop Quota. The Droop Quota is calculated by dividing the

BOX 8.1   Counting votes for elections of the House of Representatives

Zara, Alex, Clancy and Sebastian nominate for the federal electorate of Fremantle. After the election, the ballot papers are counted and there are 70 000 formal votes. In order to win the seat, the winning candidate must obtain an absolute majority of the total number of formal votes, which is 35 001 (50 per cent + 1).

On completion of the first count of the votes, it becomes evident that none of the candidates has managed to gain an absolute majority of the vote. Because Zara has the lowest number of first preference votes, she is excluded. Zara's preferences are then distributed according to their second preference. These votes are then added to the existing votes of the three remaining candidates.

The distribution of Zara's preferences following the second count of the vote does not result in any of the three remaining candidates achieving an absolute majority. Clancy, who has the smallest number of votes of the remaining three candidates, is excluded and her ballot papers are examined for their subsequent preferences. Of Clancy's 16 000 ballot papers, 10 000 have listed Alex as their third preference, and 6000 have awarded their subsequent preference to Sebastian. These votes are then added to both Alex's and Sebastian's existing votes, which allows Alex to attain an absolute majority and to claim victory in the seat.

Candidates	1st count	2nd count	3rd count	4th count
Zara	11 000	Excluded −11 000	Excluded	Excluded
Sebastian	22 000	23 000 (+3 000)	29 000 (+6 000)	29 000
Clancy	12 000	16 000 (+4 000)	Excluded −16 000	Excluded
Alex	25 000	29 000 (+4 000)	39 000 (+10 000)	**Winner**

total number of eligible votes cast in a state by the number of vacancies plus one. As a general rule, the candidate needs to attain a quota of 14.3 per cent in a **half Senate election**. Candidates who receive a quota of first preference votes are elected immediately. If an elected candidate receives more than a quota, their surplus votes are transferred to second choice candidates. All of the elected candidates' votes are transferred but at a reduced value, that is, less than their full original value. If, following the redistribution of surplus votes from elected candidates, there are still some

Half Senate election: an election in which half of the total number of Senate seats are contested. This is the norm at most federal elections. In a full Senate election all 76 Senate seats are contested. A full Senate election is rare and only occurs in the event of a double dissolution when the Governor-General dissolves both house of the Parliament.

unfilled positions, further counting is undertaken. Starting with the lowest scoring candidate, unelected candidates are excluded from the count and their ballot papers are distributed to the remaining candidates to whom the voters have given their preferences. When a candidate gains a quota following the redistribution, he or she is elected. The above process continues until all Senate positions are filled. Box 8.2 provides an overview of how the votes are calculated in practice.

BOX 8.2   How votes are counted for elections of the Senate

At the 2007 federal election for Senate seats representing the state of Western Australia, candidates needed to obtain a quota of 171 822 votes to win a seat. The quota was obtained in the following manner:

1 313 201 (formal votes) / 6 (number of seats) + 1 plus 1 = 171 822.

One of the candidates, David Johnston (LP) gained 554 531 votes and was declared elected. As the quota was 171 822, Johnston's surplus was 382 709 votes. Because it was unclear which of Johnston's votes actually elected him and which votes were surplus, all of his ballot papers were transferred at a reduced value. The transfer value is calculated by dividing the surplus by the total number of ballot papers. In this case, the transfer value was obtained thus:

382 709 (surplus votes) / 554 531 (total number of votes received)
= 0.690 148 97 (up until the 8th decimal place)

Johnston's ballot papers were re-examined so that the surplus votes could be redistributed to remaining candidates according to their subsequent preference. In this case, most of the people who voted for Johnston put Allan Eggleston as their second choice. Those votes were then multiplied by the transfer value and then reassigned to Eggleston. For example, of Johnston's 554 531 votes, 552 530 gave Eggleston their second preference, hence the following calculation was undertaken:

552 530 (number of Johnston's ballot papers that allocated a
second preference to Eggleston) x 0.690 148 97 (transfer value)
= 381 328 (votes transferred to Eggleston)

The 381 328 votes were added to Eggleston's existing votes (337), resulting in him being declared elected. However, he too had a surplus of votes (208 842). Eggleston's surplus votes were transferred in the same manner as those of Johnston (i.e. at a reduced value).

If however, all surplus votes from elected candidates are transferred and there are still some unfilled positions, further counting is undertaken. The lowest scoring candidates are eliminated and their votes are transferred according to their second preference but at full value (i.e. no calculation of a transfer value is required because the ballots have not actually contributed to the election of any candidate at this point).

Ballot structure for federal elections

Both House of Representatives and Senate ballot papers are ordinal in structure, meaning that voters are given some discretion in filling out their ballot papers. In particular, voters are permitted to make multiple marks on the ballot paper against several candidates. As we shall soon see, there is a variation in the design of Senate and House of Representatives ballot papers.

In the case of the House of Representative ballot paper, voters are required to allocate a numerical preference for each candidate listed on the ballot paper in sequential order. The failure to exhaust all preferences (that is, the voter fails to indicate a numerical sequential preference for every candidate listed on the ballot paper), renders the ballot paper *informal* and it will not be counted. The rates of informal voting at the previous five elections have averaged 4.18 per cent, ranging between a low of 3.2 per cent in 1996, to a high of 5.2 per cent in 2004. The single largest category of informal votes (50 per cent) are what the AEC terms 'Number 1 only', whereby the voter has failed to indicate a sequential preference for all candidates listed on the ballot paper. In a recent study the AEC discovered that the highest incidence of non-sequential informal votes was recorded in those states that use optional forms of preferential voting at state elections (AEC 2005, p. 15).

In the Senate, voters are presented with two choices when filling out their ballot papers. They can vote 'below-the-line', whereby the voter must register a numerical preference against the name of every candidate listed in the ballot paper. Alternatively, voters can elect to vote 'above-the-line', in which case the voter inserts the number 1 in the box of the party or group they most prefer, which is known as a Group Ticket Vote (GTV). When a voter selects this option (chooses to cast a GTV), they are handing over the right to distribute their subsequent preferences to that group they have assigned their number 1 vote. The option of casting a GTV was introduced in 1984 by the Hawke Government in response to the high number of informal votes that were occurring due to mistakes made by voters in having to indicate upwards of 50 sequential numbers against the names of candidates appearing on Senate ballot papers. Most Australian voters choose the GTV option (97 per cent) because it is much easier to indicate a number 1 against one grouping than it is to indicate a numerical preference for every Senate candidate. One of the consequences of this feature has been to convert an essentially open list Senate ticket into a close list system, thereby increasing the control of the parties over the order in which their candidates are elected.

District magnitude for federal elections

The number of candidates to be returned per seat, or district magnitude, varies between the Senate and the House of Representatives and hence the proportionality of outcomes. In the case of the House of Representatives, the nation is divided into 150 single-member electoral districts, which typically average between 80 000 and 90 000 voters per electorate. In contrast, the organisation of Senate electorates is on the basis of eight multi-member electorates that correspond to the major regional or territorial divisions in Australia. Under the terms of the Constitution, each of the states is entitled to 12 seats and each of the territories is allocated two seats. Generally, only half of the members of the Senate are voted upon at any given election. Known as a 'half Senate election', 40 of 76 Senate vacancies are contested, with the six original states returning six senators and the territories returning two senators apiece.

Research shows that the multi-member electorates used for elections of the Senate are much more likely than the single-member constituency basis of the House of Representatives to yield greater proportionality in electoral outcomes as measured by the symmetry of vote share to seats won. We will return to this issue a little later in the Issue in Focus.

Federal electoral laws

The source of electoral laws for federal elections can be located in two key articles: the Commonwealth Constitution and the *Electoral Act 1918*.

The Constitution contains a number of key provisions relevant to the operation of the electoral system and its processes. It sets down the length of the electoral term, establishing that the House of Representatives must face the people every three years and the Senate every six years. The Constitution describes the circumstances that trigger an election, namely that the Governor-General must **prorogue** the Parliament (s. 5), and writs (ss. 12 and 32) must be issued. The Constitution entrenches a modicum of electoral malapportionment. Section 26 of the Constitution guarantees the original states a minimum representative entitlement in the House of Representatives resulting in a situation whereby Tasmanian electors are over-represented

Prorogue: to terminate the term or session of a Parliament

relative to voters in other states. Similarly, s. 7 of the Constitution specifies that all of the original states are entitled to equal representation in the Senate notwithstanding population size. As a consequence of this, successful Senate candidates from the more populous states are required to achieve a much higher quota of votes than their counterparts from the less populated states. For example, Senate candidates in NSW need to attain a quota of 600 000 votes compared to 171 000 votes in Western Australia.

Virtually all of the detail pertaining to the machinery provisions for federal elections can be found in the *Electoral Act 1918*. Unlike the Constitution, which is a body of higher law, the *Electoral Act 1918* is an ordinary Act of Parliament. As a result, it is much more vulnerable to partisan manipulation by the party in government. Some of the more important matters covered under the Act include: setting out the powers, responsibilities and duties of the Australian Electoral Commission; the procedures for determining House of Representatives electoral boundaries; the threshold requirements for registering a political party; the qualifications and disqualifications for voting; establishing the criteria and procedure for eligibility to formally nominate for election; and even prescribing the day the poll must take place.

ISSUE IN FOCUS

SHOULD PREFERENTIAL VOTING BE REPLACED BY A SYSTEM OF PROPORTIONAL VOTING IN THE HOUSE OF REPRESENTATIVES?

Scholars writing about the Australian electoral system note that in the early years, Australia's political elites demonstrated a willingness to democratise elections and to be innovative with their electoral institutions (Farrell & McAllister 2006, p. 25). Australia was distinguished in this early period as the second country in the world to confer the right to vote to women, which first occurred in South Australia in 1894, before being adopted by the other colonies. Australia was also the first country to introduce the secret ballot at elections, beginning in 1856. The introduction of the secret ballot was a critical first step to reducing much of the bribery, corruption and intimidation that had previously been associated with elections (Sawer 2001, p. 4). Even today, the secret ballot is known in some countries as the Australian ballot (Lovell et al. 1998).

Despite the progressive approach adopted by Australian lawmakers in the design of Australia's first electoral institutions, the system also possessed some less than salubrious features. It was not until 1962 that Indigenous people were finally given the right to enrol and to vote at federal elections without exception. Many of the states were slow to jettison property qualifications for upper house elections, which denied the non-propertied classes representation in some Legislative Councils (Singleton et al. 2006, p. 271). Malapportionment has also been a deliberate and pervasive feature of Australian elections. It was not uncommon for rural electorates in many of the states to consist of significantly fewer voters than their urban counterparts, a feature that continued well into the 1980s (Jaensch 1995, pp. 68–71).

Some academics argue that the Australian zest to innovate has all but disappeared and that Australia is now 'a prominent and increasingly rare example of a country that is not giving serious consideration to electoral system reform' (Farrell & McAllister 2006, p. 174). Preferential voting (PV) has been used to elect members to the House of Representatives since 1918 and PR-STV was introduced more than six decades ago for Senate elections. While it is true that some reforms have been introduced over the years, such as the introduction of public funding in the 1980s (see Box 8.3), these initiatives, while significant, have not substantially altered the core dynamics generated by the electoral system.

BOX 8.3   The vexed issue of money and politics

Concerns about the ability of money to subvert politics have a long history. Orr points out that during the nineteenth century the chief concern was that politicians would use money in order to bribe the electorate. However, by the twentieth century the focus of concern had shifted to the fear that wealthy members of society were able to use money to buy favours from elected members (2004, p. 62).

Beginning in the 1980s, there were attempts in Australia to better manage the potential impact of money on electoral outcomes and, more importantly, political policy outcomes. At the federal level, one key initiative was the introduction of public funding for elections, which was implemented ostensibly to pay for some of the costs of campaigning, thereby reducing parties' dependence on private sources.

Under the federal scheme, parties are permitted to access public funds provided they register with the AEC their desire to receive such funds and then only if they attract more than 4 per cent of the first preference vote. The amount is calculated by multiplying the number of votes obtained by the funding rate, which for the 2007 federal election was $2.10 per vote for either the House of Representatives or the Senate.

However, public funding of election campaigns has not alleviated concerns about corruption. If anything, public funding has precipitated new fears about political parties 'double dipping' (i.e. receiving both public funding and political donations). One of the major complaints levelled against the scheme is that it serves to pour more money into the bulging campaign war chest of the major parties. Of the $48 million collected in public funds at the 2007 federal election, over $40 million was received by the ALP and the Liberals. The remaining $8 million was shared between 20 minor and independent candidates.

Costar argues that one of the deficiencies of the system is that parties and candidates are entitled to collect as much private funding as their campaign fundraisers are capable of collecting (2006, p. 198). Basically, the system has not lessened the party's dependence on private sources, with the major parties continuing to collect large sums from private donors. According to research conducted by Young and Tham, over 80 per cent of all funds raised by the ALP and the Liberals is still secured from private sources (2006).

One of the perverse effects of the system has been to increase the amount of money spent on campaigning. To give some kind of idea of the amount of money involved, the 2006–07 annual receipts lodged with the AEC reveal that, federally, both the ALP and the Liberals spent approximately $9 million apiece.

Some commentators object to public funding on the grounds that it is a waste of scarce public dollars that could be invested into public works or other important public services, particularly because the major beneficiaries are the already-donor-capable major parties. It effectively enables the parties to use taxpayers' funds for a private end, which is to elect their party and candidates to Parliament. It has also been linked to concerns that the system permits candidates and parties to make a financial gain from the electoral public funding system.

Nevertheless, some claim that party funding is highly beneficial and has helped to improve the electoral process. As far as they are concerned, the problem with the current system has more to do with the manner in which the scheme has been implemented than with the principle (Young & Tham 2006). One of the big benefits of the scheme is that it allows small political entities, such as minor parties and independents, to benefit, even if only retrospectively. It has provided minor parties with a much needed revenue base. It seems hardly coincidental that the organisational longevity of many minor parties has improved since the introduction of public funding.

Q Do you support the principle of public funding of election campaigns? What are its benefits and disadvantages? Should public funding be retained in its current form, modified or abolished?

BOX 8.4 The soaring cost of elections: the 2007 federal election

While democratic elections are regarded as central to the health and legitimacy of Australian democracy, they are a highly costly affair. The cost of elections has, over the years, increased substantially. The 2007 federal election, for example, cost taxpayers more than $163 million (see a breakdown of the expenses for the 2007 election below). This compares to $55 million spent in 1990. Over time, the financial costs associated with elections are imposing an ever-increasing burden on the public purse. Whereas the cost per elector in real terms in 1996 was $6.43, in 2007 it was $8.36 (AEC 2008). While it could be argued that no financial expense should be spared in order to ensure a truly democratic election, there is little to suggest that the large amounts being spent necessarily produce a better democratic outcome for the public.

Table 8.3   Breakdown of the expenses for the 2007 federal election

Expense	Amount ($)
Employee Expenses	42 517 402
Property Expenses	6 235 077
Election Supplies and Services	4 860 054
Contractors	1 945 670
Consultancy	1 265 580
Travel	2 770 215
Advertising and Promotion	29 519 430
ITC Services	10 874 985
Mailing Services	8 296 548
Printing and Publications	4 643 200
Legal Services	485 960
Other Expenses	659 347
Public Funding	49 002 639
Total	**163 076 106**

Q Do you think the amount spent on federal elections reflects the quality of the people who are elected to Parliament?

Source: AEC 2008

Australia is one of only a handful of countries that utilises preferential voting. Farrell and McAllister theorise that part of the explanation for the persistence of PV is cultural, resulting from the crystallisation of elite consensus in Australia about the desirability of PV over other forms of electoral systems that took root at the turn of the nineteenth century. They contend that the perceived superiority of PV continues to shape elite ideas about the ideal type of electoral system. Certainly, few have questioned the wisdom of the commitment to PV, which has remained, not unlike compulsory voting, a sacrosanct tenet of the Australian electoral system. The Issue in Focus considers whether preferential voting is still relevant to Australian representational needs and if it might be better replaced with a proportional system not unlike that used at Senate elections.

The introduction of PV for federal elections in 1918 is famously linked to an agreement in which a rural pressure group acceded to withdraw from the 1918 by-election in the federal seat of Flinders in exchange for the Hughes Government agreeing to repeal First-Past-the-Post (FPP) and legislate for PV. Graham argues that while there is truth to the story of the 'Flinders deal', the introduction of PV was not a 'casual expedient' but a carefully considered piece of legislation designed to create a two-party–dominant system (1968, p. 202). He claims that the implementation of PV resulted from the fortuitous coincidence of political idealism with partisan self-interest. It was thought that the two-party system it would help to create was both 'just and desirable' because it alone could drive national progress and economic development. Similarly, both the Labor and non-Labor parties saw partisan benefit in the adoption of PV. For the non-Labor forces, unable to unite under a single coherent national structure, PV would enable 'supporting groups' to run their candidates without splitting the conservative vote and handing seats to the ALP. For its part the ALP wanted a clear demarcation between the 'parties of reaction and progress' in order to simplify voter choice at the ballot box. The ALP believed that PV offered the best hope of securing such an outcome (Graham 1968, p. 212).

While a mixture of principle and major party interest accounts for the introduction of PV for elections of the federal lower house, this method is not without clear and identifiable strengths. One of its perceived virtues is that it can, under certain circumstances, enable one party to gain a clear majority of seats in Parliament. This occurs because PV is known to produce a phenomenon known as a 'winner's bonus', which is a dividend in seats that accrues to the party that accumulates the biggest share of the vote. To give some idea of how this operates in practice, at the 2007 federal election the ALP attained 43.38 per cent of the first preference vote but won 55 per cent (or 83 of the 150 seats) in the House of Representatives. The ALP received a winner's bonus of +11.62 per cent, which enabled it to claim an outright majority of seats in the lower house, something it would not have been able to do if the electoral formula produced a more proportionate outcome. Proponents of PV argue that the lack of proportionality in the ratio of vote share to seats won is an acceptable and necessary trade-off. They contend that both the public and national interest are best secured by a government able to command a single-party majority in the House of Representatives.

The other strength of PV is that it ensures strong constituent representation that allows voters to better assign responsibility for political and policy matters. The single-member electoral basis of PV engenders a clear link between the member and the constituent. It enables the elector to easily identify his or her local member, which is useful if the constituent needs to lobby their elected member or communicate a grievance. In doing so, it strengthens the accountability of the member to their constituents, helping to facilitate the system of responsible government that underwrites Australian parliamentary practice.

Preferential voting is also believed to increase the incentive for voters to cast their ballot for their most preferred candidate. It is generally assumed that most voters dislike the thought of wasting their vote. As a result, electors will avoid voting for a candidate who is unlikely to get elected, even if this is their most preferred candidate. PV is designed to avoid this situation. It enables the voter to cast their vote for their first choice of candidate safe in the knowledge that their ballot will not necessarily be wasted if that candidate is eliminated early in the count. The voter knows that should their preferred candidate be excluded early in the vote count, their second or subsequent preference will potentially count towards the election of the winning candidate. This is thought to be of particular benefit to independents and minor party candidates in two respects. First, PV counters the mentality that a vote for a minor party is a wasted vote. Second, PV can indirectly assist in boosting the minor party and independent vote because it provides disgruntled major party voters with a relatively safe place to park their vote. PV allows the disaffected major party voter to express their dissatisfaction at the ballot box without necessarily costing their most preferred party the opportunity to form government.

The strengths associated with PV are considered by some to be flaws. One of the tendencies that the literature identifies as being specific to PV (compared to PR) is that it creates conditions favourable for the existence of two major parties by imposing mechanical barriers to the success of challenger parties (see Hague & Harrop 2004, p. 153; Duverger 1959). PV has done few favours for those small parties whose voter support base is not geographically concentrated. While there are many factors that influence a party's prospects at the polls, the high electoral thresholds, combined with the single-member electoral districts, do provide a major obstacle to the election of small party and independent candidates to the House of Representatives. With the exception of the National Party, a handful of independents and the somewhat unexpected victory enjoyed by the Australian Greens at the 2002 Cunningham by-election, no minor parties have managed to win a seat in the House of Representatives since the 1930s.

Cleavage: a division within society that involves one of the primary determinants of social identity. There are groups who are aware of the cleavage and are prepared to act on the basis of their conflicting identities. The social division leads to the creation of organisations/formal institutions that represent and defend the collective identity.

It could be argued that the two-party–dominant nature of the party system is unsatisfactory given the changes that have occurred within Australian society over the past fifty years. At the time the electoral system was drafted, the necessity to implement a system that gave voice to minority interests was in many ways unimportant. The Australian population was highly homogenous and the dominant **cleavage** in society was based on a simple class dichotomy between the working class and the upper class (see Box 8.5). However, it is widely acknowledged that society is much more diverse in religious and ethnic terms, and the cleavages within society are more complex and cross-cutting than in the past. It could be argued that a new electoral system that is able to better represent Australia's growing diversity is required, particularly because PV fails an important test of political equality, favouring or over-exaggerating the will of the majority while systematically constructing impediments that potentially thwart proliferating minority interests in society.

BOX 8.5 Voters and their preferences

One of the qualities that defines the Australian voter is their fairly strong partisan attachments. Whereas the trend in other similar liberal-democratic states is partisan de-alignment, the bonds that tie Australian voters to the mainstream parties remain robust. This is not to suggest that there are some indications that voter attachments are softening. Academics have noted that Australian voters are less likely to claim strong partisan attachments and that increasing numbers are making up their minds about who they will vote for much later in the campaign. Election surveys also show that the percentage of voters who regularly change their vote from one election to the next is steadily increasing from 26 per cent in 1967 to 43 per cent in 2004 (Ward & Stewart 2006, p. 107). Nonetheless, Australian partisanship is noted for its 'stability' and habitual support for the major parties (McAllister 1997, p. 240).

The basis of Australian partisan attachments is thought to be deeply rooted in class and reinforced by a combination of factors: cultural (utilitarianism), institutional (electoral system) and political (parties, political leaders, issues). It is suggested that these attachments are handed down from one generation to the next via a subtle process of familial socialisation. McAllister argues that the 'importance of political socialisation in moulding party loyalties ... cannot be underestimated' and that it partially accounts for the fixed nature of partisan attachments (1997, p. 252).

One of the electoral implications of strong partisanship has been a tendency for Australian voters to align themselves closely with one party, particularly the three oldest continuous parties in this country: the ALP, the Liberal Party and the National Party. The basis for these attachments is thought to be founded mainly on social class, as measured by occupation status, with blue-collar and poorer members of society identifying with the ALP, affluent white-collar workers aligning themselves with the Liberal Party, and farmers/ rural communities with the National Party. While the available data suggests that occupational class seems to have a weaker association than it did previously, the influence of social class does continue to have a bearing on voter preference (Manning 2006, pp. 292–7).

Q Just as there is evidence of the effects of social class on voting behaviour, studies have also revealed a phenomenon known as the 'gender voting gap' in which women voters have displayed what Manning (2006, p. 298) refers to as a 'slight but significant and enduring' support for the Coalition over the ALP. However, more recent data shows that the gender gap is now virtually non-existent and that, if anything, women are now slightly more likely to vote for the ALP than men (Manning 2006, p. 300). What do you think might account for the fact that women voters are now more likely to vote for the ALP than the Coalition?

In light of this, it raises the question of whether elections for the House of Representatives would better served by a proportional electoral system. Proportional representation had its supporters at the time of Federation, although they had, as Graham describes, 'matched against them' the proponents of majoritarian systems. Among PR's enthusiasts were 'middle class intellectuals' and high profile politicians such as Alfred Deakin. The proportionalists were concerned about the power of party organisations and committed to the view that a stable political community could only arise if all significant social groups were given a voice in Parliament. However, the views of the proportionalists were ultimately defeated by opposing forces that feared that PR would encourage groups and individuals to pursue their narrow sectional interests at the expense of the needs of the wider community (Graham 1968, pp. 203–4).

PR was finally introduced for Senate elections in 1948. Part of the rationale for the new system was to reduce what Farrell and McAllister refer to as the 'windscreen wiper' effect, whereby one party 'wins all or most Senate seats in one election, only to lose all or most at the next election' (2006, pp. 41–2). Under the previous system (multi-member PV), the majority gained by one party was so 'extreme' and 'unrepresentative' that it 'diminished the value of the Senate as a debating house' (Crisp 1973, p. 147). However, the Chifley Labor Government also hoped that the new system would serve the party's short-term electoral needs. Fearful that it would lose the next election, the Chifley Government calculated that PR might enable the ALP to gain control over the Senate, thereby thwarting the incoming conservative Menzies Government (Uhr 1999, p. 15). While the Chifley Government's plan succeeded in denying the Menzies Government a majority in the Senate, the introduction of PR was to have unforseen electoral consequences for both the major parties in the longer term. Within a decade of the introduction of PR, minor parties and independents not only began to win Senate vacancies with greater regularity but they gained sufficient representation to gain a balance of power in the nation's powerful upper house. It should come as no surprise that both the major governing parties have at different times raised the prospect of tinkering with PR so as to reduce the likelihood of minorities in the chamber (see Bennett 1999a).

Proportional representation systems, as the name suggests, endeavour to produce electoral outcomes that closely approximate the wishes of the electorate. PR systems allocate seats in rough proportion to votes won in order to ensure a relatively 'accurate' translation of votes into seats. Do you remember the extraordinary 'winner's bonus' the ALP benefited from at the election for the House of Representatives in 2007 that was discussed earlier in this chapter? The ALP secured 43.38 per cent of the vote but claimed 55 per cent of all lower house seats. Under a proportional system, this 'winner's bonus' is significantly reduced. A comparison of the Senate contest at the same election demonstrates the very different effect that PR-STV had on representational outcomes. The ALP gained 40.3 per cent of the first preference nationwide vote in the Senate and won 45 per cent of seats. PR-STV clearly delivers a much more accurate translation of vote share into seats than PV.

Proportional systems are also credited with wasting fewer votes. This means that proportional systems increase the likelihood that all votes will in some way count towards the election of at least one candidate. To help in understanding this, consider what happens under PV. It is not uncommon that the winning candidate secures a little more than 51 per cent of the vote, even following a full distribution of subsequent preferences. As a result, 49 per cent of the vote is effectively 'wasted', or the wishes of 49 per cent of the electorate are ignored. In contrast, under PR-STV there is less likelihood of vote wastage due to the multi-member basis of the system, which generates much lower winning quotas. There is also the capacity, owing to the single-transferable-vote feature of the system, for the votes of excluded candidates to be transferred to other candidates remaining in the count. It is much more likely, therefore, that every elector's vote will contribute either in full or in part towards the election of at least one candidate.

The other strength of PR is that it improves opportunities for minority interests to win seats. Proportional systems remove some of the psychological and mechanical impediments to small party success that are found in majoritarian and plurality systems. Not only do proportional formulae typically generate much lower electoral thresholds for representation compared to majoritarian electoral formulae but they enable parties to aggregate dispersed geographical support and convert it into seats. Donovan found in his study of the Australian Senate that since the introduction of PR-STV the incidence of minor party mobilisation has increased significantly. Donovan's research shows that the number of minor parties contesting Senate elections increased at the first STV election, without ever declining to previous levels. He further discovered that 'the average number of minor parties contesting House of Representative elections has consistently lagged behind the number contesting Senate elections' (2000, p. 476). It seems that proportional representation encourages greater candidate and party participation at elections and occasionally enables minor parties and independents to win Senate vacancies.

While proportional systems ensure that the wishes of the electorate are fairly accurately reflected within Parliament, some argue that in doing so it breeds political instability because it causes the fractionalisation of the party system. Here the concern is that should minor parties proliferate, and prove successful at the polls, it would become increasingly unlikely that a single party would be able to command a governing majority in their own right. It is true that since 1979, there has only been one occasion in which a government has been able to command a majority in the Senate. However, in other Australian jurisdictions that use PR, such as for elections of the Tasmanian and ACT lower houses, it has not inevitably led to minority governments. While Tasmania has had the most experience with minority governments, Moon finds that electoral systems do not explain everything as minority governments have occurred in every state at one time or another (Moon 1995, p. 148). Nor is PV necessarily a guarantee of single-party governments, as the Western Australian state election in 2008 proved. Despite the fact that elections for the lower house are conducted using PV, neither of the major political parties managed to win a majority of the seats in the West Australian Legislative Assembly. The Liberals formed a minority government with the support of four National MPs and three independents.

This is not to say that proportional representation necessarily always produces desirable outcomes. There are weaknesses with the system, such as the fact that proportional systems obscure the link between the parliamentarian and the constituent. The philosophical underpinnings of PR systems are different from those of PV. Preferential voting is grounded in ideas of territorial representation whereas PR seeks to represent parties or interests rather than territories. This has led to concerns that it is difficult for voters to easily identify their parliamentary representative. Similarly, PR also fails to deliver on the criterion of simplicity, which is important if one believes that the electoral formula should be easy for voters to comprehend. PR is quite a complex electoral formula. The intricacies associated with calculating thresholds, as well as counting and transferring preferences, are such that it can be very difficult for the average person to grasp. Complex systems can impede transparency and also result in much slower times to declare all of the winning candidates whereas it takes only a few days before results of the House of Representatives election are known, it often takes upwards of two weeks before the Senate is confirmed.

In a more practical sense, there are two big obstacles to the realisation of PR in the House of Representatives. First, it is potentially problematic to elect two separate chambers using the same electoral method. Scholars such as Lijphart argue that there is a risk of undermining the checks and balances function performed by bicameral legislatures if the composition of the two chambers is identical, which is most likely to eventuate if the same electoral formula was used to elect both houses. Second, the major parties, those who control the all-powerful lower house, have rejected the idea of modifying, let alone repealing, the present lower house voting system. One of the key reasons that PV is unchanged since its introduction is because it has helped to sustain the dominance of the two major political groupings. It has served to create a privileged environment that protects the established parties against challenger parties and new entrants.

It true to say that none of the electoral systems we have discussed are wholly satisfactory. Some complain that PV gives undue advantage to the big governing parties and effectively sidelines minority interests. Others assert that PR confers too much power to non-major-party interests, which can make it difficult to achieve decisive legislative action in the national interest. All systems produce a bias or distortion of some form, some of which is intended and some which is simply tolerated. At the heart of the disagreement over the choice of an electoral system is a much broader theoretical and ideological debate about the type of representative system an electoral system should encourage. As Farrell explains, proponents of PR are inclined to adopt a 'microcosm' conception of representation. According to this perspective, the composition of the legislative body should closely approximate the society from which it is drawn. That is, all views, groups and interests should be given a voice in parliament. In contrast, supporters of PV subscribe to a 'principal-agent' view of representation, which prioritises the importance of good decisions and the ability of the chamber to act correctly and decisively. Because both conceptions of representation involve a normative judgment, it is impossible to argue with certainty that one system is necessarily better than the other (Farrell 2001, p. 12).

CHAPTER SUMMARY

There are three important things this chapter has attempted to convey about electoral systems. First, different electoral systems are configured to produce different types of electoral outcomes. Second, no electoral system is perfect, and all produce a distortion of some form or another. Third, there is no agreement about which electoral system is necessarily best. Judgments about what kind of electoral system is likely to produce the best type of democracy are inherently subjective and ultimately dependent on the political principles one believes should be cultivated against those that one ranks as of lesser importance.

WEBSITES

Australian Electoral Commission (AEC):
http://www.aec.gov.au/
The AEC is the body charged with responsibility for planning and managing federal elections in Australia. The site carries information about all aspects of the Australian federal electoral system.

Australian Government and Politics Database:
http://elections.uwa.edu.au/
A database of elections, governments, parties and representation for Australian state and federal parliaments since 1890.

Centre for Democratic Institutions (CDI):
http://www.cdi.anu.edu.au/index.htm
An initiative of the Australian Government, CDI provides support to developing countries seeking to democratise their political institutions.

Electoral Council of Australia (ECA):
http://www.eca.gov.au/
The ECA is the consultative council of Electoral Commissioners from the electoral authorities of the Commonwealth, states and territories.

FURTHER READING

Farrell, D. & McAllister, I. 2006. *The Australian Electoral System*. University of New South Wales Press, Sydney.

Orr, G., Mercurio, B. & Williams, G. 2003. *Realising Democracy: Electoral Law in Australia*. The Federation Press, Sydney.

The Australian Party System

THIS CHAPTER:

★ defines political parties and explains the function they perform in liberal-democratic states

★ examines the four key phases of party development

★ explores the historical development and evolution of the Australian party system.

ISSUE IN FOCUS

How relevant is the cartel party thesis to explaining new developments among Australia's major parties?

KEY TERMS

Cartel party thesis	Iron law of oligarchy	Pre-selection
Catch-all parties	Mass party	Protectionists
Electoral professional parties	National Audit Report	Rent-seeking
Free Traders	Plurality voting systems	Social movement
Interest group	Political opportunity	Tweedledum and
	structures	Tweedledee

In the wake of its third consecutive federal electoral defeat in 2001, the Australian Labor Party (ALP) commissioned a major review of the party's internal structures and processes. The stated objective of the review was to devise recommendations that would 'make the operation of our Party as attractive, inclusive and participatory as possible' (Hawke & Wran, National Committee of Review Report 2002, p. 5). The report noted concern about the party's detachment from the wider Australian community and its dwindling and increasingly alienated membership. The ALP is not alone in its concern about declining membership levels, with similar fears being voiced intermittently by both the Liberal and National Parties. The inability of the established parties to boost their flagging member ranks raises a number of interesting questions about the future of the established parties and their ability to connect to civil society.

Introduction

> Parties are inevitable. No free country has been without them. No-one has shown how representative government could be worked without them. They bring order out of the chaos to a multitude of voters (Lord Bryce, *The American Commonwealth*, 1888).

Few Australians could genuinely claim they are unfamiliar with the concept of a political party. In part, this is because Australia's political parties do their utmost to remind us of their presence. This is especially true at election time. Party members and volunteers cluster at polling booths to hand out how-to-vote cards, and regularly bombard our letter boxes with campaign paraphernalia. Party candidates door-knock the local electorate and make frequent appearances at public venues so they can 'press the flesh' with potential supporters. And the public reward parties for these mostly episodic attempts at voter engagement. Over 90 per cent of all valid votes cast at Australian elections are won by candidates who are affiliated with a party. As a result, 'government is party government' and 'legislatures are party chambers' (Jaensch 1994b, pp. 1–2).

While parties are a conspicuous and pervasive feature of Australian political life, they are a relatively new invention. They are creatures of the nineteenth century and their development coincided with the emergence of mass politics, which was facilitated by representative government and the extension of universal suffrage to working-class men, and later women. Prior to this time, parliaments were comprised of loose and fluid coalitions that lacked discipline and cohesion, and that were unsupported by an extra-parliamentary organisation (Marsh 2004). The alliances that formed within the chamber were held together by either the sheer force of personality or political exigency, and they were always temporary arrangements.

Heywood describes political parties as the 'central organising principle in modern political systems' (2007, p. 271). They are considered a symbol of political modernisation and since the 1950s most states have been governed by parties (Heywood 2007, p. 272). Parties play a central role in maintaining and lubricating the democratic process. Parties mobilise public opinion, giving both expression and coherence to the various interests found in society.

There is, however, some conjecture as to whether parties are vital to the stability of a political system. Political systems managed to function quite nicely in the absence of parties for many years (LaPalombara & Weiner 1966, p. 22). While political parties have come to be viewed as synonymous with free societies, the presence of parties far from guarantees that a political system is democratic. Parties are found in virtually all types of political systems. There are countless examples of parties tampering with an election process, refusing to relinquish political control at the expiration of their term in office and, even worse, taking power by brute force. While these are problems that no longer blight advanced democratic states, there is, nonetheless, unease about some of the activities of parties operating within these polities. As we shall see in the Issue in Focus, there are concerns that parties have become increasingly disengaged and disconnected from civil society.

This chapter begins by attempting to sketch a definition of a political party. It examines the functions that political parties perform and charts their historical evolution in advanced democracies. It then provides an overview of the Australian party system in both its historical and contemporary contexts. In the Issue in Focus, we consider the extent to which Australia's major parties exhibit the characteristics associated with the **cartel party thesis**.

Defining political parties

Before we begin this chapter, it is important to consider what we mean by a political party. Intuitively, we all know what a party is. However, attempts to produce a definition that differentiates a party from other forms of political organisation has yielded surprisingly little success. According to Ware, virtually every known definition suffers from the same affliction: there will be 'some institutions that are recognisably parties that do not conform to the definition in some significant way' (1996, p. 2). All definitions, it seems, omit some types of parties or fail to recognise some important aspect of what parties do and how they operate.

What is generally true, however, is that almost every definition acknowledges that one of the activities that defines a political party is its willingness to contest elections. Unlike **interest groups** and **social movements** with whom they are most often compared, parties are organisations consisting of people who come together with the explicit objective to field candidates for election. Political parties are typically interested in winning political power as compared to other organisations that are concerned merely to influence those who possess formal political power.

> **Cartel party thesis:** a theory that proposes that major parties will seek to consolidate their position against challenger parties by monopolising the resources of the state
>
> **Interest group:** a voluntary group or association that forms in order to influence the aims and policies of government
>
> **Social movement:** a body or group of people united by a commitment to a particular issue but which lacks a strong and disciplined organisational base. Unlike an interest group, they do not seek to influence government or the legislative process; rather they aim to influence the way the public understands and thinks about a particular issue.

BOX 9.1 The same concept, many interpretations—defining a political party

A party is a body of men united for promoting by their joint endeavours the national interests upon some particular principle in which they all agreed (Edmund Burke 1770).

Political Parties are autonomous groups that make nominations and contest elections in the hope of eventually gaining and exercising control of the personnel and policies of government (Maurice Duverger 1959).

... any group, however loosely organised, seeking to elect government office holders under a given label (Epstein 1980).

A party is any political group identified by an official label that presents at elections, and is capable of placing through elections (free or non-free) candidates for public office (Sartori 1976).

... an association that activates and mobilizes the people, represents interests, provides for compromise among competing points of view, and becomes the proving ground for the leadership ... (Macridis 1967).

A political party is an institution that (a) seeks influence in the state, often by attempting to occupy positions in government, and (b) usually consists of more than a single interest in society and so to some degree attempts to aggregate interests (Ware 1996).

Q   What, in your opinion, is both useful and not useful about these definitions? How would you define a political party?

Roles performed by parties in political life

Just as there are many different definitions to describe a political party, there is also a range of views as to the functions they perform. Some academics have compiled lists of the roles that parties undertake. As shown in Table 9.1, while there is considerable overlap in the functions scholars attribute to parties, there are also subtle differences. For example, Merriam (1923) suggests that one role of parties is to serve as 'critics' of government, which the other definitions do not include. Only Heywood's (1997) definition is explicit in its claim that parties represent the interests of its constituents in the legislative arena. Moreover, the ability of parties to undertake any of these functions varies enormously depending on the **political opportunity structures** present in any given polity. In the United States, for example, only the Democratic Party (http://www.gp.org) and the Republican Party (http://www.gop.com) perform the 'organisation of government' function, despite the existence of other parties such as the Constitution Party (http://constitutionparty.com/) and the Green Party (http://www.gp.org/).

Political opportunity structures: in this context, the specific features of a nation's political system (including the legal and electoral systems) that influence new party formation, the strategies and organisational forms that parties adopt and their electoral success

Table 9.1   Different opinions on the functions of a political party

Andrew Heywood (1997)	Anthony King (1969)	Charles Merriam (1923)	Graham Maddox (2006)	Diamond & Gunther (2001)
■ Representation ■ Elite formation and recruitment ■ Goal formation ■ Interest articulation and aggregation ■ Socialisation and mobilisation ■ Organisation of government	■ Structuring the vote ■ Integration and mobilisation ■ Leadership recruitment ■ Organisation of government ■ Policy formation ■ Interest aggregation	■ Selection of official personnel ■ Formulation of public policies ■ Conductors or critics of government ■ Political education ■ Intermediation between individual and government	■ Political education ■ Representing interest groups ■ Engines of continuous plebiscites ■ Leadership training ■ Public policy formation ■ Transmission belt linking government and the people ■ The human face of government ■ A focus of identity ■ Providing opportunities for action ■ Engendering a public consciousness	■ Recruit and nominate candidates for public office ■ Mobilise electoral support for candidates and stimulate electoral participation ■ Structure the choices among competing groups of candidates along different issue dimensions ■ Represent different social groups either symbolically or in advancing specific interests ■ Form and sustain governments ■ Integrate citizens into the nation-state and its political processes

Although there is debate about whether parties in advanced democracies remain capable and committed to performing the tasks for which they were once considered indispensable, there is little disagreement that parties continue to have a significant role in the political sphere. The accepted wisdom is that all political systems, regardless of their general character, seem to require at least one party (LaPalombara 2007, p. 143). Moreover, scholars agree that parties continue to monopolise those functions associated with the formation and maintenance of governments.

The network of parties that compete at elections, including the manner in which they interact with other parties, is referred to as a party system. While there are different methods used to classify party systems, the most common approach is to draw distinctions on the basis of number. For the most part, only those parties that consistently dominate electoral contests, that have the ability to form government either on their own or in coalition, that have the capacity to affect the tactics of competitor parties, or that possess coalition potential, will be considered significant actors within the party system (Ware 1996, p. 7). Thus, it is the competition between the dominant forces that is critical to shaping the political system and its outcomes.

The literature identifies three types of party systems (see Box 9.2). First, there are dominant-party systems in which one party is a constant component of the executive, either governing alone or in coalition. Second, there are two-party systems in which two major parties of fairly comparable size compete for government, with other parties exerting little or no influence on the formation and the policies of the government. Finally, there are multi-party systems in which governments are created out of coalitions of several parties or minority governments. There appears to be a strong correlation between electoral systems and the kind of party systems that arise. While there is ultimately little evidence that an electoral system 'causes' the number of parties, it might, under certain conditions, maintain an existing system (Sartori 2001, p. 93). Nonetheless, it tends to be the case that dominant and two-party systems flourish in countries that utilise **plurality voting systems**, and multi-party systems in those that use proportional representation (PR). Electoral systems that impose high electoral thresholds (such as plurality systems that are designed to encourage crude majorities) make it difficult for small parties to gain representation. In contrast, electoral systems that have lower electoral thresholds, such as PR, increase the likelihood that smaller parties will win seats, thus increasing the incentive for elites to compete at elections.

Plurality voting systems: refers to a voting system which ensures that candidates can win seats in parliament without having necessarily attained an absolute majority of the first preference votes cast

BOX 9.2   Party systems

Type	Advantages	Disadvantages
Dominant-party systems Definition: One party emerges as either the governing party or a fundamental element in a governing coalition. Example: Liberal Democrats, Japan, 1955–93.	Ensures policy continuity and certainty of political direction. Delivers strong government. Provides political stability. Voters can vote for the party knowing that it will not have to negotiate with other parties to get its initiatives passed. Policies will not be diluted by the politics of compromise. The party's close connection with the apparatus of the state ensures that new initiatives can be implemented quickly. Accountability is clear. Voters know who to blame for failed or poor policies.	Develops an entrenched relationship with the apparatus of the state, creating the possibility of corruption and nepotism. The creation of policies that may not reflect minority and sectional interests in society. Tendency to complacency and arrogance among members of the dominant party. Undermines the democratic spirit of the public and fosters a sense of cynicism on the part of the electorate. They become fearful of a change in government and stick to what they know. Discourages the emergence of credible and effective opposition parties.
Two-party systems Definition: Two parties have a good chance of winning public office. Example: Labour Party and Conservative Party in Britain.	Reduces opportunities for monopolistic rule. If the party wins election it does not have to negotiate with other parties in order to get initiatives through the legislative process. That is, it offers strong government. Possibility of genuine competition between parties, and with it, ensures that voters have choice between rival programs. Offers political stability and certainty within limits. That is, while the winning party can govern, it cannot become complacent due to the presence of the opposition party, which is a party-in-waiting. Tends to create moderation in policy outcomes. Accountability is clear. Voters know who to blame for failed or poor policies.	Adversarial politics in which two major parties go through the motions or ritual of opposing each other, even if they might support the initiatives put forward by their rivals. Limited program choice for voters. Voters essentially get the choice between two programs only. Electoral competition can encourage two parties to attempt to outbid each other in order to attract votes. This can encourage reckless and unsustainable policy commitments.

BOX 9.2   Party systems (*cont.*)

Multi-party systems	Creates internal checks and balances within government. Policy must survive the scrutiny of the groups that make up the governing coalition.	Accountability is less clear. It is easy for the government to side-step or to deny responsibility for policy failures by blaming other groups that make up the government coalition.
Definition: Competition between more than two political parties in which there is government by coalition.	Creates a bias in favour of conciliation and consensus in terms of policy creation. This is due to the process of coalition formation in the first place.	Policy outcomes can be seriously compromised and diluted as a consequence of attempts to develop policy that satisfies all groups that make up the governing coalition.
Example: Germany. In 2005, the Christian Democratic Party (CDU) entered into a coalition with the Socialist Democratic Party (SPD) and Christian Social Union (CSU).	Ensures that a broader set of interests are represented in policy formation.	Infighting within the governing coalition can result in a breakdown in government, which can lead to upheavals and instability.
		Coalition infighting can foster weak and indecisive government.
		Thought to be less capable of handling or managing policy change in the event of changed economic circumstances.

Q   Of the three party systems, which one do you think is more in keeping with liberal-democratic principles of government?

Sources: Heywood 1997, pp. 241–6; Axford 2002, pp. 367–70

The evolution of parties in Western democracies

Parties are living, breathing organisations, which adapt, evolve, and respond to external and internal stimuli. It is not surprising, therefore, that the nature of political parties changed dramatically over the course of the twentieth century, a time of great social transformation. During this period, developments in party characteristics were charted, and a number of party models identified. Four broad models of party organisation are considered especially important: elite parties, mass parties, catch-all parties (electoral professional), and cartel parties.

One of the earliest party types identified is *elite* parties, also known as cadre parties. The term was first articulated by Maurice Duverger (1959) to describe those parties created from within parliament and that were comprised of elected members united by a common set of concerns and interests, including a similar socio-economic background. Elite parties are often loosely structured and lacking in party members and a functional organisational structure (Hague & Harrop 2004, p. 187). In terms of policy program, elite parties are generally thought to be devoid of strong ideological convictions, even if such parties often hold very different views of the national interest. According to Krouwel, since 'all parties consisted of members of higher echelons of society … political conflict is centred on the extent of unification and centralisation of the state' (2006, p. 255). Australia's earliest political parties, such as the **Protectionists** and the **Free Traders**, conformed to this model.

Whereas elite parties were the first iteration of the modern political party, the **mass party** marks the second wave. This species of party tended to form outside of parliament by people with a strong desire to promote the election of their candidates to parliament. Mass parties aimed to integrate socially excluded groups into the political process, often seeking a radical redistribution of social and economic power within society. Because of the circumstances in which they were created, mass parties developed strong extra-parliamentary organisations and an active party membership, which often preceded parliamentary members. The parliamentary wing existed to serve the interests of the party rank and file, and the elected members were controlled by the rank and file. The organisational structure of the party was highly bureaucratic and hierarchical. Mass parties also tended to have very strong ideological convictions, believing that their political objectives could be best achieved by election to parliament. As a result, the appeal of such parties was limited to a particular set of interests: either a social class or religious denomination (Katz & Mair 1995; Krouwel 2006, p. 255). The first mass party in Australia was the Australian Labor Party (ALP), which was created to serve as the parliamentary wing of the union movement. Its formation was followed closely by the Country Party, now known as the National Party. It was to take the Liberal Party until 1944 before it managed to establish an enduring mass party structure, with its antecedents resembling the form and structure of elite parties.

In the post-1945 era, a new type of party organisation became increasingly prevalent. These parties originated from mass parties. Initially, they were identified as **catch-all parties** (Kircheimer 1966), although some later refer to

Protectionists: existed from the 1880s until 1909. This party favoured protective tariffs in order to facilitate the development of Australian industry and ensure employment. It was strongest in Victoria and in the rural areas of New South Wales. In the first elections for the Commonwealth Parliament, it constituted the largest group in the House of Representatives, although it did not have a majority in its own right. In 1909, it merged with the Free Traders to form the Commonwealth Liberal Party.

Free Traders: existed from the 1880s until 1909. This party favoured the abolition of protective tariffs and other restrictions on trade. It dominated New South Wales colonial politics before Federation. In the first elections for the Commonwealth Parliament, it constituted the second largest group in the House of Representatives. In 1909, it merged with the Protectionists to form the Commonwealth Liberal Party.

Mass party: a model of party organisation that emphasises ideology and the dominance of the party membership over both its elected members and the policies of the party

Catch-all parties: describe a model of party organisation in which ideology is subsumed by a focus on issues that are universally liked or disliked among the electorate (known as valence issues). The power of the membership over the parliamentary wing is diminished and rank and file political activism is limited.

Electoral professional parties: parties in which paid advisers, public relations experts and consultants play a key role in both election campaigning and determining party policy

them as **electoral professional parties** (Panebianco 1988). It can be argued that the success of the mass parties in achieving many of their political objectives, such as the creation of the welfare state and a more equitable distribution of resources, reduced social polarisation within society and, in doing so, sowed the seeds of their own destruction. The catch-all party did not make its appeals on the basis of narrow sectional interests within society but largely on its ability to govern in the interests of all. One of the consequences of this development was that the commitment to political principle and ideology was de-emphasised in the interests of electoral expediency. One of the key features of catch-all parties is the dominance of the parliamentary wing of the party over the extra-parliamentary branch. Unlike the mass party, the role of the membership in catch-all parties is diminished, existing only to serve the parliamentary wing. Moreover, party elites are selected not on the basis of their ideological commitments, but on the strength of their technical or managerial abilities (Krouwel 2006, p. 257). True believers are replaced by experts and new policy ideas are increasingly sought from outside the party rather than from within (see Panebianco 1988).

The most recent paradigm of party organisation is the cartel party thesis. Refined by Katz and Mair (1995), it refers to a model of party organisation that is characterised by the fusion of the party in public office with a number of interest groups,

Table 9.2   Classifying Australian parties

While parties may perform similar functions, there is a plethora of different types of parties, and many different terms that are applied to differentiate between and to group them. The task of grouping parties is done by illuminating their important characteristics, such as their electoral strength (minor or major parties), program (single-issue or broad-based parties), formation (new or old parties) and internal organisation (parties of integration or representation).

Party distinction	Distinguishing features	Examples
Major parties v. Minor parties	This distinction is not one based on the physical size of either the organisational apparatus of a political party or its membership base, but rather the size of its electoral support. Whereas a big party is one that attracts a substantial percentage of the first preference vote, a small party might reasonably be defined as one that attracts a small percentage of the vote. There is a further distinction based on a party's capacity to form government. A major party is typically one that is able to form government in its own right, while a minor party can only do so in coalition with a major party.	**Major party:** Australian Labor Party: http://www.alp.org.au/ **Minor party:** Family First Party: http://www.familyfirst.org.au/

New parties v. Old parties	This distinction is drawn between parties on the basis of the timing of their formation, the composition of their electoral support, the nature of their policy orientation and model of party organisation. 'Old' parties refer to those organisations that emerged in response to the old class struggles that dominated society prior to the 1960s. Such parties are mostly concerned with economic distribution. In contrast, 'new' parties are those that formed out of the various social movements that developed as a consequence of greater affluence in society following the Second World War. Unlike their 'old' party counterparts, these organisations are less concerned with economic distribution, focusing instead on metaphysical needs.	**New party:** The Australian Greens: http://greens.org.au/ **Old party:** The National Party of Australia: http://www.nationals.org.au/
Single-issue parties v. Broad-based parties	Parties can be categorised on the basis of the scope of their program. Does the party have a narrow issue focus or does it seek to develop policy on a broad range of issues?	**Single-issue:** What Women Want: http://www.whatwomenwant.org.au/ **Broad-based:** The Australian Greens.
Governing parties v. Non-governing parties	Not all parties are capable of forming government or have any desire to seize political power in their own right. Non-governing parties have fairly modest political goals and form in order to bring attention to a particular issue, to exert 'policy' pressure on potential parties of government, or to serve as a 'watch' on the activities of the dominant parties in parliament. In contrast, governing parties are those that have the potential to form government either in their own right or in coalition.	**Governing party:** Liberal Party of Australia: http://www.liberal.org.au/ **Non-governing party:** Australian Democrats: http://www.democrats.org.au/
Parties of integration v. Parties of representation	Parties of integration are not interested in just reflecting public opinion but in actively shaping it. They tend to be more ideologically minded. Parties of representation are pragmatic parties that wish, above all else, to maximise their votes at elections. Parties of representation are driven by electoral imperatives and attempt to maximise votes by understanding the public mood. Unlike parties of integration, they are much more interested in mobilising voters rather than converting them to their world view.	**Party of integration:** Christian Democratic Party: http://www.cdp.org.au/main.asp **Party of representation:** Australian Labor Party and Liberal Party of Australia

which forms a cartel. The *cartel* party is mainly orientated towards maintaining executive power. Members are offered even fewer opportunities for meaningful involvement in the party, with politics becoming less of means to achieve social reform but rather is seen as a profession (Katz & Mair 1995; Krouwel 2006). The key difference between the cartel thesis and other party models is the extent to which the party is dependent on the state, and not its members, for its survival. Parties monopolise the state's material and legal resources and create a competitive environment that favours the incumbents and that discriminates against challengers. According to Katz and Mair (1995), the collusion takes place at two levels: between the dominant parties and between the state and the parties. We will return to the cartel party thesis in greater detail in the Issue in Focus.

Table 9.3   Political parties in Australia

According to the Australian Electoral Commission, in 2008 there were 52 parties federally registered and separately registered in Australia. Not all of these parties are unrelated organisations, nor will every party necessarily intend to actively compete at every federal election; nor will they field candidates in every seat or even contest elections for both houses of parliament. The list changes from year to year and from one election to the next.

Australian Democrats	Liberal Party of Australia (Victorian Division)
Australian Fishing and Lifestyle Party	Liberal Party of Australia (ACT Division)
Australian Greens	Liberal Party of Australia (Queensland Division)
The Australian Greens (Victoria)	
The Greens NSW	Liberal Party of Australia (Tasmanian Division)
The Greens (WA) Inc.	
Australian Labor Party (ACT Branch)	Liberal Party of Australia (NSW Division)
Australian Labor Party (ALP)	Liberty and Democracy Party
Australian Labor Party (NSW Branch)	National Party of Australia
Australian Labor Party (Northern Territory Branch)	National Party of Australia (Queensland)
	National Party of Australia (SA) Inc.
Australian Labor Party (SA Branch)	National Party of Australia (WA) Inc.
Australian Labor Party (State of Queensland)	National Party of Australia (NSW)
Australian Labor Party (Tasmanian Branch)	National Party of Australia (Victoria)
Australian Labor Party (Victorian Branch)	Young National Party of Australia
Australian Labor Party (WA Branch)	Non-Custodial Parents Party (Equal Parenting)
Country Labor Party	
Carers Alliance	Northern Territory Country Liberal Party
Christian Democratic Party (Fred Nile Group)	Nuclear Disarmament Party of Australia
Citizens Electoral Council of Australia	One Nation
Climate Change Coalition	One Nation Western Australia
Conservatives for Climate and Environment Incorporated	Peter Andren Independent Group
	Pauline's United Australia Party
Democratic Labor Party (DLP) of Australia	Senator On-Line
Family First Party	Socialist Alliance
Hear Our Voice	Socialist Equality Party
Liberal Party (WA Division) Inc.	The Australian Shooters Party
Liberal Party of Australia	The Fishing Party
Liberal Party of Australia (SA Division)	What Women Want (Australia)

Source: AEC 2008

The evolution of the Australian party system

The Australian party system is widely regarded as a late developer among comparable Western nations. Whereas political parties emerged in other national systems quickly following the introduction of representative government and universal suffrage, it was to take thirty years for Australia to follow suit. The composition of colonial legislatures until the late 1880s was comprised of loose factions that were, in the words of Jaensch, 'complex, variable, and often hidden from public view, but essentially personal and individualistic' (1991, p. 119).

However, by 1910, a 'clear transformation' had taken place. Political parties replaced the 'old personalised systems of division' (Martin & Parker 1977, p. 1). When the change occurred it was remarkable not only because of the pace at which it proceeded, but also the ease by which parties came to dominate all aspects of the political system (Jaensch 1994b, p. 38). Moreover, the parties that competed at the beginning of the twentieth century were 'very much the descendants' of many of today's parties (McAllister 2002, p. 382). The modern-day party system has its roots deep in old class antagonisms, which continue to reverberate 'in the contest between the labour and anti-labour parties', despite the fact these divisions have begun to blur (Ward & Stewart 2006, p. 119). Today, as it was the case more than a hundred years ago, the parties that dominate the Australian party system continue to be sustained by this cleavage.

The stability of the Australian party system is considered unusual, particularly when compared to the situation in other similar advanced democracies (McAllister 2002, p. 379). The literature on Australian parties, and the major parties more especially, acknowledges that parties are 'institutionalised and reified' to extent that the 'political process' is 'dominated' by them (Jaensch 1994b, pp. 3–4). This is attributed to a number of cultural, institutional and structural factors, which have helped to maintain the stability of the party system, and reinforce the central role of the established parties in the political system. Among the factors identified as being central to this phenomenon include:

- The dynamic of the Westminster parliamentary system encourages the creation of an opposition and a government in adversarial roles. That is, the competitive logic of this system is built around the interplay between two competing blocs: a government and an opposition.
- The requirement for political survival in government, which is the maintenance of a majority in the lower house, encourages parties to remain strong and unified. The control that both major blocs have managed to establish over their MPs, and the united front they are able to present to the electorate, have served to reduce opportunities for challenger parties to present themselves as viable alternatives to the existing dominant players.

- The electoral system further encourages the bipolarity of the system. The use of a majoritarian form of voting method, combined with single-member electorates, makes it difficult for challenger parties, whose support base is not geographically concentrated, to garner sufficient support to win seats in the lower house. Without representation in the House of Representatives, a party is unable to form a government, let alone participate in a governing coalition.
- The dominant position of the two major blocs is reinforced by their ability to bend the electoral system and the laws to suit their purposes.
- The major parties have shown a remarkable aptitude in 'adapting to social circumstances' and maintaining their dominant edge in the voter marketplace (Ward 2006, p. 126; McAllister 2002, p. 384). That is, the major parties are quick to respond to the voter mood and to incorporate policies and issues that are likely to win them votes.
- The political culture and more particularly the influence of utilitarianism in Australian culture is thought to have fostered a stable party system. It has resulted, according to McAllister, in Australians viewing the political process and the institutions of which it is comprised in instrumental or practical terms. The state exists as one giant problem-solver, and parties, as agents of the state, are regarded as 'an integral part of a system of political institutions which exist solely to maximise efficiency' (McAllister 2002, p. 382). This has resulted in a quiet acceptance of the dominant parties as useful institutions.

There has been considerable debate about how best to label the Australian party system. Many scholars argue that the Australian system is a two-and-a-half–party system, consisting of two dominant parties and a significant third player. According to this formulation of the Australian party system, it is comprised of the ALP and the Liberal Party, with the Nationals counted as a third, albeit minor, actor. The National Party's half-status is derived from its independent organisational base and its ability to participate in executive government, as a result of its close relations with the Liberal Party. However, not everyone believes that the Nationals should be classified as a separate entity. Some scholars claim that the Australian party system most closely resembles a two-party system on the basis that the Nationals work in an exclusive partnership with the Liberals. Maddox supports this view, arguing that the Australian party system is ultimately 'gathered into two opposing positions' (2000b, p. 248).

However one chooses to characterise the Australian party system, one fact is indisputable: the two blocs have been an enduring and robust feature of the party system, even if there has been periods of deep instability within these parties. As Table 9.3 shows, the Australian party system is diverse nonetheless. The introduction of PR in 1949 for Senate elections has facilitated increased opportunities for minor parties to gain representation in that chamber. In recent years, there have been a number of occasions when minor parties (along with independents) have exercised the balance of power in the Senate when neither of the two main governing blocs has gained an outright majority in that chamber. Outside Parliament, minor parties have successfully used how-to-vote card recommendations to achieve policy concessions from the major parties.

BOX 9.3   A 'how-to' guide for registering a political party in Australia

Since the introduction of public election spending, political parties or groups that wish to utilise these funds are required to register with the Australian Electoral Commission (AEC). The rules for registration are found in the *Federal Registration of Political Parties Handbook* (AEC). The rules state there is no requirement for a political party to register with the AEC. However, parties who do not register miss out on a number of benefits. These include listing of party affiliation on ballot papers; access to copies of the electoral roll and the names of postal vote applicants; and ineligibility to receive electoral funding even if they meet other funding requirement hurdles.

Eligibility for registration depends on satisfying a number of criteria. First, the organisation must be a political party as defined under the *Commonwealth Electoral Act 1918*. The Act defines a political party as a body corporate or association whose objectives include the election of candidates to either house of the Australian Parliament. Second, the organisation must have a satisfactory name. The name of the party cannot be more than six words, cannot be obscene and should be unlikely to cause confusion or be mistaken with the name of a recognised political party. Third, an eligible party must take one of two forms. It can be either a parliamentary party, which is a party with at least one member in the federal Parliament, or a non-parliamentary party, which means it has a written constitution and at least 500 members who are eligible to vote at federal elections. The written constitution of the party, in addition to stating that one of the party's objectives is to facilitate the election of its candidates to public office, must also detail the terms and conditions of party membership. Fourth, the party must be able to produce the $500 application fee. In the case of parliamentary parties, party members who are Members of Parliament along with the party secretary must sign the form. For non-parliamentary parties, the registration must include the signatures of at least ten members and the signature of the party secretary. Applications for registration will not be processed during an election period, meaning in the time between the issuing of an electoral writ and the return of that writ.

Q   Is it undemocratic to require parties to pay to register for elections?

ISSUE IN FOCUS

HOW RELEVANT IS THE CARTEL PARTY THESIS TO EXPLAINING NEW DEVELOPMENTS AMONG AUSTRALIA'S MAJOR PARTIES?

While most scholars would agree with Webb that the operation of modern democracy 'would be virtually inconceivable without parties' (2002, p. 1), there would be few who view these same entities as internally democratic institutions. In the twenty-first century, the literature on parties has become increasingly subsumed by the debate about the 'decline' or 'failure' of parties (van Biezen & Korpecky 2007, p. 236). It is widely claimed that the party is in crisis in Western democracies (Hague & Harrop 2004, p. 186). This is evident across three key dimensions: programmatic convergence of the major governing parties, the erosion of party identification, and decline in membership.

Tweedledum and Tweedledee: a well-known phrase to denote two persons or things so much alike as to be practically indistinguishable

First, parties are beginning to converge in terms of platforms and policy positions. This is particularly true of the major office-seeking parties. In Australia, this phenomenon is often referred to as the **Tweedledum and Tweedledee** syndrome. There is a growing view that policy differences between the ALP and the Liberal Party have become so insignificant as to render the two parties indistinguishable. As the 2007 federal election contest so clearly demonstrated, both the major parties embraced similar positions on many areas of policy (see Marsh 2006). While this was noted by more than one commentator, the view is best put by Maiden (2007):

> The election campaign has confirmed that both sides have converged on points of micro- and macro-economic management that are of high importance to the markets. Both are committed to running surpluses over the life of the economic cycle, with a 1 per cent gross domestic surplus established as the benchmark. They both support the independence of the Reserve Bank and neither is inclined to block foreign takeovers or interfere with the markets. They have converged on the issue of climate change on the key policy position for business, a carbon trading regime, differing only on timing.

It is unsurprising, therefore, that approximately 60 per cent of Australians believe that parties do not offer voters 'real policy choices' at the ballot box (Bean & Denemark 2007, p. 69).

Second, there is evidence that voter allegiance to the major, established parties is beginning to erode. Whereas the major parties won 96 per cent of the first preference vote in the House of Representatives in 1949, this figure declined to 85.46 per cent at the 2007 polls. Until recent times, most voters strongly identified with one party, and maintained that allegiance over their lifetime. In Australia, party identification remains high but there is evidence of weakening partisan attachment. In the period 1967–2004, the proportion of the electorate who claimed to have no identification increased from 11 per cent to 23 per cent. Moreover, the number of people who claimed to very strongly identify with either major party also declined. The percentage of Coalition supporters claiming to be strong party identifiers decreased from 27 per cent to 22 per cent. Among ALP supporters, the decline in the proportion of strong identifiers was particularly dramatic, falling from 37 per cent in 1967 to 23 per cent in 2004 (Ward 2006, p. 123). The growing disaffection with parties is confirmed by polling, which shows that the broader public do not trust parties. Around 55 per cent of the public do not have much confidence in parties, with 12 per cent having none at all (Jaensch et al. 2004, p. vii).

Third, party membership is in decline. It is difficult to ascertain exact figures because most parties are reluctant to divulge this information. However, Jaensch et al. estimate that the combined party membership of the ALP, Liberals, Nationals and the Democrats is less than 2 per cent of the population (2004, p. vii). In 1939, the ALP could claim as many as 350 000 members, whereas today that number is thought to be just under 40 000 (Johns 2006, p. 47). Since 1949, the Liberals' membership has declined from 170 000 card-carrying members to 50 000 members (Ward 2006, p. 130). One of the concerns associated with shrinking party membership is that parties become more vulnerable to 'branch stacking, factional manipulation and other practices which are inimical with … Australian democracy' (Ward 2006, p. 133).

The problems that afflict Australian parties are not confined to this continent. Similar developments have been identified in other advanced democracies. One school of thought is that the public in advanced democracies have simply abandoned parties. It has been suggested that the existence of new voluntary institutions offers alternative forms of meaningful association to the public. Simply put, political parties are no longer able to compete for the time and attention of citizens who would prefer to spend their free time contributing to other organisations, if at all. Declining public interest, it is argued, has resulted from the inability of parties to adequately address the social and cultural changes that have taken place within advanced democracies. The old debates centred on class conflict have given way to concerns about cultural and quality-of-life issues that cut across the established party divisions. Individuals now seek fulfilment via membership in other types of movements, groups and interests, which, and unlike the established parties, have little connection to the social cleavages of old, and to which the mainstream parties have only 'weakly adapted'. According to Diamond & Gunther, 'mass public detachment from political parties may be generated by social, cultural, or historical factors having little to do with the current performance of parties in contemporary democracies' (2001, p. xi).

However, others contend that it is not the public who have abandoned parties but rather it is parties that have splintered from civil society. This debate has its roots in longstanding claims that mass parties, from which most modern parties have evolved, are rarely capable of subsisting as internally democratic institutions. Robert Michels (see Box 9.4) warned that as parties professionalise, many of the democratic aspects of the party's decision-making process will be stifled in the pursuit of political expediency. While this increases the possibility that a political party will be successful at electing members to parliament, and in some cases to government, it strips away opportunities for meaningful participation in the party and, in doing so, reduces public incentives for involvement.

BOX 9.4   The iron law of oligarchy

The concept of the iron law of oligarchy, formulated by German political scientist Robert Michels, is regarded as one of the most influential dictums in the literature on party organisation. Michels asserts that once a party reaches a certain size, it will eventually succumb to oligarchic tendencies, regardless of the strength of its commitment to democratic ideals. According to Michels, power will inevitably concentrate in the hands of a small party elite resulting in the exclusion of party rank and file in the decision-making process. This occurs, in part, because a small elite emerges who possess the specialisation and expertise required to manage and sustain a big, complex organisation. The leadership's 'technical indispensability' ultimately puts them in a powerful position not only in terms of the esteem in which they are held by ordinary members but because this allows them to control the allocation of the party's resources and use it for self-gain. The process is aided by the membership's apathy and 'sheep-like' dependence on the leadership (1962, p. 88).

> **Iron law of oligarchy:** in this context, it refers to a situation in which a small number of individuals control the activities of an organisation or group

Michels's proposition is heavily contested, mainly because of its methodology and reliance on psychological theories. Many commentators have been quick to point out that party elites are often riddled by factionalism and that this can prevent power from concentrating in the hands of a small and cohesive group. More recently, Koelble (1989) has argued that oligarchy is not an 'inescapable' outcome for a party and that the origins of a party ultimately influence the organisational structure it adopts. This view is supported by Rohrschneider (1994), who contends that 'new politics' parties are far less inclined to take their cues from party leaders, looking instead to local party branches.

Despite this, many continue to argue that there is truth to Michels's law. That is, within all parties, a group will emerge that dominates the operations of the party at the expense of the broader membership. Katz and Mair's cartel party thesis (discussed below) appears to provide further support for Michels's law. They suggest that one of the newest evolutionary trends in parties is the domination of the parliamentary wing at the expense of both its members and administrative branch.

Q Does it matter if parties succumb to oligarchic tendencies? Is it better to have power within the party centralised or decentralised?

A recent health check on Australia's political parties by the Democratic Audit revealed that internal democracy within mainstream parties was generally very poor. The Audit discovered that party membership was falling; the branches of parties were increasingly moribund; the parliamentary wing of the parties crafted party policy independently from the rank and file membership; party leaders enjoyed enormous clout within the party organisation; party **pre-selection** offered few opportunities for grass-roots members to influence the selection of candidates; and the process for selecting candidates is not always procedurally fair (Jaensch et al. 2004, pp. 7–24).

> **Pre-selection:** a process whereby parties select candidates who will contest an electorate under the party's banner

These concerns have been mirrored in public statements from a growing legion of former and present members of Australia's mainstream parties. Many within their ranks recognise that there is little incentive for ordinary people to join and remain committed to political parties, particularly the major governing parties. Lindsay Tanner, a senior member of the ALP, stated, 'for those without political ambitions who simply wish to make a contribution, rank and file membership of the ALP is profoundly unappealing'. He acknowledged that the average ALP member does not enjoy the right to vote in elections for senior party office-holders; has little if any access to forums of decision-making and policy debate; has participation options restricted largely to an often-boring and alienating monthly branch meeting and occasional hack work in election campaigns (Tanner 2002).

While many claim that the trends signal a decline in the ability of parties to undertake their traditional representational and linkage roles, others argue that the developments we are witnessing may not be as problematic as is often suggested. Bartolini and Mair suggest that the 'failure'-of-parties thesis is ultimately premised on a particular conception of party function that is bound to a very specific model of party—namely, the mass party model—which no longer really exists in established democracies (2001, p. 331). They contend that scholars are making judgments about modern parties against a standard that is increasingly outdated. Moreover, Katz and Mair believe that these developments far from spell the demise of party, even if there is evidence that parties have become increasingly detached from civil society.

They claim that parties have the capacity to adapt and innovate, and have begun to do so by developing strong ties to the state.

Katz and Mair have formulated a new model of party organisation, known as the *cartel party thesis*. The cartel party thesis suggests that the links between the state and parties, which were once 'temporal, contingent and loose', are now 'permanent' and ever-important to their 'legitimacy and organizational resources' (van Biezen & Kopecky 2007, p. 237). According to their theory, cartelism operates at two basic levels. First, there is inter-party collusion between bigger, politically centrist governing parties that seek to exclude smaller, radical parties from government. The bigger parties are colluding to prevent new competitors from challenging their electoral dominance. It is not that other parties are formally excluded from competing, only that the ability of such parties to access and utilise public resources is made difficult. Second, collusion is thought to take place at the level between the state and the party. Parties are using the resources of the state to fund their activities, relying less and less on party members, who are increasingly rendered irrelevant and moribund (Katz & Mair 1995).

While some reject the contention that there is anything innovative or unique in the cartel party thesis (see Koole 1996), it is regarded, nonetheless, as one of the most influential models in the party literature in recent times. It makes sense that we should examine the cartelisation thesis in the Australian context, and ascertain the extent to which it is affecting the operations of Australian parties and the competitive dynamic of the party system more generally (see Marsh 2006). To do this, we have utilised four measures against which we can explore cartelisation in Australia. The measures used are adapted from van Biezen and Kopecky (2007, p. 238):

1 the extent to which parties are dependent on the state for subventions or funds
2 the extent to which parties are managed by the state in terms of regulation of different aspects of their internal operations and activities
3 the extent to which parties display **rent-seeking** behaviour, which is loosely defined as the use of state resources to advance a party's own position and guarantee its own survival
4 the extent to which the bigger, established governing parties collude in order to block new entrants from winning seats.

Rent-seeking: to bring about a favourable transfer of goods or services from a person, group or organisation without compensation

Measure 1: Dependence on state subventions

An increasingly significant proportion of funds received by Australian political parties is derived from the public purse, that is, taxpayer sources. Millions of dollars are now given to Australian parties and the lion's share of these funds is collected by the major parties, which in many cases are able to make a profit from contesting elections. At the 2004 federal election, the ALP and the Coalition were the beneficiaries of 90 per cent of the

$42 million dollars distributed in public receipts following the election. Similarly, there is also evidence that state subventions are increasingly important to the parties' budget bottom line. For example, in the period 2000–03 approximately 18.8 per cent of the ALP's funds were derived from public election funding. Major parties and the more established parties, such as the National Party, draw a little under 20 per cent of their funds from public sources, compared to one-third in the case of the Greens and the Democrats (Jaensch et al. 2004, p. 32). At the federal level, the two big parties have benefited enormously from the receipt of state subsidies, although they still draw significant amounts from private, largely corporate sources (Johns 2006, p. 50). The ability of Australian parties to benefit from public funding schemes is augmented by regional election funding in most state and territory elections.

Evidence of cartelisation

The evidence clearly supports the proposition that the established parties in Australia are increasingly, although not completely, dependent on state subventions to finance their activities. While it is thought that taxpayer disbursements further reduce incentives for the parties to cultivate and to engage their rank and file members, the more pressing concern is that state subventions are used by the established parties to block new entrants. In the Australian context at least, there is little evidence to suggest that the use of public subsidies is being used by the major parties to freeze out challenger parties. It seems that the funding rules ensure that access to state subventions is relatively fair due to the low threshold of 4 per cent for eligibility. Scarrow (2006, pp. 363–5) finds that public subsidies do not appear to have an adverse effect on political competition or undermine the attempts of challengers to break through. While it is generally true the established parties benefit financially from access to funding, so too do smaller parties, providing them with a source of funds that can help sustain them and enable them to maintain an organisational presence between elections. Moreover, there is the view that state subventions, might be potentially disastrous for all parties in the long term. LaPalombara suggests that reliance on public funding, intended in large part to help parties to survive, is also, rather ironically, helping to facilitate their 'degeneration' (2007, p. 149).

Measure 2: State regulation of parties

Historically, Australian parties have been subject to little explicit regulation of their activities. This is due to a combination of conceptual and practical reasons. The very idea that parties should be 'controlled, or even influenced, by the state is contrary to the liberal competition of ideas, leaders and policies' (Ware 1996). Too much overt regulation, it is thought, exposes parties to the possibility of negative intervention from the state. In a practical sense, political parties, and the major parties especially, have tended to be opposed to formal regulation, particularly where it exposes their private activities to public scrutiny. While parties serve a public function, they are voluntary agencies that are engaged in a highly competitive activity. However, the introduction of public funding of elections at the federal level in 1984 necessitated statutory recognition of parties, resulting in laws to govern aspects of their activities. This has involved some legal consequences for Australian parties. Growing recognition of parties in legislation has resulted in a willingness on the part of the courts to reverse a longstanding view that the internal affairs of parties are a wholly private matter. Parties are no longer strictly regarded as being voluntary associations and, therefore, outside the reach of the courts (Bennett 2002a, p. 4).

Evidence of cartelisation

While it is true that there is growing state intervention in the affairs of parties, two points are important. First, legal regulation has been established at the instigation of the parties and, by extension, has had little effect on their freedom of action. The insertion of parties in the Constitution is a case in point. The motivation for including parties in the text had little to do with imposing fetters on how parties operate but was designed to protect their interests in the event of a Senate vacancy caused by the death or resignation of one of their members. Second, while the level of official regulation is unprecedented by Australian standards, it is minimal nonetheless. As Gauja (2005) explains, there is a

> legal requirement in Australia that political parties [be] internally democratic, or that policy formulation and candidate pre-selection involve the participation of the membership. Although registered parties require a formal written constitution under the provisions of the *Commonwealth Electoral Act*, the structure and content of the constitution are regarded as internal matters for the party to determine.

Moreover, the Courts tread carefully in such matters and do not consider the fairness of a party's rules or processes, only that they have been applied to the letter of the party's own constitution (Jaensch et al. 2004, p. 5). It is only in Queensland that legislation actually requires parties to act democratically and gives the state electoral commission the power to oversee and investigate party pre-selection ballots (Ward 2006, p. 130).

Measure 3: Rent-seeking behaviour

There is some evidence to support the view that Australian parties engage in rent-seeking behaviour. It should be noted that the phenomenon of parties plundering state resources for their own private advantage is not new. However, the arsenal of taxpayer resources that parties are now entitled to draw upon has grown exponentially, and been used shamelessly to their own, rather than public, benefit. A 2001 **National Audit Report** estimated that Australia's parliamentarians collectively received $354 million in entitlements in the 1999–2000 budget period. In 2006, the federal government substantially increased parliamentarians' printing and postal allowances. Moreover, it permitted members to roll over any unused portion of entitlement from one year to the next, which is potentially useful in building up a stock of stationery in the lead-up to an election (Kelly 2006). It also seems that there are few restrictions on how members use the resources they receive. For example, parliamentarians are permitted to use their printing allowances to produce how-to-vote cards, even though such cards serve a private, electoral purpose. Moreover, Johns (2006, pp. 57–8) points out that activities once performed by parties, such as political education, are being contracted out to government bodies, such as the AEC. In this sense, parties are increasingly adept at using the state's resources to abrogate some of the 'democratic' functions that they traditionally performed.

> **National Audit Report:** specialist public sector agency which provides auditing services to the Parliament and Commonwealth public sector agencies and statutory bodies

State resources that accrue to the party in government are greater still. Governments have access to a legion of ministerial advisers, who, unlike normal public servants, are employed at the full discretion of the government. Over the last thirty years, the number of ministerial advisory staff employed in the PM's office alone has increased from 21 to 37. There is also mounting evidence of substantial increases in government spending on advertising. Not only has the dollar amount increased, but both the timing of the spending and the nature of the campaigns funded, signal a trend towards governments using this resource to fund party-political campaigns (Miskin & Grant 2004). In 2007, it was revealed that the government was using state resources to assist in the creation of election campaign materials. Public servants had been used to compile briefing sheets that outlined how discretionary funds were spent in electorates over the government's term. This information was then used to prepare local letters and leaflet campaigns for government MPs and candidates (Mannheim 2007).

Evidence of cartelisation

While the evidence points to an increase in rent-seeking behaviour, it is also true that parties occasionally use cost blow-outs in parliamentary entitlements and in other forms of governmental expenditure to score political points against their opponents. The opposition parties are quick to apply pressure on the government to repeal or strip away some of these entitlements, even if only to embarrass the government. Opposition parties have even been known to include specific commitments to reform of government administration among their election promises. Since winning office in 2007, the Rudd government has introduced a number of initiatives designed to tighten the use of government resources, such as instituting new guidelines on government advertising expenditure and tying public funding for elections to genuine campaign expenditure to prevent parties from profiting from state subventions. While these reforms do little to roll back the resources at the parties' disposal, they remind us that there are potential limits on the extent to which the system will tolerate parties having access to taxpayers' dollars to fund their activities.

Measure 4: Major party collusion against new challengers

There is some evidence of major party collusion to block the entry and success of challenger parties, although the evidence is less impressive than in the other three categories. Major party collusion tends to be implicit and is confined to two arenas: within Parliament and in the elections.

Within the setting of Parliament, the evidence supports the contention that the major opposition party is more likely than not to support the government's bills in the Senate, despite the fact that Australian federal governments, since the 1980s, have not always controlled the upper house. Bach's study shows that approximately 65 per cent of all government bills passed through the Senate without amendment in the period 1996–2001. Moreover, of the bills that were subject to amendment, in a quarter of all cases, it was the government that proposed the amendment (Bach 2008, p. 397). It is only on rare occasions that the major opposition party refuses to support a government bill in its entirety in the Senate. The major governing parties, when possible, prefer to bypass minor parties and independents in the Senate, preferring to negotiate directly with the major opposition party.

There is also the occasional instance of opportunistic collusion between the mainstream parties outside the parliamentary context. Evidence to support such occurrences is found in the decision by the major parties to rank a high profile minor party or independent candidate seeking a seat in the House of Representatives below a major party opponent on their how-to-vote card recommendations at elections. In 1990, when popular Democrats leader, Janine Haines, contested the federal lower house seat of Kingston, the major parties ranked her last on their how-to-vote card recommendations. Haines subsequently failed in her bid to enter the House of Representatives. In 1998, Pauline Hanson found herself in a similar situation when she ran for the federal seat of Blair. Despite Hanson securing the highest first preference vote, following the distribution of ALP preferences, she was beaten by the Liberal candidate.

Evidence of cartelisation

Despite some tentative evidence pointing to collusion between the major office-seeking parties, the reality is that the major parties have not consistently colluded against challenger parties. In the main, Australia's two largest party blocs continue to see each other as their major competitor. According to Katz and Mair, there are likely to be natural barriers to collusion in adversarial systems like Australia, where the competitive dynamic of the system is built around the interplay between two major party groupings (1995, p. 17). Moreover, they argue that overt collusion can be just as damaging to the major parties' long-term electoral prospects as it can to challenger parties. Katz and Mair (1995, p. 24) contend:

> by operating as a cartel, by attempting to establish there are no clear winners and losers among the established alternatives and by exploiting their control over the state to generate resources that can be shared out among themselves, the cartel parties are often unwittingly providing precisely the ammunition with which the new protestors … wage their wars.

CHAPTER SUMMARY

This chapter has explored the role and function of political parties in modern democratic systems. It has outlined the evolution of parties in Western states, showing that the developmental trajectory of parties has moved through at least four distinct phases. The chapter also shows that parties have been an important and enduring feature of Australian political life and that the party system has been dominated by two distinct and fixed party blocs. The entrenched position of Australian parties, compared to their counterparts in other established democracies, results from the interplay of particular structural, institutional and cultural forces. In the Issue in Focus we applied the cartelisation thesis to Australian political parties. We were able to produce some evidence that Australia's mainstream parties are developing many of the characteristics associated with the cartel party model, although the transformation is far from complete, and its consequences in the medium to long term remain unclear.

WEBSITES

Australian Electoral Commission: Parties and Representatives:
http://www.aec.gov.au/Parties_and_Representatives/index.htm.
This site provides useful information in relation to Australian political parties, such as an updated list of registered parties.

International Institute for Democracy and Electoral Assistance (IDEAS):
http://www.idea.int/parties/
This is an inter-governmental organisation that supports and promotes democracy worldwide with the aim of strengthening democratic institutions and governance. One of its areas of expertise is political parties. This link provides a link to the IDEAS webpage on political parties.

Richard Kimber's Political Science Resources:
http://www.psr.keele.ac.uk/parties.htm
This is a not-for-profit website that has links to political parties from around the world.

Governments on the WWW: Political Parties:
http://www.gksoft.com/govt/en/parties.html
Much like Richard Kimber's website, this webpage provides links to political parties from around the globe.

International Political Parties Comparative Project:
http://www.janda.org/ICPP/index.htm
This project was founded at Northwestern University by Kenneth Janda under a 1966 grant from the US National Science Foundation. The website provides access to information and data on political parties.

FURTHER READING

Katz, R. & Crotty, W. 2006. *Handbook of Party Politics*. Sage, London.

Loveday, P., Martin, A. & Parker, S. 1977. *The Emergence of the Australian Party System*. Hale & Ironmonger, Sydney.

Marsh, I. (ed.) 2006. *Political Parties in Transition?* The Federation Press, Sydney.

The Australian Labor Party

THIS CHAPTER:

★ examines the way the Labor Party emerged from the Australian labour movement, and the impact this had on the internal structures of the party

★ discusses the problems the party has faced with factionalism and disunity

★ outlines the ways in which Labor has departed from the mass party model.

ISSUE IN FOCUS

What does the Labor Party stand for today?

KEY TERMS

Caucus	Neoliberalism	Protectionism
Multiculturalism	Post-materialist values	Rank-and-file membership
		The pledge

On 14 November 2007, opposition leader Kevin Rudd stood in front of a large crowd of the party faithful at Brisbane's Arts Centre to officially launch Labor's federal election campaign. The polls suggested that he was on the verge of a landslide win, which would end Labor's 11 years in opposition and propel him into Labor folklore. But Rudd was taking no chances, responding to the Howard Government's attack on Labor's economic credentials by proudly declaring that he was 'an economic conservative' (Rudd 2007b). This claim would once have amounted to heresy in a party that was formed by unions and formally committed to a socialist objective, but in 2007, the party faithful responded to Rudd's declaration with rapturous applause. This reflects the significant changes that have affected the party in recent times, and points to the ambiguous identity of modern Labor.

Introduction

In 2008, the newly elected Labor Government was riding high in the polls, with record approval ratings for new Prime Minister Kevin Rudd (Shanahan 2008). However, it was also being criticised by some political commentators for lacking a clear identity and sense of direction (e.g. Burchell 2008). In many ways, this perception reflects the fact the party has changed significantly since the late 1960s, losing its mass party characteristics and departing from its traditional ideology. This chapter will explore the origins of the Labor Party and its connection with the labour movement, the structure of the party and the extent to which it matches the mass party model, internal disunity and the role of factions, and the extent to which the party has departed from the mass party model. The Issue in Focus will examine what Labor stands for in the twenty-first century, focusing on the party's attitude towards the market, post-materialist values and federalism.

Representing labour

The Labor Party was formed to represent the interests of the labour movement in Parliament, and although it has come to represent a broader range of groups than simply unions, the close relationship between the labour movement and the party has continued into the twenty-first century. This relationship has been a source of controversy throughout Labor's history and, particularly in recent times, some within the party have questioned whether it is time to end formal links between the labour movement and the party (see Box 10.1).

The Labor Party emerged late in the nineteenth century, at a time when the Australian labour movement was growing in strength and becoming increasingly focused on transforming social conditions through collective organisation (Macintyre 2001, p. 24). There was also increasing recognition that unions' 'ability to influence wages and conditions was determined by the policies that colonial governments pursued' (Bongiorno 2001, p. 5). In the 1890s, the need to secure parliamentary representation was brought into sharp focus by the absence of social protection in dire economic conditions, and by the failure of the Maritime Strike and the Shearers' Strike (McMullin 1991, pp. 1–11; Macintyre 2001, p. 25). Of particular significance were the actions of the colonial governments, which turned on the striking unionists, using 'the legislature, the police, the army and the judiciary to abet the designs of the employers' (Macintyre 2001, p. 26). The labour movement concluded that it needed its own presence in Parliament to represent the interests of workers, and this led to the formation of labour parties in the colonies throughout the 1890s, which were dedicated to restoring workers' rights. These early parties achieved parliamentary representation in New South Wales, Victoria, Queensland and South Australia (Macintyre 2001, p. 26).

As the colonies moved closer to Federation, the colonial labour parties began to consider what role they would play in a national government. In January 1900, an intercolonial conference of labour parties was held in Sydney, with representatives from New South Wales, Victoria, Queensland and South Australia. The conference agreed to form a Federal Labor Party, and adopted a platform that outlined the key policies the new party would adopt, including 'one adult, one vote; the initiative and referendum; the total exclusion of coloured and other undesirable races; and old-age pensions' (Bongiorno 2001, p. 16).

Despite agreeing that that there would be a Federal Labor Party, each state labour party directed its own campaign, and selected its own candidates for the 1901 election (Macintyre 2001, pp. 17–18). In all, 24 Labor members were elected to the first Commonwealth Parliament, and they formed the first Federal Labor **Caucus**. These Labor MPs revised the federal platform, abandoning the call for the greater use of referendums, and adding support for a citizen army and compulsory arbitration. The first Caucus also had a crucial role in the development of the party's federal structure, which at that point was basically non-existent. The platform and the federal party architecture developed at this early stage, reflected the labour movement origins of the party, and would continue to have a major influence on the Labor Party throughout the twentieth century.

Caucus: the term used to refer to both the parliamentary Labor Party and meetings of the parliamentary Labor Party

BOX 10.1   Would Labor be better off without the union movement?

One of the major debates among Labor supporters and political commentators is over the relationship between the party and the union movement. Although the party was originally formed by the union movement, some believe that it is time to end, or at least significantly weaken, the formal ties between the two (e.g. Aarons 2008). Unions can affiliate with the party, which means that they pay an affiliation fee and participate in the party's internal decision-making procedures. In fact, affiliated unions contribute large sums to the party's finances, and they also wield much power in Labor's extra-parliamentary organisation, with strong representation at state and national executive and at Party Conferences. In addition to this, unions tend to form the basis for many of the factions within the party, and many union leaders are also factional leaders. This gives them much influence over pre-selection and party policy.

Some critics argue that trade unions have too much power in the Labor Party. This has become a particular problem in recent times because unions represent a much smaller percentage of employees than they did in this past, and this means that they wield disproportionate power within the party (Aarons 2008). Moreover, a large proportion of Labor MPs come from a union background, at least partly because union leaders often have the power to determine the outcome of pre-selection contests. The link to the union movement can also create political problems for the party. For example, in the lead up to the 2007 election, Kevin Rudd had to deal with a variety of controversies involving union leaders, including contentious remarks by Dean Mighell, the Victorian State Secretary of the Electrical Trades Union (Sheridan 2007).

In 2002, Labor leader Simon Crean sought to reform the party to reduce union power. His reforms led to a reduction in union representation at Party Conferences to ensure that there were an equal number of union delegates and branch delegates, and they also led to the introduction of a process that allowed rank-and-file members to vote on the party President. Nonetheless, these reforms did not significantly reduce union power within the party. Some continue to defend this state of affairs, stressing that the close relationship with the union movement has significant benefits for the party. Union finances, for instance, help improve its funding position, and unions provide manpower and other resources that can be used to help in election campaigns. The 2007 election illustrates this. The ACTU funded advertisements attacking the Howard Government's WorkChoices industrial relations reforms well in advance of the 2007 poll, and this campaign was credited with helping Labor win office. Lastly, the link to the union movement helps to ensure that the party will continue to exist between elections, even when it is faced with long periods in opposition.

Q What would be the costs and benefits to the Labor Party if it ended its formal ties to the union movement? What practical difficulties might stand in the way of introducing this reform?

Party structure and control

The Labor Party has always struggled to balance the demands of a democratic party structure with the need for the parliamentary party to respond to a changing political environment. The party structure was designed along the lines of a mass party. As discussed in Chapter 9, a mass party is usually formed by groups outside of parliament, and has a strong extra-parliamentary organisation with party officials and a large **rank-and-file membership** that has an important role in formulating party policy and selecting candidates. In fact, the extra-parliamentary organisation is supposed to be paramount, exercising ultimate authority over the party's parliamentary representatives. Mass parties also have a clear ideological orientation, and they are linked to a particular class or religion.

Rank-and-file membership: citizens who pay a membership fee to join the party and participate in its activities

Originally, the Labor Party fitted the mass party model well (see Parkin & Warhurst 2000, pp. 26–9). It had a strong extra-parliamentary organisation, with a large membership that reached a peak of 270 000 (equating to 7 per cent of all Australian voters) in the 1930s and 1940s. At both state and federal levels, the main policy-making bodies of the Labor Party were the state and national Party Conferences. These conferences determined the party platform, which was supposed to be binding on the parliamentary party. Rank-and-file members joined branches of the party in their local area, and could help shape party policy by passing branch motions that could ultimately be considered at Party Conferences, or they could even seek to be elected as delegates to the conference. In between Party Conferences, the party executive acted with the authority of the extra-parliamentary party.

This process placed the extra-parliamentary wing at the heart of the Labor Party, with rank-and-file members, rather than Labor parliamentarians, determining the overall policy direction of the party (Parkin & Warhurst 2000). In other words, '[p]arliamentarians were to be delegates rather than representatives; their role was to act in accordance with the instructions given them by their masters, the party rank and file and the union movement' (Bongiorno 2001, pp. 3–4). The party structures were designed to ensure that Labor MPs stayed faithful to the platform and the extra-parliamentary party when elected to Parliament. They also reflected a belief that working-class solidarity was crucial to achieving social reform, and a fear that Labor-endorsed candidates would abandon the labour movement when they were elected to Parliament, being seduced by the trappings of office and betraying the working class. The experience of the colonial labour parties illustrated the importance of these considerations. A crucial and initially controversial mechanism for enforcing obedience to the extra-parliamentary wing was **the pledge**, which all Labor-endorsed candidates had to sign. The pledge stated that the candidate would uphold the Labor platform and vote in accordance with the wishes of Caucus if he or she were elected.

> **The pledge:** an undertaking given by all Labor-endorsed candidates to uphold the party platform and the decisions of Caucus

However, in practice, Caucus has exercised more autonomy than the formal structures of the party suggested (Parkin & Warhurst 2000, pp. 28–9). This was unsurprising because Labor MPs were elected to represent a broader range of voters in their electorates than only party members, and the tension between these two demands was built into the federal Labor Party's internal structure from its inception. Nonetheless, for much of the twentieth century, Party Conference and the national executive did play a powerful role, sometimes leading to a damaging perception that the party was controlled by unionists and shadowy backroom operatives. This problem was exacerbated by the fact that the parliamentary leadership was for many years excluded from the national executive. The political problems this created were dramatically illustrated in 1963 when Labor leader Arthur Calwell and his deputy (and later prime minister) Gough Whitlam were photographed waiting for the

36 members of the National Conference to finish deciding whether to approve Labor's policy on foreign affairs and defence. This led to the famous gibe that Labor MPs were really controlled by 'thirty-six faceless men' (Faulkner 2001, p. 215; McMullin 1991, pp. 293–4).

Factions and disunity

Despite the existence of a variety of structures designed to enforce strong party discipline, internal disunity has dogged the Labor Party throughout its existence. On three occasions, the party actually split, with groups of Labor MPs quitting to side with non-Labor parties in Parliament. On each occasion, this has had disastrous electoral consequences. Although the development of the faction system in the 1980s and 1990s helped to avoid some of these problems, more recently critics have argued that factions have become too powerful, leading to the pre-selection of poor quality Labor candidates. This led some to ask, 'could Chifley win Labor preselection today?' (Ben Chifley was Labor prime minister 1945–49 and is widely regarded as one of the party's most inspirational leaders) (Cavalier 2006).

The first major split to affect federal Labor was over conscription during the First World War (1914–18) (Faulkner 2001, pp. 204–8; McMullin 1991, pp. 92–121). Billy Hughes, a Labor MP who was a member of the first federal Labor caucus, became prime minister in 1915. Fresh from a seven-month tour of Europe in 1916, and driven by a strong sense of loyalty to the British Empire, Hughes believed that Australians should be conscripted to fight in the War and decided to hold a referendum on the issue. However, there was significant opposition to conscription both in Caucus and the labour movement. After a bitter campaign, the referendum was defeated and within weeks, Caucus was debating a motion of no confidence in their leader. Hughes announced to the meeting that he would quit the Caucus, and he invited his supporters to join him. In all, 23 of 64 Labor MPs joined Hughes, who continued as a non-Labor prime minister for six years. Following this split, Labor would not form a government again for 13 years.

Labor returned to power under Scullin in 1929, but within weeks of winning the election, the Government was confronted with the Great Depression. Coming up with a policy response to Australia's dire economic predicament would once again split the labour movement asunder (Faulkner 2001, pp. 208–11; McMullin 1991, pp. 160–82). In an attempt to address concerns that Australia could not pay the interest on its loans, Scullin accepted a proposal by the Bank of England's Sir Otto Niemeyer to reduce government spending. However the labour movement was opposed to this 'harsh economic prescription, the infamous "Melbourne Agreement", which instructed governments to cut public works, pensions and wages' (Faulkner 2001, p. 208). Scullin faced particular problems in New South Wales, where Jack Lang and the State Executive directed federal MPs to oppose the Agreement. Matters were further complicated when Scullin replaced Acting Treasurer Joe Lyons, who supported the agreement, with former Treasurer 'Ted' Theodore, who did not. The end result was another Labor split, with two groups breaking off from the party, one aligned to Jack Lang (Lang Labor), and the other to Joe Lyons. The result was again electoral disaster for Labor. At the 1931 election, they lost 32 seats in the House of Representatives, reducing the number of Labor MPs in the House to just 14.

The third Labor split occurred in the 1950s when Labor was again in opposition, after the wartime governments of John Curtin and Ben Chifley (Faulkner 2001, pp. 212–13; McMullin 1991, pp. 242, 275–89). The problems began when a group of staunchly anti-communist forces who were aligned with the Catholic Church sought to combat communist influence in the labour movement, focusing on trade unions, and later the Labor Party. Tension grew within Caucus, and following an unsuccessful challenge to the opposition leader, H.V. 'Doc' Evatt, in October 1954, the Caucus was in disarray. The end result was the formation of another breakaway party—the Democratic Labor Party (DLP)—which took with it the votes of many Catholics who had previously supported Labor. Once again, the electoral costs for Labor were huge and the party remained in opposition for 23 years.

Part of the explanation for Labor's problems with internal disunity is the fact the party has always been a broad church. Ideological differences existed between Labor MPs and extra-parliamentary members even at the party's inception, as illustrated by early disagreements over whether the party should support protectionism or free trade. There were also genuine socialists in the party who supported radical social transformation, along with others who simply wanted to reform capitalism to temper some of its harsher effects. Any party with this degree of ideological diversity is likely to experience a problem with internal disunity. Ironically, this problem may have been exacerbated by the very mechanisms that were designed to enforce party discipline. Requiring that all members of Caucus sign the pledge made it more difficult to manage the tensions that inevitably rose when MPs had different opinions. In these cases, MPs who were on the losing side of Caucus debates were locked into endorsing a position they did not support, without any flexibility to depart from the party line.

In part, this problem was resolved during the 1980s and 1990s by the development of a more organised factional system. As Labor Senator John Faulkner puts it:

> The formalisation of the factions in the Caucus after Labor regained power in 1983, together with their close alignment with the Party machine, created a very effective management tool for handling Party and Caucus conflict. By the mid-1990s, power-sharing in the Caucus had evolved to the extent that elected positions in the FPLP broadly reflected internal factional balance. A spread of factional allegiances became a significant consideration when filling leadership positions (2001, p. 216).

The leaders of tightly organised factions wielded enormous power and, in effect, they were able to do deals with each other to determine which MPs would secure the coveted ministerial positions (Grattan 2001, p. 252). It also meant that the party leader could deal directly with factional bosses in advance of Caucus meetings to head off criticism from backbenchers (Grattan 2001, p. 255).

The rise of factionalism and the power shift away from the extra-parliamentary wing of the party discussed above seem to have brought Labor far greater unity and electoral success than it enjoyed for much of its existence. However, after Labor lost office in 1996, it became apparent that factionalism had major costs as well as benefits (Jaensch 2006, pp. 39–41). Because factions exercise such powerful control over party pre-selection, and because coveted positions on the Labor frontbench are generally allocated on a factional basis, it has become very difficult to have a success-ful career as a Labor MP without belonging to a faction. This becomes a problem if it means that factional loyalists are pre-selected for safe seats or appointed to the frontbench ahead of more talented individuals who lack factional support. Over time, an entrenched system of factions may also help feed internal conflict because MPs may come to care more about the success of their faction than the party as a whole (Johns cited in Jaensch 2006, p. 39).

A recent departure from factional dominance was Prime Minister Kevin Rudd's insistence that he be allowed to choose the members of his frontbench. The Labor frontbench has traditionally been determined by a caucus vote, but in practice, this meant that it was arranged by factional leaders prior to the ballot. By choosing his own cabinet, Rudd could theoretically choose whomever he wanted to serve on his frontbench, thus undermining the power of the factions. However, in the end, 'the factional make-up of … [Rudd's] front bench broadly mirrors that of the previous opposition frontbench team, which was chosen with greater factional input' (Franklin 2007). This is not surprising because leaders must try to maintain party unity and keep caucus onside to shore up their own leadership position. This means they must ensure that different groups within the party are fairly represented, otherwise they may destabilise the party and the leader. For these reasons, the existence of powerful factions within the Labor Party is likely to continue, even under a dominant prime minister such as Kevin Rudd.

Departing from the mass party model

Like other Australian political parties, Labor has suffered a steep decline in its mem-bership. This is connected to the increasing dominance of the parliamentary party over the organisational wing. As a result of these developments, Labor has departed significantly from the mass party model, although there has been a lack of change in the formal structures of the party (Jaensch 2006, p. 26). Labor's move away from the mass party model started to occur in the late 1960s when Gough Whitlam became leader of the party. Whitlam reformed Labor's internal structures, democratising the Party Conference, increasing the power of the parliamentary party (at the expense of the extra-parliamentary wing), increasing the power of the party leader (relative to caucus), and developing a series of policies that appealed to the middle class (Warhurst 1996).

Since Whitlam's time, changes have continued to occur, to the extent that Labor can no longer be regarded as a genuine mass party. In particular, the parliamentary Labor Party, rather than the extra-parliamentary wing, is now pre-eminent when it comes to determining party policy. This became apparent when the Hawke Government adopted policies on issues such as uranium mining, East Timorese independence, and privatisation that violated the party platform (Warhurst 1996, p. 246; Parkin & Warhurst 2000; Jaensch 2006, pp. 32–5). Instead of calling the government to account for disobeying party rules, conferences were held to change the platform in accordance with the wishes of the parliamentary leadership, reversing the roles that Labor's parliamentary and extra-parliamentary wings were supposed to play in determining party policy. The dominance of the parliamentary wing has now become firmly established and Party Conferences are now essentially stage-managed media events that are designed to generate good publicity for the party leader. Occasionally, the Party Conference will refuse to follow the wishes of the parliamentary leadership, as occurred in 2008 when NSW Labor's State Conference refused to support former premier Morris Iemma's plans for electricity privatisation, but such cases are very rare.

Alongside this change, Labor's parliamentary leader has become increasingly dominant. In part, this reflects the rise of television, which tends to focus attention on personalities, such as the prime minister or the opposition leader. After election victories, Labor prime ministers such as Bob Hawke, Paul Keating and Kevin Rudd had the authority to shape the policy direction of the governments they led. Even Labor opposition leader Mark Latham was given significant freedom to shape Labor policy in the lead-up to the 2004 election, although he had not led Labor to an electoral victory and had only just managed to win the leadership over Kim Beazley (Ward 2006, p. 72). The emergence of an increasingly dominant party leader is not unique to Labor. Many other political parties around the world have experienced a similar trend. However, in Australia, these changes have caused more structural problems for Labor than for the Liberal Party, which has traditionally given the leader greater autonomy.

Alongside these developments, there has been a major decline in the number of voters who are Labor Party members. While both major parties are reluctant to disclose just how low their membership is, it is estimated that Labor's membership now stands at only 50 000, which is 0.5 per cent of voters (Parkin & Warhurst 2000, p. 28; Jaensch 2006, p. 28). Moreover, election campaigns now revolve around TV rather than old-style local campaigning in which door-knocking and local events were paramount. Professional pollsters, market researchers and public relations experts have come to play a more important role in election campaigns than rank-and-file party members, leading to the notion that Labor has moved away from the mass party model to become an electoral professional party (Jaensch 2006, p. 28; Ward 2006, pp. 80–1).

Another significant departure from the mass party model relates to the financing of the party. A large proportion of Labor's funding now comes from private donations and public funding, rather than membership dues (Jaensch 2006, pp. 30–1). Unions do continue to play an important role in funding the party, but it also receives large donations from private companies, such as the Westfield Group, the ANZ Banking Group, the Coles Group, and the Westpac Banking Corporation (AEC). In addition, between 1999 and 2002, Labor received 16 per cent of its total receipts from public funding (Johns 2006, p. 51). This has led to allegations that Labor is a cartel party that seeks to use the resources of government to preserve its power, in the face of a declining rank-and-file membership. According to proponents of this view, Labor has become detached from the electorate and can no longer be considered to be genuinely representative of the working class or any other group. Instead, it is dependent on public resources to help prop up its position.

Thus, although the Labor Party still has the key organisational characteristics of the mass party—an extra-parliamentary structure of local branches with rank-and-file members, and a Party Conference that votes on a party platform—the reality is that the parliamentary party, particularly the party leadership, is dominant, the extra-parliamentary wing has declined in both size and power, and electoral professionals have come to play a crucial role both during and between election campaigns (Parkin & Warhurst 2000, pp. 26–9; Jaensch 2006, p. 25; Ward 2006, pp. 70–2).

ISSUE IN FOCUS

WHAT DOES THE LABOR PARTY STAND FOR TODAY?

As the internal functioning of the Labor Party has changed, so has the party's ideology. Modern Labor supports multiculturalism, federalism, and the market rather than the White Australia Policy, abolition of the states, and the socialisation of the means of production, which it endorsed for much of the twentieth century. Labor's departure from its traditional beliefs has led to questions over whether it actually has a distinctive ideology, or if its only commitment is to electoral success. These doubts have continued to colour early assessments of the Rudd Government. The Issue in Focus will explore these issues by examining the extent to which the party has embraced market economics, post-materialist values, and adapted to federalism.

Debates about Labor's ideological orientation are not new. Although there is general agreement that for much of the twentieth century the party was committed to reforming capitalism in order to provide a degree of social protection for citizens and a more equal distribution of wealth, things quickly become more contentious once we move beyond these general claims. One of the most long-standing debates concerns the relationship between Labor and socialism (see Box 10.2). Labor's National Constitution contains the socialist objective, which states that '[t]he Australian Labor Party is a democratic socialist party and has the objective of the democratic socialisation of industry, production, distribution and exchange, to the extent necessary to eliminate exploitation and other anti-social features in these fields' (ALP). This objective was most famously put into action by the Chifley Government, which attempted to nationalise the banks. This action was declared unconstitutional by the High Court, and Labor's stance on the issue led to the government's defeat at the 1949 election. However, Crisp's view was that in practice Labor's commitment to public ownership fell well short of a commitment to the total socialisation of the means of production and, particularly after the 1949 election, senior party figures realised that the socialist objective was unachievable without reforms to the Constitution (cited in Marsh 2006, p. 121). Nonetheless, some commentators maintain that socialism was still an important influence on Labor. It was only one aspect of the Labor tradition, sitting alongside the acceptance of an essentially capitalist economy and other values, but socialist principles motivated many of those who founded the party, and lay behind Labor's commitment to social reform for much of the twentieth century (Maddox 1989, pp. 161–81).

BOX 10.2   Ideological influences on Labor

Socialism is a political ideology characterised by a belief in equality and community, and opposition to the free market and the exploitation of workers. Socialists believe that politics revolves around conflict between different classes, and they support extensive state involvement in the economy to redistribute wealth and ensure democratic control of the means of production, particularly through state ownership. Socialists have historically disagreed on the best means of achieving their objectives with some socialists supporting a democratic path and others a revolutionary one.

Social democracy is a term that is open to a variety of interpretations. Its origins lie in the idea that socialism can be achieved through a gradual process of social reform through democratic means, rather than revolution. However, the decision to take the democratic road to socialism tended to moderate the sorts of reforms that were pursued, and modern social democrats work to reform capitalism rather than to overthrow it (Heywood 1997, pp. 49, 55–6). While they are generally committed to ideas such as equality of opportunity, social protection for all citizens through the welfare state and a higher level of government intervention in the economy, there is significant variation in their attitude towards the market. Some social democrats are very hostile to the market and support a high degree of government intervention in the economy, whereas others are much more accepting of the market and the inequalities it produces, supporting a lesser degree of intervention (Manning 1992, pp. 13–14).

Labourism emphasises the importance of electing a labour government to manage the economy in a way that looks after the interests of wage earners, rather than seeking a radical transformation of capitalism (Manning 1992, p. 14). In Australia, labourism historically entailed the White Australia policy, protectionism, wage arbitration, and the provision of a limited range of welfare benefits and services as a basic safety net.

Q Do socialism, social democracy and labourism have any relevance in twenty-first century Australia? Have these ideologies had any influence on the policies of the Rudd Government?

Another ideological influence on Labor is social democracy. This ideology can be interpreted in different ways, but it is characterised by support for government intervention in the economy in order to achieve goals such as equality of opportunity, social protection for all citizens, and a fairer distribution of social resources. Social democrats tend to emphasise the importance of developing a generous welfare state to provide social protection for all citizens. Social democracy has clearly had an influence on Labor Party thinking, including recent European debates over how to modernise social democracy to suit modern conditions (see Box 10.3).

However, the clearest ideological influence on the Labor Party, particularly during the first half of the twentieth century, was labourism. Rather than seeking a radical transformation of capitalism, labourism is based on the Labor Party winning government and managing the economy in a way that looks after the interests of wage earners (Manning 1992, p. 14). Historically, this was done through **protectionism**, which means the use of tariff barriers to protect locally produced goods against overseas imports. In theory, this fosters the development of a strong local industry and ensures the existence of local jobs for Australian workers. Labourism also involves restrictive immigration programs, such as the White Australia Policy, which prevented non-white migrants from coming to Australia, supposedly to protect workers' jobs. Another part of labourism is a regulated labour market, which relies on wage arbitration to ensure that all workers earn a wage

Protectionism: the use of tariff barriers to protect local industries against competition from overseas imports

sufficient to support a family. Welfare payments are provided, but they are only supposed to go to those who are unable to work. This approach to social protection has been dubbed the wage earners' welfare state because the government protects citizens' living standards through a regulated labour market rather than through the provision of an extensive range of welfare benefits and services (Castles 1985). Labor's support for this approach lasted for most of the twentieth century. However, the ascension of Gough Whitlam to the leadership of the Party marked a turning-point in its ideological orientation.

Embracing the market

Under Gough Whitlam, Labor won the 1972 election, and although it remained in office for only three years (1972–75), it introduced a wide range of reforms, including a significant expansion in the size of the welfare state, in order to provide welfare benefits and services to groups in the community that had previously been under-supported. This represented a significant departure from Labor's support for the wage earners' welfare state, because the government benefits provided went beyond those necessary for a basic safety net. However, this welfare reform, and other policies introduced by the Whitlam Government, were consistent with Labor's traditional willingness to intervene in the market in the interests of social justice. A notable exception to this was the decision to cut tariffs, which represented a step away from protectionism, towards a greater emphasis on the free market.

More radical changes in Labor's approach to the economy occurred in the 1980s and 1990s as the Hawke and Keating governments embraced **neoliberalism**, reducing the government's involvement in the economy by further lowering tariff barriers, introducing competition policy, floating the dollar, and deregulating the financial system. Labor also partially deregulated the Labor market, introducing a system of enterprise bargaining instead of wage arbitration. The central idea behind these reforms was to give a freer rein to market forces, an idea that is supported by the current prime minister, Kevin Rudd, who has described himself as an economic conservative. In essence, this means that he embraces the market, rather than viewing it with hostility. This change in Labor's approach to the economy seems consistent with the claim that it has departed from the mass party model, moving away from its traditional ideology.

> **Neoliberalism:** a political ideology characterised by a belief in the free market, and opposition to a large welfare state and extensive state involvement in the economy

Some Labor supporters have criticised the party for adopting neoliberal economic policy, arguing that it has betrayed its traditional values (e.g. Maddox 1989). These critics endorse what has become known as the discontinuity thesis. They argue that in becoming economic conservatives, modern Labor, starting with Hawke and Keating, has abandoned its traditional commitment to equality, and to achieving social goals other than the accumulation of wealth. Ideological convergence has occurred in Australian politics, because the two major political parties now both support neoliberalism (Marsh 2006). This has broader ramifications because it limits the choices that voters have available to them at elections.

Others have defended the party against these criticisms, emphasising that Labor governments in the 1980s and 1990s remained committed to social justice, 'refurbishing' the welfare state to protect the living standards of those who were most severely affected by the process of neoliberal economic reform (e.g. Castles & Shirley 1996). On this view, Labor has always been committed to ensuring that Australia has a strong economy, recognising that this is necessary to ensure that all Australians, including workers, enjoy a high standard of living. In an era of globalisation, achieving this objective meant opening up the Australian economy to market forces, and departing from Australia's traditional emphasis on protectionism and arbitration. While this made Australia a wealthier country, it also led to an increase in income inequality. The Hawke and Keating Governments responded to this by increasing welfare payments in order to protect the vulnerable and rectify the increase in inequality. Thus, although they crafted a new set of policies to suit a new era, Hawke and Keating Labor maintained the party's traditional commitment to both a strong economy and social justice.

The idea that Labor can support both capitalism and social justice has been attacked by Marxist critics of the party. They argue that a commitment to a strong capitalist economy means acting to maximise the profitability of companies who will demand low rates of taxation and low wages, which limits the government's capacity to redistribute income and improve the lot of workers, thereby undermining the commitment to social justice. Thus, although the Hawke and Keating Governments shifted Labor to the Right, their policies were consistent with the Labor tradition of prioritising profitability over wages and social justice at times of economic crisis (Johnson 1989, pp. 92–108).

BOX 10.3   The Third Way

In the 1990s, a number of centre-left politicians and political thinkers were drawn to an ideology known as the Third Way. The ideology was particularly associated with former British Labour prime minister Tony Blair, former United States president Bill Clinton and, at an academic level, British sociologist Anthony Giddens. The Third Way emphasises the importance of 'transcending the distinction between left and right; advancing equality of opportunity; employing mutual responsibility; strengthening communities; and embracing globalisation' (Leigh 2003, p. 10). While the exact meaning of some of these ideas is ambiguous, the general idea is that social democratic parties should modernise, embrace market economics and global free trade, while supporting strategic forms of state intervention (often in concert with private sector companies and community organisations) to ensure that all citizens have the opportunity to make the most of their talents. In addition, the emphasis on community and mutual responsibility is about ensuring that citizens take responsibility for their lives and their families by, for instance, forcing the recipients of unemployment benefits to look for jobs, or participate in education and training. The result is supposed to be a modern form of social democracy that combines a commitment to market principles and individual responsibility with a continuing belief in the importance of equality of opportunity.

While some prominent Labor figures were attracted to the Third Way (e.g. Gallop 2001; Latham 2001), it is doubtful whether it represented a genuinely new path for Australian Labor. As a number of commentators have noted (e.g. Scott 2000, pp. 1–5, 256; Crabb 2005, p. 5; also note Pierson & Castles 2002), Tony Blair visited Australia during the Hawke–Keating era and drew on the Australian experience in his Third-Way modernisation of British Labour, so the ideology may simply have been a new label for an approach that Australian Labor had already adopted. The Hawke–Keating Governments had already embraced market economics and the idea of 'reciprocal obligation' (for example, compulsory welfare-to-work schemes and labour market programs formed a key part of the *Working Nation* labour market package, which was implemented in the final term of the Keating Government). Critics in Britain and Australia also questioned whether there was any substance to the Third Way, or if it was simply 'a new label for vacuous pragmatism' (e.g. Tanner 1999, pp. 51–2). Perhaps for this reason, there was a marked drop in media and academic interest in the Third Way just five years after the term had first begun to be widely used (Leigh 2003). Whether or not the Third Way had anything to offer Australian Labor, the party did not embrace the idea, and even when Third-Way proponent Mark Latham became party leader, he rarely used the term.

Q Does the Third Way represent the modernisation of social democracy, or the abandonment of core social democratic values?

The early indications are that the Rudd Labor Government will continue in a similar vein to the Hawke and Keating Governments, presenting itself as committed to the marriage of economic efficiency and social justice. In November 2006, shortly before becoming Labor leader, Rudd published an article in the *Monthly* magazine, which briefly outlined his vision for the party. Rudd described Howard's Australia as a 'Brutopia' in which an obsession with the free market was undermining important social institutions such as the family. In contrast, he argued that social democracy is based on 'the view that the market is designed for human beings, not vice versa' (Rudd 2006). Thus, while Labor supports the market, it also believes that state intervention may be necessary to protect values such as 'equity (particularly through education), solidarity, and sustainability' (Rudd 2006).

Although it is too early to make definitive judgments about the extent of the Labor Government's commitment to these values and their policy implications, the party's opposition to the Howard Government's WorkChoices industrial relations reforms at the 2007 election is an indication that there are still important differences between Labor and the Coalition. This is also demonstrated by the way the government and the opposition have responded to the global financial crisis. While the opposition has emphasised the importance of tax cuts, the government has massively increased spending in an attempt to kick-start the economy. For Labor, this represents a departure from the dictates of neo-liberal economics, and seems more consistent with the party's traditional belief that strong government intervention in the economy is necessary. In fact, Prime Minister Rudd has argued that the crisis demonstrates that:

> the great neo-liberal experiment of the past 30 years has failed, that the emperor has no clothes. Neo-liberalism, and the free-market fundamentalism it has produced, has been revealed as little more than personal greed dressed up as an economic philosophy. And, ironically, it now falls to social democracy to prevent liberal capitalism from cannibalising itself (Rudd 2009, p. 25).

This does not mean returning to measures such as protectionism and high levels of state ownership, which Labor supported in the past, but it does mean that social democracy, with 'its capacity to balance the private and the public, profit and wages, the market and the state … once again speaks with clarity and cogency to the challenges of our time' (Rudd 2009, p. 21).

Post-materialist values

Modern Labor also stands for a variety of **post-materialist values** such as multiculturalism and environmental sustainability that have come onto the political agenda in Australia since the 1970s. These values are post-materialist in the sense that they are concerned with broader quality-of-life issues than the material standard of living. This may be further evidence that Labor has departed from the mass party model, as many associate post-materialist values with the middle class, rather than the working class, and believe that these values directly contradict traditional Labor beliefs and policies.

Post-materialist values: those values that are concerned with broad quality-of-life issues such as the environment and multiculturalism, which transcend the traditional policy focus on the economy and national security

Traditionally, Labor supported the White Australia Policy, which restricted immigration to those from a European background. However, this changed when Gough Whitlam and other Labor reformers such as Don Dunstan led the charge to remove the White Australia Policy from Labor's platform (Warhurst 1996, p. 249). Instead, Labor came to embrace a policy of **multiculturalism**, which sought to promote rather than prevent cultural diversity. Labor's support for multiculturalism continued during the Hawke and Keating years, and it looks set to continue under the Mandarin-speaking Kevin Rudd. Labor has also supported reforms aimed at strengthening Indigenous rights, such as the Keating Government's native title land-rights legislation (Warhurst 1996, p. 249), and more recently, the Rudd Government formally apologised to the Stolen Generation, sharply distinguishing itself from the Howard Government, which steadfastly refused to make a formal apology.

> **Multiculturalism:** the belief that cultural diversity is positive, and that it should be supported by the government

Labor has also aligned itself with causes such as feminism and the environment that have been advanced by new social movements (Warhurst 1996, p. 250). Once again, a key turning point was the Whitlam Government, which introduced 'economic policies such as support for equal pay for work of equal value, social policies such as child care and support for family planning and contraception, and … institutional developments such as the appointment of a Women's Adviser' (Warhurst 1996, p. 250). This has continued through to the Rudd Government, which increased the Childcare Tax Rebate in its first budget and funded the construction of more childcare centres (Lunn 2008).

Labor has also tried to distinguish itself from the Coalition by supporting more environmentally friendly policies. For example, in 1983, the Hawke Government intervened to prevent the damming of the Franklin River in Tasmania. More recently, the Rudd Government has identified itself closely with efforts to combat climate change, and the first act of the new government was to ratify the Kyoto Protocol, which again represented a major contrast with the previous Howard Government. The Rudd Government also commissioned economist Ross Garnaut to produce a report on an emissions trading scheme, which was presented in September 2008.

Some have criticised Labor for aligning itself with new social movements and the post-materialist values they advance. Particularly during the party's 11 years in opposition (1997–2007), these critics argued that post-materialist values were the concern of the affluent middle class, not Labor's traditional working-class base, or the crucial voters in marginal seats whose support the party needed to win office. Some linked this criticism to the defeat of the Keating Government in 1996, arguing that Keating's 'big picture' vision of Australia, which gave pride of place to multiculturalism and the republic, alienated many in the Australian community. In contrast, John Howard's appeal in 1996 (and at subsequent elections) was that he promised to govern 'for all of us,' rather than focusing on the interests of a narrow elite who were interested in a politically correct agenda (e.g. Brett 2004). Some in the labour movement shared this view, and thought that Labor needed to return to its working-class roots, which on their interpretation, meant placing less emphasis on post-materialist values (e.g. Thompson 1999).

However, it is important not to exaggerate the extent to which Labor has embraced post-materialist concerns. Labor's last three prime ministers, Hawke, Keating and Rudd, have all clearly viewed the economy as the number one domestic policy priority, not post-materialism, and Rudd, in particular, has been careful to avoid portraying Labor as a party of elites. An example of this was his continual use of the phrase 'working families' during the 2007 election campaign. He also took clear steps to shield Labor from the charge that it would implement a radical politically correct agenda in government, promising not to hold a referendum on the republic in his first term in office, and opposing Prime Minister Howard's proposal to hold a referendum to recognise Indigenous Australians in the preamble to the Constitution. Upon winning office, the new Labor government also emphasised the importance of practical, as well as symbolic reconciliation, and new Education Minister Julia Gillard said that it was appropriate for school history textbooks to describe the colonisation of Australia as a 'settlement' rather than an 'invasion', which was a clear attempt to distance Labor from the culture wars and disputes over identity politics. The Rudd Government also continued the Howard Government's intervention in the Northern Territory (albeit with modifications), and this suggests that it is more prepared to restrict the autonomy of Indigenous communities than previous Labor governments. It is also clear that Labor is not a radical environmental party. Rudd was strongly criticised by conservationists for refusing to ban the Gunns pulp mill in Tasmania, while its emissions trading scheme included measures to protect local industries. This suggests that although the contemporary Labor Party supports a range of post-materialist concerns, it is very sensitive to the charge of elitism and it will depart from the post-materialist path if the electoral or economic costs involved become too great. This fits with the claim that the party has become an electoral professional party whose principal commitment is to winning elections.

BOX 10.4   Who votes Labor?

Given that the Labor Party was formed as the political wing of the labour movement, it is unsurprising that its supporters have traditionally been blue-collar workers and trade unionists. Men have also been more likely to vote Labor than women.

However, these voting patterns have shifted over time, as social and economic change has occurred. In the 1970s, as Labor turned away from labourism under Gough Whitlam and embraced post-materialist values, it began to attract votes from the growing number of white-collar workers, such as teachers and public servants. Labor has also become a more appealing party to female voters (Scott 2000, 132–4). Moreover, although it has attracted greater support from women and white-collar workers, support for Labor among blue-collar voters has fallen. At the 1996 election, fewer than 50 per cent of manual workers voted for the Keating Labor Government (Scott 2000, 126–7). Some have suggested that this reflects the changes in the party's ideology.

There has also been a strong religious aspect to voting in Australia, with Protestants more likely to vote Liberal, and Catholics more likely to vote Labor. However, the Catholic vote for the Liberal Party has increased, and now both parties attract a significant level of support from Catholic voters (Bean 2000). Once again, this change may partly be explained by a shift in Labor's ideological orientation as it has embraced post-materialist causes which may at times alienate more socially conservative Catholics.

Q   **What factors account for changes in the traditional pattern of voter support for Labor?**

Federalism

Another important change in Labor's ideological orientation is in its attitude towards the federal character of the Australian political system. As discussed above, Labor's mass party structure was designed to ensure that it remained a vehicle for advancing the interests of the labour movement. The emphasis was on fostering strong internal discipline to ensure that the party remained united in its quest to achieve social reform in the interests of the working class. Labor was hostile to aspects of the Australian political system, particularly federalism, which it saw as limiting the party's capacity to implement social change once in government. Federalism disperses government power between central and state governments, and it is also linked to other power-dispersing institutions such as entrenched constitutions, judicial review and strong bicameralism. Labor supporters believed that these sorts of institutions would prevent them from being able to achieve the social reforms they desired and, consequently, a long-held Labor policy was to abolish the states. However, as Labor has departed from the mass party model and embraced, to a great extent, free market and post-materialist values, it has also become more or less reconciled to federalism.

Aside from changes in its internal workings and a more moderate ideological orientation, one of key the reasons for Labor's reconciliation with federalism is that the federal system has actually shaped the nature of the Labor Party (see Galligan 1995, p. 97). State Labor branches have operated around the country and many state

Labor governments have been formed since Federation. State Labor governments are unlikely to want to abolish themselves (and their power), and this creates internal pressure for Labor to support federalism. Australian voters have consistently rejected attempts to centralise power, and this suggests that any attempt to abolish federalism would be unsuccessful because voters would not support it at a referendum. Instead, Labor leaders realised that they were able to work within existing constitutional arrangements to achieve policy reforms, assisted by High Court decisions that have led to an increase in Commonwealth power (see Chapter 3 for further discussion) (Galligan 1995, pp. 101–9). State Labor governments have also proven their worth by helping to advance the party's objectives. In particular, Labor leaders such as South Australian Premier Don Dunstan demonstrated that state governments could advance the cause of social democracy by testing out new policy reforms, which would spread to other states if they were successful.

Not only has Labor now embraced federalism, but Prime Minister Rudd has made the improvement of federal–state relations one of his key goals in office. In fact, he campaigned hard on this issue in the lead-up to the 2007 election, arguing that as a Labor prime minister he would be able to work more effectively with the (exclusively) Labor premiers, to combat issues relating to hospital funding and the environment. Ironically, as the Coalition, which has traditionally supported federalism, has come to adopt a more centralist stance (see Chapter 11), Labor has been emphasising the benefits of greater federal–state cooperation. It will be interesting to see whether this federalist attitude persists now that Labor's monopoly on state governments has come to an end.

CHAPTER SUMMARY

This chapter has discussed the ways in which the Labor Party has departed from the mass party model, which it originally embodied. The party's internal structures were originally designed to empower the extra-parliamentary wing, and although these structures are still formally in place today, in practice, their operation has changed markedly, and power has shifted to the parliamentary leadership. Labor has also embraced neo-liberal economics, which marks a turn away from its traditional ideological commitment to high levels of government intervention in the market. This has led to debate over whether Labor has abandoned its traditional support for social justice, and whether it is any different from the Coalition in its approach to government. Modern Labor also stands for a range of new post-materialist values such as multiculturalism, Indigenous rights, feminism and environmentalism, some of which clash with the party's traditional beliefs, and which may alienate some of its traditional supporters. It remains to be seen whether the current Labor Prime Minster, Kevin Rudd, will be able to forge a clearer identity for the party in the twenty-first century.

WEBSITES

Australian Labor Party (ALP):
www.alp.org.au
The ALP's official website.

Australian Council of Trade Unions (ACTU):
www.actu.com.au
The website of the ACTU, which is the peak representative body for unions in Australia.

Australian Fabian Society:
www.fabian.org.au
A Centre-Left think-tank that is independent of, but sympathetic towards, the Labor Party.

FURTHER READING

Manne, R. (ed.). 2008. *Dear Mr Rudd: Ideas for a Better Australia*. Black Inc. Agenda, Melbourne.

Marsh, I. (ed.). 2004. *Political Parties in Transition*? The Federation Press, Sydney.

Warhurst, J. & Parkin, A. (eds). 2000. *The Machine: Labor Confronts the Future*. Allen & Unwin, St Leonards.

11 The Liberal Party

THIS CHAPTER:

★ outlines the history and organisation of the Liberal Party of Australia
★ traces the ideological orientation of Australia's non-Labor parties, including the Liberal Party, since Federation
★ critically examines the main principles of the Liberal Party including its emphasis on the parliamentary leader and the freedom of individual Members of Parliament.

ISSUE IN FOCUS

What does the Liberal Party stand for today?

KEY TERMS

Alfred Deakin
Cross the floor
Democratic Labor Party
    (DLP)

Gender voting gap
Institutionalise
Margaret Thatcher
Nationalise
Populist

Post-materialist
Robert Menzies
Social liberalism

In mid 2006, under pressure from the Indonesian Government to refuse refugee status for West Papuans fleeing their homeland, Prime Minister John Howard introduced legislation into the Commonwealth Parliament to once again change the way in which Australia treated asylum-seekers. The legislation would have prevented any asylum-seeker who arrived on Australia's mainland territory without authorisation from having their claims for refugee status heard in Australia. Since 2001, when Howard's popularity skyrocketed after he prevented the entry into Australia of asylum-seekers aboard the *MV Tampa*, the government had gradually reduced the territory on which Australian migration law applied.

Howard was surprised when a number of Liberal Party Members of Parliament made it clear that the new legislation was unacceptable and that they would cross the floor of Parliament to vote against it. One of the hall-marks of the Howard Government had been a high level of party discipline. Unlike the Menzies and Fraser Governments, when Members of Parliament on numerous occasions exercised their conscience and voted against government legislation, crossing the floor was almost unheard of under Howard. The prime minister backed down. The withdrawal of the asylum-seeker legislation was a sign that Howard's dominance of his government was slipping, and that traditional Liberal Party principles of individual conscience and social liberalism were making a comeback.

> **Cross the floor:** when Members of Parliament vote with the opposing party
>
> **Social liberalism:** a view that places less emphasis on economic freedom than classical liberalism, standing for greater social equality and individual freedom on moral issues

Introduction

When John Howard lost his seat at the 2007 election, the most successful political party in Australia's history took a leap into the unknown. The Liberal Party is a vehicle built for successful political leaders. In its two previous spells in opposition, the party had not responded well to the challenges of rebuilding public confidence in its direction. Formed in 1945, the Liberal Party's success over more than sixty years has rested on just three dominant leaders—**Robert Menzies**, Malcolm Fraser and John Howard. Between Menzies' retirement in 1966 and Fraser's appointment as prime minister in 1975, the party experienced five changes of leader. After Fraser's loss to Labor's Bob Hawke in 1983, it took six changes of leader before John Howard found an election-winning formula in 1996. The party's two periods in opposition (1972–75 and 1983–96) prior to the one that began in 2007 were characterised by a good deal of soul-searching about the party's character.

> **Robert Menzies:** prime minister 1939–41 and 1949–66

While the Liberal Party's greatest success has come from a pragmatic approach to the implementation of its preferred ideological orientation, a successful political party nevertheless requires a set of values that can inspire supporters and give direction to the parliamentary wing. The core values of the Liberal Party have always been respect for the individual, reward for hard work and support for free enterprise. Over the years, however, radically different policy prescriptions have been derived from these core values. The Menzies Government, for example, maintained high tariffs on imported goods to protect local industries from foreign competition, and maintained an interventionist industrial relations system that limited wage inequality. The Howard Government, by contrast, pursued a policy of low tariffs and sought to deregulate the industrial relations system. Neither of these policy prescriptions is at odds with the core values of the Liberal Party, but they do represent quite different approaches to economic management. The party's core values have tended to stand in contrast to the more collectivist approach of the Australian Labor Party.

This chapter explains the difficulty that right-of-centre parties in Australia have had in finding a unifying set of policies with which they could successfully combat the Australian Labor Party. It shows how the experiences of conservative parties in the first half of the century influenced the shape of the Liberal Party when it was established in the 1940s. The chapter then outlines the main features of the Liberal Party—its dependence on a strong and successful parliamentary leader, the autonomy of the parliamentary wing of the party from the organisational wing, and the nature of the party's long-running relationship with the National Party. The Issue in Focus for this chapter is the changing ideological orientation of the Liberal Party. Liberals and conservatives have always struggled for the soul of the party, with a strong dose of pragmatism from the parliamentary leadership often providing the defining characteristic of the party's approach to policy. More recently, the overturning of many of the policies of the Menzies Government and the struggle for social liberals to find a place in the party has caused some to question whether a party containing such a diversity of viewpoints can persist in the Australian party system.

Opposing Labor

One of the reasons why Australia's right-of-centre parties have always struggled to define themselves is that their identity and electoral appeal has often been about the contrast with their main rivals—the Australian Labor Party. Australian politics has featured a two-party system since 1910, when two Centre-Right parties combined to more effectively oppose Labor, which by that time was attracting nearly half of the national vote. Until the emergence of Labor as a successful political force, the right of Australia's political spectrum was divided over the question of trade protection. Colonial parliaments were similarly divided prior to Federation. The settlement of the trade issue during the first decade after Federation (through a combination of high tariffs and centralised wage arbitration) allowed Labor's opponents to find enough common ground to combine their forces into a single party (Jaensch 1994b, pp. 19–20). This combination of free-trade and protectionist Members of Parliament was known as The Fusion, and a short time later as the Liberal Party.

Just as Menzies would in the 1940s, the founders of the first Liberal Party chose the term 'liberal' in order to contrast their platform with what they argued was the threat of socialism from Labor. The modern Liberal Party, the National Party and their conservative predecessors are often referred to as the non-Labor parties, an acknowledgment of their primary purpose in the Australian political system as the alternatives to the ALP. However, while these parties have been united in their opposition to Labor, there has always been a mixture of ideological positions within them. The first Liberal Party was divided between conservatives and social liberals. The former group viewed liberalism in terms of the limited role of the state, preferring governments to restrict their activities to national defence and the rule of law.

The followers of **Alfred Deakin**, however, adopted another view of liberalism, called social liberalism, which emphasised a role for the government in unlocking the human potential in every citizen, through state-funded education, by protecting individuals from the worst excesses of the free market and by eliminating poverty (Tiver 1978, p. 21). What united these rather disparate views of the role of government was not only a dislike of the policies of the Labor Party, but also of the collectivist ethos that limited the freedom of Labor Members of Parliament to vote against an agreed party line.

Alfred Deakin: politician and leader of the movement for Australian federation. He held the office of prime minister of Australia for three terms: 1903–04, 1905–08 and 1909–10

BOX 11.1   Liberal or conservative?

This chapter often uses the word 'conservative' to describe the two parties—the Liberal and National Parties—that dominate right-of-centre politics in Australia. Many on the Right, however, consider themselves liberal rather than conservative. To make matters more complicated, there are various types of liberalism, each with an historical strand in Australian politics (see Norton 2004).

Conservatives value tradition and social stability. Conservatism can vary according to which set of values are being conserved. British and Australian conservatives have historically favoured a more interventionist economic policy than their American counterparts. There tends to be more agreement on social issues, where conservatives favour a traditional definition of the family, and tough policies against illegal drugs.

Classical liberals prefer limited government. They resist intervention by the state in both the economic and social realms. Classical liberals prefer the state to limit its activities to ensuring that citizens are treated equally under the law.

Social liberals mirror the classical liberal preference for individual autonomy. They argue, however, that the state may need to intervene in the economy to provide all citizens with equal opportunities. This may require a considerable amount of spending on welfare and education, and limits on the freedom of businesses in their treatment of employees.

Q Is the Liberal Party predominantly a conservative party or a liberal one? Why have social liberals had a limited impact on Liberal Party policies in recent decades?

While Australia's two-party system itself has been stable since 1910, the decades up until the Second World War (1939–45) saw a number of different parties fill the right side of the two-party divide. During the First World War, Labor was divided over the issue of military conscription. Prime Minister Billy Hughes (1915–23), along with a group of fellow members of the Labor Party, resigned from their party to form a government led by a new conservative party, the Nationalist Party. Once again in 1931, a new party was formed when then-Treasurer Joseph Lyons left Labor to lead yet another new conservative party, the United Australia Party (UAP). Lyons led the UAP into government that year and was prime minister until his death in 1939. In between these ructions among the largest political parties, the Country Party, the forerunner to the National Party, was formed in 1920 to represent the interests of farmers. Some scholars argue that Australia features a two-and-a-half party system or a three-party system. Others believe that, since the National Party 'invariably acts in concert with the Liberals', a two-party or bi-polar description is more apt (Ward & Stewart 2006, pp. 120–1). Regardless of how we formulate our approach to the party system, the consolidation of the Liberal Party within that system is a relatively new development.

Prior to the formation of the modern Liberal Party, then, Australia's various non-Labor parties had a number of common features. Each of those parties was distinguished more by their opposition to socialism than by any commonality of belief within their membership, and the parliamentary membership enjoyed freedom from influence from the party organisation. In addition, the sectarian divide between Protestants predominantly supporting (and joining) the conservative parties, and Catholics supporting Labor, had been established.

BOX 11.2   Who votes Liberal?

Traditionally, the Liberal Party relied on a coalition of voters from various parts of society in order to overcome the bloc of blue-collar workers habitually voting Labor. Managers, small business people, educated and professional workers, and Protestants historically favoured the Liberals. The Liberal Party also worked hard to gain the votes of women, although the **gender voting gap**, which used to favour the Coalition parties, has closed in recent decades.

Gender voting gap: the difference in voting behaviour between men and women

Post-materialist: a view that pays greater attention to issues such as the environment and human rights than economic and defence issues

Changes to the Australian economy and society since the 1970s have seen some traditionally Labor voters siding with the Liberals (and vice versa). Labor has been attracting the votes of increasing numbers of white-collar workers, such as teachers and public servants. Labor has adopted many **post-materialist** policies, closing the gap between Labor and Liberal where voters with a tertiary degree are concerned. On the other hand, the deregulation of the economy under the Hawke and Keating Labor Governments caused many blue-collar workers to become disillusioned with Labor. At the 1996 election, John Howard's Coalition captured the votes of more blue-collar workers than Labor.

One of the most striking features of the Howard Government was the number of Catholic cabinet ministers when compared with a typical Menzies cabinet of the 1950s, which comprised only one non-Protestant minister. Catholic MPs such as Tony Abbott and Kevin Andrews took high-profile ministerial portfolios under Howard. This reflects the sharper differences between the two major parties on social (rather than economic) issues. The Liberal Party has captured the votes of the old **Democratic Labor Party (DLP)** constituency. Policies such as federal aid to independent (including Catholic) schools have also been important to the trend of more Catholics voting Liberal. At the 2004 election, half of all Catholics voted Liberal.

> **Democratic Labor Party (DLP):** a Catholic-based and anti-communist party, which split from the Australian Labor Party in the 1950s

Source: Australian Electoral Study, various years

The structure of the Liberal Party

One of the defining differences between Australia's two major parties is their respective structures. For Australia's conservative parties, finding a structure that was stable, yet flexible enough to cater to a range of viewpoints, had proved difficult. Robert Menzies succeeded Joe Lyons as prime minister and leader of the United Australia Party in 1939. It was in that year that Australia, following the lead of the United Kingdom, declared war on Germany. Menzies struggled to unite his government and resigned as prime minister in 1941. At the 1943 election, with Labor's John Curtin proving an inspiring wartime leader, the UAP suffered one of the worst election defeats in Australian history. This loss was the catalyst for plans to create a stronger and more durable right-of-centre party. Previous conservative parties had been mere conveniences for ambitious Members of Parliament. Menzies and other senior conservative figures agreed that an enduring political party needed something more than their shared dislike of the Australian Labor Party. It would need a set of affirmative principles and a vibrant party organisation. The depth to which the conservative side of politics sank during the war ensured that little resistance to the concept of a new party was forthcoming (Hancock 2007, p. 53).

While the Liberal Party was to be federal (decentralised) in structure, a national organisation made up of representatives from the state divisions was designed to ensure that any differences between the state organisations would not prevent the emergence of a clear national direction. Permanent employees of the party would help develop the branch structure, provide research into policy options and seek out new candidates for public office. Representation for women on the party's decision-making bodies was designed to broaden the party's appeal (Brett 2006, p. 213). State branches set their own rules for pre-selection of candidates. It was only in 1994 that the Federal Executive was granted power to intervene in pre-selections for federal elections—an indication of the decentralised party structure.

Menzies felt that one of the problems that plagued the UAP was that it was too close to big business, and therefore unable to govern in the interests of ordinary voters. It also had no formal organisation outside New South Wales and Victoria (Hancock 1994). The new party was to feature a network of permanent party branches designed to provide a source of revenue and also to guarantee a ready reserve of volunteers for election campaigns. The Liberal Party would thus be less dependent on donations from big business. Indeed, Menzies rejected the entire notion of politics based on class warfare. 'In a country like Australia, the class war must always be a false war,' he told the nation in his famous 1942 radio address entitled *The Forgotten People*. Rather than siding with big business against the working class, Menzies saw the votes of the middle class as decisive in Australian politics. He described the middle class as 'those people who are constantly in danger of being ground between the upper and nether millstones of the false class war … the backbone of the country' (cited in Brett 1992, pp. 38–9).

The Labor Party easily won the 1946 election, which was the first electoral test for the new Liberal Party. By 1949, however, many Australians were tiring of the restrictions on markets—such as petrol rationing—that had persisted after the end of the war in 1945.

Many of the Liberal Party's candidates for office in 1949, when the party finally achieved victory, were war veterans. Robert Menzies was prime minister of Australia from 1949 until 1966, still by far the longest single stretch in the job. His long tenure was undoubtedly assisted by the postwar economic boom and the Labor Party split in the 1950s (see Chapter 10), but is also a testament to his political skills. His extraordinary success as prime minister ensured that the Liberal Party would always be synonymous with Robert Menzies.

Leadership and the Liberal Party

Another important difference between Australia's two largest political parties is the authority that the Liberal Party affords to its parliamentary leader. The most successful Liberal prime ministers—Menzies, Fraser and Howard—had quite different policy prescriptions and different ways of relating to voters. One thing they had in common, though, was the authority with which they led their parliamentary colleagues. The parliamentary leader makes the final decisions on Liberal Party policy. In government, the leader's view is rarely defeated in cabinet deliberations. John Howard ran a very disciplined policy-development process during his 11 years of government. Leaks to the media from cabinet submissions were very rare. Howard's command of cabinet was enhanced by his vast edge in ministerial experience over most of his colleagues (Weller 2007, p. 177). Howard ran a very efficient system of rewarding those who complied with his desire for government unity. In turn, the success of this strategy helped the Coalition to win elections, reinforcing the discipline of the government.

The Liberal Party leader also chooses his or her front bench team—the ministry or shadow ministry. A leader needs to be able to trust those around him. None of this is to say that Liberal Party leaders can simply dismiss any opposition from within their own party. Indeed, a secure leader will make the inclusion in the ministry of those with a different point of view, a show of strength. In addition to giving a voice to the 'broad church' of views within the party, the leader needs to ensure a balance of representation between MPs from each state in the Commonwealth as well as a blend of youth and experience. Gender balance is also becoming important. However, while the number of women in the parliamentary Liberal Party has increased at recent elections, the Howard Government only featured a maximum of two cabinet positions for women out of sixteen at any one time. These considerations mean that the leader's freedom is in practice considerably constrained.

There is a paradox in the Liberal Party's simultaneous belief in the primacy of the individual and the willingness of individual MPs to make themselves dependent on a powerful leader. Liberal MPs, successful politicians in their own right, at times subordinate themselves to their party's leader even as they decry Labor's rigid decision-making procedures. The Liberal Party's 'messiah complex', as its search for a strong leader is sometimes called, was partly a result of the long and successful period the party experienced under Menzies. The importance of the party leader has been emphasised in all Australian political parties through the advent of television, which tends to concentrate its coverage of politics on personalities rather than policy.

Yet, the Liberal Party does not **institutionalise** strong leadership. A leader must be successful by virtue of an election victory before being afforded the full authority of the party. The parliamentary party is only willing to cede its authority to a leader who has a proven connection with the electorate (Brett 2003, p. 30). David Kemp wrote in 1973 that successful political leaders are neither afraid to consult nor afraid to act alone (p. 52). They need to be secure enough in their own job to show leadership and take risks but not so removed from their followers that they lose touch with their concerns. Relying

> **Institutionalise:** the process of turning values and habits into formal and informal rules

on a successful leader to provide the party with unity and purpose ensures a power vacuum after an election loss. Table 11.1 shows that the turnover of leaders is much more frequent in opposition than in government. The Liberal Party in opposition has few formal rules to prevent leadership destabilisation and a Liberal leader who has not won an election has limited authority. By definition, an opposition leader is either unsuccessful at the previous election or new and untried. Yet, while the leader's authority is less assured while in opposition, political parties are today acutely aware that perceived divisions can be electorally damaging. Less successful leaders, as in most political parties, are at the mercy of the parliamentary party. It is for this reason that the Liberal Party has found its periods in opposition so difficult, with changes of leader commonplace. Any member of the parliamentary party can call on a vote for the leadership, making the Liberal Party leadership (as well as the ALP leadership) much less secure than in those political parties where members of the party organisation vote for the parliamentary leader, as is normally the case in Europe. In spite of Menzies' two decades as leader, the Liberal Party has one of the shortest average tenures for leaders of any political party in the democratic world (Bynander & t'Hart 2007, p. 58).

Table 11.1 Liberal Party leaders

Leader	State of origin	Years as leader (or prime minister)
Robert Menzies	Victoria	1944–66 (prime minister 1949–66)
Harold Holt	Victoria	prime minister 1966–67
John Gorton	Victoria	prime minister 1967–70
William McMahon	NSW	prime minister 1970–72
Billy Snedden	Victoria	1972–75
Malcolm Fraser	Victoria	prime minister 1975–83
Andrew Peacock	Victoria	1983–85, 1989–90
John Howard	NSW	1985–87, 1995–2007 (prime minister 1996–2007)
John Hewson	NSW	1990–94
Alexander Downer	SA	1994–95
Brendan Nelson	NSW	2007–08
Malcolm Turnbull	NSW	2008–

A popular and successful Liberal Party leader is rarely challenged by either the parliamentary party or by the party organisation. The leader's dominance in policy development, entrenched by the long run of election victories under Menzies, meant that the vigorous party structure developed at the party's founding eventually fell into decay. Policy-making in government had become a matter of problem-solving rather than political philosophy. When the Liberal Party found itself in opposition in 1972, and again in 1983, its ability to debate and develop policy had simply been lost. This lack of formal policy-development machinery in turn reinforces the importance of finding a leader strong enough to provide the party with some direction. While leaders such as John Howard sometimes choose to differentiate themselves from their opponents in the party by stressing their own set of values, leadership contests in the Liberal Party are usually about personalities and personal political connections more so than ideology.

Freedom of conscience

The non-Labor parties that were the forerunners of the Liberal and National parties could also be differentiated from the ALP by their respective party organisations. Where Labor MPs were forced to sign a pledge that bound them to decisions of the party, the anti-collectivist approach to politics of those on the right ensured that individual MPs in the non-Labor parties were granted the ability to make their own decisions on how to vote in the Parliament. It was barely noticed in the 1950s and 1960s if MPs occasionally dissented from the majority view of the party-room. The demands of a modern media environment, where differences of opinion are interpreted as division and lack of organisation on the part of the party leadership, have put this tradition under enormous pressure. Where ALP members face expulsion for voting against legislation backed by caucus, the Liberal Party has a number of ways of keeping MPs in line. The prospect of a front bench position (or the expulsion to the back bench for those already in the ministry or shadow ministry) is usually incentive enough to cooperate with the party leadership.

The impotence of the party's organisational wing is most noticeable when it comes to policy. When the party's National Conference refused to endorse John Howard's industrial relations blueprint in 2005 because the policy was in conflict with the party's long-standing commitment to federalism, the incident was barely noticed (Errington & van Onselen 2006, p. 7). It would have no influence over the passage of the legislation through the Parliament. The party organisation is important, however, when it comes to the pre-selection of Liberal Party candidates for Parliament. This in turn affects the policy direction of the parliamentary party and raises the stakes for the otherwise moribund collection of Liberal Party branches. As in the Labor Party, those small branches are susceptible to 'stacking' by one group within the party so that they can ensure that their members will make their way into Parliament.

Another dimension of the freedom of individual Liberal Members of Parliament is the absence of a formal system of factions within the party. Individual MPs can join loose groupings to strengthen support for a particular point of view, but this is an informal process. The lack of formal factions also makes changes of allegiance to new or prospective leaders easier for individual MPs. However, the development in recent decades of a de facto factional system, such as the division between the supporters of John Howard and Andrew Peacock, can be damaging. A divided party without a formal system of factions can slide into a winner-takes-all style of politics. The group with the superior numbers uses their position to gain a stranglehold over policy and senior positions—making the public stance of the party ideologically narrower than might otherwise be the case. This has been the situation in the New South Wales Liberal Party for some time. A formal system of factions has its problems, but it allows for orderly policy development and division of power within the party.

Coalition politics

Since the formation of the Liberal Party in 1945, the party has more-often-than-not been in coalition with the National Party (the renamed Country Party). The advantage for the Liberal Party of a reliable coalition partner is a more stable majority in the Parliament. The advantage of coalition politics for the National Party has been their ability to parlay a small proportion of the national vote into senior cabinet positions, including the deputy prime ministership. Men like John 'Black Jack' McEwen and Doug Anthony were formidable voices for the interests of rural Australians within Coalition governments. The two parties spent a good deal of time without a coalition agreement during the 1980s. In 1987, Queensland National Party Premier Joh Bjelke-Petersen launched an ill-fated run at the prime ministership, further souring relations with the Liberal Party. One of the things that John Howard learned from this experience and his experience in the Fraser Government as treasurer is the importance of a strong bond between the Coalition partners. His relationship with National Party leader Tim Fischer was very close during the late 1990s.

BOX 11.3   One conservative party or two?

One of the perennial issues in Australian conservative politics is the prospect of a merger between the National Party and the Liberal Party. The influence of the respective parties varies across the state divisions. The National Party has historically been strong in Queensland and New South Wales, but less so in Victoria, Western Australia and Tasmania. The Northern Territory has its own conservative entity, the Country Liberal Party. In 2006, the two parties agreed to merge at state level in Queensland but the difficulties that the merger would have placed on their federal counterparts meant that the merger did not proceed. The only National Party MP in the South Australian Parliament was even a cabinet minister in a Labor government from 2004.

The question of a merger between the conservative parties is often on the agenda because of the close and successful cooperation between the parties for long periods of time, most notably under the Menzies, Fraser and Howard Governments. Yet, long-term considerations usually outweigh any perceived benefit from a united conservative party. Australia's system of preferential voting allows the parties to allocate their preferences to each other. It is difficult to judge whether a merged conservative force would be any more electorally successful than a strong coalition. The major benefits would come in the reduced costs by eliminating duplication of party functions.

While the National Party's influence has declined in line with a drift of Australia's regional population from rural areas to the coast, the Nationals exert disproportional influence inside Coalition governments. National Party members fear losing their influence within a single conservative party. By voting as a bloc on issues such as trade and agricultural subsidies, National MPs believe they have a greater voice inside a coalition than they would have inside a merged party. The influence of the National Party in the Howard Government, though, was noticeably less than had been the case under Fraser.

The social liberals inside the Liberal Party, already under pressure from the conservative forces inside their own party, are happy to leave rural conservatives in a separate organisation. Other Liberal Party members, though, particularly those representing rural areas (and they now outnumber National Party MPs) resent the fact that important ministries such as Trade and Agriculture are automatically granted to National Party members as part of a Coalition agreement.

In 2008, the two Queensland conservative parties agreed, after an acrimonious debate, to form a single party, the Liberal National Party. The idea of a merged conservative force is one of the perennials of Australian politics. It stops inter-party bickering and allows the conservatives to fight Labor with a united front. There is little sign of a national merger, however, with the result that federal representatives of the Liberal National Party can belong to either the Liberal or National party rooms.

Q How much influence does the National Party exert from within a Coalition government? Would the influence of MPs representing rural constituencies be greater or lesser if the two main conservative parties were to merge?

Country voters have felt that their interests have not been served by the National Party, and that a greater emphasis on free trade, and a decline in services in rural areas, reflect the dominance of the Liberal Party over the Nationals within the Coalition. This represents, in part, a decline in National Party representation in the Parliament. The number of Nationals in the House of Representatives has fallen by more than half since 1984, when 21 National Party members sat in the newly-expanded House. Just ten National Party MHRs survived the 2007 election defeat. Part of the problem is the phenomenon of popular local identities winning seats from the National Party. A number of such independents have won seats from the National Party at recent elections. A more permanent problem is the threat to the National Party from the Liberal Party. Coalition agreements between the two parties prevent each party from contesting a seat held by the other. However, when MHRs retire, both parties may contest the seat. For example, when National Party leader Tim Fischer retired at the 2001 election, his southern New South Wales seat of Farrer was won by Liberal Sussan Ley.

BOX 11.4   Things are different in Queensland

Queensland is the only state or territory where the National Party has historically been more successful than the Liberal Party. Queensland has the least centralised population of the mainland states. Regional centres such as Cairns, Townsville and Toowoomba are the stronghold of the Queensland National Party. Queensland's malapportioned electoral system gave voters in some areas more than double the weight as those in city electorates between 1949 and 1992. Malapportionment was justified on the basis that rural-based MPs have more territory to cover in representing their constituents. Given the strength of the Australian Labor Party in rural Queensland, where it was founded, Queensland politics was for decades a contest between Labor and the Nationals. The Bjelke-Petersen Government, after 1983, even governed without the Liberal Party as coalition partners.

The Queensland Liberal Party fared much better in federal elections. While the state electoral system has since been changed to something closer to one vote one value, the legacy of the old system is that the Liberal Party remains a minor force in Queensland state politics. While the south-eastern Queensland urban areas are growing quickly, it has been the Nationals rather than the Liberals who have courted elderly voters in places such as the Gold Coast during state contests.

Around the country, the National Party branches are dealing with their major-party cousins in different ways. A National Party representative, Karlene Maywald, sat in the cabinet formed by Labor in South Australia after the 2006 election. In Western Australia in 2008, the Liberals and Nationals entered the state election without a coalition agreement. After a close result, the Nationals negotiated with both major parties, and exacted a substantial price in funds for regional development from the Liberal Party in return for support in the Parliament. The danger for the federal National Party in abandoning the coalition in opposition is that without a coalition agreement, the Liberal Party will contest the remaining National Party seats and probably has the resources to reduce Nationals' representation still further.

ISSUE IN FOCUS

WHAT DOES THE LIBERAL PARTY STAND FOR TODAY?

Menzies deliberately avoiding naming his new right-of-centre party the 'Conservative Party', as its British equivalent was called. His preference for the 'Liberal Party' as party label indicated a willingness to accept a greater degree of social liberalism than that found in the platforms of Australia's conservative parties between the wars. The Great Depression of the 1930s and the Second World War changed the views of many in Australian society about the role of government. The Depression underlined the need for a role for the state in creating jobs, stabilising the finance sector and providing a strong welfare system. The war effort entailed a central role for government in directing industry and mobilising resources. After the war, the Chifley Labor Government sought to consolidate this extended role for the national government in society and the economy.

While Menzies sought to differentiate the Liberal Party from Labor on some economic issues, he supported a 1946 constitutional referendum aimed at giving the Commonwealth greater power to legislate in the area of social welfare. This was an important concession in both the area of social liberalism and federalism. In unsuccessfully attempting to **nationalise** the private banks in 1947, Chifley gave Menzies the opportunity to occupy the all-important centre ground of Australian politics. Menzies could rail against Labor's alleged socialism and promote the virtues of hard work and free enterprise while keeping popular Labor policies such as welfare and a commitment to full employment. The key to the Liberal Party's success during the 1950s and 1960s, then, was a pragmatic approach to running the economy.

> **Nationalise:** when the state takes over ownership of the means of production

The Liberals under Menzies would oppose both socialism and unfettered free markets. At the Canberra Conference that helped to establish the Liberal Party, Menzies (cited in Starr 1980, p. 76) told the gathering,

> What we must look for, and it is a matter of desperate importance to our society, is a true revival of liberal thought which will work for social justice and security, for national power and national progress, and for the full development of the individual citizen, though not through the dull and deadening process of Socialism.

Yet, the words 'social justice' rarely pass the lips of a Liberal Party leader today. Up against a Labor Party no longer committed to ever-greater government intervention in the economy, the Liberal Party has had to find new ways to differentiate itself from its opponents. The postwar consensus in favour of government intervention in the economy broke down in the face of growing inflation and unemployment. The time was right for new ideas.

While Malcolm Fraser was a strong leader of the Liberal Party, winning elections in 1975, 1977 and 1980, his government was thought by many in the party to have missed an opportunity to solve the economic problems that plagued Australia at the time. The Liberal Party had found itself back in government due to the problems experienced by the Whitlam Government rather than through any resolution to the internal debates about the party's direction. Among Fraser's detractors was John Howard, who had been treasurer in the Fraser Government between 1977 and 1983. Howard and his supporters argued that the sluggish growth and high inflation experienced by Australia since the early 1970s was the result of too much government intervention in the economy. The 'dries', as they became known (mirroring a factional label in the United Kingdom, where **Margaret Thatcher**'s Conservative Government was implementing radical liberal economic ideas such as privatisation),

Margaret Thatcher: Conservative prime minister of the United Kingdom, 1979–90

advocated deregulation of the economy and cuts to taxation and government spending. By extension, the opponents of these ideas within the Liberal Party became known as 'wets'. These labels were quite simplistic, since many 'wets' accepted the need for economic reform but were concerned about the effect of free markets on the less well-off in society.

In a similar response to the nation's economic problems, the Hawke Government set about making some of the difficult decisions that the Fraser Government would not—floating the Australian dollar, reducing tariff levels, deregulating the financial system and privatising iconic Australian companies such as Qantas and the Commonwealth Bank. Howard and his supporters believed that the Liberal Party should take economic reform further and faster than Labor was prepared to do. The Liberal Party was becoming more ideologically driven just when Labor was learning the value of pragmatism. The 'dries' succeeded in ousting Andrew Peacock from the party leadership but Howard's vision proved unpalatable to the electorate and he was defeated at the 1987 election by Hawke. The high tide of the Liberal Party's promotion of economic reform was the 1993 election, where Howard's former economic advisor, John Hewson, was defeated by Labor's Paul Keating. Hewson's *Fightback!* package was initially well received as a cure for a recession-hit economy. Hewson advocated a 10 per cent reduction in government spending, deregulation of the labour market, a smaller role for government in the health system, and a Goods and Services Tax. It was the latter policy that eventually brought Hewson down.

The Coalition learnt from its experience in 1993 that they needed to be more in touch with public opinion in order to defeat Labor. John Howard proved the right man for the job when he eventually returned to the leadership in 1995. He emphasised social stability more so than economic reform. After decades of continual social and economic change, Howard's desire for Australians to be 'comfortable

BOX 11.5   The Liberal Party and think-tanks

The Institute of Public Affairs (IPA) is Australia's oldest think-tank. It was founded in 1943 with the intention of providing policy advice and fundraising assistance to the Liberal Party, although the two organisations no longer have formal ties. Two of the sons of the IPA's founder, C.D. Kemp, went on to become ministers in the Howard Government. Like the Liberal Party, the IPA has changed its ideological disposition over time, moving from supporting an interventionist economic policy to its advocacy today of free markets.

The IPA is based in Melbourne. A Sydney-based IPA was replaced by the Sydney Institute, under the leadership of John Howard's former chief of staff, Gerard Henderson. Also based in Sydney and influential in Howard Government policy on the economy and Indigenous affairs is the Centre for Independent Studies (CIS). Liberal Party members have also been influenced by organisations with a more focused agenda. Peter Costello was a founding member of the H.R. Nicholls Society, conceived in 1986 to further the cause of labour market deregulation. The Samuel Griffith Society, meanwhile, supports federalism.

The funding of these organisations is always controversial. As private organisations, they have only limited disclosure responsibilities. Money from mining companies and like-minded donors gave think-tanks such as the IPA and CIS the resources to play a higher profile in debates on economic policy during the 1980s. More recently, the IPA has promoted a sceptical view of the science behind global warming.

Q How much influence do think-tanks have on Australian political debate? Should we know more about how these organisations are funded?

and relaxed' resonated with the electorate. However, abandoning economic reform would have lacked credibility. The Liberal Party's platform included a one-third privatisation of Telstra. While this was still an unpopular policy, Labor's attacks on it were blunted by their own record of privatisation. Howard accepted that Labor's *Medicare* system was popular in the electorate and for the first time, the Liberal Party pledged to retain it. This more pragmatic John Howard won a landslide victory over Paul Keating's Labor Government in 1996.

The experience of the Kennett Government in Victoria was instructive to Howard and other Liberal Party leaders. Jeff Kennett became premier of Victoria in 1992 and set about the most radical program of economic reform seen at state or Commonwealth level. Kennett made large cuts to spending, including health and education, and privatised the state's electricity sector. The cuts to spending were unpopular, however, and Kennett unexpectedly lost the 1999 election. Howard's more pragmatic approach was proving more successful. Under Howard, the Liberal Party persisted with those economic reforms that undermined support for the Labor Party. For example, privatisation reduces the number of workers employed in the public sector. Workers in that sector have a much higher rate of trade union membership than private sector workers. The deregulation of the labour market, most notably through the WorkChoices legislation introduced in 2005, represented a more direct attack on the status of trade unions. The Howard Government steered clear, however, of other small-government values, such as cuts to welfare spending. This pragmatic approach raised the ire of some of the Liberal government's more ideological supporters but proved an election-winning formula.

BOX 11.6   Race politics

Australia is in many respects a more socially liberal country than it was a generation ago. Feminism, multiculturalism, the abandonment of the White Australia Policy, and the Indigenous land rights movement have all helped to change the face of Australian society. John Howard's brand of conservatism proved successful because it promised those sceptical of these reform movements a break from decades of constant change. Howard's promises to reduce the immigration intake and place less emphasis on Indigenous affairs were not sufficient for many Australians. A former Liberal Party candidate, Pauline Hanson, was prepared to go much further than Howard in turning back the clock. Her One Nation Party gathered a million votes at the 1998 election by promising to reduce immigration to zero, abolish what she called 'special treatment' of Indigenous Australians through the welfare system and land rights laws, and reverse the globalisation of the economy, which was by then bipartisan policy among the major parties.

In 2001, the Howard Government won back many of One Nation's supporters with a much tougher approach to asylum seekers. The government also abolished the Aboriginal and Torres Strait Islander Commission (ATSIC) in 2004. Measures to combat terrorism alienated sections of Australia's Muslim community. One Nation is no longer a political force in Australia. Howard's critics accused him of adopting Hanson's policies. While Howard was in some areas a **populist** political leader, he was also prepared to make unpopular decisions at times. In spite of increases to the immigration intake late in Howard's prime ministership, immigration was not a contentious issue at the 2007 election.

Populist: appealing to the beliefs of ordinary voters

Q How should political leaders respond to community concerns about contentious issues such as immigration? How much should we expect political leaders in a democracy to defy public opinion on issues of race and culture?

Social liberalism and conservatism

When John Howard was struggling to fend off an attack on his leadership by Queensland Premier Joh Bjelke-Petersen in 1987, he declared himself 'the most conservative leader the Liberal Party has ever had' (cited in Errington & van Onselen 2007, p. 242). Under Howard's leadership, many of the social liberals in the party were challenged for pre-selection by more conservative figures. One reason for the unity of the Howard Government was that the conservatives were ascendant in the parliamentary wing of the party. Since Howard's defeat at the 2007 election, social liberals have been more vocal, with moderate figures Brendan Nelson and Malcolm Turnbull being elected to the party leadership. Turnbull had been a leader of the Australian Republican Movement during the 1990s when Howard was the nation's foremost constitutional monarchist.

To a large extent, the Liberal Party has settled its long-running arguments over economic policy. Globalisation and privatisation are near-universally accepted in the party, along with an acceptance of the need for a welfare safety net. Kevin Rudd has attempted to exploit this unity over economic issues by accusing his opponents of supporting the 'extreme free market' policies that caused the global financial crisis (Rudd 2008). Despite such pressure from the government, divisions in the Liberal Party (and within the Coalition) now tend to centre on post-materialist issues such as global warming. Attempts by leading moderates such as Christopher Pyne to put the opposition more in touch with community feeling on greenhouse gas reduction policies have been met with resistance from the party's conservatives (Metherell 2009). Whatever their private views, neither Nelson nor Turnbull were conspicuous in overturning policies associated with Howard.

Some of Howard's critics have romanticised Menzies' liberalism in contrast to Howard's conservatism. The Howard Government threatened long-held civil liberties in the fight against terrorism. Anti-terrorism legislation compromised centuries-old principles of the legal system such as the presumption of innocence. 'The most important civil liberty,' Howard told his critics, 'is to stay alive and to be free from violence and death' (cited in Errington & van Onselen 2007, p. 335). Howard managed to stymie attempts to make Australia a republic and resisted efforts from within his own party to provide greater legal equality for those in same-sex relationships. Yet Menzies attempted to ban the Communist Party of Australia and made few concessions to the changing social mores of postwar Australia. He had his reasons for naming the Liberal Party in the way that he did, but he was a social conservative on many issues.

Towards the end of Howard's prime ministership, some of his long-time supporters such as newspaper columnists Gerard Henderson and Christopher Pearson (who had both written speeches for Howard at different points of his career) pointed out the Howard Government's lack of progress in influencing Australian culture. They criticised Howard for a lack of commitment in combating a supposed entrenched liberalism in Australia's public institutions such as universities and the ABC. Such ruminations underline a contradiction in the nature of modern conservatism in Australia and elsewhere. Are conservatives content to govern in the Menzian style, with a modest legislative program and a pluralistic view of political and social institutions? Or are conservatives reformers who seek to change economic and social arrangements to better suit their view of the world?

BOX 11.7   Is the party over?

Election losses suffered by the Liberal Party tend to lead to debates over the party's future, which is in apparent contrast to the ALP when it loses. Social liberals concerned about the growing strength of social conservatives in the Liberal Party have at times entertained the prospect of a new party. Former senator Chris Puplick (*Is the Party Over?* 1994) and ministerial advisor Greg Barns (*What's Wrong With the Liberal Party?* 2003) characterise the despair that many social liberals feel at the state of the non-Labor parties.

In spite of the stability of the two-party system, the notion of a new liberal party is not out of the question. Minor parties come and go from Australian politics. Most never achieve party representation. Those that do often begin their parliamentary representation as splinters from established parties. The Australian Democrats started their parliamentary life as a splinter group from the Liberals when Senator Don Chipp resigned from the Fraser Government. Pauline Hanson founded the One Nation Party after she was forced out of the Liberal Party prior to the 1996 election, when it was too late for the Liberals to pre-select an alternative candidate. Forming a successful political party is an expensive business. Both government funding for votes gained at each election and corporate donations to parties with a chance of winning tend to re-enforce the *status quo*.

Despair at the state of the Liberal Party was once again on display after the election loss in 2007 left the party out of government in every state and territory—the first time the Liberal Party had found itself in that position since its foundation. It was not long, though, until the popularity of Labor governments in a number of states waned, and the Liberals were able to form a government in Western Australia in 2008. Electoral fortunes tend to have cycles. Parties in opposition can go through painful periods of irrelevance to the electorate and endless debates about policy. However, opposition can also remind parties of their fundamental purpose, as they watch their opponents manoeuvre the levers of power.

Q   Is it inevitable that the conservative side of politics will always be dominated by the Liberal Party? What factors assist the ability of a party to rebuild itself after an election loss?

Federalism

In principle, federalism has the virtue of uniting the conservative and liberal wings of the Liberal Party. Conservatives are suspicious of Labor efforts to centralise power and alter the Constitution, while federalism is a natural fit for those with a preference for limited government. However, Galligan has pointed out that 'federalism is taken for granted on the Liberal or conservative side of politics and only championed when under perceived threat from federal Labor governments' (1989, p. 60). This ambivalence about federalism was underlined by the record of the Menzies government. Reflecting on his record as prime minister, Menzies noted, 'as the world becomes more complex, as international affairs engage our attention more and more, it is frequently ludicrous that the National Parliament, the National Government, should be without power to do things which are really needed for the national security and advancement' (1967, p. 24). Menzies and his successors established a pattern of centralisation of power in the Commonwealth government by the use of tied grants to states in the provision of infrastructure such as water and electricity, and in health and education. The Whitlam Government would later accelerate this use of the Commonwealth's healthy finances to fund programs in areas traditionally the preserve of the states. The only Liberal Party prime minister with a thoroughgoing commitment to federalism was Malcolm Fraser. He refused to prevent the Tasmanian Government building a dam on the Franklin River, stating that 'my government will not seek to change the balance of our federal system by subterfuge' (cited in White & Kemp 1986, p. 156). Yet, Australia's stagnant economy of the 1970s and early 1980s prevented Fraser from guaranteeing the states a fixed share of Commonwealth income.

Under John Howard's prime ministership, federalism ceased to be a central platform of the Liberal Party (Errington 2008, p. 260). Centralisation of Common-wealth power under Howard encompassed such areas as gun control; a steady stream of intervention in schools on everything from curricula to flagpoles; university management; federally funded technical colleges that duplicate state provision; numerous interventions in the laws of the territories; a national system of industrial relations; road funding allocated directly to local government; and many smaller initiatives aimed at national uniformity. Howard's approach to federalism should, however, be seen as a pragmatic one—dealing productively with premiers in areas such as water resources and anti-terrorism, and making an effort to ease the problem of vertical fiscal imbalance through the introduction of the GST.

While the Liberal Party has long had a rhetorical attachment to federalism, it is probably in the nature of Members of the Commonwealth Parliament to promote national solutions to policy problems. Federalism symbolises a wider failure of the Liberal Party to give substance to its principles of limited government. While the Liberal Party defends the principle of bicameralism, it took every advantage of its numerical majority in the Senate in the period 2005–07 to curtail legislative debate and scrutiny of the executive arm of government. Political parties are judged by the electorate according to the way in which they solve problems (or perceived problems) rather than by their adherence to political principles or democratic processes. In this environment, Liberal Party leaders pay lip service to the party's long-held principles, but not much more. It is difficult, though, to argue with the political success that Howard achieved by championing a national approach to a range of policy areas.

The conservatism of the modern Liberal Party should not be overstated. While the Howard Government pursued policies that financially rewarded stay-at-home mothers, for example, it also increased spending on child-care. Howard ensured that a woman's right to abortion did not become a partisan political issue in spite of a desire to so on the part of social conservatives such as Tony Abbott. Neither did Howard's ascendancy make Australia a more conservative place. Attitudes among younger Australians on issues such as gay marriage, for example, suggest that the conservatism associated with Howard now belongs to a previous generation. The leadership of the Liberal Party will inevitably have to deal with changing social attitudes. Just as Howard pursued a different blend of policies than his hero Menzies did, present and future Liberal Party leaders will have to redefine the balance between conservatism and liberalism in the party's platform.

CHAPTER SUMMARY

As we can see from the above discussion of the ever-changing Liberal Party policy platform, there are few principles of the party that cannot be abandoned in the name of pragmatism and electoral competition. A number of features of the Liberal Party have been consistent throughout its existence. The party depends on a strong leader to provide it with unity and direction. Individual MPs enjoy autonomy from both the party organisation and from their fellow MPs, yet party leaders have numerous methods through which to enforce party discipline. The party's core values of free enterprise and reward for hard work have taken on a number of guises over the years as leaders have responded to changes in Australia's economy and social structure, and Labor's abandonment of socialism. More problematic is the lack of an organisation that can deal with periods in opposition, when leaders lack authority and are unable to keep the party unified.

WEBSITES

Institute of Public Affairs (IPA):
www.ipa.org.au
The Institute of Public Affairs promotes free-market solutions to policy problems. It has traditionally had strong links to the Liberal Party.

Liberal Party of Australia
www.liberal.org.au
The Liberal Party website has information about the party's parliamentary team and policy platform, with links to the sites of state-based parties.

National Party of Australia
www.nationals.org.au
The National Party's website outlines the party's structure and leadership team, and highlights policies of interest to rural Australians.

FURTHER READING

Brett, J. 2003. *Australian Liberals and the Moral Middle Class*. Cambridge University Press, Melbourne.

Henderson, G. 1994. *Menzies' Child: The Liberal Party of Australia 1944–1994*. Allen & Unwin, Sydney.

Norton, A. 2004. 'Liberalism and the Liberal Party of Australia', in *The Politics of Australian Society: Political Issues for the New Century* (2nd edn). G. Stokes et al. (eds). Pearson Longman, Sydney.

12 Minor Parties in Australia

THIS CHAPTER:

★ defines the term 'minor party' and considers the various meanings of the expression
★ considers the different types of minor parties and the function they perform in a democracy
★ examines the nature of the political and electoral environment in which minor parties exist in Australia
★ provides a brief overview of the history of minor parties in Australia.

ISSUE IN FOCUS

To what extent do minor parties enhance democracy in Australia?

KEY TERMS

Balance of power
By-election

Coalition
Liberal pluralists
Preferential voting (PV)

In June 2008, four senators from the Australian Democrats delivered their valedictory speeches to Parliament. The event was a significant occasion in Australian politics. For the first time since 1977, there would be no Democrats in the nation's powerful upper house. The party that had formed to bring balance and moderation to politics through the judicious use of the balance of power in the Senate was on the precipice of electoral and political extinction. Despite the Democrats' numerous achievements over the years, its successes did not insulate it from the spectre of obsolescence. The decline of the Democrats exemplifies the fragility of Australia's minor parties and the precarious conditions under which they compete.

Introduction

Minor parties exist on the periphery of the Australian party system and go largely unnoticed by most voters. However, the presence (or absence) of minor parties says a great deal about the openness of a political system. Liberal-democratic societies embrace the ideas of plurality and choice and these are values that minor parties exemplify by their mere presence. Liberals, and **liberal pluralists** especially, believe that power in society is relatively dispersed and fragmented. The existence of minor parties is a testament to the willingness of the political community to tolerate the right of politically motivated individuals to form a party and contest elections. Just as liberals value plurality, democrats believe that citizens should possess the right to elect their political representatives. But real and meaningful choice only exists if individuals have genuine options when filling out their ballot paper on election day. In this sense, minor parties expand the political menu for voters to choose from at the polls.

Liberal pluralists: those who believe that power is diffuse and shared among many different groups in society

While it is possible to make a strong case for the importance of minor parties in liberal-democratic nations, they are often not well received in those party systems and nor are they always politically or electorally significant. As we shall see in the Issue in Focus, minor parties are sometimes the target of considerable abuse. In Australia, there is no shortage of commentators willing to declare minor parties to be undemocratic, unrepresentative and even dangerous. We will explore in greater detail the benefits and the disbenefits frequently ascribed to minor parties in the Issue in Focus. First, however, we will examine the nature of minor parties and the opportunities and constraints that the Australian political and electoral environment affords them.

What are minor parties?

When academics write about the Australian party system they do so by dividing it into two camps: the major parties (the ALP and the Liberal Party), and the others. The 'others' refers to the non-major or non-governing parties. The literature on the 'others' identifies these parties using an assortment of labels, the three most popular descriptors of which are 'minor', 'small' and 'new'.

While these tags are mostly used to distinguish the major parties from their non-governing counterparts, the three labels are loaded and occasionally imprecise. The term 'minor party' implies that such entities are peripheral to politics, and that their political and electoral impact is at best modest and at worst insignificant. However, we know that this is not always true. The National Party lacks the electoral support required to form government in its own right yet it is an active participant in executive government when in **coalition** with the Liberals. The National Party in Queensland, unlike its counterparts elsewhere in the country, was, prior to their merger in 2008, the dominant force in conservative politics and the Liberals the junior coalition partner.

However, there are a number of ways in which minor parties exert an influence over the political process. A party's ability to have an impact on political and electoral outcomes is not restricted only to its capacity to form government either on its own or in a coalition. A party can sometimes exert influence over legislative outcomes when it holds the **balance of power** in Parliament. In 2008, the Rudd government was forced into negotiations with the minor parties and an independent in the Senate in order to pass its luxury car tax when the Coalition refused to support the proposed bill. This provided an opportunity for the Australian Greens, and Family First especially, to influence both the appearance and fate of the legislation. The Australian Greens negotiated exemptions for certain fuel-efficient cars and Family First achieved concessions for farmers and tourism operators (Shanahan 2008).

Minor parties have also been known to affect the electoral tactics (strategies) of the major parties and, in some cases, have swung the outcome of an election in favour of a particular party. The Democratic Labor Party (DLP) (see Box 12.4) is widely credited with having kept the ALP out of office throughout the 1950s and 1960s because it advised its supporters to rank Liberal Party candidates ahead of ALP contestants on lower house ballot papers. Similarly, the ALP's victory at the 1990 federal polls was attributed to advantageous preference agreements it managed to negotiate with a number of environmental parties.

> **Coalition:** in Australia, the arrangement between the Liberal Party and the National Party to join forces in order to form a government
>
> **Balance of power:** when minor parties or independents can influence the passage of legislation in the Senate. The balance of power comes into play when the government lacks a majority in the Senate and is forced to rely on support from minor parties or independents in order to secure the safe passage of their bills through the upper house if the major opposition party is opposed to the proposed legislation.

The expression 'small' party also does little to clarify our understanding of the non-major parties. One of the chief difficulties with the term 'small' is that it is unclear whether we are referring to the size of a party's organisation and membership relative to the major parties, or to the size of its electoral support in absolute terms. While non-major parties do not attract anywhere near the level of electoral support won by the major parties, it is not always true that 'small' parties have a small organisational base or a small number of party members. The Nationals claim a larger membership than either the ALP or the Liberals. It is estimated that the Nationals have over 100 000 members compared to the ALP's 50 000 rank and file supporters, and the Liberals 80 000 members (Jaensch et al. 2002, p. 55). Moreover, while the membership of both the ALP and the Liberals continues to decline, some small parties, such as the Australian Greens, are recording growth in their membership numbers.

A third descriptor sometimes used to refer to non-major parties is 'new' entrants. Just prior to every federal election, a number of new parties register with the

Australian Electoral Commission (AEC). For example, the Hear Our Voice party was established in the months preceding the 2007 federal election. It was created by a disaffected member of the ALP in order to advance the political cause of women, homosexuals and the elderly. However, not all of Australia's minor parties are recent arrivals on the electoral scene. The Democrats, for example, formed in 1977. While it is evidently a much newer party than the ALP, which is over a hundred years old, the Democrats has existed for over thirty years, which hardly qualifies it as a new party. The term 'new' is also sometimes used to describe those parties that are not tied to the old class politics that previously shaped electoral contests in this country. 'New politics' parties refer to those groupings that campaign on non-economic, quality-of-life issues and that embrace open, participatory party organisational structures and processes. While some minor parties possess the characteristics that can be identified as consistent with 'new politics' parties, such as the Australian Greens, not all fit neatly into this category. Moreover, some of the major parties have been known to adopt some of the characteristics of new politics parties, especially in relation to aspects of their policies.

As this discussion clearly demonstrates, there is no best single term to apply to those parties that lack sufficient electoral support to govern in their own right. However for the remainder of this chapter, and in keeping with the preferred usage of Australian political scientists, we shall refer to them as minor parties.

BOX 12.1 Sartori and the small problem of minor party relevance

One of the issues that has preoccupied academics is what criteria should be used to distinguish between important and unimportant minor parties. Some have proposed the use of a numerical criterion based on the percentage of the vote a party manages to attract. While many favour this method, one of its chief difficulties is that the number selected is often arbitrary, and can range anywhere from 2 to 10 per cent of the vote. Notably, this method reduces the value of a party to a numerical signifier, thereby negating the possibility that the importance of a party might be connected to some other factor (Jaensch & Mathieson 2002, p. 12).

The most widely accepted standard is the one devised by Giovanni Sartori (1976). Sartori proposed that minor parties should be assessed in terms of their 'relevance'. Sartori suggested that in order for a minor party to be counted as relevant it must, at a minimum, be capable of winning seats in parliament. Once a minor party had crossed this threshold of relevance it must satisfy one of two criteria or 'rules'. Rule 1 stipulates that a minor party is relevant if it is capable of contributing towards a governing majority in the legislature. Rule 2 states that a minor party also qualifies as 'relevant' if its presence affects the tactics of party competition within the legislature and those of the major governing parties particularly.

Jaensch and Mathieson (2002) argue that while Sartori's rules are useful, they need to be modified in order to take into account the Australian electoral context. Jaensch and Mathieson rightly point out that the Australian electoral system offers opportunities for minor parties to demonstrate relevance outside of Sartori's two basic rules. They have proposed that the criteria for relevance in Australia should be broadened to include a party holding a 'numerical balance of power in the legislature'. Moreover, they believe that the system of preferential voting provides Australian minor parties with a unique opportunity to prove influential 'outside' of Parliament if they are able to harness their supporters' subsequent preferences to 'determine over time at least one of the possible government majorities' (2002, pp. 13–14).

Q   On what bases should minor parties be considered relevant?

Australia's minor parties

The electoral performance of minor parties at the federal level in Australia (and in the state arenas also) has been somewhat underwhelming. Since 1901, minor parties have formed, only to collapse quickly and spontaneously. The majority of minor parties rarely last more than one or two electoral cycles and an even smaller number manage to win seats in Parliament. The one exception to this is the National Party. Unlike other minor parties, the Nationals have achieved organisational stability and institutional longevity. The Nationals have also consistently secured the election of their candidates to the House of Representatives, and have been afforded opportunities to share in executive government, in spite of the party's small vote base.

Jaensch and Mathieson estimate that in the period between 1901 and 1996, approximately 137 minor parties contested elections for the House of Representatives. Patterns of minor party formation have been erratic, with periods of dormant minor party activity as well as periods of proliferation and mobilisation. Since the 1980s, particularly, there has been an explosion in the number of minor parties contesting federal elections. Interestingly, some of these minor parties have proven to be relatively enduring, even if they have not been more electorally successful than their antecedents. That is, quite a few of them have not vanished once the election has been held but have returned to contest subsequent elections (Jaensch & Mathieson 2002, pp. 156–8).

One commentator has identified two main drivers of minor party mobilisation in Australia. Donovan finds, first, that changes to the institutional setting, such as a change to the electoral system, which increases the prospect for minor party electoral success, can motivate elites to form a party. As a general rule, the more permissive the electoral system, the greater the strategic incentives there are for minor parties to mobilise. This can be shown to have occurred over time, since the 'number of minor parties contesting Senate elections increased with the first PR-STV election in 1949, without ever declining to previous levels' (2000, p. 476). Second, Donovan argues that periods of economic instability also seem to stimulate minor party mobilisation: 'the negative sign for the GDP variable indicates that significantly more small parties mobilised when national income had declined in the year of the election' (2000, p. 480). Ward and Stewart (2006) suggest that one factor that has potentially contributed to the increase in the number of minor parties is the introduction of the federal public funding scheme. They argue that an unintended consequence of the provision of public funding for elections is that it has encouraged independents to register as a political party in order to improve their chances of receiving such funds.

While the combination of the electoral system and economic factors are thought to facilitate the entry of new parties, what then accounts for their ability to survive in the medium to long term? The forces that give rise to the formation of a minor party are not necessarily the same as those that facilitate a party's longevity or electoral success, although they are intimately linked (Hug 2000). One possible explanation lies with the changing social and political bases of Australian society. There is some evidence that class attachments in Australia are weakening and that post-materialist values, which cut across traditional class structures, are beginning to have a greater influence on vote choice. This process is thought to be expedited by the policy 'me-tooism' of the major parties, which has helped to destabilise the bond between the electorate and the major parties (Ward & Stewart 2006, pp. 106–7). In addition, there are also greater incentives and opportunities for parties to continue operating between elections. Public funding of federal elections permits any political party that achieves more than 4 per cent of the primary vote to claim public funds to offset some of the costs associated with election campaigning. This can result in payouts totalling millions of dollars to minor parties, such as the Australian Greens, which claimed over $4 million dollars in public funds in 2007. These funds provide small parties with a much-needed revenue stream that can be invested to buttress the party's operations and activities.

However, what has been most intriguing about the history of Australia's minor parties is that none has managed to emerge as a viable alternative party of government. While more than one minor party can claim its share of success (particularly the Greens in Tasmania: see Box 12.2), the reality is that all have failed to substantially disrupt the two-party dynamic of the Australian party system. More to the point, their record of winning seats federally, in the House of Representatives, is poor. Even at the height of their electoral strength, the Democrats were unable to

By-election: a special election held between general elections to fill a vacancy caused by the resignation, death or expulsion of the sitting member

elect one their most popular and high profile party leaders, Janine Haines, to the House of Representatives. With the exception of the Nationals, minor-party candidates are only likely to win a seat in the House of Representatives at a **by-election**.

This is not to suggest that there are often very good reasons why some parties remain fringe dwellers in Australian politics. Some minor parties have limited electoral appeal, which can be due to any combination of their ideology, political philosophy (or lack thereof) or the behaviour and tactics they employ. There has been no shortage of frivolous, weird, unusual and radical minor parties over the years. Moreover, some are simply electorally unattractive because they pursue a very narrow set of policy objectives. In some cases, a party is created not with the intention of winning seats in Parliament but with some other objective in mind, such as spoiling another party or candidate's prospects of winning. More often than not, the electorate will simply ignore those parties that they identify as being vexatious.

The poor record of minor parties in Australia is also the result of powerful forces that have conspired to freeze the Australian party system and the loyalties of Australian voters. The story of minor parties in Australia is one of frustration, limited opportunities and road blocks, which arise out of the institutional and structural constraints that serve to reinforce the dominance of the two major parties. Australian voters have demonstrated a dogged reluctance to vote for parties outside the two major groupings. While there is clear evidence of a weakening of party allegiance, it remains the case that Australian voters largely remain faithful to the major parties. On average, the major parties attract more than 80 per cent of the first preference vote at elections, leaving the minor parties and independents to scramble for the electoral crumbs.

The ability of the minor parties to achieve a stable and significant core of supporters from within the electorate is frustrated by a host of factors. Mayer believes that there are very definite 'ideological' overtones that frame how minor parties are discussed and portrayed. This extends to the classification methods, such as the two-party preferred vote concept, one of the main analytical devices used to assess the outcome of elections (Mayer 1984, p. 346). The use of the two-party preferred vote concept has the effect of rendering all other parties and candidates invisible and serves to promote the view that 'minor parties are to be judged by the contribution they make to the labor/non-labor vote' (Mayer 1984, p. 352). Also, many commentators make judgments about the success or otherwise of minor parties by comparing them to the major governing parties. In doing so, minor parties are being judged against standards that they cannot reasonably be expected to meet, which is the winning of office. As a result, minor parties are typically typecast as political and electoral failures.

BOX 12.2   Minor parties in government: the Tasmanian parliamentary accord

While the Australian party system exhibits the competitive logic of a two-party system, there have been suggestions that there are forces at work that threaten this dynamic. Marsh argues that the 'strategic integrating capacities' of the major parties are under threat from the proliferation of interest groups and social movements, the catch-all policy stance of the big parties, and the erosion of voter loyalties towards the major parties. According to Marsh, these developments have created opportunities for new parties to attract higher levels of electoral support and hence new opportunities for representation in Australian parliaments (Marsh 2004).

In the early 1990s we were treated to a possible glimpse into the future when five Green independents entered into an accord with the ALP in the Tasmanian Legislative Assembly (lower house). Although not a formal coalition arrangement, the accord allowed the ALP to wrest government from the Liberals in the Assembly, despite the former having only 13 members in the 35-seat chamber. Under the arrangement, the Greens agreed to support the ALP in exchange for a number of policy concessions. According to Hutton and O'Connor, the Greens did not seek ministries because they did not wish to get locked into policy positions that they did not agree to in principle (1999, pp. 229–30). The accord ultimately ended in disaster a little more than 12 months after it had been signed, when the Greens terminated the agreement. The Greens claimed that the accord ended because of 'the betrayal' by the ALP 'over resource security legislation' (ABC *Stateline*, 10 March 2006), whereas the ALP claimed it broke down owing to a lack of 'sufficient good will and trust for it to work and bad behaviour by individuals on both sides' (ABC *Stateline*, 10 March 2006). Despite the fact that the accord was short lived, it did result in a number of policy gains for the Greens. Moreover, the Greens have indicated that should this situation arise again, they would consider entering into a similar arrangement with either of the major parties.

Q Is there anything inherently problematic with minority governments? Are claims that minority governments are unstable exaggerated? What do you believe are the advantages and disadvantages of one of the major parties being forced to govern with the support of one or more minor parties or independents?

The antipathy to minor parties is reflected in a number of different ways. For example, minor parties are frequently ignored by the free media (Mayer 1984, p. 351). While publicity doesn't guarantee that a party will prove successful, there is no doubt that it is near-impossible to attract votes if a party lacks visibility. While the big parties have ready access to the commercial media, minor parties typically lack the resources to purchase airtime or 'page space' in the popular print media. While the internet provides an alternative platform for parties to disseminate their message, the audience reach of the internet remains limited at the present time. For this reason access to free commercial media is invaluable. The problem, however, is that the media rarely bothers to attend press conferences held by small parties or publish their press releases or comment on their policies. Minor parties are only likely to attract the attention of the media if they do something outrageous, a tactic that is highly risky and that can backfire badly, serving to undermine their credibility.

Preferential voting (PV): a system whereby candidates must obtain an absolute majority of the vote to win a seat. In the event that a candidate fails to achieve this threshold, low-scoring candidates are eliminated and their votes are redistributed to remaining candidates until a final winner is declared.

Australia's federal electoral laws are not minor-party friendly. This is particularly true in respect of the electoral formula used in the all-important lower house contest, which utilises a system of compulsory **preferential voting (PV)** combined with single-member electoral districts. In order to win a seat under PV, a candidate must have concentrated geographical voter support in order to attain the 50 per cent + 1 vote needed to win a seat. With the exception of the Nationals, most minor parties have dispersed electoral support, with their supporters rarely concentrated in a particular electoral district. This makes it impossible to convert what is sometimes significant nationwide support into representation in the House of Representatives. At the 2007 federal election, the Australian Greens amassed 7.79 per cent of the nationwide first preference votes, but failed to win a single seat in the House of Representatives.

Other aspects of the electoral system, such as compulsory voting, also play an important role in reinforcing voter attachment to the major parties. It is thought that the frequency of elections (three-year cycles) forces many voters to form an allegiance to one party in order to relieve themselves of the burden of having to think about for whom they should cast their vote from one election to the next. For those minor parties that formed following the introduction of compulsory voting in 1925, this has undermined efforts to build a core constituency, which is critical if a party hopes to achieve longevity. In a study conducted by Bean and Papadakis (1995) on the electoral bases of support for Australian minor parties, they found that even successful minor parties, such as the Democrats, have an ill-defined basis of political support. One of the consequences of this is that the minor party vote is both fragile and highly volatile. Moreover, it makes it difficult for minor parties to identify who their key supporters are and how they can best connect with voters who are disposed to vote for their party (Bean & Papadakis 1995, p. 111).

BOX 12.3   Strangely successful: Australia's independents

One curiosity in Australian politics is the modest success enjoyed by independents in winning seats in the House of Representatives. Since the 1980s, independents have been growing in both electoral strength and electoral success. Interestingly, independents have proven much more successful in winning seats to the House of Representatives than their minor party counterparts, excepting the Nationals. Independents are achieving electoral outcomes that minor parties, such as the Democrats, have long coveted. Ward and Stewart posit that one of the reasons for the success enjoyed by independents may result from the fact that many independents have had a background in mainstream politics. For example, Bob Katter, member for the Queensland federal seat of Kennedy, was formerly a member of the Nationals but resigned over the party's decision to support the sale of Telstra in 2002. Another striking feature of the rise of independents is that they have tended to prove most successful in regional seats (Ward & Stewart 2006, pp. 189–90). Costar and Curtin (2004) attribute this phenomenon to the growing feelings of disenfranchisement in regional electorates, which historically have been represented by the Coalition parties.

Q What are some of the advantages and disadvantages of choosing a career as an independent member?

Minor parties are also at a disadvantage because they do not have access to the levels of financial resources and personnel that are enjoyed by the major parties. While the introduction of public funding has helped minor parties to offset some of the costs associated with contesting elections, small parties often struggle to survive. Not all parties and independents are eligible to receive the funds. Only 'registered' parties are entitled to claim the federal disbursement and even then only those parties that obtain 4 per cent of the primary vote. Also, parties obtain the payment retrospectively; that is, after the election. This means that parties are forced to look to other sources, such as donations and fund raisers, in order to raise the start-up cash to finance their campaign. However, minor parties have few corporate and private donors from whom they can solicit funds, and often only a small army of volunteers that they can call upon. In 2003–04, the ALP disclosed total receipts of $40 million, compared to the $1.1 million collected by the Greens and the $647 000 raised by the Democrats (Young & Tham 2006, p. 101). Minor parties are simply unable to match the level of election spending of the major parties, even with the assistance of state-sponsored payments.

In combination these factors not only undermine incentives for parties to form, but make it difficult for existing small parties to survive and thrive.

BOX 12.4   Categorising Australia's minor parties

Minor parties come in all shapes and sizes and represent all manner of political interests. Because of the enormous variety and sheer number of minor parties that have formed in Australia over the years, there have been some attempts to categorise them according to type. One of the most used schema in Australia is the typology devised by Richmond (1978), which categorises parties into three types: Doctrinal, Aggrieved, and Secessionist/Fragment parties. Richmond recognised that his classificatory scheme, which builds on the earlier efforts of American political scientist V.O Key, jun., was not 'perfect', and that few minor parties fall neatly into one category and can exhibit elements from all three groupings.

Doctrinal

Doctrinal parties are those that promote a rigid doctrine. Because of this, such parties are unlikely to 'affect decisions', have 'any possibility of gaining representation' and are incapable of 'supply[ing] any competition to the other parties' (Richmond 1978, p. 332).

Example: The Communist Party of Australia (CPA) formed originally in 1930 following the success of the 1917 Russian Revolution. It was created as an alternative to the ALP, which it regarded as reformist and ultimately capitalist. The party's key objectives are to replace the 'capitalist' system with a socialist government. The history of the CPA has been turbulent, surviving both proscription in the early 1940s and a number of internal factional/ideological disputes and splits. Although the CPA has failed to win seats in the federal Parliament, it has—in the estimation of some writers—proven influential, particularly in the period 1935 to the 1960s when some of its members occupied leadership positions in a number of important trade unions. More information about the party can be found on its website: http://www.cpa.org.au/.

Aggrieved

Sometimes parties form as a consequence of their discontent with the policies or performance of existing parties, and these fit into Richmond's category of aggrieved parties.

Example: The Shooters Party formed in 1992 in response to a proposal by the NSW State Government to prevent citizens from owning self-loading firearms or firearms for personal protection. The party advocates, among other things, the right of 'law-abiding' citizens to own and use firearms for legitimate purposes, including self-defence. The party currently has two representatives in the NSW Legislative Council. The Shooters contested the 2007 federal election, fielding Senate candidates in NSW (ran a joint ticket with the Australian Fishing & Lifestyle party), Victoria, Queensland and South Australia. The party captured 47 379 votes or 0.37 per cent of the national Senate vote. More information about the party can be found at its website: http://www.shootersparty.org.au/.

Secessionist/Fragment

Secessionist or fragment parties form following a split in a major party. Richmond suggests that splits are normally motivated by ideological disagreement within the party, which prompts one section or grouping of members to form their own separate party organisation.

Example: The Democratic Labor Party (DLP) emerged following a split within the ALP in the mid 1950s. Some members, many of whom were Catholics from Victoria and Queensland, left the ALP owing to concerns about the influence of communists within the party. At the height of its electoral and political success, the DLP had three members in the Senate. By 1977, the party's fortunes had taken a turn for the worse, and while it did not disband, it failed to win representation in any Parliament. In 2007, the DLP ran candidates for the Senate in every state, winning 0.92 per cent of the nationwide vote. Only in Victoria did it contest lower house seats. More information about the party can be found on its website: http://www.dlp.org.au/.

Despite the inability of minor parties to seriously challenge the dominance of the major parties in the electoral arena, there are small windows of opportunity that an astute minor party can exploit to its advantage. Since 1949, the ability of minor parties and independents to gain representation in the Senate has improved following the introduction of proportional representation (PR). One of the advantages of PR is that it lowers the threshold needed for representation. While the electoral system it replaced required a candidate to obtain approximately 33.3 per cent of the vote to win a Senate seat, under PR they only need 14.3 per cent in a normal half Senate election, or 7.69 per cent in a full Senate ballot. The benefits of the new system to minor parties and independent candidates became especially evident following the election of two DLP candidates to the Senate in 1956. Since that time, 127 minor parties and independents have taken up seats in the nation's powerful upper house. More importantly, with the exception of the period 2004–07, minor parties and independents have occupied the balance of power in the Senate since the 1980s. This has presented minor parties with occasional opportunities to shape the appearance and fate of government bills.

While PV is generally not considered the most advantageous electoral system for minor parties, it is not without some benefit. Compared to plurality electoral formulae, PV does not discourage electors from voting for minor parties. Voters can cast a first preference vote for a minor party and then allocate their subsequent preference(s) to another candidate safe in the knowledge that their vote might still contribute towards the election of the winning candidate. Similarly, because PV requires voters to distribute all of their preferences in order to register a formal vote, it does create opportunities for minor parties, through the use of how-to-vote card recommendations, to signify to their supporters a preferred ranking of candidates listed on the ballot paper. The requirement that voters must compulsorily allocate all of their preferences enables minor parties to potentially influence the outcome of the electoral contest between the major parties on a seat-by-seat basis. While the two main governing blocs continue to win virtually all seats in the House of Representatives, there has been a decrease in the number of lower house seats being decided on first preference votes. Until the mid 1950s only 10 per cent of seats required a distribution of preferences in order to determine the winning candidate (Papadakis & Bean 1995, p. 104). However, since this time, the number of seats decided on subsequent preferences has grown significantly. At the 2007 federal election, 50 per cent of seats were decided after a distribution of preferences. With the fate of many seats now being determined by the allocation of subsequent preferences, it has elevated the importance of minor parties and their supporters at elections.

Some commentators believe that the system of compulsory voting, much like PV, is also of benefit to minor parties. Richmond contends that because compulsory voting forces voters to the polls, it enables minor parties to more efficiently marshal their supporters' preferences for political and electoral gain. Not only is it 'inevitable' that minor party candidates will 'receive at least some votes' (1978, p. 322) but it allows the minor parties to use this fact to threaten, cajole or reward the major parties. Liberal Senator Nick Minchin (2001) has advocated the abolition of compulsory voting on the grounds that it 'aids' and 'abets' small parties.

Sharman et al. (2002, p. 548) have shown that in Australia, at least, a number of different types of 'preference' bargaining relationships are possible. There are four main ways that minor parties can attempt to use preferences in order to achieve their objectives:

- Small parties agree to swap preferences with each other out of ideological solidarity and to boost their mutual prospects.
- A small party and a large party agree to swap preferences for mutual electoral gain. Typically, this entails a small party agreeing to trade off their lower house preferences in exchange for the Senate preferences of the major party. This is known as a cross-house preference deal.
- A small party unilaterally denies its preferences to one of the major parties in order to punish the latter.
- A small party agrees to allocate its preferences to a major party in exchange for policy concessions.

However, given the electoral record of Australia's minor parties, it is clear that these windows of opportunity do not greatly improve their prospects for survival or success. Most minor parties will have to content themselves with remaining on the sidelines, waiting for opportunities to influence outcomes.

BOX 12.5   Australian Democrats

- *Origin*: Founded by Don Chipp, former Liberal Party minister, in 1977. Chipp put the Democrats on the map when he famously declared that the purpose of the party was 'to keep the bastards honest'. While the Democrats are more than thirty years old, the *raison d'être* of the party is unchanged and the party remains committed to keeping a watchful eye on the government of the day. In recent years, however, the Australian electorate has lost faith in the Democrats' ability to perform this role. Since 2001, the Democrats' vote has been slowly collapsing, culminating in the failure of any of its representatives to be elected to the Senate at the 2007 federal election. The Democrats, who were once recognised for their balance, independence and neutrality, are widely regarded as a spent force in Australian politics.
- *Leader of the Party as at early 2009*: Unknown.
- *Parliamentary representation as at early 2009*: One member, David Winderlich, in the South Australian Legislative Council
- *Party slogan*: Bring Back Balance
- *Estimate of party membership*: 3000+ members
- *Political ideology*: Social progressivism, environmentalism
- *Key principles (current at February 2009)*:
  - *We represent all Australians*: We are not tied to any wealthy power base— big unions, big business or powerful industrial and professional groups.
  - *We are fully democratic*: All decisions on policies and leadership positions are made by secret postal ballot in which all members equally have the right to vote.
  - *We are independent*: We have no connection with the other parties. We support their good proposals and fight their bad ones. We will not enter into coalitions and compromise our independence to secure more power.
  - *We have revitalised the Senate*: With Australian Democrat senators holding the balance of power, the Senate is now filling its true role as a House of Review, a source of initiatives, and a moderating influence on the government of the day.
  - *We look ahead*: This country must adopt long-term goals and objectives. We cannot continue to stagger along with governments unable or unwilling to make bold or unpopular moves because elections are only months apart.

□ *Our politicians have a conscience vote*: Our politicians are expected to follow party policy but they can exercise a conscience vote provided they are willing to justify it to the membership.

□ *We have plans for employment and the economy*: Like our system of government, our economy is sick. It needs more than band-aid solutions. It needs more local community involvement and control. We can no longer stand back and allow jobs to be sacrificed for the 'needs' of the market. Our economic strategies have to take account of social and environmental needs.

□ *We are concerned for the survival of the planet*: We believe the survival of our planet has reached crisis point.

□ *We are concerned about foreign control*: We want to bring Australia back under Australian control. There is too much foreign ownership of land and business, too much overseas influence in our internal economy and too much influence on our foreign policy.

□ *We offer equal opportunity for women*: We are the first political party in Australia to elect a woman as its National Parliamentary leader and to have women as a majority of Federal Parliamentary Representatives.

Source: Australian Democrats

■ *Nationwide primary vote at the 2007 federal election*: House of Representatives: 0.72 per cent (−0.52 per cent); Senate: 1.29 per cent (−0.80 per cent). Figures in brackets represent swing.

■ *Voter heartland*: South Australia

■ *Recommended reading*: Warhurst, J. (ed.) 1997. *Keeping the Bastards Honest*. Allen & Unwin, Sydney.

■ *Party website*: http://www.democrats.org.au/

Q At the 2007 federal election, the Australian Democrats suffered a fatal blow. Not only did the party's primary vote in both the Senate and the House of Representatives fall to an historic low, but the party failed to elect any of it candidates to the Senate. For the first time since 1977, there are no Democrats in the Senate. What do you think accounts for the decline in the fortunes of the Democrats? Is it a problem of 'relevance', 'leadership' or 'policy' (e.g. its position on the GST)?

BOX 12.6   Australian Greens

- *Origin*: The national organisation formed in 1992 'at a Friday night meal at a café in Newtown, Sydney' (Brown & Singer 1996, p. 84). However, it was not until 2003 that the party had chapters in every state and territory in Australia.
- *Leader of the Party as at early 2009*: Dr Bob Brown, Senator for Tasmania
- *Parliamentary representation as at early 2009*: Five senators: Bob Brown (Tas.), Christine Milne (Tas.), Sarah Hanson-Young (SA), Scott Ludlum (WA), Rachel Siewert (WA). The Greens have 20 elected members in state and territory parliaments in the ACT, South Australia, Tasmania, Victoria, NSW and Western Australia.
- *Estimate of party membership*: 8000+ members
- *Party slogan*: Take Action, Green Action
- *Key political values*: ecologism, social progressivism
- *Key principles*:
  - *Ecology*: To ensure that human activity respects the integrity of eco-systems and does not impair biodiversity and ecological resilience of life-supporting systems; to encourage the development of a conscious-ness that respects the value of all life.
  - *Democracy*: To increase opportunities for public participation in decision-making; to break down inequalities of wealth and power which inhibit participatory democracy.
  - *Social justice*: To eradicate poverty by developing initiatives that address the causes as well as the symptoms of poverty; to provide affirmative action to eliminate discrimination based on gender, age, race, ethnicity, class, religion, disability, sexuality, or membership of a minority group; to introduce measures that redress the imbalance of wealth between rich and poor.
  - *Peace*: To adopt and promote the non-aligned resolution of conflict; to develop an independent non-aligned foreign policy and a non-nuclear, defensive, self-reliant defence policy.
  - *An ecologically sustainable economy*: To develop economic policies that will ensure greater resource and energy efficiency and development and use of environmentally sustainable technologies; to reduce dependence on non-renewable resources and ensure sustainable use of renewable resources; to adopt more comprehensive social, environmental and technology assessment practices; to facilitate socially and ecologically responsible investment.
  - *Meaningful work*: To encourage, develop and assist work that is safe, fairly paid, socially useful, personally fulfilling and not harmful to the

environment; to facilitate more flexible work arrangements, on-going education, training and social welfare (including child-care).

- ☐ *Culture*: To respect and protect ethnic, religious, racial diversity; to recognise the cultural requirements of the original Australians and to assist in ensuring the achievement of Aboriginal land rights and self-determination.
- ☐ *Information*: To facilitate a free flow of information between citizens and all tiers of government; to ensure that Australians have the benefit of a locally responsible, diverse, democratically controlled and independent mass media.
- ☐ *Global responsibility*: To promote equity between nations and peoples by facilitating fair trading relationships; providing for increased development assistance and concerted international action to abolish Third World debt; providing increased green technology transfer and skills to developing countries; opposing human rights abuses and political oppression; ensuring that Australia plays an active role in promoting peace and ecological sustainability.
- ☐ *Long-term future focus*: To avoid action that might risk long-term or irreversible damage to the environment; and to safeguard the planet's ecological resources and values on behalf of future generations.

- ■ *Nationwide primary vote at the 2007 federal election*: House of Representatives: 7.79 per cent (+0.60 per cent); Senate: 9.04 per cent (+1.37 per cent).
- ■ *Voter heartland*: Tasmania
- ■ *Recommended reading*: Miragliotta, N. 2006. 'One Party, Two Traditions: Radicalism and Pragmatism in the Australian Greens'. *Australian Journal of Political Science*. Vol. 41, No. 4, pp. 585–96.
- ■ *Party website*: http://greens.org.au/

Q At the 2007 federal election, the Greens managed to achieve their fifth consecutive increase in their national primary vote. What do you think accounts for the Greens' electoral success?

BOX 12.7   Family First

- *Origin*: Founded originally by Andrew Evans, a Pastor of the Assemblies of God Church, in South Australia, some time in early 2000–02. The party was registered federally in 2004. The party has chapters in every Australian state.
- *Leader of the Party as at early 2009*: Steve Fielding, Senator for Victoria
- *Parliamentary representation as at early 2009*: 1 senator and 2 members in the South Australian Legislative Council
- *Estimate of party membership*: 2000+ members
- *Party slogan*: Put Your Family on the Political Agenda
- *Key political values*: Christianity, social conservatism, protectionism
- *Party principles*:
  - That the heroes of Australia are its Mums and Dads, who have the toughest job of all, but also the most important job of all, raising children
  - That children are our greatest gift and the future of our nation
  - That families should have genuine choice about how they balance their paid work and family life
  - That people must accept personal responsibility as well as community obligations
  - That workers who have children are parents first and workers second
  - That we must reduce the crippling number of marriage and relationship breakdowns and do all we can to support families.

Source: Family First

- *Nationwide primary vote at the 2007 federal election*: House of Representatives: 1.99 per cent (–0.02 per cent); Senate: 1.62 per cent (–0.14 per cent).
- *Voter heartland*: South Australia
- *Recommended reading*: Manning, H. & Warhurst, J. 2005. 'The Old and New Politics of Religion', in *Mortgage Nation: The 2004 Australian Election*. M. Simms & J. Warhurst (eds). API Network, Perth.
- *Party website*: http://www.familyfirst.org.au/index.php

Q The rise of Family First in Australia is viewed by many as evidence of the growing role of religion in political life, as has been the case in the United States for some years. Would you agree with the view that religion is emerging as an important issue at Australian elections?

BOX 12.8   The National Party

- *Origin*: Founded under the label of the Country Party in 1925 to defend the interests and rights of Australian farmers and rural communities. In 1947 the party changed its name to the National Party, ostensibly to widen the base of its electoral appeal. Despite this, the Nationals have experienced a consistent decline in its primary vote federally.
- *Leader of the Party as at early 2009*: Hon. Warren Truss
- *Parliamentary representation as at early 2009*: 14 members in the Federal Parliament; 18 members in the NSW Parliament; 34 members in the Queensland Parliament; 11 members in the Victorian Parliament; 9 members in the Western Australian Parliament
- *Party slogan*: Working Hard, Getting Results
- *Estimate of party membership*: 100 000+ members
- *Political ideology*: social conservatism, protectionism
- *Key principles*:
  - *Security*: We believe in security for the nation, local communities and families.
  - *Individual achievement*: We believe in private enterprise, a fair go and a balanced role for government.
  - *Strong representation*: We believe in Members of Parliament who are strong local advocates, champions for their regions and come together to act as a team.

Source: National Party of Australia

- *Nationwide primary vote at the 2007 federal election*: House of Representatives: 0.72 per cent (−0.52 per cent); Senate: 1.29 per cent (−0.80 per cent).
- *Voter heartland*: Queensland
- *Recommended reading*: Woodward, D. 2006, 'The National Party', in *Government, Politics, Power and Policy in Australia* (8th edn). A. Parkin, J. Summers & D. Woodward (eds). Pearson Longman, Sydney.
- *Party website*: http://www.nationals.org.au/

Q Over the years, there has been talk of the Nationals and Liberals formally amalgamating, especially following an election defeat. This became a reality in Queensland when the National and Liberal parties in that state merged in May 2008. Given that the Nationals' primary vote has been in decline for a number of years, is it in the party's interests to seriously consider a merger with the Liberals at the federal level also?

BOX 12.9   One Nation

- *Origin*: The party was co-founded by disendorsed federal Liberal candidate, Pauline Hanson, in Queensland in 1997. At the height of the party's success, it occupied 11 of 98 seats in the Queensland Legislative Assembly. In early 2000, Hanson left the party, and went on to contest seats in the NSW Legislative Council (2002) and the Queensland Senate (2004) as an independent. In 2007, Hanson formed the United Australia Party. Despite the loss of its prominent founding member, intra-party squabbling and de-registration, One Nation has branches in every Australian state.
- *Leader of the Party as at early 2009*: Currently does not have a national leader
- *Parliamentary representation as at early 2009*: Currently do not have any elected members in any Australian Parliament
- *Estimate of party membership*: In 1998, the party was estimated to have 25 000 members. There are no available estimates of its likely current membership numbers.
- *Party slogan*: The Voice of the People
- *Key political values*: nationalism, protectionism, social conservatism, support for private enterprise
- *Key principles*:
  - ☐ One Nation is a political party representing the people of Australia who are concerned that their will is being ignored by the two-party system. One Nation is committed to Australian sovereignty, the Constitution and Government of the people by the people for the people. Based on this view we have developed objectives and policies reflecting the will of the people. Our role as a political party is to select and recommend to the people, candidates that we feel reflect our objectives and policies and are worthy of representing them and their will as dedicated parliamentary representatives.

    Source: One Nation

- *Nationwide primary vote at the 2007 federal election*: House of Representatives: 0.26 per cent (−0.14 per cent); Senate: 0.42 per cent (−1.31 per cent).
- *Voter heartland*: Western Australia
- *Recommended reading*: Leach, M., Stokes, G. & Ward, I. 2000. *The Rise and Fall of One Nation*. University of Queensland Press, St Lucia.
- *Party website*: http://www.onenation.com.au/

Q Is it too simplistic to argue that the initial surge in support for One Nation can be accounted for solely on the basis of its position on immigration? To what extent was Pauline Hanson's persona a crucial factor in explaining the party's early success?

ISSUE IN FOCUS

TO WHAT EXTENT DO MINOR PARTIES ENHANCE DEMOCRACY IN AUSTRALIA?

It is not easy being too different from the pack in Australian politics. No entity knows this better than Australia's minor parties. Minor parties in Australia find themselves in an invidious situation. They are frequently derided on a number of different, often contradictory bases. Minor parties are accused of being radical extremists. This claim has been levelled against both the One Nation Party and the Australian Greens, albeit for different reasons. Alternatively, minor parties are declared to be impotent. Their inability to easily and consistently win seats in Australia's parliaments and the House of Representatives particularly, not to mention their failure to form a government, has led more than one commentator to declare voting for them to be a waste of a vote. However, when minor parties are afforded an opportunity to flex their muscle, they are vilified for exercising power incommensurate with their support in the electorate. This occurs most frequently in the context of their ability to trade preferences for electoral or policy gain, or when they are in a position to stop government bills from being enacted when they are in a balance of power position in the Senate.

Minor parties are rarely rewarded for their efforts at the ballot box. As discussed previously in this chapter, there are few opportunities for minor parties to transcend their status as a non-governing party. The constituency base of virtually all minor parties, suffers from any combination of being extremely small, non-existent or fickle. Most minor parties struggle to achieve a consistent level of electoral support, and fewer still have managed to marshal a core constituency. The major parties occasionally conspire against the minor parties to limit their electoral opportunities, even if the big parties have not necessarily openly cooperated with each other. In the lead-up to the 2004 federal poll, John Howard, Liberal prime minister, urged the electorate to be 'decisive' when casting their vote and to support either his party or the ALP, and not minor party and independent candidates. Moreover, minor parties lack the resources to compete against major parties that are blessed with a well-known political brand, organisational stability, experience, and significant resources to finance their campaign activities.

In spite of all the criticisms to which minor parties are frequently subjected, they continue to form in Australia and, on occasion, win representation. However, was John Howard correct when he argued that it would be bad for the country to have a parliament 'in the hands of independents' (*Weekend Australian* 2004)? Would Australian democracy be better served if there were no minor parties? In this section of the chapter we will consider the pros and cons of minor-party participation in politics, beginning with the arguments against their involvement.

The most common criticism of minor parties is that they can be a nuisance in Parliament when they are in a balance of power position in the Senate. Minor parties and independents are frequently accused of frustrating the right of a democratically elected government from pursuing its policy agenda by blocking government initiatives in the Senate. In 2008, the Rudd Government was forced to make a significant concession on its pre-election commitment to reduce the Medicare threshold for single people. The government's bill to increase the income threshold (from $50 000 to $100 000) over which singles without private health care would incur the 1 per cent Medicare levy surcharge was met with opposition in the Senate. In order to satisfy both the Family First and independent senators, the government had to reduce its planned increase in the singles' income threshold from $100 000 to $75 000, thereby denying tax relief to 70 000 taxpayers. A handful of minority actors in the Senate, who between them secured approximately 12 per cent of the nationwide first preference vote in the Senate, managed to trump the wishes of 52.7 per cent of the electorate who supported the election of the ALP to government.

Another complaint levelled against minor parties is that they can be vindictive, often using their supporters' preferences in order to prevent one of the major parties from gaining election. That is, minor parties frustrate the popular will by advising their supporters to allocate their subsequent preferences in a manner designed to injure the electoral prospects of a particular party. In the 1960s, the now-defunct Australia Party advised its supporters to allocate their subsequent preferences to the ALP ahead of the Liberal Party in an effort to force the latter to reconsider its position on Australia's involvement in Vietnam (Richmond 1978). The objective of the Australia Party's preference strategy was to punish the Liberals for supporting a war that the Australia Party opposed.

Some suggest that minor parties consume scarce and precious resources without any real tangible public benefit. While the major parties benefit from public funding, they are also the groups that win the most seats in Parliament. However, this is not true for minor parties that also access public funds to underwrite campaigns even though they frequently fail to win representation. In this sense at least, it is an inefficient allocation of public resources that might be better directed elsewhere. Related to this point, the low thresholds for eligibility to receive election funding allow minor parties to profit financially. This may encourage perverse incentives for parties to form with the intention of making money. These claims were levelled against Pauline Hanson following the 2004 federal election. More than one commentator noted that Hanson receipted $200 000 in public funds, even though—according to her annual return submitted to the AEC—she did not appear to spend a single dollar on her campaign (Orr 2007).

While there are strong arguments to support claims that minor parties are a nuisance that subvert the will of the majority and bring instability to government, there are also good reasons to regard them as important to the maintenance of Australia's democratic system. First, minor parties serve as vehicles for popular participation. Jaensch et al. (2004) suggests that many of Australia's minor parties tend to operate more democratically than their major party counterparts. It seems that opportunities for meaningful participation are more likely to occur as a member of a small party than as a member of a major party, where the contribution by most of the rank and file is likely to consist of stuffing envelopes and being used as pawns by party powerbrokers. In this sense, minor parties take us back to an almost ideal model of the participatory benefits that parties should provide.

Second, minor parties provide voters with choice on polling day. As has been noted in Chapter 9, the major parties in Australia have converged on virtually all points of policy. Policy 'me-tooism' is prevalent in the rhetoric of the major parties. Policy choice is limited and policy debate is overwhelmingly focused on economic considerations. Minor parties provide a platform for other types of issues to be canvassed, particularly those that are unlikely to be voiced in the cut and thrust of the policy exchange over economic matters between the major parties. Moreover, minor parties are more likely to put forward new initiatives and offer new ways of looking at the same old policy problems and are often important platforms to test public sentiment to certain ideas or initiatives. Minor parties identify issues that the major parties may have an interest in but avoid, fearful that it might provoke a backlash or leave them vulnerable to their major-party opponents. Minor parties can serve, therefore, as an important springboard for discussion on new or controversial policy issues. This has been true in relation to environmental concerns in recent years.

On a more practical level, minor parties have proven important in keeping the major governing parties accountable in Parliament. The major parties have much in common. They are fond of exploiting their electoral and political dominance to achieve outcomes that benefit their interests. It is for this reason that the major opposition party is sometimes reluctant to draw too much attention to activities, practices or the use of resources they hope to one day be in a position to exploit. Minor parties, in contrast, are more likely than not to be injured by major party initiatives or, alternatively, have either genuine or strategic reasons to draw attention to them. Parties, such as the Democrats, ran very important campaigns in the Senate to draw attention to instances of government dissipation and squander. While they have not always proven successful in winding back these initiatives, they have at least attempted to bring them to public attention.

It seems that there are good arguments both for and against the necessity of minor parties in a democracy. This raises an important question. How do we assess which of these camps is necessarily right and which is wrong? It seems that one's view on such matters is ultimately influenced by one's ideas about whether democracy is best served by a political system that is responsive solely to the majority of people, or one that seeks to incorporate the views and wishes of as many voters as is practical and efficacious. Like so many of the debates we have examined in this book, there is no clear cut answer to this question. If one values choice and diversity then one is likely to find in favour of the need for minor parties in a polity. However, if one believes that democracy is best served by fostering conditions conducive to the articulation of majority interest, then one might be tempted to conclude that minor parties are simply a redundancy.

CHAPTER SUMMARY

A well-known political scientist once remarked that when it comes to minor parties, being small isn't always beautiful (Mayer 1984). Mayer was not commenting on the utility of minor parties as much as he was referring to the difficulties they encounter in the Australian context. This chapter has outlined some of the institutional roadblocks confronted by minor parties and explored the small windows of opportunity that permit the more astute parties to strike back in small, but powerful, ways against the system. In the Issue in Focus we examined the much-debated topic of whether minor parties are beneficial or injurious to Australian democracy. We concluded that the position one adopts on this question is influenced by whether one ultimately supports the values of pluralism over the values of political expediency. As with many of the important questions in politics, there is no right or wrong answer: only differences of opinion about which political values and principles should be prioritised and which ones should be assigned lesser importance.

WEBSITES

The official websites for the minor parties discussed in this chapter can be found in Boxes 12.5–12.9.

Nick Xenophon (Independent Senator for South Australia):
http://www.xen.net.au/
The official website for Nick Xenophon.

FURTHER READING

Bean, C. & Papadakis, E. 1995. 'Minor Parties and Independents: Electoral Bases and Future Prospects', *Australian Journal of Political Science*. Vol. 30 (Special Issue), pp. 111–26.

Jaensch, D. & Matheison, D. 2002. *A Plague on Both Your Houses: Minor Parties in Australia.* Allen & Unwin, St Leonards.

Smith, R. 2006. *Against the Machines: Minor Parties and Independents in New South Wales 1910–2006.* The Federation Press, Sydney.

Glossary

Act of Settlement
the principal Act of 1701 governing the succession to the thrones of the United Kingdom and the other Commonwealth Realms

Activism
the legal reasoning by which contemporary social values are applied to the law

Affirmative rights
also known as positive rights: the rights to be provided something, usually by the state, for example the right to employment or free education

Alfred Deakin
politician and leader of the movement for Australian federation. He held the office of prime minister of Australia for three terms: 1903–04, 1905–08 and 1909–10

Alternative vote
an electoral system that requires voters to rank all candidates in order of preference. The candidate who receives 50 per cent + 1 of the vote is deemed elected. Also known as preferential voting.

Australian Electoral Commission (AEC)
the federal statutory agency responsible for conducting federal elections and referendums and maintaining the Commonwealth electoral roll

Balance of power
when minor parties or independents can influence the passage of legislation in the Senate. The balance of power comes into play when the government lacks a majority in the Senate and is forced to rely on support from minor parties or independents in order to secure the safe passage of their bills through the upper house if the major opposition party is opposed to the proposed legislation.

Bicameralism
parliaments that have an upper and a lower house

Bill of rights
a list of rights and liberties belonging to the people and which the government cannot trespass upon

Bipartisan
when measures have the support of the two major parties

Bourgeois democracy
a political system with minimally democratic institutions and in which capitalism is able to thrive

By-election
a special election held between general elections to fill a vacancy caused by the resignation, death or expulsion of the sitting member

Cabinet
the central decision-making body of the executive that coordinates government activity, adjudicates disputes between ministers, and allocates resources to government departments

Cartel party thesis
a theory that proposes that major parties will seek to consolidate their position against challenger parties by monopolising the resources of the state

Catch-all parties
describe a model of party organisation in which ideology is subsumed by a focus on issues that are universally liked or disliked among the electorate (known as valence issues). The power of the membership over the parliamentary wing is diminished and rank and file political activism is limited.

Caucus
the term used to refer to both the parliamentary Labor Party and meetings of the parliamentary Labor Party

Chairperson of the Committee
the person selected to chair and to manage proceedings of the Committee

Checks and balances
a system that ensures that power is divided between different institutions

Civil society
the free organisation of citizens outside the activities of the state

Cleavage
a division within society that involves one of the primary determinants of social identity. There are groups who are aware of the cleavage and are prepared to act on the basis of their conflicting identities. The social division leads to the creation of organisations/formal institutions that represent and defend the collective identity.

Clerk
the person responsible for ensuring that the business of the Parliament runs smoothly and in accordance with the procedural rules

Coalition
in Australia, the arrangement between the Liberal Party and the National Party to join forces in order to form a government

Collective cabinet responsibility
one of the conventions of responsible government; all cabinet ministers take responsibility in parliament for the decisions of cabinet. If a minister cannot publicly defend a cabinet decision, he or she must resign from the government.

Common law
the body of decisions by courts on legal matters not covered by statutes and that provide precedents for contemporary decisions

Commonwealth Gazette
the *Government Notices Gazette* is published by the Attorney-General's Department each Wednesday, except for the Christmas–New Year period. The *Gazette* contains a range of legislation, including proclamations, information about legislation, notices of Commonwealth government departments and courts, and other notices required under Commonwealth law.

Competitive elections
where the election outcome is not pre-determined and the final result influences the composition of the legislative body

Concurrent federalism
a federal system in which the tiers of government have shared or overlapping policy responsibilities

Confederation
a political system in which there is a weak central government and strong state or sub-national governments that exercise exclusive sovereignty

Conflict of interest
a situation in which a minister has the power to make decisions on an issue where they stand to gain or lose personal benefits

Consensus democracy
described by Arend Lijphart as a model of democracy that seeks to 'share, disperse and limit power'. It is characterised by inclusiveness, bargaining and compromise; endeavouring to maximise popular participation in decision-making through the establishment of rules and institutions that encourage 'broad participation in government' and 'broad agreement on policies' (Lijphart 1999, p. 3).

Consent
the permission that citizens give to governments to act on their behalf

Constitution
a document that contains the rules by which the state is organised and governed and that describes the relationship between the government and the citizenry

Constitutional Crisis of 1975
In 1975, the Governor-General took the unprecedented step of exercising his reserve powers to dismiss the Whitlam Labor Government. The Governor-General justified the dismissal on the grounds that the Government had lost

the support of the Parliament due to its failure to secure the passage of its supply bills in the Senate.

Constitutional monarchy
the combination of an hereditary but mostly powerless head of state with a parliamentary system of government

Constitutionalism
the idea that government should and must be legally limited in its powers

Conventions
informal practices that guide the operation of the constitution and which have moral rather than legal force

Coordinate federalism
a federal system in which the tiers of government have distinct responsibility for separate policy areas

Corporations power
s. 51(xx) of the Constitution, which gives the Commonwealth the power to legislate in respect of '[f]oreign corporations, and trading or financial corporations formed within the limits of the Commonwealth'

Cosmopolitanism
the belief that human beings are members of a global community with obligations to those living beyond the borders of the state in which they live

Coup d'état
the overthrow of a government by a small group

Cross the floor
when Members of Parliament vote with the opposing party

Defamation law
defamation is the false or unjustified injury to one's reputation

Democratic deficit
when notionally democratic institutions fail to reflect the views and interests of citizens

Democratic Labor Party (DLP)
a Catholic-based and anti-communist party, which split from the Australian Labor Party in the 1950s

Divisions
a device used in parliament to gauge the support of the chamber for a motion

Electoral professional parties
parties in which paid advisers, public relations experts and consultants play a key role in both election campaigning and determining party policy

Electoral roll
a register compiled by the electoral authorities that lists the names of eligible persons who are registered to vote

Electoral system
the body of rules designed to turn the votes of citizens into representation in political institutions

Elitist
a conception of democracy that sees only very limited opportunities for public participation in representative political institutions

Enlightenment
an age of rapid developments in science and philosophy

Entrenched
a constitution that is entrenched is more difficult to alter than normal law

Executive agencies
agencies that are responsible to government ministers for the delivery of services to the public

Executive branch
the branch of government responsible for carrying out the law, headed by the prime minister and cabinet

Executive federalism
interaction between the different tiers of government that primarily involves members of the executive branch

Federal Executive Council
a group of ministers who convey the wishes of cabinet to the Governor-General

Federal system of government
where political power is divided between one central, national government and several regional governments

Federalism
a division of government power between central and provincial levels

First Past the Post (FPP)
an electoral formula in which the candidate with the highest number of first preference votes is elected

Fourth Estate
a concept that sees the media in a democracy as so vital that it is often compared to that of the executive, legislative and judicial branches of government

Free Traders
existed from the 1880s until 1909. This party favoured the abolition of protective tariffs and other restrictions on trade. It dominated New South Wales colonial politics before Federation. In the first elections for the Commonwealth Parliament, it constituted the second largest group in the House of Representatives. In 1909, it merged with the Protectionists to form the Commonwealth Liberal Party.

Gender voting gap
the difference in voting behaviour between men and women

Gough Whitlam
prime minister 1972–75

Government departments
a division of the public service responsible for the administration of a given portfolio

Government trading enterprises
businesses owned and operated by the state

Governor-General
the Monarch's representative, who is the formal head of state

Great Depression
a period of record unemployment during the 1930s

Half Senate election
an election in which half of the total number of Senate seats are contested. This is the norm at most federal elections. In a full Senate election all 76 Senate seats are contested. A full Senate election is rare and only occurs in the event of a double dissolution when the Governor-General dissolves both house of the Parliament.

High Court
the highest court in the Australian judicial system. It was established in 1901 by s. 71 of the Constitution. It interprets and applies the law of Australia and is the custodian of the federal Constitution.

House of Representatives Practice
the rule book of the House of Representatives, which sets out the rules, procedures and practices to which the chamber must conform

How-to-vote card
a pamphlet printed and distributed by parties to voters on polling day that outlines the order in which a party desires their supporters to rank the candidates listed on the ballot paper

Humanism
an attempt to build a progressive and humane belief system that did not rely on religious principles

Institutionalise
the process of turning values and habits into formal and informal rules

Interest group
a voluntary group or association that forms in order to influence the aims and policies of government

Iron law of oligarchy
in this context, it refers to a situation in which a small number of individuals control the activities of an organisation or group

Issue of the writ
a document that commands an electoral officer to hold an election

James Madison
contributor to *The Federalist Papers* and fourth president of the United States, 1809–17

Jean-Jacques Rousseau
a French philosopher whose ideas about politics were integral to the French Revolution of 1789

John Locke
English philosopher most famous for his 1689 work, *Two Treatises of Government*

Joint sitting of Parliament
when both houses of Parliament

convene to debate and vote upon a bill or some other matter

Judicial review
the ability of the judicial branch to overrule the actions of the other branches of government within the limits of the constitution

Legalism
the principle that legal statutes and the constitution must be interpreted as they are read rather than according to the intentions of the authors

Legitimacy
the right to exercise power

Liberal pluralists
those who believe that power is diffuse and shared among many different groups in society

Liberalism
belief in the rights of the individual, the rule of law, and limited government

Literalist
an approach to judicial interpretation that focuses on the words in the Constitution, rather than taking into account broader principles and values

Lobbying
coined to describe people who populated the lobby of the US Congress: an attempt to influence the decisions of government officials

Magna Carta
a charter signed in 1215, which was designed, among other things, to restrain the power of the British monarchs. Under the charter, the king was required to renounce certain rights, respect certain legal procedures and accept that the will of the king could be bound by the law.

Majoritarian democracy
described by Arend Lijphart as a model of democracy that aims to concentrate 'political power in the hands of a bare majority'. It is characterised as 'exclusive, competitive and adversial'. It creates political rules and institutions, which ensure 'government by the majority in accordance with the majority's interests' (Lijphart 1999, p. 3).

Malapportionment
refers to the problem of some electoral districts containing significantly more people than others. In Australia, malapportionment has historically taken the form of deliberate rural over-representation.

Malcolm Fraser
prime minister 1975–83

Managerialism
the application of private sector principles of efficiency and goal-orientation to the public sector

Mandate
a right to act

Margaret Thatcher
Conservative prime minister of the United Kingdom, 1979–90

Mass party
a model of party organisation that emphasises ideology and the dominance of the party membership over both its elected members and the policies of the party

Ministerial responsibility
the accountability that individual ministers have to parliament for their decisions and the actions of their department

Ministers
those politicians responsible for
the development of and conduct of
government policy in a particular area

Money bills
any bill that seeks to raise money

Multiculturalism
the belief that cultural diversity is
positive, and that it should be supported
by the government

National Audit Report
specialist public sector agency which
provides auditing services to the
Parliament and Commonwealth public
sector agencies and statutory bodies

National sovereignty
the idea that each nation-state is the
supreme source of legal authority over
its territory

Nationalise
when the state takes over ownership of
the means of production

Natural monopolies
services, such as water supply, that are
most efficiently provided by a single
entity

Neoliberalism
a political ideology characterised by a
belief in the free market, and opposition
to a large welfare state and extensive
state involvement in the economy

'No confidence' motion
a motion put in parliament that censures
the government

Odgers' Senate Practice
the rule book of the Senate, which sets
out the rules, procedures and practices
to which the chamber must conform

Originalism
a form of legal interpretation that
attempts to take into account the
intention of those who wrote the law or
constitution in question

Parliamentary secretaries
the most junior members of the political
executive, who are delegated portfolio
responsibilities from ministers

Parliamentary sovereignty
the idea that the Parliament is the
ultimate source of legal authority

Parliamentary system of government
a system where the members of the
executive government are drawn from
and are responsible to an elected
legislature

Party system
refers to the interrelationship between
parties within a polity and the manner in
which they co-exist

Plurality voting systems
refers to a voting system which ensures
that candidates can win seats in
parliament without having necessarily
attained an absolute majority of the first
preference votes cast

Policy networks
formal and informal groups of
government and non-government
actors with a common interest in a
policy area

Political executive
the group of decision-makers at the
highest level of government

Political ideologies
bodies of thought, such as liberalism,
socialism or conservatism, about the way
society should be organised

Political opportunity structures
in this context, the specific features of a nation's political system (including the legal and electoral systems) that influence new party formation, the strategies and organisational forms that parties adopt and their electoral success

Political socialisation
the cumulative effect that the various institutions we come into contact with throughout our lives have on our view of the world

Populist
appealing to the beliefs of ordinary voters

Post-materialist
a view that pays greater attention to issues such as the environment and human rights than economic and defence issues

Post-materialist values
those values that are concerned with broad quality-of-life issues such as the environment and multiculturalism, which transcend the traditional policy focus on the economy and national security

Precedents
legal decisions that courts will in future use as the starting point in their deliberation in similar cases

Preferential voting (PV)
a system whereby candidates must obtain an absolute majority of the vote to win a seat. In the event that a candidate fails to achieve this threshold, low-scoring candidates are eliminated and their votes are redistributed to remaining candidates until a final winner is declared.

Pre-selection
a process whereby parties select candidates who will contest an electorate under the party's banner

Presidential system of government
a system of government that separates executive and legislative power into different branches

Presidentialisation
the notion that power centralised in the office of prime minister makes parliamentary systems more like presidential systems

Prime minister
the head of government in parliamentary systems, usually the leader of the largest political party

Private members bill
a proposed new law that is introduced to the Parliament by a person other than a government minister

Privatisation
the removal of activities from the public sector through asset sales or service contracting to the private sector

Proportional representation
an electoral system that ensures that a party's share of the seats in parliament is in accordance with its share of all the votes cast

Prorogue
to terminate the term or session of a Parliament

Protectionism
the use of tariff barriers to protect local industries against competition from overseas imports

Protectionists
existed from the 1880s until 1909. This party favoured protective tariffs in order to facilitate the development of Australian industry and ensure employment. It was strongest in Victoria and in the rural areas of New South Wales. In the first elections for the Commonwealth Parliament, it constituted the largest group in the House of Representatives, although it did not have a majority in its own right. In 1909, it merged with the Free Traders to form the Commonwealth Liberal Party.

Public–private partnerships
where private sector funding and expertise are used to build and operate public infrastructure

Rank-and-file membership
citizens who pay a membership fee to join the party and participate in its activities

Rent-seeking
to bring about a favourable transfer of goods or services from a person, group or organisation without compensation

Representative democracy
a system whereby citizens delegate power to institutions elected by the people

Republic
a form of government in which sovereignty is based on consent of the governed and whose governance is based on popular representation. Sovereignty is vested in the 'people' and exercised on their behalf by government.

Residual powers
state powers that were not granted exclusively to the Commonwealth in the Constitution

Responsible government
a system where the cabinet is responsible to the parliament and parliament is responsible to voters

Robert Menzies
prime minister 1939–41 and 1949–66

Rule of law
where all power in a society is constrained by the legal system

Semi-presidential systems
semi-presidential systems divide executive power between a president and prime minister

Senate Estimates Committee
a committee in which ministers and departmental office-holders are questioned about the activities of their departments

Separation of powers
an institutional separation of executive, legislative, and judicial functions of government

Sir John Kerr
Governor-General 1974–77

Social contract
under a social contract, the relations between citizens are part of an explicit or implicit compact

Social liberalism
a view that places less emphasis on economic freedom than classical liberalism, standing for greater social equality and individual freedom on moral issues

Social movement
a body or group of people united by a commitment to a particular issue but which lacks a strong and disciplined organisational base. Unlike an interest

group, they do not seek to influence government or the legislative process; rather they aim to influence the way the public understands and thinks about a particular issue.

Sovereignty
the right of people living within a particular geographical community to claim ownership and authority over that particular territory

Speaker
the person elected by the members of the House of Representatives to chair meetings of the chamber and to preside over proceedings. In the Senate, this office is referred to as the President.

Stakeholders
groups likely to be affected by policy changes

Statutory authorities
statutory authorities are independent public organisations created by law and accountable to parliament

9/11 terrorist attacks
a series of coordinated Islamist terrorist attacks carried out in the USA on Tuesday, September 11, 2001. Nineteen men affiliated with al-Qaeda, a network of militant Islamist organisations, hijacked four commercial airliners. They crashed one into each of the two towers of the World Trade Center in New York City, and a third into the Pentagon in Washington DC.

The pledge
an undertaking given by all Labor-endorsed candidates to uphold the party platform and the decisions of Caucus

Threshold
the minimum percentage of the vote that is required to win a seat

Tweedledum and Tweedledee
a well-known phrase to denote two persons or things so much alike as to be practically indistinguishable

Two-party system
a political system in which two parties are dominant and typically alternate between government and opposition

Universal suffrage/franchise
a guarantee of the right of all adult citizens to vote

Vertical fiscal imbalance
the disproportionate revenue-raising capacities and spending responsibilities of the Commonwealth and states

Welfare state laggard
a country with an underdeveloped welfare state that provides less social protection for its citizens than other countries

Welfare state retrenchment
a reduction in the size of the welfare state

Westminster
the name given to the British Parliament and its system of government

Whistle-blowing
actions by public servants to publicly expose corruption or mismanagement

Bibliography

Aarons, M. 2008. 'The Unions and Labor', in *Dear Mr Rudd*. R. Manne (ed.). Black Inc. Agenda, Melbourne.

Access Economics. 2005. 'Business Regulation Action Plan for Future Prosperity', Business Council of Australia, Melbourne.

Anderson, G. 2006. 'Executive Government', ch. 5 in *Government, Politics, Power and Policy in Australia* (7th edn), J. Summers, D. Woodward & A. Parkin (eds). Longman Pearson, Sydney.

Anon. 2006. 'Kevin Rudd Pushes WorkChoices, Kyoto Mandates', 26 November. news.com.au, accessed 15 January 2007.

Aulich, C. 2005. 'Privatisation and Outsourcing', ch. 4 in *Howard's Second and Third Governments: Australian Commonwealth Administration 1998–2004*. C. Aulich & R. Wettenhall. UNSW Press, Sydney.

Australian Broadcasting Corporation. 2006. *Media Watch*. Episode 31, 11 September.

Australian Broadcasting Corporation. 2006. 'Minority Government', *Stateline* program. 10 March. http://www.abc.net.au/stateline/tas/content/2006/s1588941.htm.

Australian Electoral Commission. 2005. 'Analysis of Informal Voting during the 2004 House of Representatives Election', Research Report No. 7, October.

Australian Electoral Commission. 2007. 'Electoral Advertising', *Electoral Backgrounder No. 15*, March.

Australian Electoral Commission. 2008. *Electoral Pocketbook*, Commonwealth of Australia, Canberra.

Australian Electoral Commission. 2008. *Summary of Donations Reported by Donors*. http://fadar.aec.gov.au/, accessed 21 July 2008.

Australian Labor Party. 2008. *National Constitution of the ALP*. http://www.alp.org.au/platform/chapter_17.php#17objectives, accessed 21 July 2008.

Australian Parliamentary Library. *Civil and Human Rights Law Resources*. http://www.aph.gov.au/library/intguide/law/civlaw.htm.

Australian Public Service Commission. 2002. *Values in the Australian Public Service*. Commonwealth of Australia, Canberra.

Australian Public Service Commission. 2003. 'The Australian Experience of Public Sector Reform', *Occasional Paper No. 2*. Commonwealth of Australia, Canberra.

Australian Public Service Commission, 2007. *State of the Service Report 2006–07*. State of the Service Series. Australian Government, Canberra.

Axford, B. 2002. 'Parties, Interest Groups and Public Opinion', in *Politics: An Introduction*. B. Axford, G.K. Browning, R. Huggins & B. Rosamont (eds). Routledge, London.

Bach, S. 2007. 'Mandates, Consensus, Compromise and the Senate', paper presented as a lecture in the *Senate Occasional Lecture Series at Parliament House*, 19 October, Canberra.

Bach, S. 2008. 'Senate Amendments and Legislative Outcomes in Australia, 1996–2007', *Australian Journal of Political Science*. Vol. 43, No. 3, pp. 395–423.

Bachrach, P. & Baratz, M.S. 1962. 'Two Faces of Power', *American Political Science Review*. Vol. 56, No. 4, pp. 947–52.

Barker, G. 2007. 'The Public Service', ch. 7 in *Silencing Dissent*. C. Hamilton & S. Maddison. Allen & Unwin, Sydney.

Barns, G. 2003. *What's Wrong With the Liberal Party?* Cambridge University Press, Melbourne.

Bartolini, S. & Mair, P. 2001. 'Challengers to Contemporary Political Parties', in *Political Parties and Democracy*. L. Diamond & R. Gunther (eds). Johns Hopkins University Press, Baltimore.

Barwick, G. 1996. *A Radical Tory*. The Federation Press, Sydney.

Bean, C. 2000. 'Who Now Votes Labor?', in *The Machine: Labor Confronts the Future*. J. Warhurst & A. Parkin (eds). 2000. Allen & Unwin, St Leonards, NSW.

Bean, C. 2003. 'Is There a Crisis of Trust in Australia?', in *Australian Social Attitudes: The First Report*. S. Wilson, G. Meagher, R. Gibson, D. Denemark & M. Western (eds). UNSW Press, Sydney.

Bean, C. & Denemark, D. 2007. 'Citizenship, Participation, Efficacy and Trust in Australia', in *Australian Social Attitudes 2*. D. Denemark, G. Meagher, S. Wilson, M. Western, & T. Phillips (eds). UNSW Press, Sydney.

Bean, C. & Papadakis, E. 1995. 'Minor Parties and Independents: Electoral Bases and Future Prospects', *Australian Journal of Political Science*. Vol. 30 (Special Issue), pp. 111–26.

Beattie, P. 2007. 'A Vision Beyond the Blame Game', *Griffith Review*. 19.

Bennett, S. 1996. *Wining and Losing: Australian National Elections*, Melbourne University Press, Melbourne.

Bennett, S. 1999a. *Should the Australian Electoral System be Changed?*, Department of the Parliamentary Library, Information and Research Services, Canberra, pp. 4–6.

Bennett, S. 1999b. *Australia's Constitutional Milestones*. Politics and Public Administration Group. Australian Parliamentary Library, Canberra.

Bennett, S. 2002a. 'Australian Political Parties: More Regulation?' *Research Paper No. 21*, Politics and Public Administration Group. Australian Parliamentary Library.

Bennett, S. 2002b. *The Politics of Constitutional Amendment*, Politics and Public Administration Group. Australian Parliamentary Library, Canberra.

Bennett, S. 2004. 'The Australian Senate', Research Paper No. 6. Politics and Administration Group, Australian Parliamentary Library.

Bennett, S. 2008. 'Compulsory Voting in Australian National Elections', *Research Brief No. 6*, Department of the Parliamentary Library, Canberra, pp. 1–36.

Birch, A.H. 1971. *Representation*. Macmillan, London.

Bogdanor, V. 1988. *Constitutions in Democratic Politics*. Gower Publishing, England.

Bongiorno, F. 2001. 'The Origins of Caucus: 1856–1901', in *True Believers*. J. Faulkner & S. Macintyre (eds). Allen & Unwin, Crows Nest, NSW, pp. 3–16.

Brennan, F. 1998. *The Wik Decision: Its Impact on Aborigines, Farmer and Miners*. UNSW Press, Sydney.

Brennan, G. 2007. 'The Role of the Legal Profession in the Rule of Law', Speech at the Supreme Court, Brisbane. 31 August.

Brett, J. 1992. *Robert Menzies' Forgotten People*. Macmillan, Sydney.

Brett, J. 2003. *Australian Liberals and the Moral Middle Class*. Cambridge University Press, Melbourne.

Brett, J. 2004. 'The New Liberalism', in *The Howard Years*. R. Manne (ed.). Black Inc. Agenda, Melbourne, pp. 74–93.

Brett, J. 2006. 'The Liberal Party', ch. 11 in *Government, Politics, Power and Policy in Australia* (8th edn). A. Parkin et al. (eds). Pearson Longman, Frenchs Forest.

Brett, J. 2007. 'Exit Right: The Unravelling of John Howard', *Quarterly Essay*. Issue 28.

Brown, B. & Singer, P. 1996. *The Greens*, Text Publishing, Melbourne.

Burchell, D. 2008. 'Haunted by Hasty Populism', *Australian*, 7 June. http://www.theaustralian.news.com.au/story/0,23822842-28737,00.html, accessed 21 July 2008.

Bynander, F. & t'Hart, P. 2007. 'The Politics of Party Leader Survival and Succession: Australia in Comparative Perspective', *Australian Journal of Political Science*. Vol. 42, No. 1, March, pp. 47–72.

Carney, G. 2006. *The Constitutional Systems of the Australian States and Territories*. Cambridge University Press, New York.

Castles, F.G. 1985. *The Working Class and Welfare*. Sydney, Allen & Unwin.

Castles, F.G. & Shirley, I. 1996. 'Labour and Social Policy: Gravediggers or Refurbishers of the Welfare State', in *The Great Experiment*. F.G. Castles, R. Gerritsen & J. Vowles (eds). Allen & Unwin, St Leonards, NSW, pp. 88–106.

Castles, F.G. & Uhr, J. 2005. 'Federal Constraints and Institutional Innovations', in *Federalism and the Welfare State: New World and European Experiences*. H. Obinger, S. Leibfried & F.G. Castles (eds). Cambridge University Press, Cambridge.

Cavalier, R. 2006. 'Could Chifley Win Labor Pre-Selection Today?', in *Coming to the Party: Where to Next for Labor?* B. Jones (ed.). Melbourne University Press, Melbourne.

COAG [Council of Australian Governments]. 2007. *Communiqué of Council of Australian Governments' Meeting, Melbourne, 20 December 2007*. http://www.coag.gov.au/coag_meeting_outcomes/2007-12-20/cooag20071220.pdf, accessed 7 May 2009.

Coleman, P. 1963. 'The Liberal and Country Parties Platforms, Policies and Performance', ch. 1 in *Forces in Australian Politics*. J. Wilkes (ed.). Angus and Robertson, Sydney.

Commonwealth Grants Commission. 2008. 'About CGC'. http://www.cgc.gov.au/about_cgc, accessed 30 October 2008.

Commonwealth of Australia. 2008. *Australia 2020 Summit: Final Report*. Department of the Prime Minister and Cabinet, Canberra.

Cook, I. 2004. *Government and Democracy in Australia*. Oxford University Press, Melbourne.

Coonan, H. 2003. 'The Australian Senate—From Gatekeeper To Gridlock', address to the *Australian Davos Connection Leadership Conference*, Hayman Island. http://www.treasurer.gov.au/DisplayDocs.aspx?doc=speeches/2003/010b.htm&pageID=005&min=hlc&Year=2003&DocType=1, accessed 22 July 2008.

Costar, B. 2006. 'The Electoral System', in *Government, Politics, Power and Policy in Australia* (8th edn). A. Parkin, J. Summers, & D. Woodward (eds). Pearson Longman, Melbourne.

Costar, B. & Curtin, J. 2004. *Rebels with a Cause: Independents in Australian Politics*, UNSW Press, Sydney.

Crabb. A. 2005. *Losing It: The Inside Story of the Labor Party in Opposition*. Picador, Sydney.

Craven, G. 1999. 'The High Court of Australia: A Study in the Abuse of Power', *University of New South Wales Law Journal*. Vol. 22, No. 1, pp. 216–42.

Craven, G. 2006a. 'Struggle Ahead for the States', *The Australian*, November 16. http://www.theaustralian.news.com.au/story/0,20867,20764120-7583,00.html, accessed 16 December 2008.

Craven, G. 2006b. 'WorkChoices Shipwreck', *Perspective*. ABC Radio National, 6 December 2006. www.abc.net.au/rn/perspective/stories/2006/1803817.htm, accessed 2 November 2008.

Crisp, L.F. 1961. *Ben Chifley*. Longman, Melbourne.

Crisp, L.F. 1973. *Australian National Government*. Longman, Melbourne.

Crisp, L.F. 1978. *The Australian Federal Labor Party 1901–1951*. Hale & Iremonger, Sydney.

Dahl, R. 1961. *Who Governs? Democracy and Power in an American City*. Yale University Press, New Haven.

Dahl, R. 1970. *Modern Political Analysis*. Prentice-Hall, New Jersey.

DeLue, S. & Dale, T. 2009. *Political Thinking, Political Theory, and Civil Society*. Pearson Longman, New York.

Denemark, D., Meagher, G., Wilson, S., Western, M. & Phillips, T. (eds). 2007. *Australian Social Attitudes 2*. UNSW Press, Sydney.

Diamond, L. & Gunther, R. 2001. *Political Parties and Democracy*. Johns Hopkins University Press, Baltimore.

Donovan, T. 2000. 'Mobilisation and Support of Minor Parties: The Australian Senate', *Party Politics*. Vol. 6, No. 4, pp. 473–84.

Donovan, T., Denemark, D. & Bowler, S. 2007. 'Trust, Citizenship and Participation: Australia in Comparative Perspective', ch. 4 in D. Denemark, G. Meagher, S. Wilson, M. Western & T. Phillips (eds). *Australian Social Attitudes 2*. UNSW Press, Sydney.

Duverger, M. 1959. *Political Parties: Their Organization and Activity in the Modern State*. Methuen, London.

Emy, H. & Hughes, O. 1991. *Australian Politics: Realities in Conflict* (2nd edn). Macmillan, Melbourne.

Epstein, L. 1980. *Political Parties in Western Democracies*, Transaction Books, New Brunswick, NJ.

Errington, W. & Miragliotta, N. 2007. *Media and Politics: An Introduction*. Oxford University Press, Melbourne.

Errington, W. & van Onselen, P. 2006. '"You Lucky, Lucky Bastard": The Limits of John Howard's Political Genius', paper presented to the *John Howard's Decade* conference. Australian National University, Canberra, March.

Errington, W. & van Onselen, P. 2007. *John Winston Howard: The Biography*. Melbourne University Press, Carlton.

Errington, W. 2008. 'Federalism and Liberal Thinking', ch. 16 in *Liberals and Power: The Road Ahead*. P. van Onselen (ed.). Melbourne University Press, Carlton.

Evan, H. 2004. *Odgers' Australian Senate Practice* (11th edn). Department of the Senate, Australian Commonwealth Parliament.

Evans, H. 2006. 'Democracy: The Wrong Message', Working Paper 24/06. Democratic Audit of Australia, August.

Evans, H. 2007. 'The Senate', ch. 12 in *Silencing Dissent*. C. Hamilton & S. Maddison (eds). Allen & Unwin, Sydney.

Farrell, D. 2001. *Electoral Systems: A Comparative Introduction*. Palgrave, Hampshire.

Farrell, D. & McAllister, I. 2006. *The Australian Electoral System*. UNSW Press, Sydney.

Faulkner, J. 2001. 'Splits: Consequences and Lessons', in *True Believers*. J. Faulkner & S. Macintyre (eds). Allen & Unwin, Crows Nest, NSW, pp. 203–18.

Fenna, A. 2004. *Australian Public Policy* (2nd edn). Pearson, Frenchs Forest.

Fenna, A. 2007. 'The Malaise of Federalism: Comparative Reflections on Commonwealth–State Relations', *Australian Journal of Public Administration*. Vol. 66, No. 3.

Finer, E. 1988. 'Notes Towards a History of Constitutions', in *Constitutions in Democratic Politics*. Gower Publishing, England.

Finer, E., Bogdanor, V. & Rudden, B. 1995. *Comparing Constitutions*. Oxford University Press, New York.

Franklin, M. 2007. 'Gillard to Drive Rudd Agenda', *The Australian*, 30 November. http://www.theaustralian.news.com.au/story/0,25197,22845676-601,00.html, accessed 21 July 2008.

Funnell, W. 2001. *Government By Fiat: The Retreat From Responsibility*. UNSW Press, Sydney.

Galligan, B. 1987. *The Politics of the High Court*. University of Queensland Press, Brisbane.

Galligan, B. (ed). 1989. *Australian Federalism*. Longman Cheshire, Melbourne.

Galligan, B. 1995. *A Federal Republic: Australia's Constitutional System of Government*. Cambridge University Press, Cambridge.

Galligan, B. 2006. 'Comparative Federalism', in *The Oxford Handbook of Political Institutions*. Oxford University Press, Oxford.

Galligan, B. & McAllister, I. 1997. 'Citizen and Elite Attitudes Towards an Australian Bill of Rights', in *Rethinking Human Rights*. B. Galligan & C. Sampford (eds). Federation Press, Sydney.

Galligan, B. & Morton, T. 2006. 'Australian Exceptionalism: Rights Protection Without a Bill of Rights', in *Protecting Rights Without a Bill of Rights: Institutional Performance and Reform in Australia*. T. Campbell, J. Goldsworthy & A. Stone (eds). Ashgate, Aldershot.

Galligan, B. & Sampford, C. 1997. *Rethinking Human Rights*. Federation Press, Leichhardt, NSW.

Galligan, B., Owen, H. & Walsh, C. (eds). 1991. *Intergovernmental Relations and Public Policy*, Allen & Unwin, North Sydney.

Gallop, G. 2001. 'Is There A Third Way?' in *Left Directions: Is There A Third Way?* P. Nursey-Bray & C.L. Bacchi (eds). UWA Press, Crawley, WA.

Gallop, G. 2008. 'The Federation', in *Dear Mr Rudd*. R. Manne (ed.). Black Inc. Agenda. Melbourne.

Gauja, A. 2005. 'Keeping the Party under Control: The Legal Regulation of Australia's Political Parties', *Australian Review of Public Affairs*, 11 July. http://www.australianreview.net/digest/2005/07/gauja.html, accessed 16 December 2008.

Gelber, K. 2006. 'High Court Review 2005: The Manifestation of Separation of Powers in Australia', *Australian Journal of Political Science*. Vol. 41, No. 3, September, pp. 437–53.

Gleeson, M. 1997. 'The Role of the Judiciary in a Modern Democracy', Judicial Conference of Australia Annual Symposium. 8 November. http://www.jca.asn.au/content/attachments/gleeson.html, accessed 4 September 2007.

Goot, M. 1999. 'Whose Mandate? Policy Promises, Strong Bicameralism and Polled Opinion', *Australian Journal of Political Science*. Vol. 34, No. 3, pp. 327–52.

Graham, B.D. 1968. 'The Choice of Voting Methods in Federal Politics, 1902–1918', in *Readings in Australian* Government. C. Hughes (ed.). University of Queensland Press, St Lucia.

Grattan, M. 2001. 'Caucus and the Factions', in *True Believers*. J. Faulkner & S. Macintyre (eds). Allen & Unwin, Crows Nest, NSW, pp. 250–64.

Griffith, G. 2006. 'A NSW Charter of Rights? The Continuing Debate'. *Briefing Paper No. 5*. Parliament of NSW, Sydney.

Hague, R. & Harrop, M. 1987. *Elections and Voters*, London, Macmillan.

Hague, R. & Harrop, M. 2001. *Comparative Government and Politics: An Introduction* (5th edn). Palgrave, Basingstoke.

Hague, R. & Harrop, M. 2004. *Comparative Government and Politics: An Introduction* (6th edn). Palgrave Macmillan, London.

Halligan, J. 2008. 'The Search for Balance in the Australian Public Service', ch. 2 in *Howard's Fourth Government: Australian Commonwealth Administration 2004–2007*. C. Aulich & R. Wettenhall (eds). UNSW Press, Sydney.

Hancock, I. 1994. 'The Origins of the Modern Liberal Party', *Harold White Fellow Lecture*. National Library or Australia, Canberra.

Hancock, I. 2007. *The Liberals: The NSW Division 1945–2000*. The Federation Press, Sydney.

Hancock, W. K. 1945. *Australia*. E. Benn, London.

Harris, I. 2005. *House of Representatives Practice* (5th edn). Department of the House of Representatives, Canberra.

Harrop, M. & Miller, W. L. 1987. *Elections and Voters: A Comparative Introduction*. Macmillan Education, Houndmills, Basingstoke, Hampshire.

Hawke, R. & Wran, N. 2002. *National Committee of Review Report*, Australian Labor Party, published 9 August.

Headey, B., Marks, G. & Wooden, M. 2004. 'The Structure and Distribution of Household Wealth in Australia', *Melbourne Institute Working Paper* No. 12/04.

Held, D. 1987. *Models of Democracy*. Polity Press, Cambridge.

Henderson, G. 1994. *Menzies' Child: The Liberal Party of Australia 1944–1994*. Allen & Unwin, Sydney.

Heywood, A. 1997. *Politics*. Macmillan, London.

Heywood, A. 2007. *Politics* (3rd edn). Macmillan, London.

Hirst, J. 1988. *The Strange Birth of Colonial Democracy*. Allen & Unwin, Sydney.

Howard, C. 1986. *Australia's Constitution* (2nd edn). Penguin Books, Victoria.

Howard, J.W. 2003. Address at the ceremonial sitting to mark the centenary of the High Court of Australia, Supreme Court of Victoria, Melbourne. http://parlinfoweb.aph. gov.au/piweb/view_document.aspx?ID=80649&TABLE=PRESSREL&TARGET =#pdf_desc.

Howard, J.W. 2003. 'Resolving Deadlocks', *About the House, Liaison and Projects Office of the House of Representatives*. Issue 19. http://www.aph.gov.au/House/House_news/ magazine/ATH_dec_03.htm#deadlocks, accessed 24 October 2008.

Hueglin, T.O. & Fenna, A. 2006. *Comparative Federalism: A Systematic Inquiry*. Broadview Press, Toronto.

Hug, S. 2000. 'Studying the Electoral Success of New Political Parties: A Methodological Note', *Party Politics*. Vol. 6, No. 2, pp. 187–97.

Huggins, R. 2002. 'The Machinery of Government', in *Politics: An Introduction* (2nd edn). B. Axford, G. Browing, R. Huggins & R. Rosamond (eds). Routledge, London.

Hughes, C. 2003. 'The Independence of Commissions: The Legislative Framework and the Bureaucratic Reality', in *Realising Democracy*. G. Orr, B. Mercurio & G. Williams (eds). The Federation Press, Sydney.

Hughes, O. 1998. *Australian Politics* (3rd edn). Macmillan, South Yarra.

Ionescu, G. 1988. 'The theory of liberal constitutionalism', in *Constitutions in Democratic Politics*. Gower Publishing, England.

Iorns, C. 2003. 'Dedicated Parliamentary Seats for Indigenous Peoples: Political Representation as an Element of Indigenous Self-Determination', *Murdoch University Electronic Journal of Law*. Vol. 10, No. 4.

Jaensch, D. 1989. *The Hawke–Keating Hijack: The ALP in Transition*. North Sydney, Allen & Unwin.

Jaensch, D. 1991. *Parliament, Parties and People: Australian Politics Today*, Longman Cheshire, Melbourne.

Jaensch, D. 1994a. *The Liberals*. Allen & Unwin, Sydney.

Jaensch, D. 1994b. *Power Politics: Australia's Party System* (3rd edn). Allen & Unwin, Sydney.

Jaensch, D. 1995. *Election! How and Why Australia Votes*. Allen & Unwin, Sydney.

Jaensch, D. 2006. 'Party structures and procedures', in *Political Parties in Transition?* I. Marsh (ed.). The Federation Press, Sydney.

Jaensch, D., Brent, P., & Bowden, B. 2004. *Australian Political Parties in Spotlight*. Report No. 4. Democratic Audit of Australia, ANU.

Jaensch, D. & Matheison, D. 2002. *A Plague on Both Your Houses: Minor Parties in Australia*. Allen & Unwin, St Leonards.

James, M. 1982. 'The Constitution in Australian Political Thought', in *The Constitutional Challenge*. M. James (ed.). Centre for Independent Studies, Sydney, pp. 3–36.

Johns, G. 2006. 'Party Organisation and Resources: Membership, Funding and Staffing', in *Political Parties in Transition?* I. Marsh (ed.). The Federation Press, Sydney.

Johnson, C. 1989. *The Labor Legacy: Curtin, Chifley, Whitlam, Hawke*. Allen & Unwin, Sydney.

Jordan, R. 2003. 'A Rare Form of Law Making: Legislation Made Outside Parliament', *Research Note No. 11*. Law and Bills Digest Group, Australian Parliamentary Library, 2003–04.

Katz, R. & Mair, P. 1995. 'Changing Models of Party Organisation and Party Democracy: The Emergence of the Cartel Party', *Party Politics*. Vol. 1, No. 1, pp. 5–28.

Keating, M. & Weller, P. 2000. 'Cabinet Government: An Institution Under Pressure', ch. 2 in *Institutions on the Edge: Capacity for Governance*. M. Keating et al. (eds). Allen & Unwin, Sydney.

Kelly, N. 2006. 'MPs Incumbency Benefits Keep Growing', *Democrat Audit of Australia*, Discussion Paper 26/06. Australian National University, Canberra.

Kemp, D. 1973. 'A Leader and a Philosophy', in *Labor to Power: Australia's 1972 Election*. H. Mayer (ed.). Angus & Robertson, Sydney.

Kildea, P. & Gelber, K. 2007. 'High Court Review 2006: Adjudicating Federalism', *Australian Journal of Political Science*. Vol. 42, No. 4, pp. 649–64.

Kildea, P. 2003. 'The Bill of Rights Debate in Australian Political Culture', *Australian Journal of International Rights*. No. 7. http://www.austlii.edu.au/au/journals/AJHR/2003/7.html.

Kingston, M. 2004. *Not Happy, John! Defending Our Democracy*. Penguin, Melbourne.

Kirby, M. 2004. 'Deep Lying Rights: A Constitutional Conversation Continues', The Robin Cook Lecture. Wellington. 25 November.

Kircheimer, O. 1966. 'The Transformation of the Western Party System', in J. La Palombara & M. Weiner, (eds). *Political Parties and Political Developments*. Princeton University Press, Princeton.

Koelble, T. 1989. 'Party Structures and Democracy: Michels, McKenzie and Duverger Revisited via the Examples of the West German Green Party and the British Social Democratic Party', *Comparative Political Studies*. Vol. 22, No. 2, pp.199–216.

Koole, R. 1996. 'Cadre, Catch-all or Cartel?', *Party Politics*. Vol. 2, No. 4, pp. 507–23.

Krouwel, A. 2006. 'Party Models', in *Handbook of Party Politics*. R. Katz & W. Crotty (eds). Sage Publications, London.

Kuhn, R. 2005. 'Illusions of Equality: The Capitalist State', ch. 2 in *Class and Struggle in Australia*. R. Kuhn (ed.). Pearson, Sydney.

La Nauze, J. 1972. *The Making of the Australian Constitution*. Melbourne University Press, Melbourne.

Lane, S. 2008. 'Evans Orders Review into His Own Immigration Position', on *The World Today*. ABC Radio. 19 February.

LaPalombara, J. 2007. 'Reflections on Political Parties and Political Development, Four Decades Later', *Party Politics*. Vol. 13, No. 2, pp. 141–54.

Latham, M. 2001. 'In Defence of the Third Way', in *Left Directions: Is There A Third Way?* P. Nursey-Bray & C.L. Bacchi (eds). UWA Press, Crawley, WA.

Lees, M. 1999. 'Parliamentary Reform—The Baby and the Bathwater', *A Speech to the Sydney Institute*, February 1999. http://australianpolitics.com/parties/democrats/parl-reform-lees.shtml.

Legal, Constitutional and Administrative Review Committee. 2002. *Hands On Parliament—A Parliamentary Committee Inquiry Into Aboriginal And Torres Strait Islander Peoples' Participation in Queensland's Democratic Process* (Issues Paper). Legislative Assembly of Queensland, December.

Leigh, A. 2003. 'The Rise and Fall of the Third Way', *AQ: Journal of Contemporary Analysis*. Vol. 75, No. 2, pp. 10–15.

Lewis, C. 2005. 'Police, Civilians and Democratic Accountability', *Discussion Paper No. 8*. August. Democratic Audit of Australia.

Lijphart, A. 1984. *Democracies: Patterns of Majoritarian and Consensus Government in Twenty-One Countries*. New Haven, Yale University Press.

Lijphart, A. 1999. *Patterns of Democracy: Government Forms and Performance in Thirty-Six Countries*, Yale University Press, New Haven.

Lovell, D., McAllister, I., Maley, W. & Kukathas, C. 1998. *The Australian Political System* (2nd edn). Melbourne, Longman.

Lucy, R. 1985. *The Australian Form of Government*. Macmillan, Melbourne.

Lukes, S. 1974. *Power: A Radical View*. Macmillan, London.

Lumb, R. 1965. *The Constitutions of the Australian States*. University of Queensland Press, Brisbane.

Lunn, S. 2008. 'Rebate of 50pc Helps a Return to Work', *The Australian*, 14 May.

Macintyre, S. 2001. 'The First Caucus', in *True Believers*. J. Faulkner & S. Macintyre (eds). Allen & Unwin, Crows Nest, NSW, pp. 17–29.

Macridis, R. (ed.) 1967. *Political Parties: Contemporary Trends and Ideas*, Harper & Row, New York.

Maddox, G. 1989. *The Hawke Government and Labor Tradition*. Penguin Books. Ringwood.

Maddox, G. 2000a. 'Australian Democracy and the Compound Republic', *Pacific Affairs*. Vol. 73, No. 2, Summer, pp. 193–207.

Maddox, G. 2000b. *Australian Democracy in Theory and Practice* (4th edn). Longman, Sydney.

Maiden, M. 2007. 'Me-too a Mixed Blessing for an Innovative Economic Policy', *Sydney Morning Herald*, 17 November.

Malcolm, D. 1998. 'Does Australia Need a Bill of Rights?', *Murdoch University Electronic Journal of Law*. Vol. 5, No. 3. http://www.murdoch.edu.au/elaw/issues/v5n3/malcolm53_text.html.

Maley, M. 2000. 'Too Many or Too Few? The Increase in Federal Ministerial Advisers 1972–1999', *Australian Journal of Public Administration*. Vol. 59, No. 4, pp. 48–53.

Mann, S. 2006. 'Poll finds Gloom over Terror', *The Age*, September 11.

Mannheim, M. 2007. 'PS used in "cheat sheets" for Govt', *The Canberra Times*. 10 November.

Manning, H. 1992. 'The ALP and the Union Movement: "Catch-all" Party or Maintaining Tradition?', *Australian Journal of Political Science*. Vol. 27, No. 1, pp. 12–30.

Manning, H. 2006. 'Voters and Voting', in *Government, Politics, Power and Policy in Australia* (7th edn), J. Summers, D. Woodward & A. Parkin (eds). Longman Pearson, Sydney.

Marr, D. 2007. 'Airport Whistle-blower Sentenced'. http://www.smh.com.au/news/national/airport-whistleblower-sentenced/2007/06/22/1182019345393.html, accessed 18 June 2008.

Marsh, I. 2004. 'Political Integration and the Outlook for the Australian Party System: Party Adaption or Regime Change?', *The Politics of Australian Society* (2nd edn), P. Boreham, G. Stokes & R. Hall (eds), Pearson Longman, Sydney.

Marsh, I. 2006. 'Policy Convergence Between the Major Parties and the Representation Gap in Australian Politics', in *Political Parties in Transition?* I. Marsh (ed.). The Federation Press, Sydney.

Martin, A. & Parker, R.S. 1977. 'Introduction', in *The Emergence of the Australian Party System*. P. Loveday, A.W. Martin & R.S. Parker (eds). Hale & Iremonger, Sydney.

Mason, A. 1995. 'Trends in Constitutional Interpretation', *University of New South Wales Law Journal*. Vol. 18, No. 2, pp. 237–49.

Mathews, R.L. 1977. 'Innovations and Developments in Australian Federalism', *Publius: The Journal of Federalism*. Vol. 7, No. 3, pp. 9–19.

Mayer, H. 1984. 'Big Party Chauvinism and Minor Party Romanticism', in *Australian Politics: A Fifth Reader*. H. Mayer & H. Nelson (eds). Longman Cheshire, Melbourne.

McAllister, I. 1997. 'Political Behaviour', in *Government, Politics, Power and Policy in Australia* (6th edn). D. Woodward, A. Parkin, J. Summers (eds). Addison Wesley Longman, South Melbourne.

McAllister, I. 2002. 'Political Parties in Australia: Party Stability in a Utilitarian Society', in *Political Parties in Advanced Industrial Democracies*. P. Webb, D. Farrell & I. Holliday (eds). Oxford University Press, London.

McAllister, I. & Clark, J. 2008. *Trends in Australian Public Opinion: Results from the Australian Election Study 1987–2004*. Australian National University Monograph, Canberra.

McClelland, R. 2008. An untitled speech delivered to the *Protecting Human Rights Conference*, Centre for Comparative Constitutional Studies, University of Melbourne, 3 October. http://www.attorneygeneral.gov.au/www/ministers/robertmc.nsf/Page/Speeches_2008_3October2008-ProtectingHumanRightsConference, accessed 5 December 2008.

McGregor, C. 1997. *Class in Australia*. Penguin Books, Melbourne.

McGuiness, P. 1992. 'The High Court's coup d'etat', *The Australian*, 2 August.

McKenna, M. 1996–97. *The Need for a New Preamble to the Australian Constitution and/or a Bill of Rights*. Research Paper No. 12. Laws and Bills Digest Group. Australian Parliamentary Library, Canberra.

McKenna, M. 2000. *First Words: A Brief History of Public Debate on a New Preamble to the Australian Constitution 1991–99*. Research Paper No. 16. Politics and Public Administration Group. Australian Parliamentary Library, Canberra.

McKeown, D. & Lundie, R. 2005. *Crossing the Floor in the Federal Parliament 1950–August 2004*, Research Note No. 11, Politics and Public Administration Section, Australian Parliamentary Library.

McKinlay, B. 1981. *The ALP: A Short History of the Australian Labor Party*. Richmond, Drummond/Heinemann.

McLean, I. 2004. 'Fiscal Federalism in Australia', *Public Administration*. Vol. 82, No. 1, pp. 21–38.

McMullin, R. 1991. *The Light on the Hill: The Australian Labor Party 1891–1991*. Oxford University Press, South Melbourne.

Menzies, R. 1967. *Central Power in the Australian Commonwealth: An Examination of the Growth of Commonwealth Power in the Australian Federation*. University Press of Virginia, Charlottesville.

Merriam, C. 1923. *The American Party System: An Introduction to the Study of Political Parties in the United States*. The Macmillan Company, New York.

Metherell, M. 2009. 'Liberal MPs Battle it out in public', smh.com.au. 16 January 2009. http://www.smh.com.au/news/environment/global-warming/liberal-mps-battle-it-out-in-public/2009/01/15/1231608886274.html, accessed 17 February 2009.

Michels, R. 1962. *Political Parties: A Sociological Study of the Oligarchical Tendencies in Modern Democracies*, Free Press, New York.

Mills, C. Wright. *The Power Elite*. Oxford University Press, New York.

Minchin, N. 2001. 'End Compulsory Voting says Minchin', press release, 15 May. http://parlinfoweb.aph.gov.au/piweb/Repository1/Media/pressrel/R02460.pdf.

Miragliotta, N. 2006. 'One Party, Two Traditions: Radicalism and Pragmatism in the Australian Greens', *Australian Journal of Political Science*. Vol. 41, No. 4, pp. 585–96.

Miragliotta, N. 2009. 'Small Parties and Independents', in *Government, Politics, Power and Policy in Australia* (9th edn). A. Parkin, J. Summers & D. Woodward (eds). Longman Pearson, Sydney.

Miragliotta, N. & Errington, W. 2008. 'Occupational Profile of ALP, LP and National MHRs 1949–2007: From Divergence to Convergence', paper presented at the Australasian Political Studies Association Annual Conference, University of Queensland, July 2008.

Miskin, S. & Grant, R. 2004. 'Political Advertising in Australia', Research Brief No. 5, 2004–05, Australian Parliamentary Library, Canberra.

Miskin, S. & Lumb, M. 2006. 'The 41st Parliament: Middle-aged, Well-educated and (Mostly) Male', Research Note No. 24, Politics and Public Administration Section, Australian Parliamentary Library, Canberra.

Moller, C. 2002. 'North Korea—Human Rights', in *Encyclopedia of Modern Asia*. D. Levinson & K. Christensen (eds). Vol. 4 (6 vols.). Charles Scribner's Sons, New York, pp. 355–7.

Moon, J. 1995. 'Minority Governments in the Australian States: From Ersatz Majoritarianism to Minoritarianism', *The Australian Journal of Political Science*, Vol. 30 (Special Issue), pp. 142–63.

Moon, J. & Sayers, A. 1999. 'The Dynamics of Governmental Activity: A Long-run Analysis of the Changing Scope and Profile of Australian Ministerial Portfolios', *Australian Journal of Political Science*. Vol. 19, pp. 149–67.

Mulgan, R. 1998. 'Politicising the Australian Public Service?' Research Paper No. 3, 1998–99. Parliamentary Library, Canberra.

Newman, G. & Bennett, S. 2006. 'Electoral Systems', Research Brief (Australian Department of Parliamentary Services, Parliamentary Library); 2005–06, No. 10, http://www.aph.gov.au/library/pubs/rb/2005-06/06rb10.pdf, accessed 9 January 2009.

Newspoll. 2007. 'National Security and Haneef', 07/08/2007. http://www.newspoll.com.au/cgi-bin/polling/display_poll_data.pl.

Norton, A. 2004. 'Liberalism and the Liberal Party of Australia', ch. 1 in *The Politics of Australian Society: Political Issues for the New Century* (2nd edn). G. Stokes et al. (eds). Pearson Longman, Sydney.

Odgers' Australian Senate Practice (11th edn), 2004. H. Evans (ed.) Australian Government Publishing Service, Department of the Senate, Canberra.

O'Neill, N., Rice, S. & Douglas, R. 2004. *Retreat from Injustice: Human Rights in Australian Law* (2nd edn). Federation Press, Leichhardt, NSW.

Orr, G. 2004. *Australian Electoral Systems—How Well Do They Serve Political Equality?*, Report No. 2, Democratic Audit of Australia, Australian National University, Canberra.

Orr, G. 2007. 'Pauline Hanson Cashes In on Fame', *Courier Mail*, 20 August.

Painter, M. 1998. *Collaborative Federalism: Economic Reform in Australia in the 1990s*, Cambridge University Press, Melbourne.

Painter, M. 2001. 'Multi-level Governance and the Emergence of Collaborative Federal Institutions in Australia', *Policy and Politics*. Vol. 29, No. 2, pp. 137–50.

Palombara, J. La. & Weiner, M. (eds). 1966. *Political Parties and Political Developments*. Princeton University Press, Princeton.

Panebianco, A. 1988. *Political Parties: Power and Organisation*. Cambridge University Press, New York.

Papadakis, E. & Bean, C. 1995. 'Independents and Minor Parties: The Electoral System', *Australian Journal of Political Science*. Vol. 30 (Special Issue), pp. 111–26.

Parkin, A. 2006. 'Understanding Liberal-Democratic Politics', ch. 1 in *Government, Politics, Power and Policy in Australia*. A. Parkin et al. (eds). Pearson, Sydney.

Parkin, A. & Anderson, G. 2007. 'The Howard Government, Regulatory Federalism, and the Transformation of Commonwealth–State Relations', *Australian Journal of Political Science*. Vol. 42, No. 2, pp. 295–314.

Parkin, A. & Summers, J. 2002. 'The Constitutional Framework', ch. 3 in *Government, Politics, Power and Policy in Australia* (7th edn). A Parkin, J. Summers & D. Woordward (eds). Longman, Frenchs Forest, NSW.

Parkin, A. & Summers, J. 2006. 'The Constitutional Framework', ch. 3 in *Government, Politics, Power and Policy in Australia*. A. Parkin et al. (eds). Pearson, Sydney.

Parkin, A. & Warhurst, J. (eds). 1983. *Machine Politics in the Australian Labor Party*. Allen & Unwin, North Sydney.

Parkin, A. & Warhurst, J. 2000. 'The Labor Party: Images, History and Structure', in *The Machine: Labor Confronts the Future*. J. Warhurst & A. Parkin (eds.). Allen & Unwin, St Leonards, NSW.

Passey, A. & Lyons, M. 2005. 'Voluntary Associations and Political Participation', ch. 5 in *Australian Social Attitudes: The First Report*. S. Wilson et al. (eds). UNSW Press, Sydney.

Patapan, H. 1997. 'The Dead Hand of the Founders? Original Intent and the Constitutional Protection of Rights and Freedoms in Australia', *Federal Law Review*. Vol. 25, No. 2.

Patapan, H. 2000a. 'The Howard Government and the High Court', ch. 3 in *The Howard Government: Commonwealth Government Administration 1996–98*. G. Singleton (ed.). UNSW Press, Sydney.

Patapan, H. 2000b. *Judging Democracy: The New Politics of the High Court of Australia*. Cambridge University Press, Melbourne.

Patapan, H. 2001. 'Politics, Legalism and the Gleeson Court', *Australian Journal of Political Science*. Vol. 37, pp. 241–54.

Patapan, H. 2006. 'The High Court', ch. 8 in *Government, Politics, Power and Policy in Australia* (8th edn). A. Parkin et al. (eds). Pearson, Sydney.

Peatling, S. 2007. 'Cabinet Yet to See $10 Billion Water Plan', *Sydney Morning Herald*, 14 February.

Pierson, C. & Castles, F.G. 2002. 'Australian Antecedents of the Third Way', *Political Studies*. Vol. 50, No. 4, pp. 683–702.

Pietsch, S. 2005. 'To Have and to Hold on to: Wealth, Power and the Capitalist Class', ch. 1 in *Class and Struggle in Australia*. R. Kuhn (ed.). Pearson, Sydney.

Pincus, J. 2008. 'Six Myths of Federal–State Financial Relations', CEDA. http://ceda.com.au/public/research/federal/six_myths_federal_state.html, accessed 20 February 2009.

Podger, A. 2007. 'What Really Happens: Departmental Secretary Appointments, Contracts and Performance Pay in the Australian Public Service', *Australian Journal of Public Administration*. Vol. 66, No. 2, June, p. 131047.

Prince, P. 2004. 'The High Court and Indefinite Detention: Towards a National Bill of Rights?', *Research Brief No. 1 2004–2005*. Australian Parliamentary Library, Canberra.

Puplick, C.J. 1994. *Is the Party Over? The Future of the Liberals*. Text Publishing, Melbourne.

Quick, J. & Garran, R. 1901. *Annotated Constitution of the Australian Commonwealth*. Australian Book Company, London.

Rae, D. 1967. *The Political Consequences of Electoral Laws*, Yale University Press, New Haven.

Rayner, M. 1997. *Rooting Democracy: Growing the Society We Want*. Allen & Unwin, Sydney.

Rhodes, R. 2007. 'Understanding Governance: Ten Years On', *Organization Studies*. Vol. 28, No. 8, pp. 1243–64.

Richardson, J, 2000. 'Resolving Deadlocks in the Australian Parliament', Research Paper No. 9. Politics and Public Administration Group, Australian Parliamentary Library, Canberra.

Richmond, K. 1978. 'Minor Parties in Australia', in *Political Parties in Australia*. G. Starr, K. Richmond & G. Maddox (eds). Heinemann, Victoria.

Riker, W.H. 1964. *Federalism: Origin, Operation, Significance*. Little Brown, Boston.

Rohrschneider, R. 1994. 'How Iron Is the Iron Law of Oligarchy? Robert Michels and National Party Delegates in Eleven West European Democracies'. *European Journal of Political Research*, Vol. 25, Issue 2, pp. 207–38.

Roy Morgan Poll. 2007. 'More Australians Say "Yes" Than "No" to Dr Mohammed Haneef Being Allowed To Return To Australia'. Finding No. 4202, August 24. http://www.roymorgan.com/news/polls/2007/4202/.

Rudd, K. 2006. 'Howard's Brutopia: The Battle of Ideas in Australian Politics', *The Monthly*, No. 18, pp. 46–50.

Rudd, K. 2007a. 'New Leadership for the Australian Federation: Fixing Federalism and Fixing the Australian Health Care System.' Speech to Australian Business Economists, October 4. http://www.alp.org.au/media/1007/speloo040.php, accessed 28 February, 2008.

Rudd, K. 2007b. 'Kevin Rudd Campaign Launch Speech'. http://www.alp.org.au/media/1107/speloo140.php, accessed 21 July 2008.

Rudd, K. 2008. Address to Heads of Agencies and members of Senior Executive Service. Parliament House, Canberra, 30 April.

Rudd, K. 2009. 'The Global Financial Crisis', *The Monthly*, No. 42, pp. 20–9.

Rudd, K. & Roxon, N. 2007. 'Taking Responsibility: Federal Labor's $2 Billion National Health and Hospitals Reform Plan', media statement, 23 August. http://pandora.nla.gov.au/pan/22093/20071124-0102/www.alp.org.au/media/0807/mshealoo230.html.

Russell, M. 2000. *Reforming the House of Lords: Lessons from Overseas*. Oxford University Press, Oxford.

Sartori, G. 1962. *Democratic Theory*. Wayne State University Press, Detroit.

Sartori, G. 1976. *Parties and Party Systems: A Framework for Analysis*. Cambridge University Press, Cambridge.

Sartori, G. 1997. *Comparative Constitutional Engineering*. New York University Press, Washington.

Sartori, G. 2001. 'The Party Effects of Electoral Systems', in *Political Parties and Democracy*. L. Diamond & R. Gunther (eds). Johns Hopkins University Press, Baltimore.

Saul, B. 2007. 'Between the Crime and the War Falls the Terror: Comment on *Thomas v Mobray*', *Sydney Centre Working Paper 2*. University of Sydney, Sydney.

Saunders, C. 2000. *The Parliament as Partner: A Century of Constitutional Review*. Research Paper No. 3. Australian Parliamentary Library, Canberra.

Saunders, C. 2001, *The Parliament as Partner: A Century of Constitutional Review*. Research Paper No. 3. Australian Parliamentary Library, Canberra.

Sawer, G. 1969. *Modern Federalism*. C.A. Watts, London.

Sawer, M. 1999. 'Dilemmas of Representation', *Representation and Institutional Change: 50 Years of Proportional Representation in the Senate*, Papers from a conference arranged by the Political Science Program, Research School of Social Sciences, ANU and the Department of the Senate, Canberra.

Sawer, M. 2001. 'Pacemakers for the world?', in *Elections: Full, Free and Fair*. M. Sawer (ed.). The Federation Press, Sydney.

Sawer, M. 2007. 'Democratic Values: Political Equality', Discussion Paper 9/07. Democratic Audit of Australia, Canberra.

Scarrow, S. 2006. 'Party Subsidies and the Freezing of Party Competition: Do Cartel Mechanisms Work?', *West European Politics*. Vol. 29, No. 4, pp. 619–39.

Scott, A. 2000. *Running on Empty: 'Modernising' the British and Australian Labor Parties*. Pluto Press Australia, Annandale, NSW.

Shanahan, D. 2008. 'Rudd is Mr 70 Per Cent', *The Australian*, 19 February. http://www. theaustralian.news.com.au/story/0,25197,23237263-601,00.html, accessed 21 July 2008.

Shanahan, L. 2008. 'Deal Gives Luxury Car Tax a Reprieve in Senate', *The Age*, 18 September.

Sharman, C. 1990. 'Australia as a Compound Republic', *Politics*. Vol. 25, No. 1, May, pp. 1–5.

Sharman, C. 1991. 'Executive Federalism', in *Intergovernmental Relations and Public Policy*. B. Galligan, O. Hughes & C. Walsh (eds). Allen & Unwin, North Sydney, pp. 23–38.

Sharman, C. 1999. 'The Representation of Small Parties and Independents in the Senate', *Australian Journal of Political Science*. Vol. 34, No. 3, pp. 353–61.

Sharman, C., Sayers, A. & Miragliotta, N. 2002. 'Trading Party Preferences: The Australian Experience of Preferential Voting', *Electoral Studies*. Vol. 21, No. 4, pp. 543–60.

Shell, D. 1999. 'To Revise and Deliberate: The British House of Lords', in *Senates*. S. Patterson & A. Mughan (eds). Ohio State Press, Columbus.

Sheridan, N. 2007. 'It's Not Mighell Versus Rudd', *Sydney Morning Herald*, 30 May. http://www.smh.com.au/news/national/mighell-expelled-from-labor-party/2007/ 05/30/1180205304327.html, accessed 21 July 2008.

Simms, M. 1982. *A Liberal Nation: The Liberal Party and Australian Politics*, Hale and Iremonger, Sydney.

Singleton, G., Aitkin, D., Jinks, B. & Warhurst, J. 2003. *Australian Political Institutions*. Pearson, Melbourne.

Singleton, G., Aitken, D., Jinks, B. & Warhurst, J. 2006, *Australian Political Institutions* (8th edn). Pearson Education, Frenchs Forest, NSW.

Smith, R. 1994. 'Parliament', in *Developments in Australian Politics*. J. Brett, J. Gillespie & M. Goot (eds). Macmillan, South Melbourne.

Solomon, D. 1999. *The Political High Court*. Allen & Unwin, Sydney.

Solomon, D. 2008. *The Right to Information: Reviewing Queensland's Freedom of Information Act*. The State of Queensland. June.

Spigelman, J.J. 2007. 'Judicial Appointments and Judicial Independence', Speech to the Rule of Law Conference. 31 August.

Starr, G. 1980. *The Liberal Party of Australia: A Documentary History*. Drummond/ Heinemann, Melbourne.

Stewart, J. & Maley, M. 2007. 'The Howard Government and Political Management: The Challenges of Policy Activism', *Australian Journal of Political Science*. Vol. 42, No. 2, June, pp. 277–93.

Stone, B. 2002. 'Bicameralism and Democracy: The Transformation of Australian State Upper Houses', *The Australian Journal of Political Science*. Vol. 37, No. 2, pp. 267–81.

Summers, J. 2006. 'Parliament and Responsible Government', ch. 4 in *Government, Politics, Power and Policy in Australia*. A. Parkin et al. (eds). Pearson, Sydney.

Sung Chull Kim. 2002. 'North Korea—Political System', in *Encyclopedia of Modern Asia*. D. Levinson & K. Christensen (eds). Vol. 4. (6 vols), Charles Scribner's Sons, New York, pp. 357–61.

Tanner, L. 1999. *Open Australia*. Pluto Press Australia, Annandale NSW.

Tanner, L. 2002. 'If Not Now, When?', australianpolitics.com. 5 February. http://australianpolitics.com/news/2002/02-02-05.shtml, accessed 26 November 2007.

Theophanous, A. 1980. *Australian Democracy in Crisis: A Radical Approach to Australian Politics*. Oxford University Press, Melbourne.

Thompson, E. 1997. 'The Public Service', ch. 9 in *Politics in Australia* (3rd edn). R. Smith (ed.). Allen & Unwin, Sydney.

Thompson, E. 1999. 'From the World's Democratic Laboratory to Demosclerosis'. http://pandora.nla.gov.au/nph-arch/1999/Z1999-Nov-5/http://www.realrepublic.com.au/a_page.cfm3.html, accessed 24 June 2007.

Thompson, M. 1999. *Labor Without Class*. Pluto Press Australia, Annandale NSW.

Tiernan, A. 2007. *Power Without Responsibility*. UNSW Press, Sydney.

Tilby-Stock, J. 2002. 'The Australian Democrats and Minor Parties', *Government, Politics, Power and Policy in Australia* (7th edn). J. Summers, D. Woodward, & A. Parkin (eds). Longman Pearson, Sydney.

Tiver, P.G. 1978. *The Liberal Party: Principles and Performance*. Jacaranda Press, Milton.

Uhr, J. 1998. *Deliberative Democracy in Australia: The Changing Place of the Parliament*. Cambridge University Press, Melbourne.

Uhr, J. 1999. 'Why We Chose Proportional Representation', in *Representation and Institutional Change: 50 Years of Proportional Representation in the Senate*, papers from a conference arranged by the Political Science Program, Research School of Social Sciences, ANU and the Department of the Senate, Canberra.

Uhr, J. 2001. 'The Language of Leadership: Prime Ministers as Political Institutions', Discussion Paper No. 90. ANU Crawford School, Canberra. September.

Uhr, J. & Wanna, J. 2000. 'The Future Roles of Parliament' in *Institutions on the Edge?*, M. Keating, J. Wanna, & P. Weller (eds), Allen & Unwin, St Leonards.

van Biezen, I. & Kopecky, P. 2007. 'The State and the Parties: Public Funding, Public Regulation and Rent Seeking in Contemporary Democracies', *Party Politics*. Vol. 13, No. 2, pp. 235–54.

van Onselen, P. 2007. 'Too Easy a Ride into Private Gold', *smh.com.au*. 18 June 2007. http://www.smh.com.au/news/opinion/too-easy-a-ride-into-private-gold/2007/06/17/1182018938417.html, accessed 14 September 2008.

van Onselen, P. & Errington, W. 2004. 'Political Donations and Party Fundraising: Buying Time with a Minister?' *Australian Quarterly*. Vol. 76, November–December.

van Onselen, P. & Errington, W. 2005. 'Shock Troops: The Emerging Role of Senators in House of Representatives Campaigns', *Australian Journal of Political Science*. Vol. 40, No. 3, pp. 357–71.

Walter, J. & Strangio, P. 2007. *No, Prime Minister: Reclaiming Politics From Leaders*. UNSW Press, Sydney.

Wanna, J. & Weller, P. 2003. 'Traditions of Australian Governance', *Public Administration*. Vol. 81, No. 1, pp. 63–94.

Ward, I. 2006. 'Cartel Parties and Election Campaigning in Australia', in *Political Parties in Transition?* I. Marsh (ed.). The Federation Press, Sydney.

Ward, I. & Stewart, R. 2006. *Politics One* (3rd edn). Palgrave Macmillan, South Yarra.

Ware, A. 1996. *Political Parties and Party Systems*. Oxford University Press, London.

Warhurst, J. 1996. 'Transitional Hero: Gough Whitlam and the Australian Labor Party', *Australian Journal of Political Science*. Vol. 31, No. 2.

Warhurst, J. 2007. *Behind Closed Doors*. UNSW Press, Sydney.

Warhurst, J. & Parkin, A. (eds.). 2000. *The Machine: Labor Confronts the Future*. Allen & Unwin, St Leonards, NSW.

Watts, R.L. 1999. *Comparing Federal Systems* (2nd edn). McGill-Queens University Press, Montreal and Kingston.

Weale, A. 1999. *Democracy*. Macmillan, London.

Webb, P. 2002. 'Introduction', in *Political Parties in Advanced Industrial Democracies*. P.Webb, I. Holliday & D. Farrell, (eds). Oxford University Press, Oxford.

Weber, M. 1967 [1915]. *The Theory of Social and Economic Organization*. T. Parsons (trans.), The Free Press, New York.

Weller, P. 2004. 'Parliament and Cabinet: The Centre of Government', ch. 5 in *Governing Business and Globalisation* (2nd edn). E. van Ecker & G. Curren (eds). Pearson Education, Sydney.

Weller, P. 2007. *Cabinet Government in Australia 1901–2006*. UNSW Press, Sydney.

Weller, P. 2008. 'The Public Service', in *Dear Mr Rudd*. R. Manne (ed.). Black Inc. Agenda, Melbourne.

Weller, P. & Grattan, M. 1981. *Can Ministers Cope? Australian Federal Ministers at Work*. Hutchinson, Melbourne.

Wettenhall, R. 2003a. 'Those Executive Agencies', *Canberra Bulletin of Public Administration*. No. 106, February, pp. 9–14.

Wettenhall, R. 2003b. 'Exploring Types of Public Sector Organizations: Past Exercises and Current Issues', *Public Organization Review*. Vol. 3, pp. 219–45.

White, D.M. & Kemp, D.A. 1986. *Malcolm Fraser on Australia*. Hill of Content, Melbourne.

Wicks, B. 2000. *Understanding the Australian Constitution* (2nd edn). Libra Books, NSW.

Wilkie, A. 2007. 'The Military and Intelligence Services', ch. 9 in *Silencing Dissent*. C. Hamilton & S. Maddison. Allen & Unwin, Sydney.

Williams, G. 1999. *Human Rights Under the Australian Constitution*. Oxford University Press, Melbourne.

Williams, G. 2000. *A Bill of Rights for Australia*. UNSW Press, Melbourne.

Williams, G. 2007. *A Charter of Rights for Australia*. UNSW Press, Sydney.

Wilson, S. 2003. 'Obstructing Government or Stopping Bullies: What do Australians Think about Government Control of the Senate?', *Australian Review of Public Affairs*, 13 June. http://www.australianreview.net/digest/2003/06/wilson.html, accessed 1 August 2008.

Young, L. 2006. 'Parliamentary Committees: The Return of the Sausage Machine?' Discussion Paper 28/06. Democratic Audit of Australia, Canberra. August.

Young, S. & Tham, J. 2006. *Political Finance in Australia: A Skewed and Secretive System*, Democratic Audit of Australia, No. 7, Australian National University, Canberra.

Zines, L. 1989. 'A Legal Perspective', in *Australian Federalism*. B. Galligan (ed.). Longman Cheshire, Melbourne.

Index

accountability
  ministers 101–2
  political executive 110–17
Act of Settlement 27
activism 153
Acts of Parliament 86–7
Administrative Appeals Tribunal 133
affirmative rights 29, 48
agenda setting and power 13
alternative vote 81, 163, 164, 165–6
asylum-seekers 101, 234
Australia Party 277
*Australian Capital Television Pty Ltd & New
    South Wales v. The Commonwealth* (1992)
    177 CLR 106 155
Australian Commonwealth public
    service 121, 130
Australian Constitution *see* Constitution,
    Australian
Australian Democrats 198, 203, 261–2,
    269–70
Australian Electoral Commission
    (AEC) 169, 175, 186, 198, 201, 259
Australian Fishing and Lifestyle Party 198
Australian Greens 22, 198, 258, 271–2, 276
Australian Greens (Victoria) 198
Australian Labor Party (ALP) 195, 200,
    202, 213–33
  Caucus 215, 217, 219
  and communist influences 219
  conscription (WWI) 218, 237
  departing from the mass party
    model 220–2
  embracing the market 225–8
  environmentally friendly policies 229
  factions and disunity 218–20

federalism 231–2
financing/funding 222
and government spending 218–19
ideological influences 223–4
and Indigenous Australians 230
and labourism 224
membership 203, 220
parliamentary leader 221
Party Conferences 217, 221
party structure and control 216–18
the pledge 217
post-materialist values 214, 222, 228–30
protectionism 224
rank-and-file membership (ALP) 216
representing labour 214
split 218, 219, 237–8
and social democracy 223–4
and socialism 223
the Third Way 226–7
and the union movement 215–16
what does it stand for today? 222–32
who votes for? 230–1
and women 230–1
Australian Labor Party (ACT Branch) 198
Australian Labor Party (ALP) 198
Australian Labor Party (Northern Territory
    Branch) 198
Australian Labor Party (NSW Branch) 198
Australian Labor Party (SA Branch) 198
Australian Labor Party (State of
    Queensland) 198
Australian Labor Party (Tasmanian
    Branch) 198
Australian Labor Party (Victorian
    Branch) 198
Australian Labor Party (WA Branch) 198

Australian Republican Movement   19
Australian Shooters Party   198
Australian Wheat Board (AWB)   96–7

balance of power   39, 147, 158, 183, 201,
    256, 258, 267, 276, 277
ballot papers   25, 170–2, 173, 201, 258
ballot structure (electoral system)   166–8
    federal elections   173
Barton, Edmund   108, 115, 152
bicameralism   15, 53, 56, 57, 65, 68, 75, 88,
    92, 93–4, 111, 231, 253
bill of rights   41–9, 145
    debate in Australia   44–6
    in other liberal democracies   48–9
bills   84–7
bipartisan   21, 119, 160, 250
Blair, Tony   117, 226, 227
Borbidge, Bob   156
bourgeois democracy   18
broad-based political parties   197
Burke, Brian   126
by-election   179, 180, 262
by-laws   86

cabinet   98, 100
    collective cabinet responsibility   100
    decision-making   106–10
    documents leaked to media   135
    portfolios (1901 and 2007)   108
campaign funds   176–7
Canada   49, 54, 55, 56
capitalism   18, 219, 223–4, 226, 228
Carers Alliance   198
cartel party thesis   189, 196–9, 202–11
cartelisation   206, 211
    evidence of   207, 208, 209, 210–11
catch-all parties   195, 196
Caucus   215
censure motions   80
Chairperson of the Committee   85
checks and balances   4, 9, 17, 94, 98, 110,
    138, 156, 185
Chifley, Ben   218, 219
Chifley Government   17
Christian Democratic Party (Fred Nile
    Group)   198

Citizens Electoral Council of Australia   198
civil liberties   146–7
civil society   11, 187, 189, 204, 205
Clark, Andrew Inglis   43, 44
classical liberals   237
cleavage   180
Clerk   86
Climate Change Coalition   198
coalition politics   244–6, 258
Cold War   54
collective cabinet responsibility   100
committees, parliamentary   80
common law   142, 153–4
Commonwealth Gazette   87
Commonwealth Grants Commission   62, 70
*Commonwealth of Australia Constitution Act
    1900*   38
Communist Party of Australia   146
competitive elections   162
compulsory voting   160–1, 179, 264, 268
confederation   52
conflict of interest   102
concurrent federalism   55
consensus democracy   35
consent   8, 10, 86–7, 114
conservatism   237, 251–2
Conservatives for Climate and Environment
    Incorporated   198
constitution   26
    and bill of rights   41–9
    federal   15, 29, 32, 37, 38–9, 41
    liberal   37
    monarch's   36
    rigid   37–8
Constitution, Australian   2, 13–14, 15, 18,
    25–50, 63, 99, 100, 114, 153
    and federal powers   58–9
    and High Court   143–4
    High Court interpretation   38, 59–60,
        68, 145–9
    overview of the eight chapters   34
    preamble   40–1
Constitutional Crisis (1975)   18, 92
constitutional formation and practice in
    Australia   32–3
constitutional models   26–31
constitutional monarchy   7, 27, 36, 99, 251

constitutionalism   9, 31, 32
constitutions
    of Australia (states/territories)   33
    entrenched   28
    typology of   27
    unwritten   28
    written   28–9, 33–6
conventions   14, 28, 35, 36, 97–101, 103,
    106, 114
Coombs, H.C. 'Nugget'   125
coordinate federalism   55
corporations   60
cosmopolitanism   53
Council of Australian Governments
    (COAG)   64, 69, 70
Country Labor Party   198
Country Party *see* National Party
coup d'etat   151
crossing the floor, parliamentary
    members   80, 113, 235
CSIRO   122–3
Cumulative Vote   164
Curtin, John   219

Dahl, Robert   12
Deakin, Alfred   237
decision-making and power   10, 12, 99, 125
defamation law   155
Delegate model   84
delegated legislation   78, 86–7
Democratic Audit of Australia   22, 23, 205
Democratic Labor Party (DLP)   198, 219,
    239, 258, 267
democratic deficit   11
Democratic People's Republic of Korea
    (DPRK)   30–1
democracy   2–4
    consensus   35
    bourgeois   18
    how much is too much?   9–11
    and liberalism   6, 7
    majoritarian   35
    and minor parties   276–9
    and power   12
    representative   2, 4, 5, 7–9, 11, 12, 13, 23
    where does power really lie?   12
Denmark   121

Department of Prime Minister and
    Cabinet   109, 116, 126, 133, 137, 138
Dietrich v. The Queen (1992) 177 CLR
    292   154
division of powers   58–61
divisions   80
dominant-party systems   192, 193
Downer, Alexander   97, 242
Droop Quota   170–1
Dunstan, Don   66, 67, 229, 232
Duverger, Maurice   194

economic policy   225, 237, 249, 251
economic reform   66, 67, 226, 248–50
elections, federal
    ballot structure   173
    campaign funds   176–7
    cost of   177–8
    district magnitude   174
    electoral formulae   170–2
    and first preference votes   202–3
    Group Ticket Vote (GTV)   173
    half Senate   171
    House of Representatives   170, 171,
        175–85
    Senate   171, 172–3
    voters and their preferences   181–2
    see also electoral system; voting
Electoral Act 1918   165, 174, 175
electoral formulae   162–6
    for federal elections   170–2
electoral laws 169–70
    federal   174–5
electoral professional parties   196
electoral role   169
electoral system   3, 160–85
    Australian federal system   170–5
    of Australian jurisdictions   165–6
    ballot structure   166–8
    compulsory voting   160–1, 179, 264, 268
    definition   161–70
    district magnitude   168
    First Past the Post (FPP)   163
    and first preference votes   202–3
    majoritarian   163, 164
    and minority parties   261, 264
    plurality   163, 164, 192

electoral system (*cont.*)
  proportional   8, 91, 92, 161, 163, 164,
    170, 182, 183, 184, 192, 267
  three major families   164
  threshold   163
  voters and their preferences   181–2
  why are they important?   161–70
  see also voting
elitist   12
Engineers' case: Amalgamated Society of
    Engineers v. Adelaide Steamship Co. Ltd
    (1920) 28 CLR 59, 129   146, 147
Enlightenment   5, 7
equality   19–20
Evatt, H.V. 'Doc'   219
executive agencies   123
executive branch   14, 54, 57, 63, 74, 97, 114,
    120, 122, 135, 143
executive federalism   63
executive power   96–118
  investigating the executive   111–12
  keeping political executive
    accountable   110–17
  government overload and executive
    responsibility   107–10
  origins and conventions   97–102
  and party politics   102–4
  political executive in action 104–7
  prime ministerial government   113–17
  and war   114–15
executive responsibilities   104
executive responsibility and government
    overload   107–10
executive roles and party politics   102–4

factions and disunity (ALP)   218–20
Faulkner, John   219
Family First Party   196, 198, 258, 273, 277
federal constitution   15, 29, 32, 37,
    38–9, 41
federal electoral laws   174–5
Federal Executive Council   100
federal government, structure of
    Australia's   75
federal system of government   73
federalism   9, 51–70
  and ALP   231–2
  in Australia   56–8, 64–9

concurrent   55
coordinate   55
definition   52–6
division of powers   58–61
executive   63
in a global age   53–4
and intergovernmental machinery   63–4
and liberal democracy   65–6
and Liberal Party   60–1, 253–4
redistribution   66–8
reform   64–9
and rights   66–8
vertical fiscal imbalance   61–3
Federation   14, 15, 16
First Past the Post (FPP)   163, 164
fiscal equalisation, horizontal   62–3
fiscal imbalance, vertical   61–3
Fishing Party   198
Fourth Estate   6
France   7, 9, 163, 164
Fraser, Malcolm   18, 235, 240, 242, 244,
    245, 248, 253
Fraser Government   116, 141, 142, 156,
    235, 244, 248, 252
free traders   195
freedom   20–1
freedom of conscience   243–4
freedom of information   21, 45, 133, 135
freedom of speech   6, 7, 8, 20–1, 30,
    45, 141

gender voting gap   182, 238
Germany   54–5, 56, 73
Gleeson, Murray   154
Goods and Service Tax (GST)   62
Gorton, John   242
government
  decision-making   106–7
  departments   123
  federal, structure of Australia's   75
  federal system   73
  overload and executive
    responsibility   107–10
  prime ministerial   113–17
  responsible   8, 14–16, 19, 35–6, 56, 57,
    65, 83, 91, 97, 99–101, 106, 111, 114,
    117, 118, 121, 122, 139, 144, 149, 180
government trading enterprises   123

governing political parties   197
Governor-General   14, 18–19, 36, 74–5, 87, 92, 100, 149
Great Depression   18, 218, 247
Greens (WA) lnc.   198
Greens NSW   198
Group Ticket Vote (GTV)   173

Hancock, W.K.   129
Hanson, Pauline   210, 250, 252, 275, 277
Hawke, Bob   221, 225
Hawke Government   60, 64, 128, 134, 141, 154, 155, 156, 173, 221, 225, 226, 227, 229–30, 238, 248
head of government   99
head of state   99
Hear Our Voice   198
Heffernan, Bill   157
Hewson, John   242, 248
High Court   37, 141–59
    appointments   141–2
    and Australian Constitution   143–4
    decisions   146, 158, 232
    diverse institution   150–1
    interpreting the Constitution   38, 59–60, 68, 145–9
    judges, interpretation of the law   151–8
    justices, selection of   149–50
    key decisions: common law   153–4
    key decisions: implied rights   155
    key decisions: power in the federation   147–8
    origins and function   43–5
    political criticism   157–8
    role of   149
High Court of Australia Act 1979   150
Holt, Harold   242
horizontal fiscal equalisation   62–3
House of Representatives   39
    and Constitution   76
    elections   170, 171, 175–85
    first reading   84, 85
    making laws   83–7
    power of   74, 76–7, 111
    preferential/proportional voting   175–8
    proportion of time spent considering certain categories of business   79
    role of   74, 76, 77, 78

second reading   84, 85
size   76
time spent considering categories of business   79
voting   161, 170, 171, 179, 175–85
Howard, John   15, 47, 64, 90, 96–7, 103, 106, 132, 137–8, 156, 229–30, 234–5, 240, 242, 243, 244, 248, 249–50, 251, 253–4, 276
Howard Government   1–2, 17, 22, 51, 52, 60–1, 62, 90, 101–2, 106, 109, 113, 114, 115, 124, 129–30, 132, 134, 136–8, 141–2, 147, 148, 150–1, 152, 154, 156, 157, 169, 213, 216, 228–9, 230, 235, 238–9, 241, 244–5, 249, 250, 251
how-to-vote card   167
Hughes, Billy   179, 218, 237
human rights   41, 44, 45, 46, 48, 49, 112, 148, 154, 272
human rights commissions   112
humanism   5

independents, Senate and rule of   92–4
India   54
industrial relations   51, 60, 104, 107, 113, 130, 148, 152, 216, 228, 235, 243, 253
Institute of Public Affairs (IPA)   249, 254
interest groups   22, 189
intergovernmental machinery   63–4
integration political parties   197
iron law of oligarchy   204–5

joint sitting of Parliament   39
judicial review   144

Keating, Paul   71, 103, 107, 113, 117, 137, 221, 230, 248
Keating Government   137, 154, 225–6, 227, 229–30, 231, 238, 249
Kennett, Jeff   249
Kennett Government   249
Kerr, John   18, 36
Kirby, Michael   154, 156, 157–8

labour movement and ALP   214–15
labourism and ALP   224
Lang, Jack   218–19
Langer, Albert   25

laws
    made outside parliament 86–7
    making laws in parliament 83–7
    passage through parliament 85
legalism 151
legislation 86–7, 131
legislative assemblies 72–3
legislature 71–94
legitimacy 5, 10, 15, 16, 18, 26, 89, 90, 162,
        163, 177, 206
Letters Patent 86–7
liberal constitution 31, 37
liberal democracy and federalism 65–6
Liberal Party 200, 202, 234–55
    cabinet ministers 239
    classic liberals 237
    coalition politics 244–6
    conservatives 237
    core values 235
    and economic reform 248–50
    federalism 60–1, 253–4
    formation 235
    freedom of conscience 243–44
    industrial relations reform 60–1
    leaders 242
    leadership 240–3
    membership 203
    opposing labor 236–8
    is the party over? 252
    post-materialist values 238, 251
    pre-selection of candidates 239–40
    Queensland 246
    race politics 250
    social liberalism and conservatism 251–2
    social liberals 237
    structure of 239–40
    and think-tanks 249
    what does it stand for today 246–54
    who votes liberal? 238–9
    and women 238, 239, 241
Liberal Party (WA Division) Inc. 198
Liberal Party of Australia 198
Liberal Party of Australia (ACT
        Division) 198
Liberal Party of Australia (NSW
        Division) 198
Liberal Party of Australia (Queensland
        Division) 198

Liberal Party of Australia (SA Division) 198
Liberal Party of Australia (Tasmanian
        Division) 198
Liberal Party of Australia (Victorian
        Division) 198
liberal pluralists 257
liberal-democratic system 20, 82, 94
    Australia 13–16
liberalism 2, 4–7, 20, 31
    and democracy 6, 7
Liberty and Democracy Party 198
List System (Highest Average) 164
List System (Largest Remainder) 164
literalist 59
lobbying 11, 21, 126–7, 132, 138
Locke, John 5
Lyons, Joe 219, 238, 239

McGinty v. Western Australia (1996) 186
        CLR 140 155
McMahon, William 242
Mabo v. Queensland (No. 2) (1992)
        175 CLR 1 154
Madison, James 8, 53
Magna Carta 27
major political parties 196
    collusion against new challenges 210–11
majoritarian democracy 35
majoritarian electoral system 163, 164
malapportionment 91
managerialism 124
mandate 15
Mandate model 84
mass party 195
Maywald, Karlene 246
media 112
Menzies, Robert 235, 239–40, 241, 242,
        247, 251, 253–4
Menzies Government 16, 146, 150, 182,
        235–6, 253
Mills, C. Wright 12
Minister of State for Immigration and Ethnic
        Affairs v. An Hin Teoh (1995) 183
        CLR 273 148
ministerial responsibility 101
ministers 98
    buying time with 105–6
    holding to account 101–2
    and power 109

minor political parties   196, 256–79
  Australia   260–75
  and Australian democracy   276–9
  Australia's independents   265
  categorising Australia's   266–7
  in government (Tasmanian parliamentary
    accord)   263
  relevance and Sartori   259–60
  Senate and rule of   92–4
  what are minor parties?   257–60
monarch's constitution   36
monarch's power   74–5
money and politics   176–7
monopolies   129
Montesquieu, Baron de   31
Moore-Wilton, Max   137
multiculturalism   229

9/11 terrorist attack   47
National Audit Report   209
National Health and Hospitals Reform
    Commission   69
National Health Reform Plan   69
National Party of Australia   198, 200, 203,
    244–6, 257, 260, 274
National Party of Australia (NSW)   198
National Party of Australia
    (Queensland)   198, 246, 258
National Party of Australia (SA) Inc.   198
National Party of Australia (Victoria)   198
National Party of Australia (WA) Inc.   198
national sovereignty   53
nationalisation   247
natural monopolies   129
Nelson, Brendan   242, 251
neoliberalism   225
new political parties   197
New Zealand   4, 49
'no confidence' motion   74
Non-Custodial Parents Party (Equal
    Parenting)   198
non-governing political parties   197
Northern Territory Country Liberal
    Party   198
Nuclear Disarmament Party of Australia   198

Odger's Senate Practice   77
old political parties   197

ombudsmen   111
One Nation   198, 250, 275, 276
One Nation Western Australia   198
ordinances   86
originalism   152

Parliament, Australian   74–87
  anatomy of   74–7
  censure motions   80
  committees   80
  consent   8, 10, 86–7, 114
  devices to scrutinize   80–1
  formation   74
  four faces   77–83
  institutional design   91–2
  legislative function   77
  legislative power   74–5
  making laws   83–7
  member crossing the floor   80, 113, 235
  parliamentary privilege   81
  passage of laws   85
  and political executive   110–13
  procedure   81
  questions   81
  and Senate   88–94
  urgency debates   81
  and war   114–15
  and women   23, 82, 241
parliaments, state   15
parliamentary committees   101, 111–12,
    123, 125
parliamentary privilege   81, 157
parliamentary scrutiny   81
parliamentary secretaries   104
parliamentary sovereignty   57
parliamentary system of government   3,
    7–8, 73–4, 110–13
participation in politics   21–3
party politics and executive roles   102–4
party systems   165, 193–4
  dominant-party systems   192, 193
  multi-party systems   98, 192, 194
  two-party systems   21, 165, 179, 180,
    192, 193, 200, 236, 237–8, 261, 262,
    263, 275
Pauline's United Australia Party   198, 275
Peacock, Andrew   242
Peter Andren Independent Group   198

pledge, the (ALP)   217
plurality voting system   163, 164, 192
Podger, Andrew   139
policy-making and the public service   125–8
political executive   97
    in action   104–7
    investigating   111–12
    keeping accountable   110–17
    and war   114–15
political ideologies   6
political institutions, Australian   16–23
political opportunity structures   190
political parties   187–211
    in Australia   196–8
    cartel party thesis   189, 202–11
    classifying Australian   196–7
    defining   189–90
    dependence on state subventions   206–7
    different opinions on the functions of   191
    evolution of the Australian party
        system   199–201
    evolution in Western democracies   194–8
    and first preference votes   202–3
    governing v. non-governing   197
    integration v. representation   197
    iron law of oligarchy   204
    major   196
    major party collusion against new
        challenges   210–11
    membership   22, 203
    new v. old   197
    registering in Australia   201
    rent-seeking behaviour   208–10
    roles performed by   190–4
    single issue v. broad-based   197
    state regulation   207–8
    see also individual parties; minor political
        parties
political socialisation   13, 181
political systems   8–9
    Australian   14
    Australia's liberal-democratic   13–16
    liberal and democratic features of
        selected   4
politics
    and money   176–7
    participation in   21–3
    and women   197, 198, 229, 238, 241, 259
populist   250

portfolios   104
post-materialist values   214, 222, 228–30,
        238, 251, 261
power
    as agenda setting   13
    and declaration of war (Parliament/
        executive)   114–15
    as decision-making   10, 12, 99, 125
    and democracy   12
    division of   58–61
    of ministers   109
    as political socialisation   13
    prime minister   115–17
    what is?   12
precedents   146
preferential voting (PV)   82, 161, 163, 164,
        168, 170, 173, 184, 244, 260, 264
    House of Representatives   179, 175–85
presidential system of government   3, 7,
        8–9, 54, 73–4, 99, 114, 117
presidentialisation   117
pre-selection   205
pressure groups   22
Prime Minister   14, 118
    Department of   116
    power   115–17
prime ministerial government   113–17
privatisation   120, 129
procedure, parliamentary   81
producer groups   22
promotional groups   22
proportional representation   8, 91, 92, 161,
        170, 182, 183, 184, 192, 267
    Single Transferable Vote (PR-STV)   164,
        165, 166, 170, 176, 183, 261
proportional voting   19, 163, 154
    House of Representatives   175–85
prorogue   174
protectionism   224
protectionists   195
public policy, influencing   126–7
public sector, structure and values of
        Australian   121–5
public sector organisations
    examples of Commonwealth   124
    types of   123
public service   119–39
    Australian Commonwealth   121, 130
    job security   136

and policy making   125–8
politicised, allegations of   136–9
reform   131–6
shrinking public sector   128–30
size   130
structure and values of Australian public
    sector   121–5
types of public sector organisations   123
women   127–8
Public Service Act 1999   122, 136
public-private partnership   123
Pyne, Christopher   251

Queen, power of   74–5, 100
Queensland Legislative Council   15
question time   112
questions, parliamentary   81

race politics   250
rank-and-file membership (ALP)   216
referendum   3, 4, 16, 19, 29, 32, 36, 37–8,
    39, 44, 57, 69, 86, 90, 144, 152, 215,
    218, 230, 232, 247
registering a political party in Australia   201
rent-seeking   206, 208–10
representation political parties   197
republic   19
Republican referendum (1999)   36
residual powers   58
responsible government   8, 14–16, 19, 35–6,
    56, 57, 65, 83, 91, 97, 99–101, 106, 111,
    114, 117, 118, 121, 122, 139, 144,
    149, 180
representation, theories of   83–4
representative democracy   2, 4, 5, 11, 12,
    13, 23
    types of   7–9
Rousseau, Jean-Jacques   5, 6
Royal Commissions   104, 112
Rudd, Kevin   69, 115, 120, 138, 214, 220,
    221, 225, 227, 228, 230, 232
Rudd Government   69, 70, 82, 105, 106,
    108, 119, 127, 132, 136, 209, 222,
    229–30, 258, 277
rule of law   6, 10, 40, 143, 236

Sartori, Giovanni   29, 259–60
Scullin, James   218–19
sectional groups   22

semi-presidential systems   9
Senate   39, 88–94
    balance of power   183, 201, 256, 258,
        267, 276, 277
    control of   113
    committees   85, 113
    and Constitution   76
    elections   171, 172–3
    expression of democratic will   88–94
    half Senate elections   171
    making laws   87
    power of   71, 74, 76–7, 80, 88–94
    role of   74, 77, 78, 80
    rule of minority parties and
        independents   92–4
    size   76
    time spent considering categories of
        business   79
    voting   91, 92, 170, 172–3, 184, 267
Senate Estimates Committee   112–13
Senator On-Line   198
Senior Executive Service (SES)   134, 137
Single Transferable Vote (PR-STV)   164,
    165, 166, 170, 176, 183, 261
single-issue political parties   197
Snedden, Billy   242
social contract   5, 7
social democracy and ALP   223–4
social liberalism   235, 237, 247, 251–2
social liberals   236, 237, 245, 251, 252
social movement   11, 189, 229, 263
social reform   66–7, 196, 217, 223, 231, 232
Socialist Alliance   198
Socialist Equality Party   198
socialism and ALP   223
sovereignty   29
Speaker of the House   85
stakeholders   126
state parliaments   15
state regulation of parties   207–8
statutory authorities   122, 123
Sweden   120
Switzerland   4, 57

2020 Summit   119
Tampa, MV   234
*Tasmanian Dam case: The Commonwealth v.
    Tasmania* (1983) 158 CLR 1   147, 148
Tasmanian parliamentary accord   263

taxation legislation 152
terrorists 147
Thatcher, Margaret 248
think-tanks 249
Third Way (ALP) 226–7
Thomas v. Mowbray (2007) 237 ALR 194
  146, 158
threshold 163
Trustee model 84
Turnbull, Malcolm 242, 251
Two-Ballot System 163, 164
two-party system 21, 165, 179, 180, 192,
  193, 200, 236, 237–8, 261, 262, 263, 275

Uniform Tax case: South Australia v.
  The Commonwealth (1942) 65
  CLR 373 147
union movement and ALP 215–16
United Australia Party (UAP) 238, 239
United States 4, 8–9, 29, 48, 55, 56, 74,
  117, 122, 138, 143–4
United Kingdom 4, 9, 14, 32, 49, 57, 73,
  117, 121, 144
universal suffrage/franchise 161
urgency debates, parliamentary 81

vertical fiscal imbalance 61–3
vote, right to 160
voters and their preferences 181–2
voting
  alternative 81, 163, 164, 165–6
  compulsory 160–1, 179, 264, 268
  and first preference votes 202–3
  gap, gender 182, 238
  Group Ticket Vote (GTV) 173
  House of Representatives 161, 170, 171,
    179, 175–85
  how-to-vote card 167
  preferential voting (PV) 82, 161, 163, 164,
    168, 170, 173, 179, 184, 244, 260, 264

Senate 91, 92, 170, 172–3, 184, 267
Single Transferable Vote (PR-STV) 165,
  166, 170, 176, 183, 261
and women 32, 175, 188, 238
see also electoral systems; proportional
  representation

web sites 23, 49, 70, 94, 118, 139, 159, 186,
  211, 233, 254, 279
Weber, Max 120
welfare state laggard 67
welfare state retrenchment 67–8
Wentworth, William Charles 15
Western democracies, evolution of parties
  in 194–8
Westminster parliamentary system 15, 32,
  35, 54, 80, 83, 89, 121, 122, 124, 125,
  127, 136, 138, 199
What Women Want (Australia) 198
whistle-blowing 136
White Australia Policy 222, 224, 229, 250
Whitlam, Gough 18, 125, 217, 220–1, 225,
  229, 230
Whitlam Labor Government 18, 92, 125,
  132, 134, 150, 225, 229, 248, 253
Wik Peoples v. Queensland (1996) 187 CLR 1
  154
Williams, Daryl 157
women
  and ALP 230–1
  and the Liberal Party 238, 239, 241
  and parliament 23, 82, 241
  and politics 197, 198, 229, 238, 241, 259
  in the public service 127–8
  and the vote 32, 175, 188, 238
WorkChoices case: New South Wales v. The
  Commonwealth (2006) 229 CLR 1 51,
  52, 68, 148, 152, 156

Young National Party of Australia 198